POPULATION POLICIES AND PROGRAMMES

José Donayre, M. D., Project Coordinator

Principal Contributors

Tevia Abrams   Sethuramiah Rao

Abdul-Muniem Abu-Nuwar   Pierre Severyns

Ruth Akumu   R. Paul Shaw

Alan Keller   Oscar J. Sikes

Atiqur R. Khan   Mallica Vajrathon

Pedro P. Villanueva

POPULATION POLICIES AND PROGRAMMES

Lessons Learned from Two Decades of Experience

Edited by NAFIS SADIK

Published for

UNITED NATIONS POPULATION FUND

BY

NEW YORK UNIVERSITY PRESS

New York and London

Note

The designations employed and the presentation of material in this publication do not imply the expression of any opinion whatsoever on the part of the United Nations Population Fund concerning the legal status of any country, territory, city or area of its authorities, or concerning the delimitation of its frontiers or boundaries.

The term "country" as used in the text of this report also refers, as appropriate, to territories or areas.

In the text and tables, the designations "developed" and "developing" countries or "more developed" and "less developed" countries are intended for convenience and do not necessarily express a judgement about the stage reached by a particular country or area in the development process.

Copyright (c) 1991 by UNFPA

Library of Congress Cataloguing-in-Publication Data

United Nations Population Fund.
    Population policies and programmes: lessons learned from two decades of experience / edited by Nafis Sadik.
        p.   cm.
    Includes index.
    ISBN 0-8147-8553-0 (cloth)
    ISBN 0-8147-8554-9 (paper)
    1. United Nations Population Fund. 2. Population policy. 3. Population research. I. Sadik, Nafis. II. Title.

HB849.4.U55 1991   91-12388
363.9--dc20   CIP

CONTENTS

Part One: Programming and Policy Concerns

Part Two: Regional Perspectives

Part Three: Agenda for the Future

ANNEX

TABLES

FIGURES

BOXES

FOREWORD

In the course of the last two decades, the population field has been transformed. When the United Nations Population Fund (UNFPA) finally became operational in 1969, after a long international debate, intervention in population was still loaded with the potential for controversy. Few countries considered population policy a necessary part of their development armoury. Fewer still thought it proper for governments to become involved in decisions about family size.

Yet 1969 was the turning point in a process which has changed attitudes and promoted decisive action in every part of the developing world. The international community is unanimous that population is an essential component of development policies; nearly all governments assist family planning directly or indirectly, either as a health measure or as a means to influence population growth. The discussion today is not whether governments should be involved in population matters, nor about how policy should be implemented. Increasingly the debate is about how the resources are to be found to carry out policies on which all are agreed.

UNFPA has played its part in this transformation. As we reached our 21st year, it seemed appropriate to stand back and assess how far the world has come in population; how far there is still to go; and what means are most appropriate to achieving the goals of the international consensus. This study is the result.

Our research has left no doubt that the need for action in the population field is more urgent than ever. Better population data and analytical techniques have made possible the examination in depth of population growth, size and structure, and better understanding of their social and economic implications; population intervention is agreed to be both necessary and valuable; population programmes are more comprehensive and effective than ever before; the awareness and availability of family planning services are at an all-time high: yet the sober fact is that additions to world population are running at some 95 million a year. Between 1989, UNFPA's 20th anniversary year, and the end of the century, another billion people will be added to the planet's human cargo. Recent concern for the future of development, and indeed for the future security of the entire global ecosystem has been greatly increased by the knowledge that 6.25 billion people will enter the 21st century.

In November 1989, with the support of the Government of the Netherlands, UNFPA organized the International Forum on Population in the 21st Century (Amsterdam) to bring the implications of its Review and Assessment exercise to the attention of governments. The Forum called upon developing countries and the international assistance community to strengthen their resolve to achieve specific targets in health, family planning, education and the condition of women. The "Amsterdam Declaration" has been duly noted by the United Nations Economic and Social Council and the General Assembly. Its message -- that if the *medium projection is to be attained, with a stable population of "only" 10.2 billion people a century from now, the effort and resources devoted to fertility decline will need to be doubled in the next ten years -- has found a receptive audience. The next decade will test the world's determination to act; it may decide the future of the planet as a home for human beings.*

Nafis Sadik
Executive Director
United Nations Population Fund

March 1991

ACKNOWLEDGEMENTS

The major part of the work presented in this book reflects the experience and insights of UNFPA staff in analyzing the voluminous literature on population programmes as well as the information emerging directly from the programmes themselves. The main responsibility for the design and conduct of the study fell on UNFPA's Technical and Evaluation Division and its Technical Branches. These were, in particular, responsible for the sectoral analysis while the Geographical Divisions carried the task of organizing the regional reviews. We would like to register here our special gratitude to the following UNFPA officers for the quality of their contribution and the dedicated manner in which they carried these onerous demands without reducing their attention to their regular obligations.

Technical and Evaluation Division: José Donayre, Chief; Kerstin Trone, Deputy Chief; Pierre Severyns, Chief, Maternal and Child Health and Family Planning Branch; Sethuramiah Rao, Chief, Population Data, Policy and Research Branch; Oscar J. Sikes, Chief, Education, Communication and Youth Branch; Tevia Abrams, Senior Technical Officer; Abdul M. Abu-Nuwar, Technical Officer; Ruth Akumu, Technical Officer; Alan Keller, Technical Officer; Atiqur R. Khan, Senior Technical Officer; Y.O. Lee, Technical Officer; R. Paul Shaw, Senior Technical Officer; Mallica Vajrathon, Senior Technical Officer; Pedro P. Villanueva, Technical Officer.

Information and External Relations Division: Jyoti Singh, Chief; Alex Marshall, Chief, Editorial, Publications and Media Services Branch.

Africa Division: Lamine N'Diaye, Chief; George Nsiah, Programme Officer.

Arab States and Europe Division: Roushdi El Heneidi, Chief.

Asia and Pacific Division: Raheem Sheikh, Chief; Henna Ong, Chief, East and South East Asia Branch.

Latin America and Caribbean Division: Hugo Corvalán, Chief; Nerina Perea, Programme Officer.

Prof. Mercedes Concepción accompanied us for most of the process of the Review and Assessment, providing us with all of her unusual skills, technical, administrative and motivational in all phases of the study.

We would also like to acknowledge the patient and consistent work of the numerous research assistants and secretaries involved in this exercise. In particular, we would like to thank Ravi Fernando, Beverley Kerr and Luz Pereira; research assistants, Luisa Jimence, Administrative Branch and Rosemarie Cruz, Isabel Clostre, Chandra Conte and Beatriz Martinez; secretaries in the Technical and Evaluation Division, for their efficient support and generous giving of their time and energies. Similarly, Barbara Ryan, who was responsible for the editing of the manuscript, for her remarkable skills and the ease with which she addressed stylistic, consistency and substantive issues in the presentation.

A large number of people contributed comments and observations to this book in different opportunities. Some responded to requests from the Fund with suggestions and insights which were incorporated into the text whenever possible. Others participated in special expert groups called for discussing preliminary drafts of the sector papers. Others still worked as consultants in the preparation of country case studies and regional reviews. We would like to extend our special gratitude to them. Their affiliations are as of the date of their participation in the Review and Assessment. We apologize for any inaccuracies as verification of the information was not entirely possible. They are listed as follows:

Gwendolyn J. Acsadi, USA
Aderanti Adepoju
Sultana Alam, Bangladesh
Anthony Bennett, Institute for Population & Social Research, Thailand
Josayne Blanchard, UNESCO
Fathi Botros, FAO
George Brown, The Population Council
David Burleson, UNESCO
Arthur M. Conning, CELADE
George Brown, The Population Council
David Burleson, UNESCO
Leonard Dawson, University of North Carolina
J. de Jong-Gierveld, Netherlands University Demographic Institute
G. Farooq, ILO
Mahmoud Fathalla, WHO
Moye Freymann, University of North Carolina
Lawrence Green, Kaiser Family Foundation
Jack Harewood, Trinidad and Tobago
Alejandro Herrin, University of the Philippines
Fernando Hurtado, UNFPA
J. A. Johnston, ILO
N. O. Kabwasa, UNESCO
Nathan Keyfitz, International Institute for Applied Systems Analysis
Karol J. Krotki, University of Alberta
Eric R. Krystall, JSI Research and Training Institute, Kenya
Luis Leñero-Otero, Instituto Mexicano de Estudios Sociales, A.C.
G. López-Escobar, Corporación Regional de Población, Colombia
Sheila Macrae, UNFPA
Milos Macura, Ekonomski Institut, Yugoslavia
Maher Mahran, National Population Council, Egypt
M. Maidey
G. Martinez, National Population Council, Mexico
Kanwar Mathur, UNESCO
Walter Mertens, USA
Chisale Mhango
Marvellous Mhloyi, University of Zimbabwe
Paul Micou, USA
K. V. R. Moorthy, UNFPA
Alfonso F. Morejon, University of Havana
Donald Morisky, University of California, Los Angeles
Ellen Mouravieff-Apostol, Internation Federation of Social Workers
Axel Mundigo, WHO
Manfred Oepen, Friedrich Naumann Foundation, Germany
Lautaro G. Ojeda, Facultad Latinoamericana de Ciencias Soc., Ecuador

Abdel-Rahim Omran, USA
Angèle Petros-Barvazian, WHO
Phyllis Piotrow, Johns Hopkins University, USA
Malcolm Potts, Family Health International, USA
Jawarat Porapakkham, Mahidol University, Thailand
Iqbal Qureshi, Canada
Hamish Richards, David Owen Centre, England
Jacques Rioux, Le Centre Hospitalier de l'Université Laval, Canada
Mouna Saman, UNESCO
William Schellstede, Family Health International, USA
Michael P. Todaro, Population Council, USA
Manuel Urbina, Ministry of Health, Mexico
Clayton Vollan, United States Agency for International Development
Elizabeth Wollast, Université Libre de Bruxelles, Belgium
Nicholas Wright, Robert Wood Johnson Medical School, USA
Hugh H. Wynter, University of the West Indies, Jamaica
Yasar Yesilcay, College of Science, Sultan Qaboos University, Turkey
Margot Zimmerman, Programme for Appropriate Technology in Health, USA

Participants in Expert Groups:

Ronny Adhikarya, FAO
Joop Alberts, FAO
Chris Allison, ODA, United Kingdom
S. Kumar Alok, Ministry of Health and Family Welfare, India
D.Alopaeus-Stahl, Ministry of Foreign Affairs, Sweden
Carlos Aramburu, INANDEP, Peru
Andrew Arkutu, UNFPA
Oladele Arowolo, Lagos State University
Fama Ba, UNESCO
Reynaldo Bajraj, CELADE-ECLAC
Sylvia Balit, FAO
Loana Barbosa, Ministry of Foreign Affairs, Brazil
Mark Belsey, WHO
Désirée Bonis, Ministry of Foreign Affairs, Netherlands
John Boongaarts, Population Council
Manfred Bretz, Population Register
Noel Brown, UNEP
Eric Callway, ODA, United Kingdom
Bruce Campbell, Royal Tropical Institute, The Netherlands
Bruce Carlson, World Bank
Rami Chabra, India
Souad Chater, Tunisia
John G. Cleland, London School of Hygiene and Tropical Medicine
Susan Cochrane, World Bank
Leonardo de la Cruz, UNESCO
Julie Davanzo, USA
Alberto De Caterina, Permanent Mission of Italy to the United Nations
Linda Demers, CIDA, Canada
Ramiro Echeverria, Fundación Eugenio Espejo, Ecuador
Ann Ehrenreich, Permanent Mission of Denmark to the United Nations
Susan Eisendrath, University of California, Los Angeles
Charles Ejiogu, United Nations
E. El Wardini, UNESCO
Ibrahim El-Etriby, National Population Council, Egypt
Nuray Fincancioglu, Turkey

Wilhelm Flieger, University of San Carlos
Roland J. Fuchs, UN University
Francis Gendreau, Centre Français sur la Population et le Développement, France
Hubert Gerard, Université Catholique de Louvain and CIDEP, Belgium
Duff Gillespie, United States Agency for International Development
Wilma Goppel, UNFPA
K. Gnanasekaran, United Nations
Alan Hancock, UNESCO
Donald Heisel, United Nations
Julia Henderson, USA
Michael Heyn, UNFPA
Alan Hill, London School of Hygiene and Tropical Medicine
K. Ikegami, JOICFP
A. Joukhadar, UNESCO
Takeshi Kagami, Permanent Mission of Japan to the United Nations
Meba Kagone, Burkina Faso
Shenadu Kar, University of California Los Angeles
Carol Kazi, USA
E. Kennedy, FAO
Alan Kondo, UNESCO
Rolf Korte, Gesellschaft fur Technische Zusammenarbeit
C. Kunii, JOICFP
S. K. Kwafo, Ghana National Family Planning Programme
Eddy Lee, ILO
Massimo Livi-Bacci, IUSSP
Hedi M'Henni, Office National de Famille et de la Population, Tunisia
Gordon MacArthur, U.S. Agency for International Development
Elizabeth Maguire, U.S. Agency for International Development
Halfdan Mahler, IPPF
Gibson M. Mandishona, Central Statitiscal Office, Zimbabwe
Nydia Maraviglia, World Bank
A. Marcoux, UNFPA
Khalid Mardini, Minister of Health Syria
Parker Mauldin, The Rockefeller Foundation
Rafael Mazin, UNESCO
Alhaji S. A. Musa, National Population Commission, Nigeria
Masood Nabi Nur, Population Division, Pakistan
S. Naicken, FAO
Hans Narula, UNICEF
Susan Newcomer, Planned Parenthood Federation of America
A. Ofstad, NORAD, Norway
Shirley Oliver, Margaret Sanger Center, USA
Alfred Opubor, Multimedia Associates, Nigeria
Paulo Paiva, CEDEPLAR/UFMG,Brazil
Jairo Palacio, UNESCO
Kosit Pampiernas, Nat'l Economy & Social Development Board-Thailand
John Parsons, UNFPA
G. Perez-Ramirez, United Nations
John Pilbeam, Permanent Mission of Australia to the United Nations
Samuel Preston, University of Pennsylvania, USA
K.V. Ranaganthan, USA
Corazon Raymundo, University of the Philippines
Michael Sachs, USA
Atif Saghayroun, National Council of Research, Sudan
Fred Sai, World Bank
E. Salim, Population and Environment, Indonesia

Emmerich Schebeck, World Bank
Rolf-Dieter Schnelle, Permanent Mission, Federal Republic of Germany
Sheldon Segal, The Rockefeller Foundation, USA
William Seltzer, United Nations
R. C. Sharma, UNESCO
K. Springer, UNDP
Lyra Srinivasan, UNDP
Krishnamurthy Srinivasan, International Institute for Population Sciences, India
B. Maxwell Stamper, USA
Riad Tabbarah, ESCWA
Penporn Tirasawat, Institute of Population Sciences, Thailand
Alfred Ukaegbu, UNESCO
Raul Urzua, UNESCO
Margaret Valdivia, USA
D. J. van de Kaa, Netherlands Institute for Advanced Study, WASSENAAR,
    and University of Amsterdam
Carl Wahren, OECD
Bradman Weerakoon, IPPF
Du Xiangjin, State Family Planning Commission, China
S. Yagi, JOICFP, Japan
Sun Hee Yun, Johns Hopkins University, USA

NOTE ON SOURCES OF DATA

The primary source of population data for this book is the United Nations Population Division in the Department of Economic and Social Affairs of the United Nations Secretariat. Unless otherwise indicated, references in the text to demographic data are from the Population Division's World Population Prospects: 1988 (United Nations publication, Sales No. E.88.XIII.7), medium variant of the projections. The Department of International Economic and Social Affairs is also the source of the information shown in annex table 2, from its Global Population Policy Data Base. Another publication of the Population Division, Levels and Trends of Contraceptive Use As Assessed in 1988 (United Nations publication, Sales No. E.89.XIII.4), is one of the primary sources of data on contraceptive use.

Notes to each chapter appear at the back of the book.

Explanatory Notes to Tables

The following symbols have been used in the tables that are based on United Nations sources:

A point (.) is used to indicate decimals.

Two dots (..) indicate that data are not available or are not separately reported.

A dash (--) indicates that the amount is nil or negligible.

A hyphen (-) indicates that the item is not applicable.

A minus sign (-) before a number indicates a deficit or decrease, except as indicated.

Details and percentages in tables do not necessarily add to totals because of rounding.

EXPLANATORY NOTES

This volume of observations and conclusions focuses on action programmes, what makes them work, and what will make them work better in future. The study consisted of three desk reviews in population policy development; maternal and child health and family planning; and population information, education and communication. The reviews were discussed at five expert group meetings. To bring out the distinctive character of regional experiences in population programmes the Fund also commissioned special reviews for Africa; the Arab States; Asia and the Pacific; and Latin America and the Caribbean. At the same time national experts undertook case studies in Ecuador, Egypt, Kenya, Mexico, the Philippines, Thailand, Tunisia and Zimbabwe, the results of which were incorporated in sectoral and regional assessments.

The findings of the Review and Assessment were first discussed in January 1989 by a group of country representatives, United Nations Specialized Agencies, non-governmental organizations and experts. In May 1989, the Fund reported to the 37th session of the Governing Council, highlighting the need for international co-operation and increased financial resources to achieve the medium demographic projections for the year 2000.

This volume is structured according to the elements of the Review and Assessment study. Part I reflects the three sectoral studies, analyzing current experience and pointing out possible approaches. Part I ends with a review of issues which apply to the entire population field: the most important are political commitment, coordination and the status of women. This section also assesses the cost of reaching Amsterdam's principal target: the medium variant population projection of the United Nations.

Part II consists of the regional reviews of sub-Saharan Africa, the Arab States, Asia and the Pacific, and Latin America and the Caribbean. A short review of the evaluation of population programmes in each region is followed by a summary of constraints and favourable factors, and consideration of future perspectives.

Part III, an Agenda for the Future, discusses international cooperation and coordination as essential for the most effective use of resources, and closes with a section on programmes, presenting multiple options for national and international action.

INTRODUCTION

Recorded history offers no parallels to humanity's success at survival and reproduction. In retrospect, it is phenomenal that the world's population mushroomed from 1 billion people in the year 1800 to more than 5 billion by 1990. It is even more staggering to imagine planet earth with yet another 3 billion within the next 30 years--as projected by the United Nations.[1] Surely this is testimony to human ingenuity and progress in combatting disease, food shortages and famines, natural disasters such as drought and floods, and a host of other restraints on full human potential.

Yet, in many parts of the world, unbalanced population growth and distribution are swamping the capacity of societies to cope with ever increasing numbers of people. Each day, the world's population swells with an additional 220,000 people. By the year 2025, the planet will have to support upwards of 8.5 billion (according to United Nations medium variant projections). Of this growth, 90 per cent will be occurring in developing countries--precisely where rising standards of living and education frequently elude the poor--thus contributing to a massive economic gulf between regions of the world with slow-growing populations and those with fast-growing ones.

The nature of this gulf, its complex causes and consequences, has prompted a great deal of attention to the costs and benefits of population growth. Indeed, it is safe to say that population growth and change has produced a twentieth-century paradox. On the one hand, population growth is an acknowledged engine of socio-economic growth and development whereas, on the other, imbalances in population growth and distribution are exacerbating land and food shortages, leading to environmental degradation and outpacing the provision of needed health, educational and housing services.

Furthermore, as poor and rich countries come into closer contact through international trade, migration and sharing of technologies, the interaction of unbalanced population growth and resources in one nation can produce negative spill-over effects in neighbouring nations. Population growth may have once been an issue of national sovereignty alone, but today it has far-reaching implications for wise use of natural resources, preservation of the environment, and sustainable development on a truly global level.

It is this recognition that has prompted so many Governments, non-governmental agencies, scientists, politicians and individual citizens to express growing concern over the effects of unbalanced population growth and distribution. According to monitoring reports produced by the United Nations Population Division in 1987 and 1989, for example, more than 60 per cent of the Governments of less developed countries perceived their population growth rates as "too high" in 1988, compared with only 25 per cent in 1974 (for data on individual countries in 1987, see annex table 2). Equally significant, at least 90 per cent of less developed countries perceived their populations' distribution--involving concentrations in major cities or rapid rural-to-urban migration--to be unsatisfactory.[2] At the root of these perceptions is a growing awareness that population trends have an impact on development, especially on the ability of Governments to provide needed health, educational and housing services. Such concerns have been widely echoed in the proceedings of international forums such as the 1974 World Population Conference, the 1984 International Conference on Population, deliberations of regional Parliamentarian meetings on population and development, and the priorities of national development plans of a great many countries.

To understand and implement more favourable patterns of population growth and distribution, resources have been mobilized on many fronts. This effort has taken the form of in-depth research and policy analysis on the causes and consequences of population growth and distribution; the evolution of national population policies and strategies to tackle the problems involved; growing collaboration between governmental and non-governmental agencies in population matters; renewed emphasis on people's participation at the community and local level; recognition of the imperative of strengthening the role of women; and more effective political commitment at all levels of societal organization.

In financial terms, international assistance for population matters has been mobilized to the extent that it now stands at approximately $600 million annually. In addition, total national expenditures for family planning and related activities are roughly estimated to have surpassed $2.5 billion annually.

In view of the above, it is hardly an exaggeration to say that the "population field" has arrived at a crossroads. Innumerable studies have explored or reflected on the problems as well as on the virtues of proposed solutions. Literally thousands of population projects, country programmes and policies have also been implemented, monitored and evaluated, yielding insights as to what works and what does not, at both country and regional levels. Furthermore, assessments of "unmet needs" have prompted greater scrutiny of the adequacy of available financial resources for meeting the challenges ahead. Increasingly, those resources are being deemed inadequate.

It is time for a stock-taking, therefore, a distillation of wisdom based on experience. The United Nations Population Fund (UNFPA) has chosen to review this experience for several reasons. First, since it became operational in 1969, UNFPA has been the world's major multilateral population agency. Hence, it is in a position not only to assess accomplishments of action-oriented programmes over the last 20 years but also to identify obstacles to the smooth functioning of such programmes. Second, in the company of many other international, national and non-governmental agencies, UNFPA seeks forward-looking strategies to tackle future challenges. The concern here is both to distil a sharper appreciation of what works and to anticipate more fully the requisites of comprehensive approaches to solving population problems in countries shackled by limited infrastructure, low productivity, poverty and massive indebtedness. Third, UNFPA seeks to identify a broader substantive base for joint programming and inter-agency co-operation so that resources can be more effectively mobilized at the global, regional and national levels.

Such a task, obviously immense, could not be undertaken without a great deal of preparation to clarify the scope, aims and methodology. Not surprisingly, therefore, planning unfolded in stages. At the outset, it was decided that the stock-taking should focus largely on components of action-oriented population programmes. This is in keeping with the Fund's mandate and its particular expertise in the population field. That expertise includes knowledge of the process by which the concerns, objectives and priorities of population programmes are determined at the national level, regional or global level; what is needed to lay the substantive, technical, institutional and policy groundwork to implement such programmes; how different components of such programmes--such as research findings, awareness creation and service delivery--should ideally interact to bring about intended effects; and what kinds of socio-cultural, political, economic, planning and administrative obstacles might be encountered.

It was also decided at the outset that such a stock-taking should be as extensive as possible--reaching globally. That is, it should distil project and programming experience from a diversity of countries in Africa, Latin America and the Caribbean, Western Asia, and Asia and the Pacific. It should incorporate lessons learned by other agencies undertaking population activities, whether international, national or non-governmental organizations (NGOs). And, it should seek, where possible, to identify broad generalizations about problems, approaches, successes and shortcomings that have a basis not only in programming experience but in research findings as well.

In view of these broad aims, it was decided to call the UNFPA stock-taking a "Review and Assessment of the Population Field". Perhaps the most difficult decision in conducting the Review and Assessment was a methodological one--how to categorize a vast amount of information in ways that would be manageable and functionally indicative of important components of population activities.

After several possibilities were considered, each with different merits, it was finally decided to group population activities and approaches into three substantive categories: "Population Data, Policy and Research", "Maternal and Child Health and Family Planning", and "Information, Education and Communication". No pretense is made that these three sectors capture all population-related activities. However, they remain desirable because they are used extensively by

UNFPA; they are familiar to many funding agencies dealing with population and related issues and, as will be evident, they reflect the logic of comprehensive, integrated population programming itself.

Thus, as a glance at the organization of this book reveals, major findings of the Review and Assessment are organized into three chapters, reflecting the three categories mentioned above. These substantively oriented chapters are followed by an analysis of common issues and by shorter regional reviews, each offering background information on the scope of population activities in a major geographical region of the world. Finally, conclusions and recommendations flowing from the Review and Assessment are provided in the concluding chapters.

Perhaps the most direct way of conveying what this study has to impart is to identify its intended audience. For all readers, it is hoped that the study will stimulate interest in population issues by providing a global review of approaches and accomplishments in the population field over the last 20 years, as well as challenges that lie ahead. For specialists, it is further hoped that the Review and Assessment will prove useful as a consolidation of information on population problems, Governments' perceptions of such problems, successful approaches to tackling them and obstacles requiring further understanding. For those agencies providing population assistance, it is hoped that the Review and Assessment will serve as a guide, a record of experience, that will contribute to improvements in population programmes at national, regional and global levels. It is also hoped that the study will speak to the international community about the urgency of joint programming and inter-agency co-operation in preparing forward-looking strategies, as well as the need for greater mobilization of financial resources to achieve them.

The reader should be equally aware that a compendium of encyclopaedic proportions would be required to do justice to all aspects of the population field. Many such aspects simply fall outside the scope of this inquiry, including the history of thinking on population matters; philosophical debates on the role of population in socio-economic progress or stagnation; and detailed methodological approaches needed to determine the precise causal relationship of population variables to, for example, the formation of investment capital, environmental degradation or intersocietal conflict.

Nor does this book set out to collect data to assess a particular linkage between population and non-population variables or to undertake surveys to fill gaps in knowledge. Rather, the strength of the Review and Assessment is that it draws on published and unpublished research, along with project and programming experience, accumulated in UNFPA archives during the past 20 years or so. This knowledge has been complemented by the insights and experience of UNFPA staff members, as well as the rich and varied suggestions of a great many experts and officials of other development agencies who were asked to share their knowledge with UNFPA. The expertise represented by these individuals spans population planning and policy-making, management and delivery of family planning services, public health and education, demography, sociology, economics and related specialties.

Above all, the Review and Assessment shows that population issues are truly interdisciplinary and multifaceted. Population variables--mortality, fertility, migration--not only affect but are affected by a multitude of development variables such as--income growth and equality, employment growth and distribution, settlement patterns, resource use and environmental conservation, and so forth. To prepare for sustainable development in the future, therefore, fuller integration of all population variables into national development planning will be necessary. As this Review and Assessment shows, the process of doing so promises to be not only immensely challenging but also profoundly rewarding, by improving prospects for families and their Governments to enhance their social and economic well-being.

Part One:

Programming and Policy Concerns

2. Elements of Population Policy-Making

Introduction

Most developing countries now consider population matters important to their national development,* and a large majority directly or indirectly support measures to influence one or more population variables. Financially, developing countries are contributing substantially to population programmes** as well. Notwithstanding wide variations from one country to another, developing countries are currently contributing an estimated 67-75 per cent of the total funds expended annually on their population programmes.[1]

These impressive gains in tackling population problems have several sources. The World Population Plan of Action (WPPA), unanimously adopted at the 1974 World Population Conference in Bucharest, provided the policy framework. This was reaffirmed at the 1984 International Conference on Population in Mexico City. International multilateral and bilateral organizations, non-governmental organizations (NGOs) and others played a catalytic role.*** Most importantly, the political will and commitment of a large number of developing countries to solving their own population problems fostered awareness and action.

---

* In the literature, the term "development" has been used to signify a goal, an instrument or an indicator, or both a cause and a consequence of social progress. Development may mean economic growth, social transformation or cultural progress--in short, a broad range of individual and collective contributions to society. It may be impossible to provide a universally accepted definition of the term. In this review, development is used to signify all actions aimed at enhancing the individual's potential for personal growth and for contributing to society. The collective performance of members of a society can be taken to represent societal development.

** The term "population programmes", often used interchangeably with "population activities", may be defined in the broadest sense as comprising all activities related to the determinants and consequences of population trends, including economic, social, demographic, biological, geographical, environmental and political aspects. However, the field of international population assistance employs a narrower meaning, defining the population aspects of development "as the causes, conditions and consequences of changes in fertility, mortality and mobility as they affect developmental prospects and the human welfare resulting therefrom".[2] This review generally uses the narrower definition of population programmes.

*** However, international agencies and other organizations providing population assistance have not necessarily supported every aspect of population-related activities. Most, for instance, have placed greater emphasis on maternal and child health and family planning (MCH/FP) programmes than on population redistribution programmes. In addition, most agencies have viewed efforts that are aimed primarily at reducing mortality, improving general health conditions or strengthening overall statistical services as outside the core of population programmes.

The policy-making process in brief

Demography emerged as a field of public policy with the adoption of the WPPA in 1974. Since that time a large body of demographic knowledge has been produced on the causes and socio-economic and political consequences of mortality, fertility, family planning, internal migration, population distribution and international migration. Yet demographic knowledge has not yet been fully used in policy-making and planning. This chapter examines key elements in the process of policy-making to identify achievements, obstacles and opportunities for bringing that body of knowledge to bear on population-related policies.

Policy-making in the field of population relies upon several discrete but interrelated activities: population data collection and analysis, research, dissemination, policy formulation, policy planning, policy implementation and evaluation. These activities are illustrated as parts of a loop in Box 1. Many agencies, including UNFPA, have used the scheme represented in Box 1, or a variant of it, as a framework for the design of their population assistance activities in developing countries. However, individual agencies may give different weight to each of the specified activities.

3

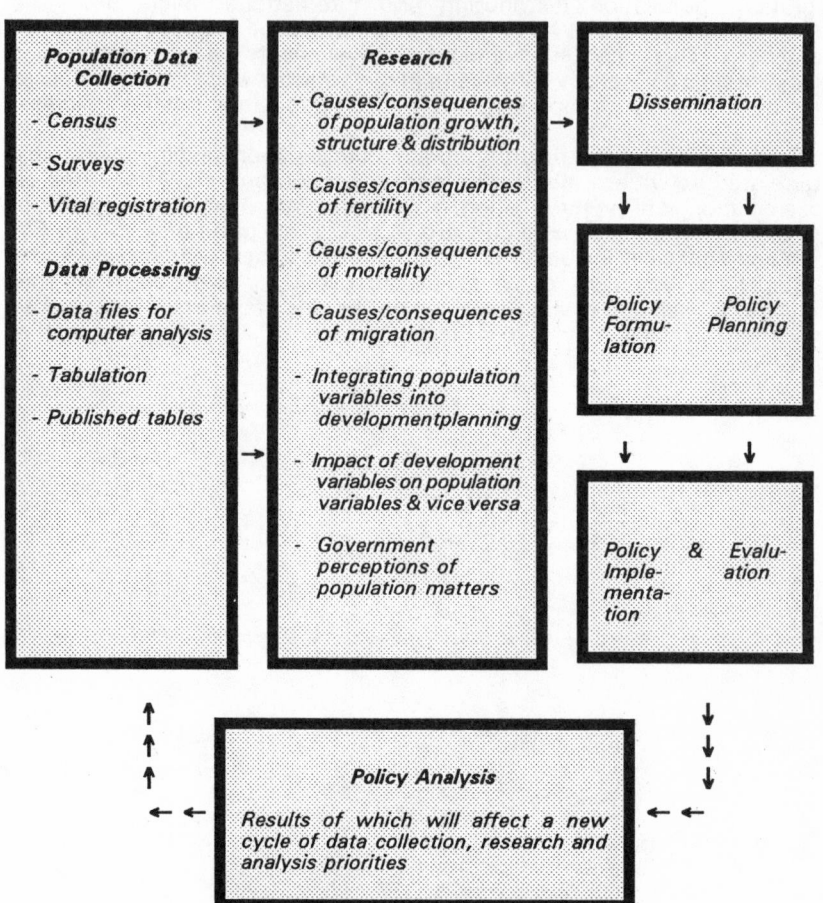

Box 1

INTERRELATED ACTIVITIES IN POPULATION POLICY-MAKING*

Population Data Collection
- Census
- Surveys
- Vital registration

Data Processing
- Data files for computer analysis
- Tabulation
- Published tables

Research
- Causes/consequences of population growth, structure & distribution
- Causes/consequences of fertility
- Causes/consequences of mortality
- Causes/consequences of migration
- Integrating population variables into developmentplanning
- Impact of development variables on population variables & vice versa
- Government perceptions of population matters

Dissemination

Policy Formulation   Policy Planning

Policy Implementation   &   Evaluation

Policy Analysis
Results of which will affect a new cycle of data collection, research and analysis priorities

---

*   <u>Source</u>: Diagram adapted from the United States Agency for International Development, "Overview of A.I.D. Assistance in Population Policy Development" (Washington, D.C., Policy Development Division, 1985), unpublished, p. 3.

Effective policy formulation relies upon an in-depth analysis of each country's population and development situation based upon accurate data, competent analysis and relevant research. Most of the activities in the policy loop overlap with one another; in addition, the possibilities of feedback from each activity into another are many.

Data collection - A fundamental activity in the entire process of research and policy analyses. Timely, reliable data from censuses, surveys and vital statistics systems not only facilitate national, regional and global policy-related research but also provide an accurate basis for designing detailed population policies and programmes and for planning at macro- sectoral and sub-national levels.

Research - Information on the causes and consequences of fertility, mortality, migration, population growth, structure, composition and distribution as well as on the operational and methodological aspects of integrating population variables into development planning and the impact of development policies and projects on demographic variables.

Dissemination - The processes whereby knowledge gained through population research reaches those responsible for development planning and policy formulation in appropriate formats.

Policy formulation - Policies and specific activities aimed at achieving objectives directly or indirectly. For example, international agencies concerned with population matters often focus policy formulation on substantive or geographic priorities, whereas a national population commission may focus on a particular policy reflecting the internal interests of a sovereign nation.

Policy planning - The applications of population information and research findings in policy makers' efforts to improve or design new policies. Policy planning engenders an understanding of the immediate benefits and costs of health and longevity, fertility and migration, and the long-term potential for realizing development gains from different kinds of population interventions.

Policy implementation and evaluation - The translation of policies into programmes, measures or instruments; organizing the human, financial and institutional resources necessary for achieving policy goals; and undertaking continuous assessment, monitoring and evaluation of policies and programmes.

Policy analysis - A continuing activity drawing on research, policy planning, implementation and evaluation to help identify issues that are insufficiently understood or overlooked in policy development and to determine the types of data and analyses needed to improve the knowledge base.

Though each of these activities is an important area in and of itself, this chapter focuses on the contribution of such activities to policy formulation, which is dependent upon a dynamic feedback from these complementary activities. Specifically, the chapter examines four critical elements in the policy loop: research, policy analysis, policy planning and data collection. Another element in the loop is dissemination--communicating the knowledge gained in population research to planners, policy makers and national leaders in clear and appropriate formats. This is touched on only briefly in this chapter because it is a major topic in Chapter 4. Similarly, policy implementation is covered in much detail in later chapters dealing with maternal and child health and family planning as well as with information, education and communication.

Because policy analysis has much in common with research, these two topics are treated together. The next topic, integrating population variables into development planning and population planning, is one of the most challenging current tasks. Data collection, the final topic, serves both research and policy analysis and, like policy analysis, is a continuous process.

Role of research and policy analyses in policy-making

Research and policy analyses, though integral to population policy-making (see Box 1), are neither automatic nor simple elements in the policy development process. Research provides information on the causes and consequences of fertility, mortality, migration, and population growth, structure and distribution. It is also concerned with the operational and methodological aspects of integrating population variables in development planning, and the impact of development policies and projects on demographic variables. Policy analysis draws upon research to (a) identify the analytical issues that are insufficiently understood or insufficiently represented in policy development, (b) determine types of data and analyses needed to produce a better knowledge base and (c) improve the use and dissemination of research results in population programmes. The findings reviewed below are presented not as a comprehensive summary of the state of research but rather as indicators of how research and analyses have been applied to action programmes in the field of population.

Findings on fertility

Population-related research and policy analyses have pursued multiple objectives in advancing knowledge about fertility. One of the earliest research tasks was to determine the prevalence of family planning and to identify the countries in which fertility rates were perceived as high, low or satisfactory. Later goals were to ascertain the proximate determinants of reproductive behaviour and to identify the socio-economic and geographic correlates of different fertility patterns.[3] In addition, research and policy analyses have continued to identify types of population-related activities that would help couples attain their desired family size and, at the same time, help Governments achieve their population growth targets within given resource constraints.

To obtain information on knowledge, attitudes and practice (KAP) of fertility and family planning, more than 400 surveys were undertaken between 1960 and 1980. To identify how fertility rates were being--and continue to be--perceived, the United Nations employed a series of surveys--Population Inquiries--designed to obtain Governments' assessments of the status of population matters in their countries. Over the past decade these Inquiries have found that more and more Governments of developing countries favour lowered fertility rates. For example, in 1974, only 41 Governments of developing countries favoured lower rates; by 1986 the number had grown to 67 (Table 1). (For individual countries, see Annex-Table 2.)

7

Table 1

DEVELOPING COUNTRIES FAVOURING LOWER FERTILITY RATES, BY AREA OF RESPONSIBILITY OF REGIONAL COMMISSIONS, 1974-1986
(Number of countries)

Area of Responsibility of Regional Commission	Year 1974	1986
Economic Commission for Africa	11	31
Economic and Social Commission for Asia and the Pacific	16	19
Economic Commission for Latin America and the Caribbean	13	15
Economic and Social Commission for Western Asia	1	2
Total	41	67

Sources: Adapted from *World Population Trends, Population and Development Interrelations and Population Policies, 1983 Monitoring Report, Vol. II,* (United Nations publication, Sales No. E.85.XIII.2), p. 187; *World Population Trends and Policies, 1987 Monitoring Report* (United Nations publication, Sales No. E.88.XIII.3), p. 14.

However, reducing fertility is not a universal goal. Among developed countries, for example, no Government perceived its fertility rate as too high, and almost 30 per cent perceived their fertility rates as too low (1986). Even among Governments of developing countries, almost half of 131 surveyed (1986) perceived their fertility rates as satisfactory (38 per cent) or as too low (10 per cent).[4]

Rationales for family planning policies

Even though not every country aims at reducing fertility, a strong rationale now exists for providing family planning education and services in all countries. This rationale has emerged from three major findings: that discrepancies exist between desired and actual family size; that birth-spacing helps reduce infant mortality and fertility; and that safe family planning contributes to maternal and child health (see chapter 3 for details).

In all countries surveyed by the World Fertility Survey (WFS), a large proportion of women wanted to delay or prevent a birth--a finding that provides strong support for continuing cost-effective MCH/FP programmes.[5] Wider acceptance of family planning is partially attributable to policies that have avoided equating family planning with "population control". A sound rationale for family planning programmes involves the provision of services and supplies to prevent unwanted births and high-risk pregnancies, to help bring about wanted births and to diagnose and treat infertility. It also involves providing education about responsible parenthood, including the timing and spacing of births.

Many Governments have formulated family planning policies for health, demographic, developmental or human rights reasons. Some Governments have sought to reduce the incidence of unwanted births and high-risk pregnancies, thereby reducing the incidence of maternal and child mortality and morbidity. Several studies produced by The Population Council and other organizations reveal that family planning policies and programmes have assisted this aim by exerting independent effects on fertility. These effects have been achieved by (a) providing information and education on health implications of the timing, spacing and number of births, and (b) providing services that enable couples to avoid unwanted or poorly timed births and to realize desired births. However, without parallel improvements in socio-economic development, the impact of programmes is greatly reduced.[6] The improved methodologies developed and applied by organizations such as The Population Council, the United Nations Population Division and the International Union for the Scientific Study of Population (IUSSP) have permitted measurement of the relative contribution of the various effects noted above.

It is now possible to conclude that family planning programmes have played a significant role in the decline of crude birth rates. Though declines vary greatly among major regions of the world (Table 2), between 1950-1955 and 1980-1985 the average crude birth rates among less developed countries fell from 44.6 to 31.8. Over the same period, the average number of children per woman as measured by the total fertility rate (TFR) declined from 6.2 to 4.1.

Table 2

CRUDE BIRTH RATES, WORLD AND REGIONAL AVERAGES, 1950-1985

	1950-1955	*1970-1975*	*1980-1985*
World	37.4	31.5	27.7
More Developed Regions	22.6	16.7	15.2
Less Developed Regions	44.6	37.1	31.8
Africa	48.9	46.7	45.5
Latin America	42.5	35.3	30.9
North America	24.6	15.7	15.6
Asia	42.9	34.8	28.4
Europe	19.8	15.7	13.4
Oceania	27.6	23.8	20.6
Union of Soviet Socialist Republics	26.3	18.1	19.1

Source: *World Population Prospects: 1988* (United Nations publication, Sales No. E.88.XIII.7), Table 6, pp. 118-120, 122, 124.

Governments have justified their support of family planning information and services because of the economic benefits such activities produce. Although consensus is lacking on the contribution of fertility reduction to the growth of per capita income or to gross national product (GNP), it is widely agreed that families and societies as a whole have benefited from fertility reductions. At the family level, for example, reduced fertility can lead to better schooling and nutritional opportunities for children.[7] In the society as a whole, reduced fertility can result in less rapid degradation of such resources as air, water, soil, and species of plants and animals, and less pressure on resources provided by the society, such as schools.[8]

Influences on fertility reduction

A common thread in the findings of research and policy studies is that social and economic development underlies fertility decline, although the processes influencing the timing and pace of this decline are imperfectly understood. These influences appear to be the result of interactions among population policies, development policies and cultural factors.[9] Programmes to reduce fertility or to influence desired family size have thus far relied too much on biological and demographic paradigms or on narrow economic frameworks. As yet, however, there is little understanding of how social, economic, political and cultural structures and institutions interact to produce the motivation for reducing fertility.

Confusion over an appropriate framework for explaining fertility behaviour has produced confusion over expected impacts of population interventions *per se* on fertility. For example, a study comparing fertility decline in the Republic of Korea with that in Costa Rica emphasizes the role of political commitment in ensuring sustained fertility decline.[10] Another study, based on a review of the literature on fertility declines in less developed countries, emphasizes the importance of social development and the spread of new ideas.[11] Still another study, which reviews the contributions of social science research to the population sector, focuses on the role of culture and social institutions in fertility change.[12] In addition, several researchers argue that exposure to external markets (trade), liberal import policies (new technologies, literature) and urbanization (including the influence of modern mass media) exert powerful independent effects on fertility reduction.[13] Indeed, without these influences, they argue, population and development interventions along traditional socio-economic lines--more jobs for women, better housing, old-age security--may do little to affect fertility. This rationale poses a serious challenge to advocates of slower urban growth and economic "conservatism" in developing countries.

Importance of women's education

Research funded by the World Bank, UNFPA, Canada's International Development Research Centre (IDRC) and other institutions reveals that women's education is the most consistent correlate of lower fertility;[14] and a mother's education is more strongly correlated with fertility reduction than is a father's education. The reasons are several. Increased education for a woman delays marriage, increases the probability of her working away from home, provides her with greater access to family planning information, changes her interest in spending her time raising children, affects reproductive behaviour through several "cognitive pathways" and, as discussed below, reduces infant and childhood mortality.[15]

The considerations above have two important implications for policy. Governments that want to reduce population growth now have a strong additional rationale for emphasizing population education and

11

communication programmes for women in formal schooling as well as through informal and non-formal education. The rationale is "additional" in the sense that the education of women should be a goal of development by itself. The second implication is that Governments that are now investing heavily in schooling, particularly to increase female enrolment, should anticipate the effects of such schooling on fertility and the demand for family planning services. In poor countries, improved education may at first produce an increase in fertility--as a result of improved diet, child care and so on--but will then result in a sustained fertility decline.

Though rarely employed, crude methodologies are now available for translating the effects of educational investments on future fertility reductions, and thus for examining the implications for family planning services. To illustrate, in Arab countries an IDRC-financed study--which uses education and fertility data, projections of female enrolments, and national development plans' investments in education--predicts that couples in the region will have attempted to avert some 13 million births between 1975 and 1995.[16] Though much work remains to be done to perfect the research techniques involved, it is none the less possible to anticipate the demand for family planning services and to remedy likely shortages.

Influence of socio-economic status

Another research task is to establish that fertility reduction among the poorest sections of a population will indeed reduce income inequality. The relationship, which tends to be assumed, should be empirically tested by a thorough study of the life histories and the social, economic, health and demographic status of acceptors and non-acceptors of family planning methods. The link between fertility, education and income inequality could be a keystone in population programming. As research and policy analyses have revealed, users of family planning services are often concentrated among upper classes of societies, among certain ethnic groups, and among women who tend to be at the end of their reproductive cycle. The problem, as is true also for mortality, is one of identifying the appropriate targets. In Mexico, fertility has reportedly fallen rapidly in rural areas because that is where the national programme, aimed at the rural poor, was focused from the outset. In Malaysia, ethnic and educational differentials in the use of family planning have been substantially narrowed because public family planning services have been readily available across ethnic and educational groups.[17]

One reason for the lack of focus on income inequality problems is a traditional concern of Governments--sometimes an obsession--with income growth at the national level and corresponding neglect of the linkages between fertility and the economy among the poorest segments of the population (for example, the landless). As identified in a review of Ford Foundation programmes, this neglect is often the result of superficial research relying on national-level statistics that are available on the populations easiest to reach.[18] What is needed, rather, are

12

"disaggregated" data and analysis concerning relatively disadvantaged groups.

Findings on mortality

By historical standards, mortality declines since 1945 have been extraordinarily rapid. In 1950-1955, life expectancy was below 50 years of age in approximately 96 countries, and infant mortality rates were above 125 per 1,000 live births in 91 countries. The 1974 World Population Conference recommended that all countries strive to reach life expectancy levels above 50 years of age by 1985. By 1985-1990, all but 22 countries had reached this goal. However, United Nations Population Inquiries leave little doubt that reducing mortality should continue to be a priority: Governments of more than three quarters of all developing countries perceive their rates of life expectancy as unacceptable.[19]

Government public health programmes have played a major role in mortality declines. Studies of both demographic and health interventions show that anti-malarial programmes along with vaccination and immunization, oral rehydration and nutritional supplementation programmes have had important impacts on mortality, and the potential gains from these and related programmes have yet to be exhausted. In assessing relative contributions to mortality declines, the International Review Group of Social Science Research on Population and Development distilled the following conclusions: (a) half the decline in infant mortality rates derives from public health measures relying on new and inexpensive medical techniques, such as vaccination; (b) one third of the decline stems from control of environmental problems associated with influenza, pneumonia, bronchitis etc.; and (c) slightly less than one tenth (9 per cent) of the reduction is attributable to control of diarrhoeal diseases through improved water supplies, sewage control etc.[20]

Population research and policy analyses have contributed in several ways to the decline in mortality. First, research has helped to identify the groups with the highest mortality rates--those who most need intervention. This accomplishment rested on advances in civil registration and the collection of vital statistics and analysis of socio-economic and geographical differentials in infant and childhood mortality, morbidity and life expectancy. Second, research has identified correlates of mortality differentials--among them, mother's and father's education, marital status, rural/urban residence and economic activity status.[21] Third, research has identified the types of population activities that can significantly affect the proximate or intermediary mechanisms correlated with mortality.

Influence of birth-spacing on infant and child mortality

Analyses of the relationships between infant mortality and lactation amenorrhoea, birth intervals, subfecundity and foetal wastage have benefited action programmes to combat mortality.[22] One major research finding is that of a causal relationship between birth intervals and infant and child mortality. WFS data indicate that short birth intervals often raise the risk of infant mortality by 50-100 percent.[23]

The relationship between birth-spacing and mortality constitutes a strong justification for integrating family planning education, information and services as instruments for reducing infant and child mortality. Not only have maternal and child morbidity and mortality been directly improved through birth-spacing, but women's health has been indirectly improved. Other effects are also apparent, such as improved physical and mental development of youngsters, with long-term benefits in human capital investment.

Influence of mother's age on infant, child and maternal mortality

Another important finding is that of the link between the mother's age and both maternal and child health and mortality. Studies show that babies born to mothers younger than 16 years are much more likely to die in the first month of life. The pattern of early mortality for babies of young women seems little changed even when indirect socio-economic influences are controlled. Thus the relationship appears to stem primarily from biological causes.[24] Likewise, babies born to mothers older than 40 are more likely to die in infancy. In this case, however, no known biological mechanism has been established as the cause. As for birth order, many studies confirm the conventional observation that first births are more likely than second or third births to have higher mortality. This applies particularly among younger mothers. Maternal morbidity and mortality are similarly affected.

The above findings underscore the importance of family planning programmes for the very young, as is being emphasized in special projects aimed at adolescents and youth. Apart from their value in reducing fertility and improving maternal health and well-being, family planning programmes for older mothers are equally important for the health and survival of babies. The causal relationship found between birth-spacing and reduced infant and child mortality also implies that policies raising women's marriage age will lead to reduced infant mortality. The implications of these findings are that programmes should provide health care early in infancy for babies of very young mothers and should monitor the condition of babies of older mothers throughout infancy.[25]

Influence of mother's education on infant, child and maternal mortality

An increasing body of evidence suggests that child care practices in the household are key variables in child mortality and are favourably influenced by a mother's additional years of education.[26] Research and policy analyses have shown that the mother's level of education both directly and indirectly influences exposure to health risks and responses to a sick child.[27] In India's Kerala state and in Sri Lanka, for example, studies indicate that women's educational attainment adds to their self-assurance, which in turn makes them more ready to take the initiative in seeking medical care for a sick child and demanding that good care be

14

available in the local community.[28] Mothers with more education tend to maintain improved personal and household hygiene; have more knowledge of disease and nutritional processes; are more likely to use modern health services and to have changed birth intervals. Such mothers are also better household managers, and their family income is more likely to have increased. Women's educational attainment can also bear indirectly on maternal mortality.[29]

These findings have created an important rationale for enhancing women's opportunities in population and development (see Box 2). They also justify the expansion of female access to education as an instrument for reducing infant and child mortality as well as for reducing fertility. Full support should thus be continued for education and communication programmes for schoolgirls and older women with the explicit goal of reducing mortality.

Box 2

WOMEN, POPULATION AND DEVELOPMENT

The International Conference on Population, held in Mexico City in 1984, and the World Conference to Review and Appraise the Achievements of the United Nations Decade for Women: Equality, Development and Peace, held in Nairobi in 1985, confirmed a global consensus regarding the close relationship between women's roles, on the one hand, and demographic and development goals, on the other hand. Both Conferences emphasized the need for the international community to increase support of activities aimed at improving women's situations as an important aspect of the overall development process. Furthermore, recommendations adopted at both Conferences urged Governments to take the measures necessary to facilitate the involvement of women in all phases of national development. Neither national economic nor demographic goals could be achieved, it was noted, without taking into account the specific contributions of women and their needs.

Improvement of the status of women is an important issue *per se*. Moreover, it has even greater significance in the context of the UNFPA mandate because it influences and is influenced by a number of demographic factors, such as fertility and maternal and infant mortality patterns. In addition, because of their dual productive and reproductive roles, women require attention to their special needs as mothers and the consequential demands upon them in this dual responsibility. UNFPA has always emphasized that women's aspirations and their decisions are vital to an effective population policy and that more women should take part in decision-making both in the family and in the community.

The importance attached to the need for special efforts to promote women's participation and the incorporation of their specific concerns into policies and programmes has led to the formulation and implementation of concrete policies and strategies to enhance the status of women in the context of population programmes. To implement the Fund's policies in regard to the integration of women's interests into all population activities, UNFPA has emphasized two complementary approaches: (a) promotion and support of activities required to ensure the participation of women and the incorporation of their interests in all programmes and projects; and (b) support of projects specifically developed to benefit women, as well as inclusion of specific components benefiting women in other projects where appropriate.

These two approaches proceed simultaneously. In the context of UNFPA work, specific projects are those designed explicitly to benefit women. In these projects, activities are recognized as having a direct bearing on improving the situation of women. The activities include education, training, skill development, economic activities, child care and community participation. Specific projects also include activities aimed at increasing the awareness of policy makers, political leaders, the media and the public of the importance of women's issues. They include the identification of constraints to the full participation of women in the development process. As a result, measures can be designed to overcome those constraints, and institution-building activities can be undertaken to strengthen the capacity of national women's organizations to participate fully in development activities. Moreover, such activities can assist women's organizations in expanding their roles beyond the traditional ones and to become advocates for women.

Despite many achievements in recent years, it is clear that much more remains to be done to ensure the full incorporation of gender issues into all aspects of population as well as other developmental programmes. For example, it has usually been assumed that, because maternal and child health and family planning and many information, education and communication activities are addressed mostly to women, these activities are automatically gender-sensitive and meet the needs of women. Evaluations have shown, however, that programme quality has often been seriously wanting because the specific needs of women--for example, culturally sensitive modes of delivery, appropriate hours and location of services, and confidentiality--have not been considered in the design and the implementation of project activities. Women have seldom been consulted or involved in needs identification, programme development and management, or decision-making.

Another sector of population programmes where progress has been noteworthy in regard to gender-specific issues--but also where much more needs to be done--is the field of data collection and analysis. Increased efforts are required to ensure the collection, analysis and dissemination of data dissaggregated by gender. In this regard, the need for identifying accurate indicators of the actual situation of women in specific areas should be emphasized. Only with this type of information can policies and programmes aimed at improving the situation of women and increasing their participation in developmental efforts be planned and progress measured.

Influence of socio-economic status on mortality and fertility

Another major finding of research and policy analyses is the extremely high mortality rates among the poorest subgroups in populations. In Bangladesh and India, data indicate that child mortality rates among families of landless workers (agricultural labourers) are 50 per cent higher than those among owner/worker families and close to three times those of land-owners (see Table 3). Data on the fertility response to death rates (elasticities) show rates 50 per cent higher among landless families than among land-owning families (see Table 4). Research and policy analyses clearly identify the need to focus efforts on disadvantaged population subgroups in countries where economic and health conditions are apparently interacting to produce a high mortality-fertility trap.

Table 3

MORTALITY IN SELECTED AGE GROUPS (BOTH SEXES), BY OCCUPATION OF HOUSEHOLD HEAD, MATLAB, BANGLADESH, 1974-1977

Occupation of household head	Death rates per thousand population	
	1-4 yrs.	15-44 yrs.
1974 - 1977 Average:		
Agricultural Labourer	42.9	3.6
Owner/worker	27.5	2.4
Landowner	15.9	2.2
1975 Famine Year:		
Agricultural Labourer	57.9	5.7
Owner/worker	35.7	3.5
Landowner	14.5	3.2

Source: Stan D'Souza and A. Bhuiya, "Socio-Economic and Mortality Differentials in a Rural Area of Bangladesh", *Population and Development Review*, vol. 8, No. 4 (December 1982), p. 761.

Table 4

FERTILITY RESPONSE TO DEATH RATE AMONG RURAL HOUSEHOLDS, BY LANDHOLDING STATUS, INDIA, 1970-1971

	Female Age Group	
Landholding Status	*40-44 Yrs.*	*45-49 Yrs.*
	Elasticities *	
1. Landless	.136	.167
2. Landowners	.088	.113
3. Ratio (1)/(2)	1.55	1.48

Source: BCM. T. R. Sarma, "Demand for children in rural India", in *Fertility in Developing Countries*, G. M. Farooq and G. B. Simmons, eds. (London: Macmillian, 1985), p. 359.

One reason the poorest groups are not benefiting from efforts to reduce morbidity and mortality is that data are lacking on where these disadvantaged groups are. For the same reason, analysis of the relative impacts of medical, MCH/FP and socio-economic improvements on health conditions of these groups has been limited. But the unavailability of data is not the only problem. Population programmes and funding agencies pay far more lip-service to "disaggregation" and to specifying targets of relatively disadvantaged subgroups than to concerted efforts to understand and resolve their predicament. As a result it is impossible to tell (a) whether current country programmes are assisting those most in need, (b) whether assistance to the poorest subgroups, e.g., the landless,

---

* An "elasticity" relates the percentage change in one variable, such as "children ever born", to the percentage change in another, such as the child mortality rate. In this table, the elasticity of .136 for women aged 40-44 years in landless families means that for every 1 per cent change in the child mortality rate among landless couples, the number of children ever born to these families will change .136 per cent. The difference in elasticities between landless and land-owning families (a ratio of 1.55 in this table implies that increases or decreases in fertility are more responsive to changes in child mortality among landless families than land-owning families.

is sufficient to overcome debilitating effects of their socio-economic situation, or (c) whether and to what extent the problem is being neglected because of emphasis on targets and strategies that are aimed at aggregates.

Hence the relationship between efforts to reduce mortality and actual declines in mortality within target groups remains poorly understood. The complexity is compounded because individual motivations for reducing morbidity and mortality are difficult to quantify. In addition, notwithstanding national commitment to solving a particular problem, the resources channelled for that purpose may be insufficient.

Findings on migration and population distribution

A strong consensus has emerged that problems of migration should be the focus of intensified research, policy analyses and programmes to improve population distribution. The WPPA (1974), the Report of the International Conference on Population (1984) and several United Nations Population Inquiries have indicated that population distribution is of urgent concern to most countries. By 1985, more Governments sought policies to modify migration (72 per cent of 170 countries) than they did policies for any other population problem. In developing countries, governmental concern over migration problems took second place only to concerns over mortality reduction. In Africa, 65 per cent of Governments sought interventions to decelerate or reverse migration; in contrast, 47 per cent sought interventions to reduce fertility. Almost every internal assessment by population assistance agencies has recommended attention to migration as a priority area of research, policy analyses and programme development.[30]

Ramifications of migration and population distribution problems

One reason for this consensus is that problems of population distribution and migration have powerful intersectoral ramifications, particularly on rates of urban growth. Mushrooming cities in many less developed countries are largely the result of rural-urban migration and natural increase rates (fertility minus mortality) of new migrants. Pressure on urban planners and policy makers to provide health, education and housing services has been unprecedented. The cost to urban environments is often visible in depletion of the agricultural lands near towns and cities for squatter settlements and shanty towns; in environmental degradation affecting urban water supplies, green spaces etc.; and in congested transportation, health and school systems. Indeed, unanticipated migration can redistribute population in ways leading to rapid population growth and related problems far beyond what would be attributable to fertility alone.

Rapid rural-urban migration also has important effects on age distribution and the labour force and manpower development in rural and urban areas. It is well known that migration from rural areas tends to be selective of relatively young, better educated residents. This tendency

19

can rapidly alter the age and human-capital distribution to the disadvantage of labour-force productivity. The idea that migration from rural areas has often kept those left behind on a treadmill of inequality and underdevelopment has fueled debate on what is to be done. Research and policy analyses have also found that migration affects fertility not only directly, but also indirectly, through its impact on income inequality.

Finally, persistent problems associated with international migration have intensified the concerns about migration. Some of these problems are outside the scope or mandate of international population programmes and agencies: they cut across national boundaries, are not politically neutral or require international consensus for their resolution. These include the so-called brain-drain and shortages of skills in origin countries--problems that frequently motivate Governments to criticize the policies, or lack of policies, of other Governments. On the other hand, problems of channelling remittances earned by foreign workers to productive investments in their home countries, or unfavourable treatment of "guest workers" and their families in host countries, usually involve domestic policies and thus entail measures to resolve them.

Against this background, several research and policy studies question the relatively little attention given to migration. One explanation is that migration has traditionally been viewed as tangential to "population concerns", whereas concerns over mortality, fertility and rapid population growth occupy a more central place. Another explanation is that migration interventions entail "action" programmes or costly capital outlays to finance projects to resettle populations, to undertake politically sensitive agrarian reforms or to build "counter-magnet" cities as an alternative to residence in principal cities.

Increasingly, however, Governments are realizing that migration is central to all population-development interrelationships. Equally important, migration--and thus income distribution, congestion, environmental degradation and fertility--can be influenced in ways that do not entail costly capital outlays. Often, problems in the spatial distribution of the population arise from unintended effects of development policies. As detailed below, these policies include national economic policies concentrating investments on urban centres while simultaneously discouraging rural-urban migration; poorly planned decentralization policies for industry and job creation; and inadequate population and migration planning in agrarian reform and resettlement schemes.[31]

Unintended effects of fiscal and development policies

One of the priority topics for population research and policy analyses is the hidden effects of certain development policies on the behaviour of population variables and the performance of population policies. Population specialists usually equate distortionary fiscal policies with "urban bias"--that is, whether for reasons of favouritism, elitism or political pressure, national development expenditures tend to be concentrated on urban areas, which thereby become more attractive to rural residents seeking to improve their economic and social welfare. Development economists, on the other hand, view urban bias as only one of several reasons for the draw of urban areas. Equally important are discriminatory price policies that keep "farm gate" prices down, thus reducing rural incomes and job creation; preferential tariffs for industry or discriminatory tariffs for agriculture that worsen terms of trade between rural and urban areas and thus motivate rural-urban and rural-rural migration; and negligent tax policies that reduce incentives to develop transport, storage and marketing systems in rural areas.[32] The potency of these distortionary measures on rural and agricultural incentives has been forcefully argued by the World Bank.[33]

Effects of migration on rural women

Consider a question posed by a department head of a major international agency: "How can there be a labour shortage in rural agricultural areas in several African countries when rapid population growth is supposed to be a problem?" One answer is that distortionary agricultural pricing has so reduced incentives for farming that adult males migrate in search of better paying jobs. The irony is that their absence contributes to higher fertility by placing pressure on their wives to have more children to assist on the farm.[34]

In addition, studies conducted by the Food and Agriculture Organization of the United Nations (FAO) of many developing countries--Botswana, Mozambique and the Sudan, for example--show that socio-legal conditions of rural women can be heavily compromised when policies unintentionally promote the migration of adult male family members out of rural areas.[35] In some countries, women tend not to have legal rights over land or full votes in rural co-operatives, even though they are the *de facto* heads of households.[36] Such constraints deny them resources for farm investment and the full powers of farm management and thus limit their capacity for improving their socio-economic situation. Programmes of population education and training for rural women may be hindered if the indirect effects of migration and women's socio-legal constraints are not considered.

Effects of remittances

The argument has often been made that the benefits of migration to individuals result in negative returns at the societal level, in the form of urban congestion, depletion of rural skills and brain drains. Yet, policy analysts are just beginning to decipher the important role of remittances in producing net costs and benefits. Within developing countries, it is not unusual for 15-35 per cent of rural family income to consist of remittances from migrant family members.[37] In 1980, migrant remittances to nine relatively poor labour-exporting countries in North Africa and the Middle East were approximately $5 billion, representing 24 per cent of their combined value of exports.[38]

21

Few Governments have systematically designed policies and strategies to channel remittances into productive investments. Studies by the International Labour Organisation (ILO), FAO, IDRC, the World Bank, and Harvard University's Migration and Development Programme reveal that remittances contribute to food security and housing for families, farm investments and reduction of income inequality.[39] In contexts of rural stagnation, migration for remittances may help reduce rural-urban income inequality, help families prosper and thus contribute to fertility changes. On the other hand, as discussed above, the migration of male household heads may place pressure on their families to have more children to help manage family activities or businesses. Similarly, landless families may pursue larger families to promote remittance strategies through rural-rural and seasonal migration. Thus migration for remittances may either contribute to, or undercut, objectives of policies advocating fertility reduction. As Governments have few mechanisms for dealing effectively with these issues, there is a clear role for research and policy analyses.

Effects of interventions

Efforts to control urban population growth--through policies to restrict rural out-migration or urban in-migration, to develop urban counter-magnets and alternative growth poles, or to transfer and resettle urban populations--have been relatively unsuccessful. As many studies show, the policies have seldom been well conceived, well implemented or sufficiently integrated with other development policies.[40] Furthermore, many such interventions are extremely costly (new cities, land reclamation and resettlement), thus reducing incentives for assistance from population funding agencies. At the same time, some advocates of urbanization have questioned the wisdom of such interventions. They point to urban areas as centres of modernization and industrialization, catalysts for development. These centres, it can be argued, are vital receiving points for migrants who might not otherwise be fully used in stagnant rural areas. Furthermore, a shift of a country's population through migration from rural to urban areas may accelerate "modernization", prompting individuals to be more open to suggestions for planning their life course, including the planning of their families. Finally, a 1979 study of urban growth in less developed countries[41] illustrates that policies affecting natural increase as well as policies affecting migration have a strong influence on urban growth.[42] Thus the provision of family planning services may effectively reduce population growth in urban areas.

Perhaps the greatest confusion in devising policies for this area stems from an "unnatural" alliance of policies to redistribute incomes and benefit the poor, on the one hand, and policies to promote rapid economic growth through efficiency-oriented investments, on the other. That is, Governments themselves may be unclear about whether and to what extent their agendas to promote the social welfare of all citizens are consonant with urgent priorities of economic policies.[43] Furthermore, the goals of international aid agencies might actually conflict with governmental priorities, depending on the extent to which their assistance is guided largely by social welfare criteria (grants only) or is dependent on

22

recipient Governments' assuring rates of return on foreign assistance (e.g., loans).

Needs for data

One reason why few Governments have been able to modify internal migration substantially[44] is that policies have been built on highly incomplete data and analysis. It is impossible to conduct salient policy analyses of migration, or to prescribe interventions to modify it, without ascertaining the characteristics of origin and destination areas, particularly areas of high "expulsion" and "attraction." This knowledge is needed for analyses of rural-rural migration, circular migration and stage migration--all of which may function as a substitute for "permanent migration"[45]--as well as of determinants of international migration.

However, surveys of migrant characteristics *per se* are now abundant. Hundreds of surveys have been undertaken to measure characteristics and consequences of migration from rural to urban areas, between cities and between countries. Several reviews of the literature have produced profiles of migrants' age distribution, educational characteristics, occupational and marriage status, residence patterns etc.[46] In addition, major guidebooks have been produced on techniques of measuring and analysing migration.[47] This extensive body of research may be used to generalize about migrant characteristics and consequences of migration for the rural areas of origin and the urban areas of destination. In the areas of origin those effects include, for example, the depletion of relatively educated, skilled workers; in the urban destination areas they include impacts on labour markets and demand for services.

Notwithstanding this body of research, an understanding of the characteristics of migrants only begins to uncover the causes of migration. Migrants react to "structural" characteristics at the places of origin and destination. Those characteristics in turn give rise to relative deprivation between places, determined by the free market economy (growth of local employment, wages); government expenditures on housing, water, schools; the political economy (long-lasting inequalities in land ownership), the political climate and a range of amenities.

A knowledge of the structural characteristics and their effects on relative deprivation, fiscal policies and the role of remittances would produce a deeper understanding of motives for migration. However, to capture rigorously the effects of structural characteristics on migration flows, it is essential (a) to establish, in censuses and migration surveys, places of previous and current residence, duration at current residence and destination and (b) to obtain reliable data on a host of societal and economic variables depicting origin and destination areas. Few developing countries have this information. Furthermore, even when structural effects are evaluated at one time within the same country or region, their significance may shift over time--often because the social and economic processes generating migration are later altered by the migration itself.

23

The design of appropriate policies thus depends upon continuous monitoring of these shifts.

As discussed above, research in general has already contributed much to the policy process.[48] However, the application of specific research findings to policy and planning needs to be greatly enhanced by improving the substantive character of research as well as by strengthening institutional arrangements. The following sections of this chapter deal with these needs.

Role of population planning and integration in policy-making

In the past three decades, most developing-country Governments have given special attention to socio-economic development, adopting development plans as the chief means for translating goals into specific programmes. According to the ILO, during the 1950s and 1960s, when developing countries were just beginning to adopt a planning approach, national development plans served primarily as guides to the use of resources in the public sector. Since then, however, national development plans have become much broader, providing most developing countries with "comprehensive and authoritative statements of medium- and long-range development goals, policies and programmes in major socio-economic spheres".[49]

Most development plans also make some reference--however incidental or superficial--to population matters.[50] Not only do Governments recognize that population variables affect, and are affected by, socio-economic variables, but many are attempting to ensure that their plans reflect these relationships. According to the United Nations Fifth Population Inquiry, 62 Governments of developing countries report having treated population variables in socio-economic planning exercises. Of these Governments, 45 report having given a specific unit in the planning system the responsibility for considering population variables in the planning process.[51]

Yet, despite the widely acknowledged interrelationships between socio-economic development and population, the treatment of population variables and policies in development planning continues to be rudimentary. The report of the 1984 International Conference on Population states that national development policies, plans and programmes as well as international development strategies should be formulated on the basis of an integrated approach that takes into account the interrelationships between population and development.[52] To date, however, efforts to achieve integration have concentrated primarily on the numerical implications of population trends in terms of socio-economic needs, according to a group of experts who examined projects designed to bring about integration. The group concluded that population variables have been treated exogenously in projections of consumption, production, employment and other socio-economic variables.[53]

Although development planning provides a logical and comprehensive framework for introducing population factors into socio-economic development plans, there are conceptual, methodological and practical problems. One problem is the diversity of political, social and economic situations across countries, which may preclude the creation of a uniform approach to integrating population variables into development planning. Each country has development goals and strategies that make its attempts at integration unique. Moreover, the strategies and relevance of development planning itself are so varied that "integrated population and development" may never acquire universal meaning.

Definitions of integration

The concept of integration itself has taken on new meanings since it was first introduced in the World Population Plan of Action (1974). Sometimes the term has been used to describe demographic trends in population size, growth, composition and distribution in national development plans. Sometimes the term has signified the harmonization of population policies with development policies on macro-economic variables, social sectors or regional or spatial factors. Sometimes it has meant the process of considering specific interrelationships between population, resources, environment and development factors in the design of development policies and programmes.

A 1983 seminar organized by UNFPA defined integration as an approach that involves "considering systematically and taking into account explicitly in the planning process, population factors insofar as they significantly influence or are influenced by other variables relevant to development plans".[54] The seminar also specified the twofold aims of integration: (a) to improve the general quality of development planning; and (b) to promote awareness among both planners and policy makers of the need to adopt population policies consistent with development objectives.[55]

The term is used in this chapter to mean the explicit consideration of population variables in development planning, by taking into account both the impact of population factors on development and the implications of development goals, strategies and programmes for population variables. Operationally, this definition means that population variables and goals need to be made endogenous to development planning.

Approaches to integrating population and development planning

Conceptual difficulties notwithstanding, countries have attempted integration[56]--some in simple and practical ways, others in more complex and comprehensive ways. Some have adopted demographic-economic modelling; others have considered the interrelationships between population factors and other important variables in a single field, such as employment and human resources development, agriculture and rural development, or health and family planning. The discussion of approaches below is followed by an examination of certain fundamentals that seem to be necessary regardless of approach. These fundamentals are (a) reliable measures of demographic factors and related variables; (b) basic understanding of interrelationships between demographic and developmental variables; (c) appropriate methodologies; (d) well-trained personnel; and (e) appropriate institutional arrangements.[57]

26

Projections

Demographic contributions to development planning typically consist of demographic information and alternative population projections as part of different planning scenarios. It may be a surprise, however, to learn that until 1974 fewer than half the development plans in developing countries were based on scientific projections of the population by age and sex. Today, the number of plans using population projections is much greater, partly because of the availability of projection software packages for microcomputers. It is also partly because of the simplicity of preparing numerical projections, in contrast to more complex, expensive macro-economic and sectoral demographic-economic planning models.

Population projections have helped planners acquire perspectives not only on the future size, but also on the age structure, composition and distribution of populations, thus enabling them to analyse the magnitude of changes and to calculate the implications of differing population scenarios for specific variables--such as food, housing, schooling and health, including family planning--in socio-economic development planning.

Many opportunities arise for integrating population and development variables in the course of preparing population projections. However, several difficulties have become apparent in projections of non-demographic variables. Few developing countries have undertaken regular long-term projections of social and economic variables, and without such information, it is impossible to link population projections to projected changes in the key socio-economic determinants of fertility, mortality and migration. A consistent series of population and socio-economic projections, with even a simple feedback between the two, is basic to integration of demographic and development variables.*

Single-sector versus multi-sectoral approaches

Some countries have tried to integrate population variables into development planning by concentrating on a priority field, such as employment, health or education. This single-sector approach does not include attention to how the integration activity affects related sectors other than the priority one. Other countries have employed a multi-sectoral approach, which requires simultaneous consideration of interrelationships between population and other development variables in all selected sectors at the specific planning level. More comprehensive than the single-sector approach, the multi-sectoral approach is also much more complex and requires more sophisticated tools.

---

* The United Nations Population Division is compiling a "Manual on the Integration of Population Variables in Development Planning", which includes a series of methods or models for preparing demographic and socio-economic projections needed for a national development plan. The Manual also includes methods for projecting demands for outputs of several socio-economic sectors--agriculture, industry, health, education, human settlements and manpower--as well as sectoral resource requirements.

<u>Modelling</u>

To understand and draw upon the interrelationships between population and development, planners have turned to modelling, and recent years have seen renewed activity in constructing new models or in reformulating existing demographic-economic (population and development) models. These models have served as a framework to study the interrelationships between population and development variables, to prepare a consistent set of economic and population projections, and to evaluate consequences of alternative demographic and socio-economic development policies. In contrast to traditional or simple projections, models relate population variables to socio-economic variables through a matrix of interrelationships and perform simultaneous projections.

At the country level, Mali and Rwanda have attempted to integrate population factors into sectoral development plans through modelling. A successful model prepared by an international agency is the FAO "Computerized Agricultural and Population Planning Assistance and Training System" (CAPPA), a package of methodological and research information designed to help planners learn how to integrate agricultural, rural development and population components into planning. Adapted for microcomputers, CAPPA emphasizes the impact of alternative population dynamics on agricultural-demand patterns and on production potential. In the past, macro-economic models have been used in Jamaica, Kenya, Malaysia, the Philippines, Thailand and Yugoslavia, sometimes at national universities rather than at government planning institutions.

Sectoral models have been used more than macro-economic models because they are less complex, more sensitive to medium-term population changes and less dependent upon large amounts of information, requiring only enough data to establish interrelationships between demographic factors and the particular development variables of the sector. Hence, the data-processing equipment needs are simpler. Planners can work interactively with the model on a microcomputer. Other advantages are that the impact of demographic factors on sectoral development variables is easier to demonstrate and the results and constraints are easier to understand. In contrast to sectoral models, macro-economic models require information about development variables in all sectors, if all the intersectoral relations are to be modelled.

Notwithstanding the progress in population-development modelling, models are currently being used principally for study and research and only rarely for planning or policy formulation.

Critical needs

As mentioned above, regardless of the approach adopted, any success at integrating population factors with development planning seems to depend upon the availability of reliable information, an understanding of relationships, the selection of appropriate methodologies, well-trained personnel and appropriate institutional arrangements.

Reliable and timely measures of demographic factors

One important obstacle to the integration of population variables into development planning is the lack of data. However, the problem seems not to be a lack of population information in general. As discussed in the previous section, many countries already possess a wealth of demographic and socio-economic data collected over the years through censuses, vital registration systems and special surveys. Though more data are needed on certain topics, it is the lack of reliable and timely information for planning that is causing a problem. In addition, planners and other users need the data presented in understandable formats.

In many developing countries, data-processing capabilities are still hindered by shortages of qualified staff and physical difficulties such as power interruptions and lack of equipment maintenance. These problems have led not only to delays in data-processing and dissemination but also to increased cost. Census tabulations in many developing countries are produced three to five years after the enumeration. By the time data are tabulated, questions about the cost of printing and paper often arise. If the census findings have already been published, they are seldom widely disseminated: statistical offices tend either to curtail the number of tables included in the census reports or to cut down on the number of copies printed. Thus, data users have limited access to detailed data and in many instances have to pay the cost of any special tabulations they require.

In addition, census and survey reports often fail to meet the actual needs of various users. Statistical offices need to identify and involve potential users in the early stages of census or survey planning to ensure that the tabulation plan is responsive to user needs. Tapes or diskettes with sample data as well as technical reports, executive summaries, graphic presentations, maps, special tabulations and data bases should be disseminated to researchers and other users. Recent technological advances--microcomputer technology for on-line access to data bases; Compact Disc-Read Only Memory and other optical media, particularly for storage and dissemination of large data sets where on-line access facilities do not exist; and software for the rapid and accurate retrieval of data--greatly facilitate the dissemination of data.

There is also a need for computer-based demographic accounting frameworks that can project at disaggregated levels--such as by age, sex, education, location--the size of the population and labour force, school attendance, educational attainment and numbers of people in need of health or family planning services. Migrant status, employment status, land ownership and other socio-economic classifications are also necessary for national and regional development planning.[58]

29

Understanding the relationship between population and development

Thus far, inadequate attention has been given to the understanding of the relationship between population and development. Instead, demographic data tend to be tacked on to development assessments.[59] Moreover, most impact assessments rely heavily on population-related criteria: Have Governments adopted a population policy? Has a population unit been established in a national planning ministry? Have reductions in mortality and, subsequently, fertility been assisted by family planning services, education etc.? In one country, an impact assessment of a major population and development programme judged success only in terms of numbers of new users of contraceptives and changes in desired family size.[60] Though affirmative answers to these questions may well indicate that population concerns are entering development planning, they bear only indirectly on the *relationship* between population and development itself.

Understanding the role of population in the development process requires answers to questions such as the following: (a) To what extent are population issues exogenous rather than endogenous to national development plans? (b) In countries in which mortality, fertility, migration and income inequality are strongly related, to what extent are population programmes aimed at disadvantaged subgroups? (c) To what extent do population programmes focus on the causes of population and development problems, aiming to alter those that can reasonably be expected to increase the prospects for development? (d) To what extent are the consequences of development policies, such as structural adjustment policies, anticipated, particularly in their effects on the most vulnerable population groups, food security, infant and maternal mortality, education of women, and prospects for achieving sustainable populations and for preventing environmental degradation?

A fuller understanding of the two-way interaction between population and development will also depend upon explicit representation of the population-development linkages that are assumed to benefit development. The benefits to development are often assumed or only vaguely specified in many projects, as in "population and development projects" in Burkina Faso, Egypt, Mexico and Senegal. When a project is vague about the linkages between population variables, such as migration, women and employment--or simply assumes the connections exist--it becomes impossible to ascertain and evaluate the project's impact.

An additional shortcoming is that few systematic attempts have been made to evaluate the representation of population in national development plans. Cross-sectional and time-series analyses would help establish correlations between the representation of population variables in such plans and population funding (absolute dollars), on the one hand, and the existence of a population unit in a national planning ministry, or the existence of a formal population policy, on the other. Aside from a Population Council review more than a decade ago,[61] no systematic work has been undertaken or published in this area.

Programmes to integrate population into national development planning rarely take into account the adverse effects of non-complementary population and development policies on socio-economic gains. Although most reviews of population research and policy analysis cite the need to consider impacts of development projects on population as well as impacts of demographic trends on development, recognition of this issue is usually an afterthought.[62] Recently, however, agencies that are assisting population activities have begun to recognize this gap.[63] A review of population and development planning by the Economic and Social Commission for Asia and the Pacific (ESCAP) concludes that the treatment of harmful demographic consequences of policies adopted for other purposes has been inadequate.[64] ESCAP cites the example of a rice export premium policy applied by the Government of Thailand, which produced an unplanned demographic consequence by distorting rural-urban terms of trade, contributing to unabated migration of villagers to towns and cities. Moreover, such policies often have unexpected reverberations. Lower farm-gate prices for agricultural products tend to reduce farm family incomes, thus constraining the hiring of landless workers on family farms. Wherever infant mortality and fertility are high and employment and income opportunities for women are already low, such policies can produce famine-like conditions for landless families and, consequently, a rural exodus.

To move ahead in this area will require additional research and policy analysis.   Methodologies need to be devised for anticipating the demographic consequences of development policies and for identifying counter-productive policies.   Until then, there is every reason to expect that many development policies may inadvertently continue to affect population goals adversely.

Identification of appropriate methodologies

Even in the narrowest sense of integration--meaning that population variables such as size, growth and composition be treated as exogenous to development goals, policies and programmes--the relevance of population factors in development planning can be greatly enhanced by undertaking and presenting alternative population projections.[65] The more explicit inclusion of the linkages between two or more demographic variables and socio-economic planning depends upon sufficient data and a thorough understanding of indirect as well as direct linkages. For this purpose, better models of development, which adequately reflect the relevance of population factors, are needed.

The choice of approach to integration depends on various criteria, the most important of which are the goals of integration; the availability of resources--technical staff, data and data-processing equipment; and the adequacy of institutional arrangements.   Integrated population and development activities in a regional or spatial context can be undertaken at the regional or subnational level. In projects in Mexico and Senegal, for instance, population factors and policies were integrated with regional and

31

socio-economic development plans. A comprehensive methodology for implementing both the single-sector and the multi-sectoral approaches is still being developed.

Training

Many assistance agencies, as part of their efforts to help developing countries become   self-reliant in research and policy analysis, have supported research and training at specialized population and development centres, interregional demographic institutes, universities and national institutions. For example, UNFPA funds several demographic institutions in which the training programme includes a module on population and development.   In addition, the Centre for Development Studies, Trivandrum, India; the Catholic University at Louvain, Belgium; and the Institute of Social Studies at The Hague in the Netherlands now offer specialized and concentrated training in population and development interrelationships.

Much remains to be done, however, to ensure adequate training in population and development policy and planning. The first challenge is to gear the type of training proposed in project plans to the type of substantive skills actually required. Many population projects, seeking to ascertain the impact of population variables on the economy--for example, the relationship between an aging population and the fiscal carrying capacity--include provisions for training at specialized demographic institutes because of the lack of national expertise in these areas. For example, dozens of plans for projects concerned with complex economic-demographic interrelationships have recommended master's degree or doctoral training in demography *per se*. Solid training in economics is required as well. A related problem is that many programmes designed to produce professionals with solid economic and demographic skills tend to be filled much more often by those with backgrounds in demography and statistics than by those with backgrounds in socio-economic development planning. This practice is not conducive to fostering integration of research and policy analysis in national economic development planning ministries. The UNFPA Global Programme of Training in Population and Development was established specifically to help correct the problem.

Course materials should be developed to promote understanding and communication on this poorly understood subject for all levels of population research and planning--for advanced researchers, policy analysts, project designers and field officers. At present, course materials seldom adequately treat the integration of population factors into development planning. In addition, appropriate training materials, including microcomputer simulation programmes to illustrate population dynamics at the sectoral level, are in short supply. Again, training materials usually treat population variables and their consequences as highly aggregated, exogenous processes. When they do treat them as endogenous, the materials are unnecessarily complex. The types of manuals needed would contain systematic, step-by-step instruction in population and development interrelationships.

Institutional arrangements for population planning

Recognizing the importance of strengthening the institutional setting, several countries have established national population councils at cabinet level and population units as co-ordinating and operational bodies under the councils; others have placed population units or divisions in planning institutions; still others have set up population units in sectoral ministries or in regional development planning bodies (see Box 3).

Box 3

INTEGRATED POPULATION AND DEVELOPMENT PLANNING IN POPULATION UNITS

One of the primary objectives of UNFPA assistance to population and development planning is to enhance the capacity of Governments to undertake their own planning and integration efforts. Between 1969 and 1985, funding to strengthen national institutional capacity accounted for approximately 33 per cent of UNFPA funds in support of population and development projects.

Two yardsticks for measuring a country's commitment to population concerns are the establishment of a national population commission and a population unit. A population commission usually functions as a high-level policy-making body, whereas population units tend to be directly responsible for the day-to-day work of integrating population variables into development planning. According to United Nations surveys, by 1983, 61 population units had been established. Of the 51 countries classified as members of the United Nations Economic Commission for Africa, 36 per cent had population units. The corresponding percentages for the remaining Economic Commissions were 39 per cent for Latin America, 46 per cent for Eastern Asia, 8 per cent for Western Asia and 31 per cent for Europe. However, nearly half of the 170 countries represented by these regional commissions have not yet established a population unit.

That population units facilitate the integration of population and development is clear. Those countries with the strongest population units--in terms of staffing, appropriate institutional location and longevity--had the best record for integrating population concerns into development planning. By carving out an institutional niche, preferably in a national planning ministry, population units represent a focal point for population expertise and for assessments of the implications of population growth and distribution patterns for development targets (e.g., needed food supplies, medical facilities, schools, housing). As a physical entity, population units typically house population reference materials and can be used to organize seminars, promote apprenticeships and training. They also promote interaction among economists and demographers, thus helping to enrich and broaden development perspectives.

Although the existence of a population unit or council does not guarantee that population factors will be adequately incorporated into development planning, it does represent an important and necessary step towards integration. Most external assistance for this purpose has been devoted to strengthening or establishing population units to help Governments integrate population variables into development plans at national and subnational levels, through projects executed primarily by the ILO and the United Nations Department of Technical Co-operation for Development (UNDTCD). Many ILO-executed projects for strengthening institutional capacity--including those in Cape Verde, Mali, Nicaragua, Somalia and the United Republic of Tanzania--have focused on the creation of population and human resources units in national planning ministries and departments of population and human resources. UNDTCD has executed relevant projects in El Salvador, Honduras, Rwanda and Senegal. National Governments have executed still other projects in Ecuador and Mexico.

Some critical questions about institutionalization are still unresolved:

(a)   Where, within the government structure, should a population unit be located?

(b)   Should only one population planning unit be established at the central level in the planning ministry or should there be population units within each of the sectoral population-related ministries?

(c)   What types of institutional arrangements will be required and would be most suitable at subnational and regional levels?

(d)   What should the population unit do?

(e)   How should the network of planning-related units be built up at different levels and different sectors, and what hierarchical and functional linkages should be created between all units?

(f)   What legal status should the population unit have?

(g)   How many personnel should the population unit have, with what professional backgrounds?

A review of several country programmes and projects reveals that the functioning of planning units has been hampered because of the following: (a) lack of knowledge and information on population among planners; (b) a shortage of adequately trained personnel, particularly those trained in methodological and technical aspects of the population unit's work; (c) insufficient or inadequate training programmes; (d) lack of institutional experience (methodologies, guidelines, procedures) to create, implement and evaluate the population unit itself; (e) competition of population issues with other socio-economic development issues for the planners' priorities;

(f) lack of communication between planners and demographers about the integration of population variables into development planning; (g) insufficient collaboration between planning and research institutions; and (h) shortage of financial resources for implementing programmes other than family planning. Another problem has arisen in countries without a population policy or without a consensus on the role of population in development planning. Lacking a clearly defined institutional framework, population units have been unable to set working priorities or to concentrate on activities that would contribute most to integration objectives.

Despite these and other constraints, population units are increasingly playing an important role in integration efforts. Whatever the institutional model, it is clear that for effective integration of population and development planning to take place, there must be a network of local capabilities in data collection, research and analysis on population and development interrelationships, policy formulation and programme development, and population and development planning.

Role of population data collection
in policy-making

Information about a country's population, growth, characteristics, living conditions, spatial distribution and physical resources is vital for rational policy formulation and planning. For this reason, the collection and analysis of population data constitute a fundamental part of the web of policy-related activities (see Box 1). Over the past two decades, many countries have made demonstrable progress in obtaining such data. Yet, as discussed below, much remains to be done to bring the data fully to bear on population policy-making.

Planners need population data and information to assess demographic trends; to assess the socio-economic situation of women; to design population policies, strategies, programmes and projects; to integrate population factors into development planning; to monitor and evaluate the effectiveness of policies and programmes in light of national development goals; and, as discussed in chapter 4, to help promote population awareness among government decision makers and the population at large.[66] All these tasks require a vast body of information and statistical series, which, in turn, require viable national statistical organizations as well as training and research in demographic and statistical methods.

Types of data needed

The types of data needed for population policy-making include socio-economic and health as well as demographic data, and range from data on individuals, households and families to the community and society. Four broad types of data can be distinguished: stock data, flow statistics, community-level data and programme data.

Stock data

Stock population data are the data from censuses and surveys. Usually undertaken at 10-year intervals, population and housing censuses provide information for all administrative divisions of a country down to the smallest recognized area. Censuses also yield the sampling frame for successive surveys. The data from censuses serve as benchmark statistics against which changes over the decade can be assessed. Examples of census data include information on population size; growth; distribution by sex, age, place of birth and residence (geographic levels); educational attainment and school enrolment; marital status and age at first marriage; fertility; mortality; economic activity; employment; occupation and industry; household structure and composition; and housing characteristics. Censuses can also provide data on minorities and special groups such as women, the elderly and youth.

36

In addition to censuses, surveys have become integral data-collection activities. Surveys help planners measure short-term changes at national levels or in large areas; they also provide detailed data on particular topics. For example, household surveys are often used to collect data on such topics as underemployment, which may not be covered in any detail in the census. Surveys such as the Contraceptive Prevalence Survey (CPS), the Demographic and Health Surveys (DHS) programme, the National Household Survey Capability Programme (NHSCP) and the World Fertility Survey (WFS) (see Box 4) have provided needed data on a variety of topics, including fertility and pregnancy history; knowledge, attitude and practice of contraception; breast-feeding; mortality; migration; family formation and dissolution; disability; school enrolment and educational attainment; economic activity; employment, occupation and industry; and income and expenditures.

Box 4

INTERNATIONAL SURVEYS

World Fertility Survey

The World Fertility Survey (WFS) was established in 1972 by the International Statistical Institute in collaboration with the United Nations and the International Union for the Scientific Study of Population. UNFPA, the United States Agency for International Development (USAID) and, in later years, the United Kingdom Overseas Development Administration (ODA) contributed substantially to the project. Policy makers and planners have relied on WFS data for reliable information on current fertility levels in preparing population projections, evaluating the effect of national family planning programmes and assessing social and demographic change within a country. Data have been analysed on both a country-specific and a cross-national basis. One unique contribution of the WFS has been the series of analyses on such topics as estimates of fertility levels, trends and determinants; fertility and family structure; breast-feeding; sterilization; contraceptive use; and infant and child mortality. By 1983, 42 developing countries had participated and 20 developed countries had collaborated with the WFS.

Demographic and Health Surveys

The Demographic and Health Surveys (DHS) programme was initiated in 1984 as a five-year follow-up to the WFS and Contraceptive Prevalence Surveys (CPS) programmes. Funded by USAID, DHS is being implemented by The Institute for Resource Development, a wholly-owned subsidiary of the Westinghouse Electric Corporation, as well as The Population Council. The project is providing financial and technical assistance for 35 surveys in Africa, Asia and Latin America, as well as for 25 analytical studies of DHS data. Intended as a primary source of international population and health information for policy makers and the research community, DHS aims at providing surveyed countries with data and analyses on major health phenomena and on family planning, fertility and mortality. It also helps participating countries develop the technical

37

skills and resources necessary to conduct demographic and health surveys. DHS has contributed an integrated microcomputer software package--Integrated System for Survey Analysis (ISSA)--for capturing, processing and tabulating survey data.

National Household Survey Capability Programme

The National Household Survey Capability Programme (NHSCP) was launched in 1979 in response to two resolutions of the United Nations Economic and Social Council stressing the importance of continuous and integrated household surveys for providing essential information on economic, social and demographic conditions of people in developing countries. The Programme is co-sponsored and supported by the United Nations, the United Nations Development Programme, the World Bank, the United Nations Children's Fund and UNFPA, with participation of the United Nations regional commissions and specialized agencies in implementation. The principal aim of NHSCP is to help developing countries obtain a continuing flow of integrated statistics for their development plans, policies and administration. Simultaneously, the Programme serves to build up permanent survey apparatus. As of August 1987, 28 countries were implementing NHSCP.

Data generated by censuses and surveys along with vital statistics compiled from civil registration and population registers, discussed below, constitute the base for demographic analysis. Hence they are fundamental for understanding, comparing and projecting the levels, trends, differentials and interrelationships of demographic, health and socio-economic factors.

Flow statistics

Still another type of data is the population flow statistics continually recorded by administrative record systems, such as those of health and education ministries and civil registration. In education, for example, the records system of education ministries keeps counts of the number of students enrolled in schools by level, gender, age and geographic location, along with drop-out levels. The health records system compiles data on, *inter alia*, the number, characteristics and diagnoses of hospital patients and out-patients. The records system for primary health care registers important information on immunization, nutrition, pre-natal and post-natal care, and contraceptive use. The civil registration system--in the form of complete registration, sample registration or dual registration--captures vital events--births and deaths within small areas. Population registers also provide flow data on birth, death, migration and sometimes on marriage and divorce.

Flow data are needed for monitoring population changes at national and subnational levels. They are also used for evaluating population and development programmes and policies for a country as a whole and for sectors, as the data generated by these systems can be presented at different administrative and geographic levels.

Community-level data

Data on the infrastructure and on community services include information on the availability of schools, hospitals and clinics, maternal and child health care and family planning centres, water supply, electricity, day-care centres, sewerage, transportation, telephones, recreation facilities, libraries, social centres, banking and private-sector services. These data are used both in planning and in evaluating programmes and projects, particularly for designing social marketing family planning programmes.

Programme data

Programme data include family planning statistics, financial data by source and level of expenditures, institutionalization and technical capacity and capability of concerned national offices, staff availability and level of training, staff turnover, and ratio of staff to project beneficiaries in local areas, co-ordination mechanisms, and other indicators of programme and project achievements. These data are indispensable for evaluating and assessing the accomplishments of population programmes and projects.

Achievements in population data collection

Censuses and surveys

Before the 1980 round of population censuses,* only about 70 per cent of the world's population lived in countries in which the population had been enumerated. After the census in China and the censuses of 22 countries under the African Census Programme (see Box 5), the estimated percentage rose to about 95 per cent. In addition to the valuable data gained from censuses, single-round retrospective sample surveys, such as the WFS, CPS and DHS programmes, have helped planners identify levels, trends and differentials in fertility and infant and child mortality.

Box 5

AFRICAN CENSUS PROGRAMME

The African Census Programme (ACP) was launched in 1971, in response to a series of recommendations and resolutions by various United Nations bodies and at the request of a number of African countries

---

* Because countries may undertake their censuses in different years, the census "round" is the term used to indicate decennial censuses held within 10 years on either side of the year indicated. Thus, the 1990 round encompasses all censuses held from 1985 to 1994.

39

that could not participate in the 1970 round of censuses because of inadequate technical and financial resources.

The long-range objective of ACP was to assist African Governments in creating a capacity for conducting all types of demographic data-gathering operations. A related aim was to stimulate the development of vital statistics registration systems. ACP was designed to provide information not only on the present structure of the population--age, sex, urban/rural residence etc.--but also on the components of population change--fertility, mortality and migration. Another goal was to provide in each country a group of experienced technicians able to plan and conduct censuses and surveys. By building up national cadres of officials trained in demographic data-gathering techniques, ACP helped Governments use data from censuses, surveys and vital registration systems in their economic and social development planning.

Of 22 African countries requesting UNFPA assistance under ACP, 15 had never had a complete census of their population. The combined population of the 22 countries was estimated to be 167 million at that time, or approximately 45 per cent of Africa's total population. UNFPA also assisted countries that did not participate in ACP in carrying out censuses during the period.

The United Nations served as the executing agency for the Programme. A team of regional advisers was attached to the Economic Commission for Africa's Statistics Division and to what was then the Population Programme Centre. In addition to ACP support of the regional advisory team, UNFPA projects for population censuses in ACP countries included the assignment of more than 40 resident experts in such fields as census organization, tabulation, data collection, cartography, sampling, data-processing and data analysis, as well as short-term consultancies. Fellowships were provided for training technical and administrative personnel of the countries concerned.

A UNFPA evaluation of ACP covering 9 countries--Burkina Faso, Cameroon, the Congo, Côte d'Ivoire, Liberia, Madagascar, Senegal, Somalia and the Sudan--indicated that, despite many problems, reliable population data were available for many countries for the first time, and cadres of trained technicians and administrative personnel were in place. A review of the 1980 round of censuses indicated the needs for more attention to sampling techniques; strengthened institutional frameworks; a census cartography programme; evaluation and analysis during preparatory activities; more formal quality-control procedures; improved coverage of special population groups; a comprehensive document on editing specifications; and continued training of more data processing staff and of national staff in various aspects of censuses and surveys, including management.

Censuses and surveys in developing countries have generally employed tested methodologies and documentation schemes, including tabulation plans, made available chiefly through the efforts of the United Nations Statistical Office, the International Statistical Institute (ISI) and the U.S. Bureau of the Census. Further, the availability of United Nations, public-domain and commercial software and the adaptation of that software for microcomputers have contributed much to the timely recording, editing, tabulation, dissemination and analysis of census and survey data (see Box 6). These advances have aided developing countries in overcoming many problems in data-processing. Today, microcomputer software is also available for statistical and demographic analysis and projections and for computer map digitization and data retrieval.

Box 6

MICROCOMPUTER SOFTWARE PACKAGES

Software packages--and microcomputer software packages in particular--have greatly eased the burden of data-processing. A wide range of microcomputer software for population activities is now available, either commercially or through the United Nations and other public-domain organizations and agencies. Examples of software by area of application follow:

Census planning - CENPLAN, a software for establishing the census calendar and estimating the cost, time and manpower requirements for each census operation is being developed by the International Statistical Programs Center (ISPC) of the U. S. Bureau of the Census.

Data capture - Software for effective data capture and validation includes PC-EDIT of the United Nations; CENTRY, produced by ISPC; the Data Enter Package for the East-West Population Institute; and two commercial packages, RODE-PC and ENTRY POINT.

Data edit - Packages for editing data include UNPC-EDIT, Consistency and Correction (CONCOR) of ISPC and Data Enter of the East-West Population Institute.

Data cross-tabulation - Packages for summary cross-tabulations from statistical data, some producing camera-ready tables, include the United Nations PC-COXTALLY and the CENTS 4, produced by ISPC.

Integrated software - For data capture, validation, editing and tabulation, software includes the Integrated Microcomputer Processing System (IMPS) of ISPC and the Westinghouse Integrated System for Survey Analysis (ISSA).

Demographic analysis - Software for demographic analysis includes the Fertility Analysis Package of the East-West Population Institute, the U.S. Census Bureau's Microcomputer Programs for Demographic Analysis (MCPDA), UNDTCD-SMPD, the United Nations Software Package for Mortality Measurement (MORTPAK-LITE) and the CELADE PANDEM.

41

Population projections - Software for projecting population, using mainly the standard cohort component projection methods, include The Futures Group DEMPROJ-Population Projection and RAPID-Population Projection, the ESCAP/POP, The Population Council FIVFIV--SINSIN--Population Projection, the National Institute for Demographic Studies Animated Pyramids for demonstrating demographic projections, the CELADE PRODEM, and the United Nations PROS.

Statistical analysis - Software for a range of statistical functions--descriptive statistics, regression, variance analysis, time-series analysis, multivariate analysis, graphics etc.--includes the SPSS, SAS and SYSTAT.

Population data base - Software for the development and management of data bases and for data retrieval at small areas or levels supported by enumeration area maps, includes CELADE REDATAM, PICK and ORACLE, COMPUSHEET, CDATA, TIGER and SUPERMAP.

Population planning - Software for population planning and training in population and development includes the CELADE Long-run Planning Model for Personal Computers (LRPM), The Futures Group Demographic Projection Model for Development Planning (DPMDP), and the ILO Microcomputer-based Training Module: Planning for Population, Labour Force and Service Demand (TM-1).

Population and health - Software for setting family planning targets and health planning includes The Population Council's Target-Setting Model; the Research Triangle Institute's Integrated Population, Family Planning, and Health Planning Model; and the University of Michigan's Health/Population Model (DYNPLAN).

Training documents and manuals such as FLORENCIA, Atlantida, Popstan, and the documentation for the WFS and the NHSCP are contributing much to the technical knowledge of statisticians in developing and developed countries alike. As a result of collaboration between UNFPA, the United Nations Statistical Office, the United States Agency for International Development (USAID) and the International Statistical Programs Center (ISPC) of the U.S. Bureau of the Census, Popstan--generally regarded as the best training documentation on population censuses--is now being augmented with methods for microcomputer processing of census and survey data. The United Nations Statistical Office is designing methods of population data-base management. All these efforts are influencing the institution-building of statistical offices.

Internationally comparable data

Progress has also been made in establishing standards for the collection, tabulation and analysis of population data. The need for internationally comparable data was recognized as early as 1853 by the first International Statistical Congress, which called for "international classification of causes of death for use in vital statistics".[67] The League of Nations and its Health Organization--now the World Health Organization (WHO)--were among the other organizations contributing to the body of definitions, classifications, standards and methods. Their efforts constituted the earliest strategies for improving the completeness, quality and comparability of population data, in general, and vital statistics, in particular. With the establishment of the United Nations, responsibility for improvement in the international comparability of statistics was assigned to the Economic and Social Council and the Statistical Commission. Since then, the United Nations has continued to make recommendations on decennial housing and population censuses as well as on civil registration and sample surveys. The ILO is responsible for providing international classifications of occupations.

In censuses, the comparability of population data has been improved through the use of standard definitions and classifications of households, family, economic activity, industry and occupation, marital status, literacy, place of usual residence etc. The comparability of data on fertility and family planning behaviour has been much improved through the use of WFS survey instruments and standard data tapes. The widespread availability of these high-quality, comparable data sets has permitted many advances in research on fertility and family planning. The comparability of vital statistics has been advanced by the United Nations formulation of principles and recommendations and the WHO international classification of causes of death and morbidity, including the definition of live births and still births.

Application of programme data

The use of population data for population programme development is relatively better than the use of research findings in policy and planning. A detailed survey of countries participating in the WFS, for instance, showed that an overwhelming majority have used WFS findings to strengthen official family planning programmes; public health activities and programmes on women's status; population projections; and the teaching of demography.[68]

Data collection needs

Despite these significant advances, the need continues for obtaining certain types of data for policy-making, improving the quality of data and eliminating wasteful duplication of effort and resources.

43

Data on special subgroups

A major problem is the shortage of reliable data on certain subgroups--among them, women, nomadic populations and minority groups. Data on women are lacking in a number of developing countries in Africa, Asia and the Middle East. Many countries do not collect data by gender, and others do not tabulate data separately for each sex. In addition, data on migration are lacking. The most common method of enumerating nomads is to conduct the enumeration at fixed sites (e.g., water points)--a method resulting in widespread omissions. Consequently, many African countries conduct censuses in two time periods, at one time for the settled population and at another for nomads, with drawbacks affecting both the cost and the quality of the census undertaking. The methods for collecting census and survey data on relatively rare events, such as maternal mortality and deaths of young adults, also require improvement.

Reliable birth and death data

According to an assessment made for the United Nations Demographic Yearbook,[69] more than half the countries in the world lack reliable data on births and deaths. Almost 80 per cent of African countries, 56 per cent of South American countries and 80 per cent of Asian countries reported unsatisfactory (less than 90 per cent coverage) coverage of births. Death registration is even lower.

Because the civil registration system has not yet been developed or is incomplete, many developing countries now employ sample surveys for obtaining vital statistics. With the development of a satisfactory civil registration system, they could reduce dependence--and therefore expenditures--on sample surveys and, at the same time, realize the benefits of having continuous data for every geographic subdivision of the country. However, the impediments and obstacles to complete registration of vital events are considerable; otherwise, all countries would long ago have had the benefits of national vital statistics. Lack of adequate budgetary support; inadequate legal bases; administrative problems affecting supervision and control arising out of the unco-ordinated involvement of several agencies in the registration system; low priority assigned to registration work by administrators and policy makers, resulting in indifferent performance; public attitudes towards civil registration; inaccessibility of local registration offices; lack of trained manpower; and inconsistent legal and statistical definitions--the list of problems is long.[70] Without a strong national commitment to push through the urgently needed reforms, and high-level support for the development of a national civil registration and vital statistics system, no significant progress can be expected in civil registration and vital statistics systems in most developing countries. Every country has an obligation to protect the birthright of its citizens by providing proper documentation of the vital events. Governments that lack adequate national vital statistics for national social and economic planning need to recognize, as a matter of policy, that civil registration and vital statistics are essential for the achievement of national well-being.

Even before complete coverage of the civil registration systems is obtained, existing data could be fruitfully exploited by ensuring that key variables (e.g., mother's age, age and gender of a deceased person, place of birth or death) are included in the registration data. Another step would be to produce detailed tables on births, shown by mothers' characteristics, and on deaths, shown by a variety of personal and demographic attributes. Such tables would greatly increase the scope for analysing registration data. Improved coverage of birth and death registration statistics could be achieved by linking registration with the primary health care reporting system or other health administrative records systems.

Multilateral agencies are attempting to co-ordinate a strategy for improving civil registration and vital statistics and for providing needed technical assistance. A co-ordinating committee has representatives from UNFPA, WHO, the United Nations Statistical Office, the Pan American Health Organization (PAHO), the International Institute for Vital Registration and Statistics (IIVRS) and other interested agencies and organizations.

Quality of data

In most developing countries, mapping for censuses and surveys still requires better planning and more time and funds as well as qualified staff. Seldom do the census offices have base maps. Maps generated for one census are sometimes lost by the time the next surveys or censuses take place. Also, the existing maps rarely cover the total area. Constrained by the high cost and technical complications of aerial photography, census offices in such countries tend to prepare maps from scratch. The cartographic work, based on rough sketching, seldom adequately reflects zones and boundary delineations, leading to coverage errors that inevitably weaken the basis of the sampling frame.

Moreover, quality controls and measurements of content and coverage errors are seldom undertaken, nor is the magnitude of content error presented along with the census and survey data. Procedures for improving data quality are seldom followed and, consequently, the demographic analysis provides the only measure of data quality. Finally, despite many advances in data collection, mortality data lack comparability, principally because of the failure to adhere to uniform international classifications. Migration data also lack comparability, for the same reason but additionally because of the complexity of the phenomenon and the lack of comparable data on immigration and emigration.

Duplication and underuse of data

In every country, a multitude of public and private agencies collects a variety of population data on a routine basis and in special surveys. As a result some efforts are duplicated. In addition, many opportunities for

45

interpretation and analysis of data are missed. Apart from the classic sources of demographic data--principally censuses and civil registration statistics--the data collected by, for example, ministries of health could be used for assessing demographic trends. Some modification of the methods of collecting and analysing these data could be made at relatively low cost. In addition, sample surveys, large and small, could be used more effectively to supplement census data, perhaps even leading to lower costs by allowing simplification of the census questionnaire. More innovative uses of available sources of demographic data would add significantly to a country's knowledge of demographic levels, trends and differentials. It is also important for Governments to co-ordinate more effectively all statistical activities carried out by the various ministries' statistical units.

Priorities for future population data collection and analysis

The development of a permanent capacity for collecting, processing, analysing and disseminating all kinds of statistics and statistical services to cater to the needs of all kinds of users is a dynamic process. Through the concerted efforts of Governments and multilateral and bilateral organizations, a few developing countries have already attained a high level of statistical capability and are largely self-sufficient. Others have acquired a moderate national capability. Still others are in early stages of developing their national statistical capabilities. Despite the considerable variations from country to country, certain priority needs in generating population data and developing institutional capacity can be identified. For countries that are without appropriate legislation, the enactment of law may be the primary need. In addition to legal and institutional foundations, however, there are pervasive needs for enhancing control over resources, for staffing and training, and for dealing with methodological and technological advances. All these challenges have implications for international assistance.

Need for institutionalization and legal foundations

Many Governments in developing countries create *ad hoc* census offices and cartographic units so close to the time of the census or survey that no adequate preparatory activities, not even mapping, can be carried out. Moreover, statistical offices in many countries function in the absence of a Statistical Act. Such Acts establish the mandate for the office to co-ordinate statistical activities and to collect, process, evaluate, analyse and disseminate population data through censuses and surveys. A Statistical Act generally also specifies the periods for conducting these activities and provides guarantees of the confidentiality of individual data. Even in countries that do have such Acts, the legislation is sometimes flawed: some laws have no provisions for national committees of users and producers to set priorities and establish data requirements and, even more important, some have no provisions for government appropriation of required funds.

Managing costs and controlling resources

Recently, cost considerations as well as concern for the burden imposed on the public have led a number of industrialized nations to begin considering alternatives to population censuses. One country, Denmark, has used statistics based on administrative records in lieu of a census; several countries are using sampling techniques or mini-censuses to obtain data to supplement the few items included in the census on a 100 per cent basis. To reduce the heavy cost of a population census, research is needed on the costs, benefits and difficulties of different ways of producing reliable population data quickly. Continuous training and transfer of technical knowledge will thus remain a priority.

In some developing countries statistical offices suffer not only from inadequate budgets but also from lack of control over the financial resources, which are under the authority of the permanent secretary of the ministry in which the statistical office is located. As Governments opt for more quantitative procedures in planning and administration, they should incorporate statistical development programmes into their national development plans and earmark clearly adequate funds.

Staffing and training

Many developing countries suffer from a persistent and rapid turnover of staff. With too few qualified statisticians and data-processing staff to start with, statistical offices are set back even more by the loss of qualified personnel who leave for better job opportunities elsewhere, in part because of the large salary differentials between the private and public sectors. Given the length of time required to replace experienced staff, their loss is seldom offset by training and new recruitment. An additional problem is that some statistical offices currently lack staff with adequate management skills to build an effective statistical programme. This deficit has led to inadequate co-ordination of national statistical activities, poor liaison with data users and slow production of results. Executive training as well as appropriate training materials are needed to overcome this problem. In addition, guidelines on management issues, offering appropriate examples, are called for.

The provision of suitable training for individuals in national statistical offices, planning ministries, universities and research institutes must also be a priority in attempts to enlarge the capacity for carrying out detailed analyses of censuses, surveys, vital registration and other relevant demographic data. Initial assessments of data from various sources as well as detailed analyses of the collected data will help to identify gaps and problems--knowledge that will be valuable for improving data collection and analysis efforts.

Developing methodological and technical capability

Statistical offices in most developing countries need to give greater priority to adapting statistical standards and methods to national conditions. This would help them overcome problems caused by the transfer of technical knowledge, including standards and methods, principally from the United Nations and industrialized nations, without timely or proper adaptation.

Increasing attention will also be needed to meet the challenge posed by new technologies for statistical activities, including remote sensing imagery for constructing maps and geographic statistical frames; audio and video technology for census and survey training and for publicity campaigns; "lap-top" and hand-held computers for interviewing; minicomputer and microcomputer technology for data capture, editing, tabulation, analysis, and dissemination, including the use of Compact Disc-Read-Only Memory; and optical mark readers and optical character readers. The application of these technologies has presented numerous problems, including cost, accessibility to developing nations, training and maintenance, software development, control and data security (that is, confidentiality). Research is still required to solve problems associated with remote sensing imagery for frame construction. Research will likewise be needed to solve problems of confidentiality, control, and the handling and linking of large data sets associated with microcomputers. Special attention should be paid to co-ordinating the development of easily learned microcomputer packages for data-processing and analysis and for establishing data bases and data banks. Detailed documentation and adequate training are priorities.

Problems of statistics on special groups

The methodology for enumerating and analysing data on migration and special subgroups--nomads, semi-nomads, refugees, other minority groups and rare events, such as maternal mortality, needs to be improved, as does the compilation of social indicators, including those on the status of women.

Implications for external assistance agencies

Much progress has been made in the co-ordination of the technical assistance of multilateral and bilateral agencies for the 1990 round of population and housing censuses, particularly for sub-Saharan Africa. In monthly meetings, a co-ordinating committee with representatives from the World Bank, the U. S. Bureau of the Census, USAID, UNFPA and the United Nations Statistical Office reviews the funding status and implementation of censuses, ensuring that efforts are not duplicated. Because countries vary greatly in their capacities, the neediest countries must be identified for priority assistance in data collection, processing, evaluation, analysis, dissemination and application.

Conclusions and recommendations

Population research, policy analyses and planning, and data collection have all contributed to the advancement of knowledge about the determinants and consequences of population change. The challenge now is to identify specifically where and how the population policy process needs to be strengthened or modified to fit future needs.

Research and policy analyses

Despite the growing body of knowledge about fertility, mortality and migration, developing countries often lack most or many of the ingredients needed to formulate knowledge-driven policy--among them, political will, appropriate knowledge, enough properly trained experts and strong institutional arrangements.   Two broad sets of factors--political and substantive--seem to be the main causes.[71]

The political factors include cultural, ideological and social issues. It has been argued that the use of demographic knowledge by political decision makers is determined less by the quantity and quality of demographic data than by the character of the political and bureaucratic systems of the State.[72] Policy decisions are essentially political in nature and tend to reflect ideological preferences and values of the political decision makers.

The substantive problems include the lack of quality and timeliness of available data; unavailability of data on small areas; inappropriateness of data and information for population and development planning; population research findings that are not easily usable by planners because they have not been adequately translated into policy makers' language; and a dearth of solid findings on interrelationships between population variables and development factors.

Severe population problems may well require bold interventions to overcome them, but first the nature of the problems must be fully understood. To uncover the consequences of demographic change for geographical regions, social classes, the environment and sectors such as agriculture, health, education and employment, it is necessary to move beyond vague, unproven assertions that highly aggregated population-development relationships exist. The effort should focus on obtaining more precise empirical evidence to support cause-and-effect relationships at disaggregated, sectoral levels. If the data needed for this work do not exist, disaggregated data need to be collected, tabulated and analysed.

There is little evidence that population assistance programmes are effectively reaching those among the poorest classes of society, where women are trapped on a reproductive treadmill of high fertility, high infant mortality and ill-health. This is perhaps the one area in which population assistance can contribute most to economic development *per se.*

49

Another need is to identify the relative effects of health interventions and socio-economic policies on mortality. A range of thresholds needs to be established to determine the mix of health and MCH interventions as well as socio-economic programmes likely to produce favourable mortality reduction. Establishing such ranges may be unachievable by traditional multivariable analysis of secondary data sources; rather it may require "hands-on" impact-analysis projects in which inputs can be differentially controlled and evaluated.

The important interrelationship between gender roles and demographic behaviour is another research priority. How can women's role as a catalyst in population behaviour be enhanced? For example, what aspects of a formal education system provide women with independence of thought and action, underlying their motivation to reduce family size or adopt contraceptive methods? Can these aspects be identified and then communicated through non-formal systems of education? This is important because in some countries there are strong cultural barriers to sending girls to school.

What decision-making processes among husbands, wives and different generations are affecting major demographic outcomes, such as decisions on family size, spacing of children, and access to population education and services? An important issue here concerns communication between parents about the costs and benefits of children in different socio-economic contexts.

For programmes aimed at changing mortality, fertility or migration among the poor, more research is needed on costs versus benefits. A fundamental issue is whether to expand resources to reach the rural poor- -which can be extremely costly due to logistical problems or small benefits if acceptance levels are low. An alternative is to reach urban dwellers of higher socio-economic status, which would entail lower costs, particularly in programmes with cost-recovery mechanisms, and rely upon relatively higher benefits due to higher levels of acceptance. The answer to such resource-allocation questions may depend partly on the particular region of development or the infrastructure.

Migration issues, as noted earlier in this chapter, have been relatively neglected. Research and policy analyses are needed on the consequences of migration on sending and destination areas; on how migration affects redistribution of the supply and demand for food, urban/rural infrastructure, and fiscal carrying capacity; and on how remittances sent from an urban to a rural area or to a country of origin promote development, particularly in rural areas. An important issue here is that migration can redistribute population in ways that produce rapid population growth and environmental degradation far in excess of that attributable to natural increase alone. Other important research questions are how rural-urban and other forms of migration, such as rural-rural, circular, or stage migration, differ by gender. And, finally, what social,

50

economic and legal opportunities or constraints does the migration of males produce for female family members left behind?

The lack of complementarity between development policies and population policies has become apparent, as development policies continue to have indirect, negative effects on population variables, detracting from the success of population programmes. Fiscal policies, for example, are distorting economic incentives in rural areas, resulting in low employment growth and fostering inequality between rural and urban income, fertility differentials and excessive rural emigration. Planners and researchers alike need to ascertain the extent to which population policies for fertility, mortality and migration are being adversely affected by macro-policies such as monetary or fiscal policies.

Every country has programmes or policies that can be expected to affect fertility, mortality and migration directly or indirectly. Wherever possible, programmes and policies should have built-in provisions for assessing that impact, which would require (a) attention to developing an adequate population data base and research design, (b) analysts equipped to perform the analysis, and (c) incentives to having such analysis performed. Because these ingredients are seldom all present, institutional arrangements should be sought to ensure attention to them when programmes are designed.

The dearth of policy analysis and programme-related research on population variables is the result not only of the absence of institutions specializing in policy and programmatic research but also of an acute shortage of well-trained professionals in this discipline. If the content of research and policy analysis is to be substantially refined and new modalities identified to ensure that findings are applied to policy formulation and programme development, one programmatic implication is the necessity for a short-term training course on the dynamics of policy analysis. Other measures will also be needed to enhance developing countries' institutional capacities for formulating, evaluating and modifying population strategies and programmes through policy analysis.

A United Nations study[73] of data from 81 developing countries shows that the use of demographic information in the formulation of population policies depends in part on the existence of governmental institutions with significant responsibilities in this area. For effective policy formulation, institutions would need to produce demographic information and knowledge, to undertake research on population and development interrelationships and to incorporate such knowledge and research findings into policy formulation and development planning.

Integrating population variables in development planning

In most developing countries, Governments recognize that population variables affect, and are at the same time affected by, other socio-economic development variables. However, no consensus has been reached on the meaning of integrating population and development planning. Because neither the concept nor the scope of integration is clear, as yet, articulating the aims and scope of integration is of utmost priority. Related to that complexity is the nature of population and development phenomena themselves and the host of variables they include. Moreover, relationships between the two sets of phenomena can and often must be considered at micro-, community, macro- and spatial levels, as well as over time. As discussed, neither the statistical methodologies nor the data needed to treat them are readily available.

Also, the expanding scope of development planning itself poses a challenge for integration. In the 1950s, development planning was focused on economic planning; in the 1960s and 1970s, social planning was added; in the 1980s, population planning was included. For the 1990s, considerations of population, resources, environment and development are foreseen. Another major complexity is that of different time or planning horizons when demographic objectives are meshed with economic ones. Whereas development plans usually cover four to six years--a period within which economic and social changes can be realized--demographic changes will become visible only after a much longer time.

A chief concern of planners in developing countries is the allocation of resources within the public sector and the influence on resource allocations within the private sector. The decisions on allocations are made and implemented in an annual time-frame. This constitutes the "investment plan". Though the decisions are generally made annually, they should also be based on long- and medium-term situation-analysis and prospectives. The emphasis on short-run decision-making does not mean that medium and long-term factors should be ignored. Because short-term planning functions affect, and are affected by, population factors in the distant future, any analysis of the role that demographic variables should play in the planning process should clearly distinguish between the period when decisions are to be made and the period when their consequences will be felt.

The lack of research insights, particularly research based upon econometric analyses of population variables, has hampered efforts at integration. One basic problem is the absence of agreed-upon methodologies for research on population and development interrelationships or for the application of research findings to policy-making and planning within the context of short to medium-term development planning. A related concern is the lack of appropriate data and population analysis for planning. Planners have not been provided with population data and research in a technical language and format that are familiar to them, e.g., as elasticity coefficients, capital-output ratios or production functions. Many such efforts have come from the demographic perspective, principally the translation of exogenously prepared population projections into quantitative demands for sectoral planning. Furthermore, given the lack of econometric analysis of economic-demographic interrelationships in most developing countries--analysis that requires both methodological development and empirical work--incorporating population variables into development planning will continue to be difficult.

Other concerns arise concerning the establishment or strengthening of institutional arrangements for integration. Although many countries have created population units for this purpose, many questions of structure and purpose are still unresolved. A major impediment to the success of the institutional arrangements that have already taken place to integrate population and development planning is the lack of qualified specialists in population and development. Also, political instability and changes in development plans over short periods of time can pose major obstacles to the adequate incorporation of population variables in development planning.

The initiation of specialized training programmes for integrating population and development will help bridge the present hiatus. However, success will depend upon a clear understanding of the meaning and aims of integration; a deep national commitment to achieving this integration; efficient machinery to effect, monitor and evaluate the process; and competent staff to carry out activities. Here lies the challenge for national Governments and international organizations alike.

Data collection and analysis

Greater attention should also be paid to institutionalizing activities related to data collection and analysis, to developing low-cost methods of data collection and to incorporating technological developments with a view to enhancing the quality and timeliness of statistics for policy and planning.

All but a few countries have taken a national census; basic descriptive analysis of population is now available for a large number of developing countries; the dynamics of fertility and contraception are better understood today in many countries through the World Fertility Survey programme, demographic and health surveys, and other field investigations; and the availability of trained census statisticians in the developing countries has also greatly improved. Future demands on data collection will arise from policy, planning and programme considerations. Increasingly, policy and programme interventions will need to be aimed at special target groups--women, landless labourers, urban poor, youth, the elderly and others. To meet these needs, data collection, tabulation and analysis should become more gender-specific and more sensitive. In addition to timeliness, the essential requirement is that the data be disaggregated for population subgroups, and then integrated between different social and economic sectors. In this way, for example, an educational campaign to reduce fertility could be based on information about the consequences of high fertility among various population subgroups for the individual, family, community and nation. The availability of integrated statistics will be fundamental in the formulation and evaluation of programmes for these special groups.

53

There is also a need to adapt rapidly and efficiently to technological developments in data compilation. For the full exploitation of technological advances--not only for processing data, but also for experimenting with new methods of data collection and analysis--a well-designed plan of human resources development and training is required. It is essential that human resources planning as well as software development and hardware manufacturing keep pace with technological advances.

The collection of population data cannot continue to be an *ad hoc* and irregular activity. Whether through the censuses, vital registration systems or sample surveys, population data collection needs to be fully integrated into a country's statistical machinery. Thus institutionalization of population data collection and analysis within the national statistical machinery is of the highest priority.

Implications

These and other substantive concerns identified above have major implications. First and foremost, if the policy development process is--as it ought to be--based upon scientific data, research and analysis, there should be strong political commitment, institutional support, budgetary provisions and a willingness to use the findings. Next, the quality and content of research and analysis should be improved, and a research agenda, including critical unresolved research issues with programmatic underpinnings, should be developed in the area of population. Moreover, the contribution of data and research to policy and planning activities in developing countries should be assessed periodically. Training activities need to be closely re-examined, and a cost-effective strategy designed for training specialists to implement the policy development process. Finally, Governments, international and bilateral organizations and NGOs should support, in a co-ordinated fashion, institutional development for data collection, research, analysis, planning and policy formulation. Developing countries have different institutional capacities, and thus technical co-operation should be tailored to meeting particular needs in institutional development.

3. Maternal and Child Health and Family Planning Programmes

Introduction

Why family planning?

Until a few decades ago, societies rarely expended public resources for individuals and couples who wished to control their fertility. In the second half of this century, however, dramatic social and technological changes took place. The rapid emergence of family planning (FP) programmes was one of the most significant of these new developments. At present, more than a hundred countries throughout the world provide either direct or indirect support for family planning services.* The most widely accepted justifications for doing so are the health benefits of family planning for mothers and children; the relationship between population and development; and the right of couples and individuals to make informed decisions about their own fertility.

This chapter focuses on family planning because that service is most closely related to the UNFPA mandate and because other agencies have extensively reviewed other aspects of maternal and child health (MCH) care.** However, because MCH and FP services are frequently delivered in an integrated fashion, many of the observations below regarding FP service delivery and management are equally true of MCH in general.

Health benefits

The health justification for providing family planning is based on the adverse effects of unregulated fertility upon the health and welfare of families and communities, and particularly of women and children. Although women have died in pregnancy and childbirth in every generation, only recently has attention been focused on the nature and

---

* Family planning offers individuals the means to have the number of children they want at the intervals they desire. Therefore, it embraces two types of services, one for the spacing and prevention of births for those who otherwise would have too many children and the other for helping infertile couples to have the children they desire.

** Women, during the reproductive period of their lives, and young children are especially vulnerable to health problems requiring preventive and curative attention. Maternal health care encompasses information and services provided to women of reproductive age and related to their reproductive function. Child health care refers to services provided to infants and children less than five years old. Together these services are usually labelled maternal and child health care. Family planning is an essential component of MCH services.

extent of the tragedy and has pertinent information become available. The International Safe Motherhood Conference held in Nairobi in 1987 brought the critical issue of maternal deaths to the world's attention, calling upon all nations to prevent needless loss of life and to improve maternal health. At present, half a million maternal deaths occur annually during pregnancy and childbirth.[1] About 99 per cent of these take place in the developing world, particularly in urban slums and rural villages, where women experience poor health, ignorance, poverty, low social status and limited access to essential health care, including FP services.

Maternal mortality rates vary from country to country and region to region. For example, in northern Europe, there are typically 2 to 9 maternal deaths for every 100,000 live births, whereas in some parts of Africa there are more than 1,000 deaths for every 100,000 live births.[2] Most developing countries have maternal mortality rates ranging from 300 to 800 per 100,000 live births. The lifetime risk of dying because of a pregnancy-related condition is 1 in 48 for women in developing countries, whereas it is only 1 in 1,462 in developed countries (see Annex Table 1).

The mother's age and the number and spacing of pregnancies are three central factors associated with susceptibility to death and pregnancy-related morbidity. In most developing countries women under the age of 15 are five to seven times more likely to die during pregnancy or childbirth than are women in the 20-24 age group.[3] Women who have had five or more pregnancies and women who are 15-19 years or over age 35 also face substantially higher risks than those in the 20-24 age group. Women who become pregnant within two years of giving birth face higher risks than do women who space births more than two years apart. Additionally, pregnancy can exacerbate many pre-existing chronic conditions, such as heart disease, hypertension, diabetes and hepatitis, all of which can indirectly cause maternal death. Another factor related to maternal deaths is unsafe abortion. Throughout the world, unplanned pregnancies often end in abortions, performed legally or illegally. The World Health Organization (WHO) reports that unsafe induced abortions are responsible for as many as 50 per cent of the maternal deaths in some regions.[4] Although the exact number of abortions is unknown, estimates range from 40 million to 60 million per year.[5] It is calculated that 20-30 per cent of the pregnancies that occur world-wide each year end in abortions, and many women have undergone more than one.

Infant mortality follows the same pattern as that of maternal mortality. On average, infant mortality rates are 10 times higher in the developing than in the developed world.[6] In developing countries, approximately 10 million infants' deaths and another 4 million children's deaths occur each year. Plotted on a graph according to the age of the mothers, infant mortality usually assumes a "U" or "J" curve form, indicating higher risks at maternal ages of under 20 and over 35. Infant mortality varies by birth order, with higher risks for the first-born child than for the second, and mortality rates climb steeply for children born after the third or fourth child. Rates are also higher when pregnancies have been closely spaced.[7]

In sum, maternal and infant deaths are closely correlated with pregnancies that are too early, too late, too many and too close. Thus, in light of the interrelationships between fertility patterns and abortion on the one hand and maternal mortality and morbidity on the other, the extension and improvement of family planning services could reduce maternal mortality and morbidity significantly. Although consensus has not been reached on the magnitude of the impact of family planning on infant and child mortality, family planning has the potential for preventing many needless deaths.

Social and economic development benefits

The social and economic development rationale for family planning is popular in countries where high population density or population growth rates are considered constraints on development. The report of the 1984 International Conference on Population in Mexico City describes well the relationship between population and national development, noting that "social and economic development is a central factor in the solution of population and interrelated problems" and "that population factors are very important in development plans and strategies and have a major impact on the attainment of development objectives".[8]

The exact magnitude of effects and the specific nature of population and development interactions are not yet completely understood. Studies and experience suggest, however, that high population growth rates can exacerbate socio-economic development problems by placing additional burdens on attempts to improve food production, housing, education and health facilities, and job opportunities. Thus, the search for solutions to development problems is likely to be slowed when socio-economic advances are weakened by a rapidly growing population. Many Governments in the developing world, perceiving that rapidly growing populations are complicating the efforts to improve social and economic well-being, have accepted family planning as one element in their strategies for bringing about socio-economic development. In this context, research on fertility determinants and on the impact of women's participation in the labour force has pointed to the crucial roles of female education and employment in reducing fertility.

Basic human rights

The basic human rights rationale for family planning is also widely accepted by most of the countries providing family planning services. The 1974 World Population Plan of Action (United Nations World Population Conference, Bucharest, 1974) and the International Conference on Population (Mexico City, 1984) provided reminders that all couples and individuals should be able to decide freely and responsibly the number and spacing of their children. At those meetings, Governments were called upon to ensure that their citizens have access to family planning information, education and services so that they may effectively exercise this right.

Increasingly, governmental and societal consensus is emerging in regard to the right of all individuals to seek to improve the quality of their lives for themselves and their children through family planning. The World Conference to Review and Appraise the Achievements of the United Nations Decade for Women: Equality, Development and Peace, held in Nairobi in 1985, reaffirmed women's rights to plan their families for the sake of their health. Additionally, it is increasingly accepted that women should be able to exercise their right to take advantage of educational, vocational and employment opportunities, thus contributing directly to social and economic development. To do so, they must be able to control their fertility.

Current family planning practice
and future needs

Current rates of contraceptive prevalence

The history of organized programme efforts to promote the practice of family planning is a relatively recent one. Although in some countries the policy originally tended to be based on the grounds of demographic and socio-economic development, the health rationale soon assumed an equally important role. In the last 20 years programme efforts for promoting family planning practice have expanded significantly. UNFPA has been a major source of support for family planning during this period.

As a result of expanded services, contraceptive prevalence (defined here as the proportion of all women 15-49 years old living in union who practise contraception) in the developing world has risen significantly.[9] Prevalence in developing countries, estimated at 9 per cent in the early 1960s, had risen to 48 per cent in 1987 (as compared with 71 per cent in developed countries). If China is excluded, the rate in developing countries is still calculated at 35 per cent, representing significant growth over the period.

Individual country-level achievements are also impressive: e.g., contraceptive prevalence rates increased in Brazil, from 32 per cent in 1970 to 65 per cent in 1986; in Malaysia, from 9 per cent in 1966 to 51 per cent in 1984; in Mauritius from 25 per cent in 1971 to 75 per cent in 1985; in the Republic of Korea, from 9 per cent in 1964 to 70 per cent in 1985; and in Sri Lanka, from 34 per cent in 1975 to 62 per cent in 1987.[10]

Given the positive effects of family planning referred to in the introduction to this chapter, it is appropriate to review in more detail the degree to which contraception is currently practised around the world. The following presentation draws heavily on the work of the Population Division of the Department of International Economic and Social Affairs of the United Nations Secretariat. The Division routinely estimates contraceptive prevalence for a large number of countries from family planning programme service statistics and from surveys of fertility, contraceptive prevalence, and knowledge, attitude and practice of family planning (KAP). The Division's 1988 update of such estimates, given the varying dates for which the most recent country-level data are available, portrays the situation on average as of mid-1983.[11]

Developed countries

In countries with a relatively high degree of economic development, contraceptive prevalence rates generally exceed 60 per cent (see Table 5). The average prevalence for these countries, weighted by population size, is 71 per cent. Such levels of contraceptive use are associated with a replacement-level total fertility rate (TFR) of 2.1 or less in 22 of 24

59

countries for which data are available. Only in Poland and Romania are replacement levels of fertility even slightly exceeded.

Table 5

TOTAL FERTILITY RATES, CONTRACEPTIVE PREVALENCE AND PATTERNS OF CONTRACEPTIVE USE IN 24 DEVELOPED COUNTRIES

Country	Total fertility rate (1985)	Contraceptive prevalence (%)	Sterilization Female (%)	Male (%)	Pill (%)	Intrauterine Device (%)	Condom (%)	Other supply methods (%)	Nonsupply methods*(%)	Abortion rate per 1,000 women 15-44
Austria	1.6	71	1	0.3	40	8	4	3	15	--
Belgium	1.6	81	--- 17---		32	8	6	--	17	--
Bulgaria	2.0	76	1	1	2	2	2	--	69	61.9
Canada	1.7	73	31	13	11	6	8	2	4	13.0
Czechoslovakia	2.1	95**	3	--	14	18	13	1	46	34.5
Denmark	1.4	63	--	--	22	9	25	4	4	18.4
Germany	1.4	78	10	2	34	15	6	1	10	6.4
Finland	1.7	80	4	1	11	29	32	1	3	12.1
France	1.9	79	--- 5---		27	10	6	---31---		14.9
Hungary	1.8	73	--	--	39	19	4	1	11	37.1
Italy	1.6	78	1	--	14	2	13	2	45	19.0
Japan	1.8	64	8	2	1	4	45	1	18	84.2
Netherlands	1.5	77	8	11	38	10	7	--- 3---		5.6
New Zealand	1.8	69	11	9	29	4	8	--	10	9.7
Norway	1.7	71	4	2	13	28	16	2	6	15.9
Poland	2.3	75	--	--	7	2	14	3	49	16.5
Portugal	2.0	66	1	0.1	19	4	6	3	33	--
Romania	2.2	58	--	--	1	--	4	1	53	90.9
Spain	1.8	59	4	0.3	16	6	12	---21---		--
Sweden	1.7	78	--- 3---		23	20	---25---		7	17.7
Switzerland	1.5	71	---16---		28	11	8	2	6	--
United Kingdom	1.8	83	14	14	24	7	17	3	8	12.8
USA	1.8	68	17	10	14	5	10	6	6	27.4
Yugoslavia	2.1	55	--	--	5	2	2	3	43	70.5
Developed countries	2.0	70	7	4	13	6	13	2	25	--

Source: Data presented are from most recent sources available. On average they represent the situation as of mid-1983. The total fertility rates represent averages for the periods 1980-1985 and 1985-1990, from medium variant estimates in *World Population Prospects: 1988* (United Nations publication, Sales No. E88.XIII.7); contraceptive prevalence data are from *Levels and Trends of Contraceptive Use as Assessed in 1988* (United Nations publication, Sales No. E.89.XIII.4); abortion data are from Christopher Tietze and Stanley K. Henshaw, *Induced Abortion: A World Review 1986*, 6th ed. (New York, The Alan Guttmacher Institute, 1986).

---

* Non-supply methods generally refer to traditional methods.

** Ever-use (percent who named a method "most often" used since married life).

In the majority of today's more developed countries, the beginnings of a fertility decline predated the introduction of modern fertility-regulating methods. Early decreases were achieved through changes in age at marriage and through traditional contraceptive methods, including abstinence and withdrawal. As modern contraceptives were developed, a number of these countries, especially those in Western Europe, North America, and Australia and New Zealand, opted to make this technology readily available through government programmes, private-sector programmes and sometimes both. The populations of these countries responded, substituting modern methods for traditional ones. Other countries, however, including most in Eastern Europe and to some extent Spain and Portugal, have been slower in making modern technology, including surgical sterilization, readily available; consequently, they remain heavily reliant on traditional methods.

In countries where people rely significantly upon traditional methods (classified in Table 5 as "non-supply" methods), the incidence of abortion is generally higher than it is in countries where large proportions of the population employ modern methods (see Table 5). For example, in the 6 countries in which more than 30 per cent of the population depend on traditional methods, 4 have abortion rates of more than 30 per 1,000 fertile-age women annually, whereas only 2 have less. On the other hand, in the 10 countries in which the use of traditional methods is low (less than 20 per cent), only 2 have abortion rates of more than 30 per 1,000. Thus, available evidence suggests that, on balance, traditional methods are subject to more frequent failures than modern ones, and that abortion is one means of compensating for method failure. Even in countries with considerable dependence on modern methods, abortion as a back-up for method failure remains at significant levels, although it is lower than when there is high reliance on traditional methods. In Hungary and the United States of America, for example, with overall prevalence levels exceeding 60 per cent and relatively little dependence on traditional methods, annual abortion rates still exceed 25 per 1,000 women aged 15-44; only two countries, the Netherlands and New Zealand, have rates below 10 per 1,000.

In countries with a variety of methods available, oral contraceptives, intra-uterine devices (IUDs) and condoms are popular. Contraceptive sterilization plays an important role in approximately half of the developed countries except in Eastern Europe, where it is generally unavailable.

No developed country reports prevalence of more than 83 per cent, and levels as low as 55 per cent are associated with replacement-level fertility. These findings strongly suggest the existence of a "natural maximum" contraceptive prevalence level of approximately 80 per cent. It would appear that in most societies, including those in the developing countries, at least 20 per cent of women are pregnant, are waiting to become so, or perceive themselves or their partners to be infertile.

Developing countries

Developing countries vary more than their economically more developed counterparts in contraceptive prevalence levels (see Table 6). For example, Brazil, China, Colombia, Costa Rica, Mauritius, Panama, the Republic of Korea, Sri Lanka and Thailand have prevalence figures comparable to those in more developed nations. However, they have not yet reached replacement levels of fertility, presumably because of differences in effectiveness of contraceptive use, in breast-feeding practices, in nuptiality and in incidence of induced abortion. At the other extreme, rates in most of sub-Saharan Africa, parts of the Middle East and a number of Asian countries are so low as to have had little or no impact on fertility.

Table 6

TOTAL FERTILITY RATES, CONTRACEPTIVE PREVALENCE AND PATTERNS OF CONTRACEPTIVE USE IN 76 DEVELOPING COUNTRIES*

Country	Total fertility rate 1985-1990	Contra- ceptive prevalence (%)	Sterilization Female (%)	Sterilization Male (%)	Pill (%)	Intra- uterine Device (%)	Condom (%)	Other supply methods (%)	Non- supply methods** (%)
Africa									
Benin	7.0	9	--	--	0.2	0.1	0.1	0.1	9
Botswana	6.3	28	2	--	10	5	1	1	9
Burundi	6.3	9	--	--	--	--	--	1	8
Cameroon	5.8	2	--	--	0.2	0.2	0.2	--	2
Cote d'Ivoire	7.4	3	--	--	0.4	0.1	--	--	2
Egypt	4.8	30	2	--	16	8	1	1	1
Ethiopia	6.2	2	..	..	..	..	..	..	..
Ghana	6.4	10	0.5	--	2	0.3	1	2	4
Kenya	8.1	17	3	--	3	3	0.3	1	7
Lesotho	5.8	5	1	--	1	0.1	0.1	0.2	3
Liberia	6.5	6	1	--	3	1	0.1	0.5	1
Mali	6.7	5	..	..	..	..	..	..	..
Mauritania	6.5	1	0.2	--	--	--	--	0.1	0.5
Mauritius	1.9	75	5	--	21	2	11	7	30
Morocco	4.8	36	2	--	23	3	0.5	0.4	7
Nigeria	7.0	5	0.1	--	0.2	0.1	--	0.2	4
Rwanda	8.3	10	--	--	0.2	0.3	--	0.4	9
Senegal	6.4	12	0.2	--	1	1	0.1	0.2	9
Sierra Leone	6.5	4	..	..	..	..	..	..	..

---

* Most recent data available at time of preparation of this paper vary from 1979-1988. The average date is about 1983.

** Non-supply methods generally refer to traditional methods.

Table 6 *(Continued)*

Country	Total fertility rate 1985-1990	Contraceptive prevalence (%)	Sterilization Female (%)	Sterilization Male (%)	Pill (%)	Intrauterine Device (%)	Condom (%)	Other supply methods (%)	Non-supply methods* (%)
Africa (Continued)									
Somalia	6.6	2	..	..	..	..	..	..	..
South Africa	4.5	48	8	--	15	6	---17---		3
Sudan (north)**	6.4	5	0.3	--	3	0.1	0.1	0.1	1
Tunisia	4.1	41	12	--	5	13	1	2	7
Uganda	6.9	1	--	--	--	--	--	--	--
Zimbabwe	5.8	38	2	0.1	23	1	1	1	12
Asia and Oceania									
Afghanistan	6.9	2	--	--	1	0.4	0.2	---0.2---	
Bangladesh	5.5	25	8	2	5	1	2	1	7
China	2.4	74	27	9	5	30	2	0.5	1
Fiji	3.2	41	16	0.1	8	5	6	0.3	6
Hong Kong	1.7	72	20	1	19	3	15	5	8
India	4.3	34	---21---		1	0.4	4	--- 7---	
Indonesia	3.3	48	3	0.2	16	13	2	10	4
Iraq	6.4	14	1		9	1	1	2	2
Jordan	7.2	26	4	--	8	8	1	0.3	5
Lebanon	3.4	53	1	--	14	1	7	--	35
Malaysia	3.5	51	8	0.2	12	2	8	1	22
Nepal	5.9	14	6	6	1	0.1	1	0.5	--
Pakistan	6.5	8	2	--	1	1	2	1	1
Philippines	4.3	45	11	1	6	2	1	0.3	24
Rep. of Korea	2.0	70	32	9	4	7	7	---11---	
Singapore	1.7	74	22	1	12	--	24	---14---	
Sri Lanka	2.7	62	25	5	4	2	2	3	22
Syria	6.8	20	0.3	0.1	12	1	1	2	5
Thailand	2.6	66	22	6	20	7	1	9	2
Turkey	3.6	51	1	--	8	7	4	3	28
Yemen	7.0	1	0.1	0.1	1	0.1	0.1	--	--
Latin America and Caribbean									
Antigua/Barbuda	2.9	39	--- 9---		16	5	2	6	2
Barbados	2.0	46	14	0.2	17	4	5	5	2
Bolivia	6.1	26	3	--	3	4	--	2	15
Brazil	3.5	66	27	1	25	1	2	0.5	9
Colombia	3.6	65	18	0.4	16	11	2	5	12
Costa Rica	3.3	69	---14---		21	8	13	---13---	
Cuba	1.7	60	--	--	7	37	7	9	..

*   Non-supply methods generally refer to traditional methods.

**   Data available only for northern Sudan.

63

Table 6 *(Continued)*

Country	Total fertility rate 1985-1990	Contra- ceptive prevalence (%)	Sterilization Female (%)	Sterilization Male (%)	Pill (%)	Intra- uterine Device (%)	Condom (%)	Other supply methods (%)	Non- supply methods* (%)
Latin America and Caribbean (Continued)									
Dominica	2.9	49	---15---		16	2	4	10	2
Dominican Rep.	3.8	50	33	0.1	9	3	1	1	3
Ecuador	4.7	44	15	--	8	10	1	2	8
El Salvador	4.9	47	32	--	7	3	1	--- 4---	
Grenada	2.9	31	2	--	8	3	8	7	3
Guadeloupe	2.2	44	12	--	10	4	6	--	12
Guatemala	5.8	23	10	1	4	2	1	1	4
Guyana	2.8	31	8	0.1	9	6	3	2	3
Haiti	4.7	7	1	0.1	2	0.2	0.5	0.2	3
Honduras	5.6	35	---12---		13	4	1	--- 5---	
Jamaica	2.9	51	11	--	19	3	8	8	3
Martinique	2.1	51	13	--	17	3	4	2	12
Mexico	3.6	53	19	1.0	10	10	2	3	8
Montserrat	2.9	53	--- 2---		31	11	3	6	0.3
Nicaragua	5.5	27	7	0.1	10	2	1	2	4
Panama	3.1	58	33	--	12	6	2	2	4
Paraguay	4.6	45	4	0.1	14	5	2	4	16
Peru	4.5	46	6	--	6	7	1	2	23
Saint Kitts/Nevis	2.9	41	--- 3---		20	4	6	5	4
Saint Lucia	2.9	43	---11---		21	1	4	3	3
Saint Vincent	2.9	42	---12---		13	2	8	4	2
Trinidad/Tobago	2.7	53	8	0.2	14	4	12	6	8
Venezuela	3.8	49	8	0.1	15	9	5	1	12
Less developed countries	3.9	45	15	5	6	10	3	1	5

Key: -- indicate that the amount is negligible. (see Note on Sources of Data, pp. xv.)
.. indicate that data are not available or are not separately reported.

Source: Most recent contraceptive prevalence data available at time of
preparation vary from 1979 to 1988. The average date is about
1983. Total fertility rates are 1985-1990 projections from *World
Population Prospects: 1988* (United Nations publication, Sales No.
E.88.XIII.7); contraceptive prevalence data are from *Levels and
Trends of Contraceptive Use as Assessed in 1988* (United Nations
publication, Sales No. E.89.III.4).

Few developing countries have sufficiently reliable data so as to permit
analysis of the interaction between patterns of contraceptive use and
abortion.   However, with regard to the former, in most developing

---

* Non-supply methods generally refer to traditional methods.

countries, excluding those of Africa, contraceptive sterilization is significant. Once programmes are under way, it would appear that if sterilization is offered, it may be expected to contribute one third or more of contraceptive prevalence. In sheer numbers of users, the IUD is the second most prevalent form of contraception, largely because of its prominence in the China programme. If the China experience is excluded, however, this method is relatively less significant except in several Latin American and Caribbean countries and Tunisia. Hormonal contraceptives play a greater role than the IUD in the majority of developing countries. In only a few of those same countries are condoms used by more than 10 per cent of the population, despite their theoretically increasing importance in disease prevention.

Although "invisible" in Table 6, because its users do not necessarily consider it a contraceptive method, breast-feeding remains the single most important determinant of marital fertility in several regions, including much of Africa and the Indian sub-continent. Future reductions in incidence or duration of breast-feeding, then, would be expected to produce dramatic increases in fertility unless offset by gains in the use of reliable contraceptive methods. For example, in Pakistan, if the long intervals of breast-feeding were to decline to those currently found in Latin America, contraceptive prevalence would have to rise from the present level of less than one tenth to almost one third simply to hold fertility constant. Because in many developing countries, breast-feeding is at levels that cannot be expected to rise and because fertility also remains at high levels, especially in Africa, reductions in fertility can be achieved only by increasing the age of marriage or by the use of reliable contraceptives.

Contraception in the future

Current contraceptive prevalence levels, especially in developing countries, are well below those required to meet national demographic or health goals, including a reduction in the continued toll of illegal or unsafe abortions.

Projections of need

Simply to maintain prevalence at the projected 1987 rates of 71 per cent in developed countries and 48 per cent in developing countries, the number of protected couples would have to increase by almost 100 million, from 459 million to 559 million by the year 2000 (see Table 7). Because most of the growth in population occurs in the developing countries, more than 90 per cent of the increase in numbers of protected couples must be achieved there.

Table 7

COUPLES IN UNION, CONTRACEPTIVE PREVALENCE AND CONTRACEPTIVE USERS, 1987 AND 2000

	1987 (Estimates)			2000 (Projections)		
	Total couples (millions)	Contraceptive prevalence (%)	Contraceptive Users (millions)	Total couples (millions)	Contraceptive prevalence (%)	Contraceptive Users (millions)
More developed	188	71	134	196	70	139
Less developed	675	48	326	874	48	420
TOTAL	**863**	**53**	**460**	**1070**	**53**	**559**

Source: United Nations Population Fund, Technical and Evaluation Division.

A second technique of estimating additional needs for family planning draws upon data from the World Fertility Survey (WFS) as well as contraceptive prevalence, demographic and health surveys from a wide variety of developing countries. These sources imply that, with the exception of China, an average of 20 per cent of married women do not want another child but are not using contraception. Prevalence figures, which differ widely from country to country and are generally lower in sub-Saharan Africa and the Middle East than in other regions, therefore suggest the need to extend contraceptive protection from the 35 per cent of couples now using contraceptives to at least 55 per cent. This implies an increase of 92 million users over those projected from the 1987 population base.

To lower the TFR to 3.3 in developing countries by the year 2000--a goal in accord with the United Nations medium variant population projection--likewise requires tremendous efforts. In developed countries the number of contraceptive users would need to grow only by the 5 million figure indicated in Table 7; in contrast, in developing countries contraceptive protection would have to increase from 326 million couples in 1987 to 493 million by 2000.[12]

Although the task just described is immense, given average annual additions of about 1.6 points to prevalence rates in developing countries over the past decade, it would appear to be achievable if the necessary political support and resources are applied. Africa, after more than doubling the current number of users from 16 million to 40 million, will still have prevalence of only 27 per cent and a TFR of 5.5, whereas East Asia, where figures reflect principally the Chinese experience, will have fallen below replacement-level fertility on the strength of extending contraceptive protection to 34 million more couples than are currently covered. In purely arithmetical terms, the most daunting challenge is faced by South Asia and Oceania, which must add 91 million to those protected (see Table 8). Of course, the figures cited refer only to those users required at any given moment in the year 2000 to achieve the specified demographic target. Because turnover is relatively high among users of temporary methods, more couples than the number indicated would have to be using contraception at some time during the year in question.

Table 8

TOTAL FERTILITY RATE, CONTRACEPTIVE PREVALENCE AND CONTRACEPTIVE USERS IN DEVELOPING COUNTRIES UNDER ASSUMPTIONS OF UNITED NATIONS MEDIUM VARIANT POPULATION PROJECTIONS, 1987 AND 2000

	1987 (Estimates)			2000 (Projections)		
	Total fertility (millions)	Contraceptive prevalence (%)	Contraceptive Users (millions)	Total fertility (millions)	Contraceptive prevalence (%)	Contraceptive Users (millions)
Developing countries	3.9	48	326	3.3	56	493
Africa	6.2	16	16	5.5	27	40
East Asia*	2.4	74	152	2.0	78	186
South Asia and Oceania**	4.4	39	120	3.6	52	210
Latin America and Caribbean	3.6	59	38	2.9	67	57

Source: United Nations Population Fund, Technical and Evaluation Division.

* Excluding Japan.

** Excluding Australia and New Zealand.

Financial implications

To speak of the costs of reaching any of these goals is of necessity highly speculative. Even estimates of current expenditures are inconsistent because of varying definitions of what costs should be attributed to provision of family planning services. Nevertheless, among those who have attempted to bring some order out of available information, a consensus has emerged on estimates of 1988 annual expenditures in developing countries, excluding China, of approximately $2 billion for family planning activities. Of this total, external agencies provide approximately $500 million, the Government of India perhaps $500 million, other developing-country Governments an additional $500 million, and users spend approximately $500 million to obtain private-sector services. It has been calculated that China's budget for family planning is approximately $1 billion.[13]

Projections of funding needs are subject to even greater uncertainty than estimates of current expenditures. Will provision of services in Africa cost more or less than it does in other regions? There, fewer professional medical and paramedical staff are available than in Asia and Latin America and greater reliance must be placed on non-professional community workers. What will the effects of inflation be over the next decade? Will the costs of raising contraceptive prevalence from 30 to 60 per cent be similar, more, or less expensive than those associated with increments from 10 to 30 per cent?

Perhaps the simplest technique for forecasting financial requirements is to calculate future costs in terms of today's average annual cost per current contraceptive user (about $10 in developing countries) and of necessary growth in numbers of users. Thus, just to maintain current levels of contraceptive practice (as depicted in Table 7), expenditures in developing countries would have to rise from the current $3 billion to $4.2 billion in constant dollars by the year 2000. Other authorities suggest that $10 will prove too low and that $18-$20 is more realistic.[14] If $20 is used, maintaining current prevalence would cost $8.4 billion in constant dollars by 2000. If $10 and $20 set the probable range, to lower total fertility rates to 3.3 (see Table 8) by 2000, expenditures would have to rise from current levels to between $5 billion and $10 billion in constant dollars by 2000.

Yet another goal--to extend services in developing countries outside China to the estimated 92 million unprotected couples who do not desire another pregnancy--would require expenditures up to $1-$2 billion annually beyond the $2 billion already spent in those countries. Both of these sets of calculations coincide reasonably well with earlier ones. For example, the World Bank (1984) estimated that for the world to reach a total fertility rate of 3.3 by the year 2000, annual public-sector expenditures in developing countries including China would have to rise from a 1980 level of $2 billion to $5.6 billion (1980 constant dollars) by 2000.[15]

All of the estimates above may ultimately prove conservative, as they take into account only direct costs of delivering family planning services. They exclude costs of other primary health and MCH care, which are often linked with those of family planning under integrated, multi-purpose delivery systems. Given the importance of attaining the goals but the uncertainty of obtaining financial resources of the magnitude cited above, cost-effective strategies for demand generation and service delivery are clearly necessary.

Macro-environmental factors affecting
provision of services

Changing behaviours as deeply ingrained as those relating to human reproduction presents a formidable challenge even under optimal conditions. Unfortunately, in a number of developing countries those convinced of the necessity of providing MCH/FP services face one or more macro-environmental factors that seriously interfere with meeting this objective.

Political commitment

To have a reasonable chance for success, MCH/FP programmes require considerable political support at the highest governmental levels as well as in the relevant ministries at the central, provincial and district levels. Political commitment enhances the probability of success through the assignment of priority in the allocation of financial and human resources, the mobilization of ministries with central and peripheral roles in programme efforts and the legitimization--particularly of family planning--through demonstration of the convictions of the country's leadership to the population.

As of 1987, of 131 developing countries surveyed, 99 provided direct support for family planning and 14 claimed to provide indirect support. Only 4 developing countries officially opposed family planning altogether. The combined population in these 4 countries amounts to less than 0.5 per cent of the world total. A somewhat larger number of countries--14--although permitting family planning, have no official policy supporting it and do little or nothing to promote the delivery of services. However, no country in this group has a large population; a total of approximately 70 million live in these countries.[16] In another survey of 134 countries, 37 espoused policies to reduce demographic growth rates, and 33 favoured provision of services on health or human rights grounds. Approximately 76 per cent of the population of the developing world reside in the former group and 17 per cent in the latter.[17]

Nevertheless, it is important to recognize that within these two groups of countries, the degree and impact of political commitment differ widely. Although in some, frequent vocal support is accompanied by the allocation of the financial and human resources necessary to make family planning programmes work--for example, China, Indonesia, Mexico and Tunisia--in others, such as the Philippines, there has been no assignment of true priority status to family planning programmes. In countries in the latter group, delivery of services, to the extent that it must depend on governmental support, clearly represents a formidable challenge.

70

Budgetary support

A crude indicator of the degree of political commitment may be found in the financial support provided for family planning. Experience in developing countries indicates that making family planning services readily accessible and gaining widespread acceptance of them require significant investment of financial resources, although of a much lower magnitude that those needed for other development and social service interventions in such fields as education, health infrastructure, irrigation, transportation and energy generation. As noted previously, current expenditures in developing countries are on the order of $3 billion, of which approximately $1 billion is spent in the Chinese programme. This figure needs to be seen in context, however, if it is to convey a sense of the priority assigned to family planning.

The health sector as a whole, to which responsibility for family planning is often assigned, is rarely a powerful one in commanding a high proportion of developing-country budgets. It tends to constitute 1-10 per cent of governmental budgets. Moreover, family planning is usually assigned a small portion of the total health budget.[18] Despite the exceptions--Bangladesh, India, Indonesia, Pakistan and the Philippines--in most countries family planning receives less than 10 per cent of the health budget.

As a result of the relatively small shares of fiscal expenditures going to health and the low proportions of total health funds going to family planning, only a small fraction of 1 per cent of total governmental expenditures is devoted to family planning. This pattern is replicated in external assistance. Less than 1 per cent of funds available for development are earmarked for family planning, no doubt largely reflecting the priorities of assistance agencies. To some extent, however, this situation reflects the degree of demand for family planning support exerted by the developing countries themselves.

Table 9 presents data for 3l countries on the annual per capita expenditure for family planning programmes and the proportion contributed by the developing countries themselves. Because programme accounting practices differ greatly, as do procedures for attributing costs to family planning in multi-service programmes, these figures are no more than broadly indicative. None the less, the median amount is $0.5l, with a range of from $0.l9 in the United Republic of Tanzania to $3.20 in Swaziland. The most recent annual expenditures do not relate directly to contraceptive prevalence levels or to declines in fertility rates, partly because these two variables are subject to the influence of cumulative expenditures over many years and partly because outlays normally vary at different stages of the programme. An additional reason is that high expenditures do not necessarily ensure the creation of demand or of services that the population views as accessible and of acceptable quality. Relatively low budgets that are well spent can sometimes achieve greater impact than larger, poorly directed ones.

Table 9

ANNUAL PER CAPITA FAMILY PLANNING PROGRAMME EXPENDITURE

Country	Year	Contraceptive prevalence (%)	Total current U.S. cents	LDC* Government share U.S. Cents	(%)
Bangladesh	1980	25	51	25	49
Colombia	1983	65	26	14	51
Costa Rica	1980	68	149	113	76
Dominican Republic	1980	50	64	5	8
Ecuador	1980	44	78	56	71
Egypt	1980	30	81	27	33
El Salvador	1980	47	163	125	77
Ghana	1980	10	24	11	44
Guatemala	1980	25	128	76	59
Haiti, Republic of	1980	7	66	21	31
Honduras	1980	35	81	11	14
Indonesia	1983	48	46	34	74
India	1982	34	45	36	81
Jamaica	1980	51	218	105	48
Kenya	1980	17	72	23	32
Korea	1980	70	46	42	91
Liberia	1980	61	16	33	28
Malaysia	1980	51	79	60	76
Mauritius	1982	75	91	66	72
Mexico	1980	53	88	69	78
Nepal	1980	15	74	29	39
Panama	1980	59	234	136	58
Paraguay	1980	45	65	8	12
Peru	1980	46	30	7	23
Philippines	1983	44	43	25	58
Sierra Leone	1980	..	44	4	9
Sri Lanka	1980	62	42	8	20
Swaziland	1980	..	320	23	7
Tanzania	1980	..	19	6	34
Thailand	1983	65	27	18	67
Tunisia	1980	41	36	10	28

Source: Dorothy L. Nortman, "Family planning programme resources: focus on funds", in *Organizing for Effective Family Planning Programs*, Robert J. Lapham and George B. Simmons, eds. (Washington, D.C., National Academy Press, 1987) pp. 116-117.

* Least developed country. (LDC)

The share of family planning expenditures provided by the developing countries themselves varies from 7 to 91 per cent. Programmes that have existed in countries for a relatively long time tend to depend less on external sources; the same tendency is found in programmes in countries with stronger economies. The majority of countries surveyed depend on external sources for more than half of the small amount spent on family planning, a further indicator of the relatively low priority that many countries assign to family planning.

Even committed Governments, however, may find it difficult to make the necessary resources available for maternal and child health in general and family planning in particular. Uncertainties in the world economy, generally low levels of development, over-dependence on limited exports and unreliability of prices for them, the external debt crisis--plus a variety of other socio-economic forces--present formidable obstacles. In addition, in many cases the rate of population growth itself creates a drag on economic development. Moreover, political instability sometimes introduces elements of uncertainty to the extent that medium and even relatively short-range planning becomes impossible. In the most severely affected countries, these conditions lead to paralysis of all types of social spending.

In countries where economic conditions are more favourable, family planning is still given relatively low priority in resource allocation. At least 3 of 10 countries for which trend data are available show absolute declines in the Government's per capita expenditures during the economic crisis of the 1980s. Two other countries manifest increases below inflation rates.[19] Were data available from a larger, more representative sample, the proportion of countries with these patterns might be even larger.

In addition to the above constraints, in some countries--Egypt and the Philippines, for example--funds for family planning are delivered to "executing" ministries, typically the health ministry, in the form of block grants with no required line budgets or activities. Many analysts believe this practice reduces the availability of funds for the original purpose.

For all but a few countries (including some for which more external funding is available than existing infrastructure can readily absorb), financial resources for family planning range from being moderately to seriously inadequate for meeting goals of widespread accessibility and acceptance. A few programmes control sufficient resources, or make such efficient use of what they have that they come reasonably close to the goal of universally accessible services. In such cases, they would undoubtedly be able to reach these goals even faster were their budgets moderately increased. Yet, even these privileged programmes do not count on all the resources they could effectively and efficiently apply in reaching their family planning objectives. At the other extreme, many programmes have such limited budgets, or make such inefficient use of what they have, that at best they are able to offer services to small segments of their populations.

Shortages of financial resources negatively affect MCH/FP programmes in several ways. In many cases, programmes are unable to attract and hold qualified managerial and service personnel, a point treated later in this chapter. Frequently, the service network cannot be expanded beyond limited, usually urban, areas. Pilot projects that have been sustained by external agencies and that have proved successful in delivering services often cannot be replicated, at least with the same intensity of inputs, on a wider scale. In the worst cases, they cannot even be maintained by Governments (for example, Liberia and Sierra Leone) when external assistance ends. Finally, in countries with economies hard hit by recession, the recurring cost burdens of personnel, supervision and transportation, and basic drugs and contraceptives have proved difficult to bear.

With regard to recurring costs, declines in local economies leading to freezes on government hiring, as in the Dominican Republic and the Philippines, have often made it impossible to absorb central or provincial-level managerial and service-provider posts. Such posts were supported by external agencies for a short term under the assumption that the Governments would take over this responsibility. Many government programmes (in Jamaica, Nigeria, the Philippines and Senegal, among others) were initiated under the philosophy that such services should be offered to the population free of charge. This practice made it difficult to recover costs, leaving governmental or private agencies unable to develop other sources of revenue for meeting local-currency recurring costs and hard-currency expenditures for equipment, drugs and contraceptives. Additionally, the surge of world prices leaves non-petroleum-producing countries like the Niger, the Philippines and Sierra Leone at a great disadvantage in their ability to fuel and maintain vehicles for supervision and logistics.

Immediate programme strategy for "living with" economic constraints, in the worst cases, has amounted to holding service delivery points to a minimum, retaining only those staff capable of exerting the greatest political pressure (typically administrators, physicians and paramedical personnel), reducing or eliminating commitments to non-civil service staff (usually village outreach workers), reducing supervision, and "allowing" persistent shortages of drugs and contraceptives. The programme then risks becoming one with personnel but with practically no services.

Legislation

Another indicator of the degree of political commitment is the extent to which laws have been drafted or redrafted in such a way as to favour easy accessibility of family planning services. In this regard, progress has been significant over the last 20 years. Many countries--particularly those among the francophone group, which previously had the least favourable legal environment--have liberalized their laws to permit advertisement and distribution of contraceptives. A pioneer among them was Tunisia, which in 1961 repealed the former colonial law that prohibited contraceptive

74

advertisement. Among the francophone countries to follow suit were Mali (1972), Cameroon and Senegal (1980), Côte d'Ivoire (1982) and Lebanon (1983); Burkina Faso in 1986 abrogated laws that had made contraceptives illegal. Other countries that liberalized contraceptive distribution and sales include Italy and Spain (1978) and Mexico (1984). Ireland legalized contraception in 1929, though its availability is restricted.

Availability and use of oral contraceptives have been greatly facilitated recently by the elimination of prescription requirements in such countries as Antigua and Barbuda, Bangladesh, China, the Dominican Republic, Grenada, Iraq, Jamaica, Nepal, Pakistan, the Philippines, the Republic of Korea, Sri Lanka and the Territory of Hong Kong. In the United Kingdom, one cycle of pills can be obtained in an emergency without a prescription. In many other countries, prescription requirements are not rigidly followed in practice. Also, some countries have amended laws to permit distribution of oral contraceptives along with barrier methods and occasionally injectables by non-physicians, such as nurses, midwives, "barefoot doctors", health visitors and even community health workers. Trained non-physicans in Bangladesh, Barbados, Chile, China, Morocco, Mexico, Pakistan, the Philippines, the Republic of Korea, the Territory of Hong Kong, Thailand and Turkey are allowed to insert IUDs.

There has been a trend towards adopting a more liberal import policy on contraceptives. Contraceptives have been exempted from import duties and/or tariffs by many countries, e.g., Bangladesh, Egypt, Jamaica, the Republic of Korea, Sri Lanka, Thailand and Tunisia.

Voluntary sterilization is currently the most frequently used method of contraception world-wide. In most countries it is permitted by specific legal provision or because there is no law against it. Only in a few countries is sterilization prohibited either by statutory law or by regulatory restrictions. Those countries include Myanmar (formerly Burma), Chile, Peru, Saudi Arabia and Somalia. Many countries recently liberalized their laws or regulations to permit sterilization, e.g., Denmark, Spain and Turkey in 1973; Austria, 1974; Iceland and Sweden, 1975; Norway, 1977; Iraq, 1980; Ecuador and Côte d'Ivoire, 1982.[20]

Receptivity to family planning

It has been argued that where socio-economic conditions are favourable, once family planning services are made available in acceptable form, use should be relatively automatic. Even in the absence of services, the argument continues, such populations will, through traditional methods and induced abortion, begin substantially to lower their fertility. In such settings, "demand" for services is seen as largely already present; programmes may devote most of their efforts to meeting, rather than creating, demand.

It has also been maintained that some countries--or at least substantial proportions of their populations--are unreceptive to family planning, perhaps so much so that until social conditions are altered investment in such services would be wasted. The reasons are many, including a low degree of socio-economic development, high infant mortality, low educational levels, low status of women, high value of children as present-day producers and future providers of old-age assistance, extended family responsibility for child care and other cultural and religious factors. This hypothesis must be considered. Evidence from several countries with long-standing FP programmes but little change in their fertility rates--Ghana, Kenya and Pakistan are leading examples-- would seem to support it. In countries where spontaneous demand seems relatively slight, programme managers ignore at their peril the necessity for creating demand and tailoring services to cultural conditions. At the same time, the quality and accessibility of services bear examination in such settings.

On the other hand, perhaps stronger evidence supports a counter-hypothesis that even in supposedly "unreceptive" countries, considerable demand for family planning exists already or can be generated. Pilot projects in countries once labelled "resistant"--Bangladesh, Haiti, Kenya and Zaire--have been successful. Also, several national-scale programmes have flourished in countries such as Mexico where, for social and cultural but not economic reasons, social scientists had predicted the population would not respond.

Within each category of countries with similar socio-economic indicators, fertility declines have been steeper wherever family planning programme efforts have been greater (see Table 10, in which fertility declines are taken as a proxy for contraceptive prevalence). Additionally, given equal programme effort, the higher the socio-economic status of the country the greater the impact of its programme. Thus both development and programme efforts are important, and the latter seem worthwhile regardless of a country's socio-economic condition, as also indicated in cost-benefit studies of FP programmes. These studies, on balance, show more benefit in economic progress from investment in family planning than in other types of development programmes.[21] Thus, the evidence does not favour withholding support for family planning until social conditions change. Even in relatively "unreceptive" settings, fertility and health indicators can be improved by well-conceived family programme efforts. Additionally, the very lack of family planning often delays the types of social changes held to be necessary for its acceptance.

Table 10

CRUDE BIRTH RATE DECLINES 1965-1980, BY 1970 SOCIAL SETTING AND 1972-82 PROGRAMME EFFORT: 91 DEVELOPING COUNTRIES AND AREAS

Programme Effort, 1972-1982*

Strong	Decline (%)	Moderate	Decline (%)	Weak	Decline (%)	Very weak or none	Decline (%)	Total
Social Setting ** **1970: High**								
Singapore	43	Cuba	59	Brazil	27	Lebanon	27	
Hong Kong	40	Colombia	35	Mexico	22	Paraguay	14	
Rep. Korea	30	Chile	32	PDR of Korea	20	Peru	11	
Taiwan, China	30	Panama	28	Venezuela	14	Kuwait	8	
Jamaica	30	Costa Rica	24			Jordan	4	
Mauritius	28	Trinidad/Tobago	23			Libya	0	
		Fiji	18					
Mean	**34**	**Mean**	**31**	**Mean**	**21**	**Mean**	**11**	**25**
Social Setting'' 1970: Upper Middle								
China	43	Thailand	37	Turkey	34	Mongolia	9	
		Malaysia	30	Egypt	12	Nicaragua	7	
		Philippines	23	Guatemala	7	Algeria	5	
		Domican Rep.	21	Ecuador	7	Syria	3	
		Tunisia	19	Morocco	6	Congo	0	
		Sri Lanka	18	Honduras	6	Ghana	0	
		El Salvador	11	Iran	2	Zaire	0	
						Zambia	0	
						Iraq	0	
Mean	**43**	**Mean**	**23**	**Mean**	**11**	**Mean**	**3**	**12**

---

* Programme effort 1972-82 is measured by averaging the 1972 and 1982 scores after appropriate weighting because the scales were different (0-30 and 0-120). Formula used (2 x 1972 + 1/2 1982). The means are weighted by population size, 1980.

* * Social setting is defined by adult literacy, primary and secondary school enrolment, life expectancy at birth, infant mortality, gross national product per capita, proportion of males 15-64 employed in non-agriculture and proportion of population living in cities of 100,000 or more.

Table 10 (Continued)

Strong	Decline (%)	Moderate	Decline (%)	Weak	Decline (%)	Very weak or none	Decline (%)	Total
Social Setting'' 1970:		Lower Middle						
		Indonesia	28	Haiti	11	Kampuchea	14	
		India	17	Pakistan	9	Burma*	6	
		Vietnam	10	Kenya	0	P. New Guinea	5	
						Dem. Yemen	3	
						Bolivia	2	
						Côte d'Ivoire	1	
						Nigeria	1	
						Senegal	0	
						Liberia	0	
						Madagascar	0	
						Mozambique	0	
						Uganda	0	
						Cameroon	0	
						Saudi Arabia	0	
						Zimbabwe	-1	
						Lesotho	-4	
Mean	--	**Mean**	19	**Mean**	7	**Mean**	2	5
Social Setting' 1970: Low								
				Bangladesh	0	Mauritania	6	
				Nepal	-1	Lao PDR	5	
						Burundi	4	
						Afghanistan	3	
						Benin	3	
						Guinea	2	
						Togo	2	
						Niger	1	
						Cen. Afr. Rep.	0	
						Chad	0	
						Ethiopia	0	
						Malawi	0	
						Rwanda	0	
						Sierra Leone	0	
						Sudan	0	
						Tanzania	0	
						Burkina Faso	0	
						Yemen	0	
						Somalia	0	
						Mali	-1	
Mean	--	**Mean**	--	**Mean**	0	**Mean**	1	1
Total Mean	35	**Total Mean**	25	**Total Mean**	11	**Total Mean**	3	11

Source: Robert J. Lapham and W. Parker Mauldin, "The effects of family planning on fertility: research findings", in *Organizing for Effective Family Planning Programs*, Robert J. Lapham and George B. Simmons, eds. (Washington, D.C., National Academy Press, 1987), pp. 668-670.

---

*   Now Myanmar.

78

Finally, as discussed above, financial support for family planning constitutes a minuscule portion of development spending. Redirecting available funds away from family planning would not significantly increase those for other development aims, nor would it significantly accelerate desired social changes (and hence would not speed changes in fertility "caused" by socio-economic development). It would, however, delay changes in reproductive behaviour.

Nature of government organization

In some developing countries governmental organization is extremely centralized and relatively rigid, lacking the flexibility and capability for rapid response necessary for effective and efficient operations. The ministries typically responsible for MCH/FP activities (planning, treasury, health, education) are seldom freer of such over-centralization than is government in general. Occasionally, over-centralized Governments discourage NGOs and the private sector from delivering services. In other developing countries, histories of regional and ethnic separation or autonomy have led to regional, provincial and local disregard for national policy for family planning or other matters. These countries are characterized by the lack of a reliable apparatus for transmitting and enforcing government policy from centre to periphery.[22]

Degree of socio-political stability

In several developing countries, among them Afghanistan, Angola, El Salvador, Ethiopia, Mozambique and Nicaragua, civil war has made it difficult even for committed Governments to provide the necessary resources and maintain a widespread network of MCH/FP services. In others, chronic instability in political leadership has led to uncertainties regarding policy, strategies and resources and hence to minimal development of services.

Geography and infrastructure

In some developing nations, many people live in widely dispersed rural areas, sometimes occupying mountainous, riverine, desert or jungle terrain. Population dispersion calls for an extensive network of service points, which may drive programme costs up while reducing cost efficiency. Where difficult geography and dispersion are accompanied by relatively underdeveloped transportation and communication infrastructure, creation of MCH/FP service delivery, logistics and supervision systems is extremely challenging.

Approaches to service delivery

With the objective of expanding family planning coverage and, to some extent, that of other MCH services, programme managers have encouraged the involvement of public, governmental or quasi-governmental organizations and private sectors. They have employed various modes of service delivery and, within them, various forms of organization, bringing differing styles of management to the task.

Public and private sectors

The responsibility for public-sector involvement in service delivery has most commonly belonged to ministries of health. In some cases special bodies have been established outside these ministries for this purpose-- for example, the Population Welfare Division of Pakistan. The private sector encompasses a wide variety of non-governmental organizations (NGOs), including voluntary non-profit institutions, such as the affiliates of the International Planned Parenthood Federation (IPPF); both non-profit and for-profit social marketing programmes; and private practitioners and pharmacies in the commercial sector.

No consistent trend may be discerned across countries as to which sector typically became the first to undertake the delivery of family planning information and services. In some countries, the private sector came first. The pioneering efforts of private family planning organizations, especially IPPF affiliates, were often crucial in legitimizing family planning to the degree that Governments were later able to assume a role. In many other nations, however, including those with no private sector, the public sector initiated such efforts.

Regardless of which sector initiated family planning efforts, pressures have normally followed to involve the other sector to maximize the availability of services. Additionally, private-sector participation is often sought because of its flexibility and capacity for more innovation than Governments can provide. Moreover, the constraints on national health budgets make cost abatement through privatization attractive. Table 11 shows the degree to which the two sectors have contributed to family planning in various countries.

Table 11

CONTRACEPTIVE USERS, BY
SOURCE OF METHOD
(Percentage)

Country	Public	Private	Year
Africa			
Burundi	75	25	1987
Liberia	31	69	1986
Mauritius	80	20	1984
Nigeria	53	47	1986
Senegal	46	54	1986
Zimbabwe	60	40	1984
Latin America			
Brazil	27	73	1986
Colombia	43	57	1984
Costa Rica	41	59	1984
Dominican Republic	48	52	1977
Ecuador	67	33	1974
El Salvador	33	67	1976
Guatemala	37	63	1987
Mexico	54	46	1982
Paraguay	50	50	1977
Middle East			
Egypt	29	71	1984
Iran	65	35	1978
Jordan	37	63	1985
Morocco	39	61	1974
Tunisia	79	21	1983

Table 11 *(Continued)*

CONTRACEPTIVE USERS, BY
SOURCE OF METHOD
(Percentage)

Country	Public	Private	Year
Asia			
China	100	0	1982
India	95	5	1984
Indonesia	78	22	1987
Malaysia	53	47	1984
Philippines	56	44	1981
Republic of Korea	56	44	1985
Singapore	75	25	1978
Sri Lanka	88	12	1987
Taiwan	74	26	1986
Territory of Hong Kong	57	43	1984
Thailand	81	19	1987

Source: Adapted from John A. Ross, and others, *Family Planning and Child Survival in 100 Developing Countries* (New York, Colombia University, Center for Population and Family Health, 1988). Table 27. Interested readers should refer to original Table for accurate interpretation of data.

Styles of management and types of delivery

In the early years of many programmes, management was often characterized by charismatic leadership, informal structure, flexible procedures and varying degrees of adapability to crises and opportunities. This style was evident particularly in countries where private organizations initially led the way in family planning, but also to some extent in public-sector programmes. As the size of programmes increased and the controversy over family planning abated, this style has tended to become replaced by one characterized by a greater tendency towards management by objectives--the "making" of opportunities rather than simply responding to them--along with formal organizational structures, stricter delineation of functions and more rigidly defined procedures.

At least four modes of service delivery have evolved, the first three of which have been employed at various times in both public and private sectors: clinic-based services, community-based delivery (CBD), social marketing and regular commercial distribution. In some places all approaches have been used for delivery of such MCH services as oral rehydration, food supplements and pre-natal care, in addition to family planning. Clinic-based services refer here to those provided by public or private hospitals, clinics and health post facilities, and occasionally by mobile units, typically staffed by medical or paramedical personnel. Generally located in urban and semi-urban areas, such facilities normally offer the full range of contraceptive methods available in the programme.

Where populations have no easy access to such infrastructure, the need to bring services closer to those requiring them has been recognized. One response has been the creation of community-based programmes in which local residents are trained to provide information and some of the contraceptive methods in the programme. In some programmes, residents undertake other maternal and child health measures, using their homes or space donated by the community as a base of operations. The desire to increase the availability of services at the village or household level and to make them more acceptable because they are being delivered by peers has led to a proliferation of CBD programmes. The earliest community agents were the "barefoot doctors" who delivered basic health care in China during the 1950s and 1960s. Later examples of CBD were developed by private family planning associations in Colombia and Brazil. CBD programmes currently exist at more than 70 locations in some 40 African, Middle Eastern, Asian, Latin American and Caribbean countries.[23]

Community workers have also been successful in undertaking simple health interventions such as oral rehydration therapy, pre-natal screening, immunization, nutritional education and environmental sanitation. In family planning, most CBD programmes--among them the earliest ones in Brazil, Colombia and the Republic of Korea--offer oral contraceptives and barrier methods, usually including condoms. The delivery of family planning services--particularly the pill--by non-physicians was initially resisted by the medical establishment, which had not been sufficiently sensitized and convinced of the safety of this new approach. However, the early programmes demonstrated safety and largely won over medical support.

Community distribution of oral contraceptives has been successful in countries as diverse as Indonesia, Mauritius, Sri Lanka and Thailand, to name a few. At present, it is widely accepted that risks associated with oral contraception under both CBD systems and under medical direction are much less important than those associated with childbirth for most women in developing countries.[24] Certainly they are negligible when compared with the risks of illegally induced abortions. In 1987, these facts were highlighted at two major international conferences held in

Nairobi, the Safe Motherhood Conference and the International Conference on Better Health for Women and Children through Family Planning.

Men and women, married or unmarried, users or non-users of contraceptives, traditional birth attendants (TBAs), and malaria workers--all have served as agents in CBD programmes. For training and supervision, such programmes have traditionally been seen as requiring the backstopping of a medical-paramedical infrastructure. They are often directly linked to the governmental or NGO clinic infrastructure as an outreach arm.

Social marketing programmes are characterized by the sale of oral and barrier contraceptives at subsidized, below-market prices. Some programmes also offer oral rehydration salts and other simple maternal and child health remedies. Distribution networks have included pharmacies, groceries, refreshment stands and barber and beauty shops. Social marketing programmes were first tested in the late 1960s by the Indian Government, which promoted the subsidized sale of Nirodh condoms. Since then, many programmes have been launched in some 30 countries in Asia, Africa, the Middle East, Latin America and the Caribbean, supported by the United States Agency for International Development (USAID). Social marketing programmes have successfully distributed contraceptives through existing commercial channels in such countries as Bangladesh, Egypt, El Salvador, Honduras, India, Jamaica and Nepal. A variant on such programmes is represented in the move to establish community-based, not-for-profit pharmacies in such countries as Bangladesh, Haiti and Honduras.

Although clearly, under certain conditions, well-managed and well-publicized social marketing programmes can reach between 5 and 15 per cent of all couples of reproductive age, questions about their impact on family planning practice remain. Among these are whether social marketing can be effective at the early stages of programme development before family planning has been legitimized by other means and whether limits exist to prevalence generated by this source.[25]

Regular commercial distribution includes the efforts of private physicians and paramedics and the non-subsidized market-price sale of contraceptives and other maternal and child health remedies in pharmacies and other commercial outlets. A variant observed in the Republic of Korea involves governmental payment of fees to private practitioners who perform such functions as IUD insertion and sterilization.

Organization

The mode of service delivery--whether it is clinic-based or community-based, social marketing or commercial distribution programmes--may be structured in a vertical or integrated fashion. These terms may refer either to how programmes are managed or to how services are delivered, or to both.

Vertically managed programmes are those employing a managerial structure aimed at a single purpose, such as family planning, MCH or malaria control. A vertical approach was often the initial pattern in Asia, where Governments facing serious population problems assumed responsibility for family planning programmes earlier than did those in other regions. Services were provided through the public health system, as in India, or through separate agencies reporting to a high-level co-ordinating board, as in Indonesia and the Philippines. A common element under vertical management is the deployment of managerial staff with exclusive responsibility for one service, most often family planning. In contrast, under integrated management, the goals of the entire organization encompass several types of services, MCH and family planning, for example, and managerial staff have responsibilities for the entire spectrum of services.

Vertical services have taken a number of forms. Services may be delivered at single-purpose sites by single-purpose workers or at multi-purpose sites either by separate service staff or by regular health staff devoting separate service areas and hours to family planning. In some countries, even in remote and somewhat inaccessible areas, a separate time period is allotted for family planning consultations held by physicians receiving extra pay. In extreme cases, the health network is duplicated by a family planning programme with a competing, better paid staff.

When family planning is offered in an integrated fashion, it is usually coupled with other MCH services and sometimes an even broader primary health care package. In rural settings, family planning has often been paired with one or more simple health interventions, such as oral rehydration, malaria eradication or parasite control. This approach has been tried in several programmes of the Japanese Organization for International Cooperation in Family Planning, Inc. (JOICFP).

Under the rubric of integration, the literature on development planning occasionally recommends the addition of family planning to agricultural, industrial and social work programmes as well as the more usual combination of family planning with other health services. One particular form of such integration, which incorporates the advantages of private-sector participation and the convenience of community-based distribution, is the employment-based family planning programme. The concept is not new, having been pioneered by manufacturers and plantations in India as early as the 1950s, but it is now attracting more attention. In Egypt and Nigeria, contraceptives are being sold in factories. Commonly, as in Kenya, the Philippines and Zaire, large businesses offer family planning services along with other health or social services for their employees and dependents. At times, labour unions--in Indonesia and Turkey, for example--have developed such programmes. Other organizations, such as the social security system in Latin America and the military in the Republic of Korea and Thailand, offer on-the-job family planning services.

Occasionally, the distinction between vertical and integrated programmes becomes blurred, as when family planning services are

85

offered in a separate consultation room by a specific staff member but in the context of an MCH unit. To complicate analysis further, vertical management approaches are frequently employed in programmes that are largely integrated at the service level, as in Mexico's and Indonesia's clinical programmes.

In the late 1960s and early 1970s, major international organizations and lending agencies channelled financial resources to health ministries to encourage vertical family planning programmes. It appeared preferable to create additional single-purpose organizations to ensure that resources earmarked for family planning would not be diverted into other programmes and that family planning clientele would not become "lost" in health services with other, especially curative, priorities. The success of disease-specific health programmes, such as malaria eradication or smallpox control, further motivated the adoption of a vertical approach.

The vertical family planning programmes were effective in countries with densely settled, highly motivated populations generating a strong demand for services, such as China and Indonesia. Such programmes were costly and poorly attended in some other locations. The organizational costs incurred by vertical structures, such as duplication of existing health networks or tensions between externally assisted FP programmes and poorly funded government-supported MCH programmes, led to a reversal of the favour enjoyed by the vertical approach.[26] By the end of the 1970s, the vertical approach had lost ground, progressively giving way in a number of countries to an integrated approach.

Additionally, as programmes matured, more pragmatic policies emerged. Heightened interest in the consumers' perceptions put emphasis on getting information and services to users by a variety of channels, including existing health networks. The first World Population Conference held in Bucharest (1974) promoted a wide acceptance of the notion that family planning is one of the necessary interventions to improve population welfare. The International Conference on Primary Health Care held in Alma-Ata (1978) further spread the idea that primary health care still requires full commitment and co-operation on the part of all govenrment sectors.[27] The Alma-Ata report, among the minimum services to be provided by primary health care, listed family planning as a component of MCH services.

Over the years a consensus has emerged within the national and international community that specialized population activities are legitimate but that involvement of the health sector is also important for several reasons: to ensure training, supervision and medical back-up to non-medical delivery systems; to provide those methods that cannot be delivered by non-medical delivery systems; and to serve as a forum for the promotion of family planning. Additionally, it has been argued that to separate family planning from those services offered by the health sector is to deprive individuals of their right to an important health measure. Other advocates of integration have variously reasoned that people are more likely to accept family planning if the service is offered in the existing environment of health services, and that MCH services afford a unique opportunity for promotion of family planning.

Despite the trend towards integration, at least within governmental health systems, debates have continued between advocates of different modes of service delivery and different organizational approaches. The question of which modes of service delivery are most appropriate is addressed in detail later in this chapter. All have effectively contributed to contraceptive prevalence in certain national contexts. When resources are available, it seems probable that an ideal approach for most contexts would entail employment of all four modes--clinic-based, community-based, social marketing and commercial sector--in varying combinations depending on national circumstances.

Notwithstanding heated disputes over the ideal form of organization-- vertical versus integrated--evidence indicates that in most settings the key factor is not the form of organization but rather how well programmes are planned and managed. For example, vertically managed programmes have been effective in Indonesia and Mexico but have produced meagre results in Pakistan, whereas integrated programmes have failed to meet expectations in Egypt but have been highly successful in Thailand.

In many, if not most, contexts, integration is not required to produce significant family planning acceptance. In controlled studies, vertical programmes have produced prevalence levels equal or superior to those of integrated approaches. However, the relative simplicity of vertical programmes is offset by the loss of opportunity for promoting family planning at one of the moments when the population is most receptive; that is, when receiving MCH care. Furthermore, in many, if not most, national settings, integration can be more cost-effective than creating new categories of single-purpose workers, at least when the focus is the delivery of both family planning and the remainder of basic MCH services. Such integration must nevertheless be carried out carefully.

Thus it would appear that both integrated and vertical forms of organization can yield desired results when programmes are well managed and that local circumstances will dictate the best formula. Within many national contexts both approaches may make an important contribution. As noted in one analysis of the structural issues affecting delivery:

■ "Where the density of the user population is high and the technology being provided is familiar, a low-cost strategy will be most effective when implemented through a vertical structure. Volume will be high, and the major constraint will be clinic capacity. This is the case with oral contraceptive distribution programs operated in urban areas by national family planning programs.

■ "Where the density of the user population is low and the technology is familiar, a low-cost strategy will be most effective when implemented through an integrated structure. This is most likely to occur in rural areas, where the cost of a free-standing family planning clinic is not justified.

■ "Where either the density of population is low or a technology is unfamiliar, a segmented strategy, that is, a strategy that seeks to use different approaches for different target groups in the population, will be most effective when implemented through a linkaged structure, that is, a structure closely tied in with local institutions. The most common example is the community-based program, in which key actors are not part of the family planning organization, but rather part of the village . . . . It can be further hypothesized that these programs will be more effectively managed if the organization provides a high degree of independent decision authority to program workers and administrators working at the field level".[28]

Current and future contraceptive technology

The World Fertility Survey has demonstrated that in many countries gaps exist between knowledge and use of family planning methods and between the family size that people desire and their use of family planning. Closing these gaps and meeting the contraceptive needs of the twenty-first century will be enormous tasks.

The effectiveness of family planning services is highly dependent on the quality of contraceptive technology offered to millions of males and females at all stages of their reproductive lives in varied social, cultural and religious environments. Although the current array of contraceptive methods is far from perfect, scientific advances in the safety and effectiveness of fertility control methods during the 1970s and 1980s have been considerable. These include lower-dose oral contraceptives with fewer side-effects and health risks, more effective copper-clad and hormonal IUDs and improved techniques of sterilization. Additionally, a new method has been introduced--the Norplant contraceptive device, in which hormone-releasing rods implanted under the skin provide long-term, effective protection from pregnancy. Norplant, developed by The Population Council's International Committee for Contraception Research (ICCR), has proved widely acceptable in extensive field trials among women who wish to avoid pregnancy over a long period without surgical sterilization.

Overview of existing contraceptive methods

The ideal contraceptive--one that is absolutely safe, simple to use, totally effective, easily and quickly reversible, inexpensive, self-administered and widely available without a medical visit--will probably never exist. Evaluation of current contraceptive methods has to take into consideration three important attributes: *effectiveness*, *health risks* and the *health benefits* associated with use other than those conferred by avoiding pregnancy (non-contraceptive benefits). In a paper presented at the International Conference on Better Health for Women and Children through Family Planning, Nairobi (1987), M. F. Fathalla classified the different contraceptive methods into five "attribute" categories:

a) Methods that are completely effective and that carry no health risks or non-contraceptive benefits. Complete abstinence is the only method in this category.

b) Methods that are associated with neither health risks nor benefits, but that are not highly effective, e.g., withdrawal (coitus interruptus) and periodic abstinence (natural family planning).

c) Methods that are not highly effective but are associated with no health risks and with non-contraceptive health benefits: male and female barrier methods--condom, diaphragm, spermicide which offer protection against sexually transmitted diseases (STDs) and their consequences-- and breast-feeding, which provides health benefits for the infant.

d) Methods that are associated with certain health risks, certain non- contraceptive health benefits and a high degree of effectiveness: hormonal contraception in the form of pills, injectables and implants.

e) Methods that are associated with certain health risks, have no non-contraceptive health benefits and have a high level of effectiveness: the IUD and methods for male and female surgical contraception.[29]

Obviously, there can be no overall ranking of the different methods in terms of risk-benefit ratio because their values vary among populations and individuals at different stages in life. For example, where maternal mortality and morbidity levels are high, as they are in most of the developing countries, the risk of oral contraceptives is lower than the risk of pregnancy, and thus method-effectiveness is of prime importance. Similarly, effectiveness is of vital importance if there is a specific medical contra-indication to pregnancy or a higher than usual health risk, such as child-bearing too early, too often or too late.

Effectiveness of existing contraceptive methods

One way of assessing the effectiveness of different contraceptive types is to examine failure rates (see Table 12). The range of effectiveness relates to both the degree of dependence on recurring user actions and the efficacy of the method itself. The most effective methods having failure rates of less than 1 per cent, such as injectables, implants and surgical contraception, do not require the user to take frequent action. In contrast, IUDs are somewhat less effective than those three methods because the user has periodically to verify the presence of the device (and can eventually remove it) and because the mechanism of fertility regulation is less effective than the mechanisms involved with the first three. Combined oral contraceptives are even less effective because they require a more consistent commitment on the part of the user; they are nevertheless vastly superior to coitus-related methods such as the barrier ones.

Table 12

CONTRACEPTIVE FAILURE RATES
IN DEVELOPED COUNTRIES

Contraceptive method	Failure rates per 100 users
Natural family planning	10 - 30
Barrier methods:	
Condoms	3 - 15
Diaphragms	4 - 25
Spermicides	10 - 25
Hormonal contraception:	
Combined oral contraceptives	1 - 8
Injectables and implants	less than 1
Intra-uterine devices	1 - 5
Surgical contraception	less than 1

Source: W. P. Mauldin and S. J. Segal, *Prevalence of Contraceptive Use in Developed Countries* (New York, The Rockefeller Foundation, 1986), p. 18.

The least effective contraceptive methods are the natural family planning ones. Among those, the contraceptive effectiveness of lactation depends largely on its duration and on breast- and supplementary feeding patterns. The failure rate is generally estimated between 3 to 7 per cent during amenorrhoea. Behavioural methods most dependent on a couple's motivation, such as periodic abstinence and withdrawal, carry the highest risk of unplanned pregnancies.

Health risks associated with contraceptive methods

Surgical contraception

The risks of surgical contraception are similar to those of any minor surgery and are usually limited to a short post-operative period. Vasectomies are safer than tubectomies, and few long-term effects have been described in association with either procedure. Based on some animal studies, a concern was raised regarding the development of an immune response to the sperm antigen among vasectomized men and its possible harmful health effects.[30] However, evidence from recent human studies has effectively dispelled the doubts in this regard. In women, the ratio of ectopic pregnancies occurring in rare tubal occlusion failures is relatively higher than average.

Injectable contraceptives and implants

No serious health risks have been reported for injectables or implants provided under hygienic conditions. Nevertheless, WHO has warned that non-sterile injections of all types can transmit infectious diseases such as hepatitis B and AIDS. Controversy about whether long-acting injectables cause cancer arose because two species of laboratory animals, beagle dogs and rhesus monkeys, given large doses of Depo-provera (DMPA) or Norethisterone Enanthate for a long time, developed tumours of the breast and endometrium. Recent case control studies of women, conducted by WHO, as well as clinical research in Canada, Thailand and the United States of America found no link between DMPA use and cancer of the breast, endometrium, ovary or liver.[31] Among the adverse effects of both injectables and implants are changes in menstrual patterns, irregular bleeding and spotting. Reported lasting reproductive effects are that some women experience a delay of several months in ovulation or conception after discontinuing the injectables. The contraceptive effect of Norplant wears off quickly once the implants are removed.[32]

Combined oral contraceptives

The major health risks known to be associated with oral contraceptives combining both oestrogen and progestogen are increased incidence of cardio-vascular diseases, increased risk of developing a rare liver tumour (hepatocellular adenoma) and, in lactating women, a reduction of milk volume detrimental to infants.

Cardio-vascular diseases include venous thrombosis with potential pulmonary embolism, stroke and myocardial infarction. In the United Kingdom the overall mortality risk from cardio-vascular diseases was initially reported as 26.8 deaths per 100,000 woman-years in pill users versus 5.5 deaths for non-users. A later analysis of the Royal College of General Practitioners (RCGP) concluded that the increased mortality risk was concentrated in pill users over 35 years of age who smoke.[33] Indeed, studies in the United States of America have shown a very low

92

risk of mortality, between 1 to 3 deaths per 100,000 method users, among the non-smoking pill users under 35.[34]

The RCGP study found the frequency of deep vein thrombosis, which could potentially lead to thromboembolism, to be four times higher in pill users than in non-users, whereas the less serious superficial vein thrombosis was twice as frequent among pill users. Overall, the excess mortality caused by thromboembolism among pill users has been estimated to be 1 to 3 deaths per 100,000 woman-years.[35] Both thrombotic and haemorrhagic strokes have been associated with oral contraceptive use. The initial suspicion that the oestrogen component of the combined oral contraceptive caused cardio-vascular complications led to wide reduction of the oestrogen content of the pill. However, later investigations attributed venous complications to oestrogen and attributed arterial complications (such as stroke or myocardial infarction) to the progestin component of the pill.[36] The experts now advise use of the pill with the lowest possible progestin content compatible with an effective oral contraceptive. In fact, the occurrence of heart attack appears to be related to the effect of the proportion of oestrogen/progestin on the blood lipids. The early RCGP study in the United Kingdom indicated that the risk of death by heart attack was 8.1 per 100,000 woman-years among pill users versus 2.5 among non-users. More recent analyses showed the mortality risk was highest among older, smoking pill users.[37] One study found a 3.5 times increased risk of myocardial infarction among current pill users as compared to non-users, with a persisting higher risk among former users who had taken the pill for more than 10 years, a finding possibly related to the use of high-dosage oestrogen pills initially marketed in the 1960s.[38]

Although pill use is associated with hepatocellular adenomas, they are of little public health significance: in the United States of America they affect only 3 out of 100,000 long-term users.[39]

Potential but not conclusively documented health hazards of oral contraceptives are breast cancer after prolonged early use, carcinoma of the uterine cervix in long-term users, malignant melanoma in long-term users, primary hepatocellular carcinoma in long-term users, gall-bladder disease, chronic inflammatory bowel disease, impairment of fertility and foetal malformations if these contraceptives are taken inadvertently during pregnancy. The evidence is still insufficient to permit definitive conclusions.

Despite the health risks cited above, for the great majority of women in developing countries using oral contraceptives is so much safer than undergoing pregnancies that as a public health measure these contraceptives should be made available without prescriptions.[40] Nevertheless, under ideal circumstances information would be available on contra-indications and on other contraceptive methods so that women for whom oral contraceptives represent a greater than average risk (especially smokers and those over 39 years old) might seek alternatives.

Intra-uterine devices

IUDs are associated with various health hazards, including heavy menstrual blood loss, uterine perforation, septic abortion and pelvic inflammatory disease (PID). The problems of blood loss and uterine cramps have been less severe and less frequent since the introduction of smaller copper-coated devices. Uterine perforation occurs in 1 of every 800 to 1,000 procedures, mostly as the result of faulty insertion technique.[41] Spontaneous abortions occurring with an IUD in place are likely to be complicated by infection. Thus, this event, as well as a diagnosis of STD, is an indication for the immediate removal of the device. The risk of PID is serious because one episode of infection, even if treated, causes infertility in approximately 10 per cent of all cases. Overall, IUD users are about twice as likely to develop PID as non-users. The increased risk is mainly concentrated in the first few months after insertion and thereafter in women exposed to STDs by having a past history of PID, multiple partners or a non-monogamous sexual partner. However, the risk of tubal infertility stemming from STD is not increased in copper-IUD users living in monogamous sexual relationships.[42]

There is no evidence that IUDs increase the risk of ectopic pregnancy. However, the IUD offers less protection against ectopic than against intra-uterine pregnancies. Thus, in the relatively infrequent cases when an IUD user accidentally becomes pregnant, the pregnancy is more likely to be ectopic than it is in a non-user. Among IUD users 3 to 4 per cent of pregnancies are ectopic, whereas among the public the corresponding figure is 0.8 per cent. The possibility of ectopic pregnancy must always be considered in cases of contraceptive failure.[43] In recent years, significant improvements in the design of IUDs have resulted in greater effectiveness and fewer side-effects. The addition of copper has led to smaller size with a concomitant reduction in complications while maintaining or enhancing effectiveness. Studies have led to further development regarding the optimal amount of copper to be included in IUDs. Consequently, copper T380A, 380Ag and Multi-load 375 represent significant improvements over earlier generations of IUDs.

Behavioural and barrier methods

No proven health risks are associated with periodic abstinence, coitus interruptus or barrier methods.

Non-contraceptive health benefits

Health benefits beyond those attributable to avoidance of pregnancy fall within three categories and vary in different users or populations.

Preventing sexually transmitted diseases

A world-wide change in sexual behaviour and a growing incidence of STDs have made the role of barrier methods in the prevention of STDs increasingly important. The emergence of the human immunodeficiency virus (HIV) infection further dramatizes the significance of this health benefit. Besides decreasing the health risks of STD transmission to sexual partners or foetuses and new-borns, condoms and, to a lesser extent, spermicides and diaphragms offer some protection against localized lesions in the lower genital tract and against cancer of the cervix, according to a number of studies.

Reducing menstrual problems

Hormonal contraceptives, particularly the combined oral contraceptives, have been credited with favourable effects in preventing or reducing menstrual problems, iron-deficiency anaemia, benign breast diseases, functional ovarian cysts, epithelial ovarian cancer and endometrial cancer. The health benefits also include the prevention of ectopic pregnancy by preventing pregnancy itself.

Furthering health of the new-born

The health benefits of lactation amenorrhoea concern mainly the new-born in terms of nutrition, prevention of infection and benefits associated with spacing pregnancies.

Future contraceptive technology

Besides Norplant, which is rapidly becoming available, and the vaginal hormone-releasing ring, which may soon become so, several long-acting progestin-releasing methods are in various stages of development and testing. Biodegradable implants, injectable microspheres and capsules, all of which share the disadvantage of disrupting menstrual patterns, may become available in the 1990s.

Monthly injectables being developed will minimize menstrual changes by adding an oestrogen to the progestin. Two new monthly injectables supported by WHO research, Cycloprovera and HRP 102, promise to be highly effective and acceptable because of bleeding patterns more like normal menstrual cycles. Vaccine development is still a long-term prospect.

By contrast, new anti-progestogen agents such as RU 486 used in conjunction with prostaglandins may be expected to be popular in some settings and to place significant training and logistics demands on programmes that use them. Anti-progestogens are steroidal compounds with a chemical structure comparable to progesterone. Because of this resemblance, RU 486 competes for binding to the cellular progesterone receptor, thus inhibiting the normal biological effects of progesterone on the uterus. The availability of a non-invasive method for the termination of early pregnancy that can be self-administered under supervision of qualified personnel has clear advantages, but moral and ethical considerations will no doubt arise. These will have to be addressed in the light of local, cultural and social values and practices. In France, RU 486 has obtained government approval and is currently available on a limited scale under medical supervision.

In addition to new methods, improvements in existing ones, such as decreasing the number of Norplant rods, hormone-releasing IUDs and more effective barrier methods, may be expected to increase effectiveness and acceptability of contraceptive technology. However, none of the new methods, with the possible exception of long-lasting implants and RU 486, nor the modifications to existing ones that may realistically be expected in the coming decade represent the magnitude of "breakthrough" of oral contraceptives in the late 1950s and early 1960s. Programme managers probably will face the 1990s with no revolutionarily new contraceptive tools at their disposal.

The relatively slight possibilities of another breakthrough are in part a function of biological limitations and in part an outcome of the research environment. Because the private sector has gradually withdrawn from investigation in reproductive biology over the last 10-15 years, funding for contraceptive research and development has not increased in constant dollar terms since the early 1970s. The pharmaceutical industry is devoting little effort to developing contraceptives suitable for use in developing countries, not only because development and testing are costly but also because they expose companies to product liability risk. Furthermore, since the ideal product should be long-lasting and inexpensive, there is little promise of a significant return on investment. Much of the burden for development and testing, therefore, must fall on public-sector organizations, such as ICCR, which developed the copper-T IUD and Norplant.

In the future, contraceptive development will have to rely even more on joint public-private ventures, on single-product companies and on increased collaboration and co-operation in the public sector. Not only is more money required in the public sector, but a better co-ordination of funding for promising approaches is vital to ensure the most effective use of scarce resources available to the seven major international public organizations concerned: the Contraceptive Development Branch of the U.S. National Institute of Child Health and Human Development, the WHO Special Programme of Research and Research Training in Human Reproduction, The Population Council's ICCR, Family Health International, the Program for the Introduction and Adaptation of Contraceptive Technology, the Contraceptive Research and Development Programme at the Eastern Virginia Medical School of Hampton Roads and the International Organisation for Chemical Development.

Socio-cultural background research and attitudinal studies of users in early clinical trials will continue to be essential so that methods can be modified to elicit greater acceptability as early as possible in their development. Ultimately, solutions regarding liability issues may have to be found in the United States, and increasingly in the rest of the world.

Implications for health planners and programme managers

At present and for the foreseeable future it is only realistic to work with technologies that are currently available, while getting ready to distribute the new long-acting steroids as rapidly as possible and ensuring that early experience with anti-progestational agents be reviewed objectively at the country level. With the increasing use of different methods in different populations, the needs for safety surveillance will continue, as will the requirement for further social and behavioural research. Additionally, greater attention needs to be given to appropriateness of methods according to stage of life-cycle and relationship to breast-feeding. A method categorized as inappropriate for a particular stage of life may still be appropriate for certain individuals in special circumstances. Table 13 shows "average" indications of appropriateness.

Table 13

APPROPRIATENESS OF CONTRACEPTIVE METHODS BY STAGE IN REPRODUCTIVE LIFE

Contraceptive method	Reproductive life stage		
	Before first birth (delay)	After frist birth (spacing)	Completion of family
Oral contraceptives	MA	A	LA
Injectable	A	MA	LA
Long-acting steroids e.g. Norplant	A	A	MA
IUD	LA	A	MA
Condom	MA	A	LA
Vaginal spermicide	A	A	LA
Contraceptive sponge	A	LA	LA
Diaphragm/cap	A	A	LA
Periodic abstinence	A	A	LA
Sterilization	LA	LA	MA

Key: **MA** - more appropriate   **A** - appropriate   **LA** - least appropriate

Source: Adapted from J. Hutchings, G. Perkin and L. Saunders, "The effect of Contraceptive Technology on the Programme Environment", in *Organizing for Effective Family Planning Programs*, R. J. Lapham and G. B. Simmons, eds. (Washington, D. C., National Academy Press, 1987).

Appropriate channels for delivery of contraceptive methods vary in accordance with the amount of training required by the provider. For example, sterilization is generally viewed as requiring physician participation. Initially, while implants are still in early stages of introduction, physician involvement has also been the norm. IUD insertion and removal, although in many programmes still the responsibility of physicians, has in some cases been successfully delegated to nurses and midwives. Injectable contraceptives are delivered by both medical and paramedical personnel; the delegation of this responsibility to cadres with even less training has generally been resisted. Because of the risks associated with unskilled provision of these methods, as well as abortion, delivery systems are limited to locations where trained providers are present--principally within existing networks of hospitals, clinics, health posts and, in some cases, mobile units. Other methods that are less dependent on the providers and have little or no risk when self-prescribed and self-administered by the user are, of course, appropriate candidates for distribution through a broader range of outlets. Table 14 highlights appropriate channels of distribution for the various types of contraceptives.

Table 14

RATING OF DELIVERY SYSTEMS FOR
VARIOUS CONTRACEPTIVES*

Contraceptive method	Clinic based delivery	Community -based distribution	Commercial distribution (usually subsidized)
System (hormonal)			
Oral	LA	A	A
Injectable	A	A	A/LA**
Long-Acting Steroids e.g. Norplant	A	I	I
Barrier			
Condoms	LA	A	A
Vaginal spermicide	LA	A	A
Diaphragm/cap	A	I	I
Contraceptive sponge	LA	A	A
Surgical			
Male sterilization	A	I	I
Female sterilization	A	I	I
Abortion/MR	A	I	I
Intra-uterine device (IUD)			
Inert	A	I	I***
Copper	A	I	I***
Periodic abstinence	A	I	I

Key: A - appropriate LA - least appropriate I - inappropriate or not

Source: Adapted from J. Hutchings, G. Perkin and L. Saunders, "The effect of contraceptive technology on the programme environment", in *Organizing for Effective Family Planning Programs*, R. J. Lapham and G. B. Simmons, eds. (Washington, D. C., National Academy Press, 1987).

---

* This table highlights various delivery system strengths by indicating contraceptive methods they are well suited to promote. A designation of less appropriate does not suggest that a delivery system should not offer that method, but rather that the method may be provided more effectively through another system.

** Different countries have different views on the appropriateness of delivering injectable contraceptives through subsidized commercial distribution systems.

*** IUDs could be sold commercially, with buyers taking them to a trained private midwife or physician for insertion.

Health planners and managers should keep in mind that availability, in and of itself, does not ensure acceptance and continued use of contraceptive methods. Acceptance is determined by a number of factors including individual preference, the influence of suppliers on demand, and availability. It is also determined by perceptions, whether correct or incorrect, of the advantages and disadvantages of particular family planning methods. Users' perceptions about the safety of contraceptive methods often deviate from scientific evidence, tending to be influenced by adverse publicity and unconfirmed rumours. Moreover, wherever cultural pressures encourage child-bearing, clients tend to ignore the risks associated with pregnancy and childbirth.

Alarming rumours and false safety issues affect usage of all methods but tend to have relatively little effect on the use of barrier and other less effective non-hormonal, non-invasive methods. In many instances, perceptions about the side-effects of hormonal methods are incorrect. Studies show that oral contraceptives are especially and consistently misunderstood all over the world: negative side-effects, such as the birth of abnormal babies, are persistently and incorrectly attributed to these methods while many positive physical effects, such as prevention of ovarian and uterine cancers, are generally unrecognized. These misconceptions must be corrected to permit genuine "informed choice" about whether to contracept at all and, if so, what method to use.

Clients' concerns and questions do not end at initial acceptance. The possibility of minor side-effects requires either careful pre- and post-acceptance counselling when the method is delivered through clinical services or ready availability of information through other sources when community-based and commercial marketing outlets are employed. Such sources include mass media, informational inserts accompanying the method, pharmacists and village health workers.

Conveying such information is complicated by cultural differences: what is viewed as negative in some cultures may be viewed as positive in others e.g., changes in menstrual volume. The possibility of major side-effects, which is related to health status and other client characteristics, justifies the screening of all new acceptors at initial visits in the clinical setting. It also justifies public awareness campaigns regarding methods to be distributed beyond the clinic network, to prevent potential users with contra-indications from choosing an inappropriate method. Thus, as mentioned earlier, smokers should be advised of the alternatives to oral contraceptives. Furthermore, accessible back-up medical services must be provided for treatment of the few major side-effects that occur.

Users' judgements and concerns are heavily conditioned by such factors as sex roles, belief systems, levels of interpersonal communication between partners, literacy and educational levels, intergenerational factors and personal habits and attitudes towards various aspects of sexuality. Additionally, each method of family planning has unique characteristics of varying importance to different clients. In general, effectiveness, safety, side-effects and ease of use appear to be the most salient ones, but the importance of any characteristic will vary widely by age, culture and individual perception. Thus, to ensure widespread acceptance and continuation of contraception, the programme manager faces the highly complicated challenge of making contraceptives widely available in culturally appropriate ways while ensuring that potential and actual users are exposed to accurate information required to generate and sustain motivation. Because most users and potential users are women, the "user perspective" should reflect the concerns of women. To carry out these tasks successfully, managers need the support of research aimed at revealing the population's perceptions and fears of the service delivery system, the contraceptive methods it offers, and actual experiences with the methods as well as of epidemiological investigations that monitor method safety.

Strategic issues

Although the criteria are subjective, most observers would agree that family planning programmes in Colombia, China, Indonesia, Mexico, the Republic of Korea and Thailand have been relatively successful. Close observation further suggests that successful programmes have most, though not necessarily all, of the following characteristics: effective political support; widespread, easily accessible services; multiple public and private delivery systems; a broad choice of contraceptive methods; personnel systems ensuring reasonably adequate and motivated labour forces; sound strategies for financing programme activities; relatively strong information, education and communication (IEC) efforts; logistics systems for timely delivery of adequate supplies and equipment; strategic planning and flexibility; effective supervisory systems; and well-functioning management information systems and research and evaluation mechanisms. With the exception of the range of contraceptive methods, all these characteristics are equally necessary for the success of other maternal and child health interventions.

The impact of some of these factors on programmes may be seen in Table 15, which presents 1983 scores on a number of the characteristics mentioned above, together with contraceptive prevalence rates about the same time. Although more recent ratings indicate improvements in some programmes, the 1983 data correspond to most of the available data on contraceptive prevalence and hence are useful here in demonstrating the relationships between components and prevalence. In the table, the policy and stage-setting activities that are scored include official government policy, favourable statements by leaders, political infuence of leaders supporting the family planning programme, official policy on age at marriage, import laws and legal regulations regarding contraceptives and their advertisement in mass media, involvement of agencies and ministries in addition to the ministry of health and relative size of in-country programme budget.

Table 15

FAMILY PLANNING PROGRAMME COMPONENT
SCORES FOR 99 COUNTRIES,
AND CONTRACEPTIVE PREVALENCE
1977-83 IN 72 COUNTRIES

Effort level and Country	Policy and stage-setting score	Service and service related score	Recordkeeping and evaluation score	Contraceptive prevalence Rate (%)	Contraceptive prevalence Year of estimate
Maximum Possible Score	32	52	12		
Strong					
China	31.0	40.3	6.8	69.0	1982
Republic of Korea	23.5	37.3	10.5	58.0	1982
Singapore	21.3	39.6	10.0	71.0	1977
Indonesia	24.5	40.6	11.2	48.0	1980
Colombia	19.5	34.0	11.0	51.0	1980
Territory of Hong Kong	17.7	30.2	11.4	80.0	1977
Mauritius	25.5	35.3	8.8	50.6	1981
Sri Lanka	21.3	35.1	7.1	57.0	1982
India	26.0	32.2	7.2	32.4	1980
Mexico	22.7	31.1	7.8	40.0	1979
Moderate					
El Salvador	17.9	32.6	7.0	34.4	1978
Thailand	16.7	27.5	8.6	59.0	1981
Tunisia	19.8	25.4	7.5	32.0	1978
Bangladesh	18.6	28.5	5.1	19.2	1979
Jamaica	21.0	22.6	6.2	55.0	1979
Philippines	18.2	27.0	5.6	45.0	1978
Dominican Republic	17.2	27.9	5.7	47.0	1983
Viet Nam	16.8	27.3	5.9	21.0	1982
Cuba	8.6	28.8	5.4	79.0	1980
Malaysia	18.9	18.4	8.7	42.3	1981
Panama	13.8	16.6	8.3	62.0	1979
Fiji	16.9	25.0	4.2		
DPR of Korea	18.3	24.0	2.5		
Trinidad and Tobago	16.9	19.2	6.0	55.0	1977
Weak					
Chile	14.2	19.0	8.2	43.0	1981
Brazil	11.6	18.7	8.0	50.0	1981
Pakistan	18.8	14.5	6.3	6.4	1979
Egypt	16.1	19.8	3.0	25.0	1980
Nepal	17.7	15.6	5.0	7.0	1981
Haiti	14.3	15.3	5.1	19.0	1977
Morocco	12.6	16.5	4.9	27.0	1983
Ecuador	11.7	14.8	3.7	40.0	1982
Costa Rica	10.3	12.0	4.4	66.0	1981
Lebanon	6.0	18.0	5.2		

Table 15 (Continued)

Effort level and Country	Policy and stage-setting score	Service and service related score	Recordkeeping and evaluation score	Contraceptive prevalence Rate (%)	Contraceptive prevalence Year of estimate
Weak (Continued)					
Venezuela	12.7	14.6	2.8	49.0	1977
Turkey	19.3	8.2	3.5	40.0	1978
Guatemala	5.6	11.5	5.5	25.0	1983
Samoa	13.3	12.0	3.6		
Kenya	13.7	12.7	3.8	7.0	1977
Zimbabwe	11.0	14.8	1.7	14.0	1979
Botswana	12.0	11.5	1.5		
Guyana	6.4	14.9	0.9		
Gambia	16.6	8.7	1.9	1.0	1977
Papua New Guinea	12.8	9.2	3.1	5.0	1982
Cyprus	6.0	13.3	3.4		
Honduras	7.7	10.2	1.8	27.0	1981
Algeria	13.5	10.1	5.2	7.0	1978
Rwanda	16.7	8.3	2.0		
Senegal	10.3	10.4	3.0	4.0	1978
Tanzania	11.1	11.7	2.1	1.0	1977
Peru	9.7	7.6	2.5	43.0	1981
Liberia	14.1	6.8	2.3	1.0	1977
Very Weak or None					
Nicaragua	4.7	9.3	2.7	9.0	1977
Ghana	10.1	7.6	2.1	10.0	1979
Uganda	12.2	5.4	2.0	1.0	1982
Democratic Yemen	7.5	9.2	1.5		
Mozambique	9.8	4.7	1.9		
Zambia	10.1	5.5	1.4	1.0	1977
Sierra Leone	8.0	6.3	1.3	4.0	1978
Jordan	5.2	3.0	1.4	26.0	1983
Congo	10.1	5.3	1.4		
Lesotho	8.6	6.3	0.9	6.0	1977
Togo	6.1	7.5	2.3		
Guinea-Bissau	6.0	7.8	0.8	1.0	1977
Zaire	4.9	5.4	2.5	3.0	1978
Nigeria	5.9	5.8	1.3	5.0	1981
Benin	3.9	5.0	2.9	20.0	1981
Mali	4.5	5.1	2.1	1.0	1977
Afghanistan	4.7	6.5	0.5		
Iran	4.1	4.8	2.0	23.0	1978
Syrian Arab Republic	5.4	3.9	1.6	20.0	1978
Burundi	9.5	1.7	0.4	1.0	1977
Central African Republic	6.9	3.6	1.0		
Somalia	6.0	3.6	1.1	2.0	1978
Madagascar	2.8	3.3	1.2		
Cameroon	3.4	4.3	0.4	3.0	1978
Paraguay	2.7	2.0	0.2	39.0	1979
Yemen	5.6	1.5	0.2	1.0	1979

Table 15 *(Continued)*

Effort level and Country	Policy and stage-setting score	Service and service related score	Recordkeeping and evaluation score	Contraceptive prevalence	
				Rate (%)	Year of estimate
Very Weak or None (Continued)					
Sudan	5.7	2.8	0.2	5.0	1978
Bolivia	2.5	5.0	0.9	23.6	1981
Chad	5.0	2.9	0.0	1.0	1977
Ethiopia	2.5	3.1	1.0	2.0	1978
Malawi	4.0	1.4	0.3	1.0	1977
Côte d'Ivoire	3.8	0.6	0.4	3.0	1980
Kuwait	3.1	1.0	0.0		
Niger	3.0	1.1	0.2	1.0	1977
Guinea	2.3	2.1	0.2	1.0	1977
Burkina Faso	3.8	0.9	0.2	1.0	1977
Burma*	1.0	0.0	0.0	5.0	1978
Mauritania	1.3	1.4	0.0	1.0	1981
Iraq	2.0	0.8	0.0		
Oman	0.8	0.0	0.4		
United Arab Emirates	0.8	0.0	0.2		
Saudi Arabia	0.0	0.8	0.4		
Equatorial Guinea	0.0	0.5	0.0		
Libyan Arab Jamahiriya	0.0	0.0	0.0		
Democratic Kampuchea	0.0	0.0	0.0	0.0	1982
Lao PDR	0.0	0.0	0.0		
Mongolia	0.0	0.0	0.0		
Total (weighted by population size)	21.7	28.0	6.1	42.4	
Total (unit weights)	10.5	12.6	3.4	25.1	

Source: Adapted from W. Parker Mauldin and Robert J. Lapham "The measurement of family planning inputs" in *Organizing for Effective Family Planning Programs*, Robert J. Lapham and George B. Simmons, ed. (Washington, D.C. National Academy Press, 1987) pp. 564-567

Service and service-related activities include involvement of private-sector agencies and groups; use of civil bureaucracy; proportion of the country covered by CBD and social marketing programmes; extent of coverage of new mothers by post-partum programmes and of the general population by home-visiting field-workers; adequacy of

---

* Now Myanmar.

administrative structure at national, provincial and district levels; adequacy of training programmes for different types of staff; extent to which staff actually carry out assigned tasks; sufficiency of logistics and transport; adequacy of supervision; frequency and quality of use of mass media; and employment of incentives and disincentives.

Record-keeping and evaluation activities focus on the degree of development in the systems of recording, reporting and evaluation and also on the extent to which results are applied to decision-making.

These factors and prevalence appear to be directly related. Yet a large gap exists between recognition of the apparent importance of the components mentioned above and their degree of development in specific national contexts. In most developing countries there is considerable room for improvement. In countries that have had relative success, as well as those that have not, several of the challenges to programme managers seem predictable. If not dealt with effectively, each of these may slow the progress of family planning. In extreme cases, inability to develop appropriate responses may lead to stagnation or even to declines in prevalence rates at levels well below what policy makers consider desirable.

Some of the most common strategic issues faced by those who would expand and improve family planning services are discussed below, along with a summary of what has been learned about responses to them. Some of these issues stem at least partially from the unfavourable macro-environmental conditions described earlier; others arise independently.

Political commitment

The principal objectives of family planning programmmes are to generate demand where it does not already exist and to develop and maintain services to meet that demand. As suggested earlier, political commitment is a requisite for success in that it "produces" the economic and human resources necessary and legitimizes the actions required. Ideally, political support will have developed before programme efforts are launched and will continue throughout their lifetime. However, programmes are sometimes initiated in the absence of support. The task of proponents then becomes that of generating commitment at all governmental levels in favour of family planning. Steps found effective in this task include conducting and disseminating studies that demonstrate the negative consequences of unregulated fertility or high demographic growth rates for maternal and child health and for socio-economic development. Cost-benefit analyses and modelling of future socio-economic trends have also proved effective in convincing the political leadership. Finally, efforts to persuade grass-roots organizations, such as women's groups and labour unions, of the importance of family planning for health and social development in some cases have resulted in their becoming effective pressure groups to demand more and better services.

Demand generation

In many developing countries, including the majority of those in the Middle East and sub-Saharan Africa, spontaneous demand for family planning and some other MCH services is relatively low.   Lack of knowledge of what benefits may be obtained and where services are available impedes acceptance; so too do inaccurate perceptions of the efficacy and safety of various contraceptive methods. Even in countries where demand is significant, lack of knowledge regarding correct method use and side-effects contributes to method failures and discontinuation. Consequently, the design and implementation of IEC programmes for the community at large and for specific "target groups" and users of family planning services are critical for programme success.   They are also essential for making meaningful the right of potential users to an "informed choice" about services and specific contraceptive methods. The issues involved are treated extensively in the population education and communication sections in Chapter 4.

Accessibility of services

World-wide experience has shown that easily accessible services are necessary if programmes are to achieve relatively high contraceptive prevalence and hence to contribute significantly to national demographic or health objectives. Ensuring extensive accessibility of services is also necessary for other MCH interventions.   For example, in relatively successful family planning programmes, such as those of Indonesia and Thailand, the number of available distribution points per 1,000 married women exceeds 2.0. In Bangladesh, this figure drops to .07, in Pakistan to .09, and in sub-Saharan African countries just beginning to offer services, it is even lower.   The relationship between availability and contraceptive prevalence is treated later in this chapter.[44]

To expand accessibility, programme managers must often overcome a variety of pressures. In many developing countries in all regions, governmental social services focus disproportionately on certain elite groups, in particular, on urban working and middle classes.   Such concentrations are typical in the health sector, where the bulk of budgets goes to supporting curative services in urban hospitals and health centres. Although the need to change this disproportionate investment has been widely recognized and underscored in such documents as the 1978 Alma-Ata Declaration on primary health care, the more privileged groups have resisted changing the present distribution.   To promote a change of priorities with the health sector, data should be provided demonstrating the negative impact on health and the low cost-effectiveness of the current patterns in distribution of resources.

In some countries pressures to retain physician control of family planning have also slowed progress in making services widely available, though this is somewhat a phenomenon of the past. However, abundant evidence demonstrates that trained non-physicians can safely and effectively   deliver   barrier   and   hormonal   (oral   and   injectable)

107

contraceptives. They can also perform IUD insertions for the great majority of couples who want and need them. Thus, wherever a shortage of physicians, their concentration in urban areas, or their preoccupation with other tasks limits the population's access to needed services, managers should strive to delegate responsibility for such methods to non-physicians. At the same time, programmes should rely on medical back-up for handling serious side-effects and changes to methods that can be provided only by physicians.

Not only should paramedical and village health personnel be prepared to offer family planning and other MCH services to the general population, but they should also be taught to recognize individuals for whom pregnancy represents a high risk because of special medical, age or parity characteristics. They should make special efforts to encourage such individuals to use contraceptives, and, if pregnancy occurs, refer them to more highly trained and better equipped personnel for care. Systems for teaching even relatively unskilled health workers to screen for such conditions have been extensively developed by WHO under the "risk approach".

Historically, many programmes began by making services available in free-standing urban clinics, readily accessible only to limited segments of the urban population. In parts of Africa, access is even further restricted because a significant portion of the clinical infrastructure is operated by religious groups opposed to family planning. In most contexts, therefore, given the limited infrastructure and the difficulty sometimes experienced in obtaining family planning services at multi-purpose clinics, the clinical approach alone will not lead to high coverage rates. Unless these clinics are supported by outreach workers and supplemented by other sources of services, their "passive" approach will sometimes fail to generate significant demand, especially where the majority of the population resides in surrounding rural areas (as in Kenya).

Successful programmes have risen to this challenge by developing "multi-source" strategies to promote services and make them widely available. Such strategies usually include supplementing clinical with post-partum family planning services at all units where births are attended, forming CBD networks and involving the private sector in furthering government goals. Such schemes have significantly increased prevalence, especially in rural areas--even, on a pilot basis, in countries otherwise considered "resistant" to family planning, such as Bangladesh, Haiti, Kenya and Zaire.

The private sector has proved a vital adjunct to government efforts to extend the accessibility of services, and hence contraceptive prevalence. These sources--NGOs such as family planning associations, private pharmacies, physicians and social marketing schemes--are responsible for half or more of existing prevalence in many countries, especially in Latin America (Brazil, Colombia and Mexico). Removing the barriers to the commercial sector's ability to acquire and sell contraceptives allows it to contribute importantly to government goals. The potential for extending contraceptive availability under either social or regular commercial marketing lies in the tremendous numbers and geographic dispersion of possible outlets. In Bangladesh, for example, more than 100,000 retail outlets could participate in contraceptive delivery, as could the many Sarisari stores (small variety shops) in the Philippines. Other efforts to engage the private sector in family planning and thus increase accessibility have entailed paying special fees to private physicians for delivery of services (as in the Republic of Korea), creating communal pharmacies, and establishing service delivery at the work-place, with economic backing from the business or the union (as in Indonesia and Turkey).

To increase accessibility and availability of contraceptives is not simply a matter of multiplying service points but also of providing an extensive variety of contraceptive options. Because of differing individual preferences and requirements and because of divergent needs at different life-stages, multiple contraceptive alternatives increase the probability that couples will find methods acceptable to their needs. Sterilization, for example, is inappropriate for young marrieds who want more children, whereas oral contraceptives may be a poor choice for older, high-parity women. Research indicates that, at least under conditions of low to moderate prevalence, the provision of additional contraceptive alternatives increases use rates.[45] Despite such evidence, however, programme progress has been restrained because of limited contraceptive choice in India, Nepal, several South Pacific and numerous African countries. It has been argued that even relatively successful programmes such as Indonesia's have achieved less than they otherwise might have because of the low availability of contraceptive sterilization.

The answer to the strategic question about the optimal contraceptive method mix is not a simple "make all methods extensively available". Where administrative capacities are not highly developed, concentration on wide accessibility of a few methods may yield greater results than a more ambitious initial strategy. Once again, the case of Indonesia illustrates the impressive results attained by focusing delivery capacity on a few methods. Once such a strategy has been effectively implemented, however, other contraceptive alternatives must be made available. Otherwise prevalence can reach a plateau at undesirably low levels. Administrative and service capacity should increase in a gradual and orderly fashion to ensure that personnel receive requisite training and that delivery of methods already in the programme is not disrupted or weakened by broadening the method mix made available. Finally, making a wide range of methods available should not be taken to mean offering many variants of each method. Programmatic evidence suggests that providing too many types of oral or injectable contraceptives leads to complications in logistics systems, shortages of stocks, frequent changes in prescriptions, confusion among providers and clients and discontinuation of use. Thus, a few representatives of each type of method should be carefully selected, perhaps no more than two or three types of oral contraceptives, for example.

Factors that discourage broadening contraceptive alternatives include uncertainty about safety (especially of injectables), religious objections to method (IUD, sterilization, all "non-natural" methods), supposition of socio-cultural resistance to certain methods (IUDs in some Muslim countries), costs inherent in introducing methods into programmes when staff have not had training in their use (Norplant, injectables) and lack of sufficient acceptors to justify training (IUDs, sterilization, Norplant). Solutions aimed at overcoming such impediments include disseminating international data on the safety and efficacy of methods, conducting small-scale pilot tests of methods in countries unconvinced about their acceptability, retraining service personnel to combat misconceptions regarding methods and, in some cases, developing local manufacturing capability to ensure contraceptive supplies.

Development of an adequate financial base

Almost all MCH/FP programmes suffer to a greater or lesser degree from scarcity of financial resources, as mentioned earlier. Given current economic and political realities, it will generally be necessary to combat resource constraints simultaneously on two fronts. On the first, research demonstrating the negative impact of unregulated fertility on health and socio-economic development as well as research on the costs and benefits of investment in family planning has proved effective in convincing Governments to make resources available. This applies particularly to countries that have never made a significant political commitment to family planning. In other countries where political commitment has been made, where the leadership is convinced of health and development rationales but where that commitment may be ebbing, demonstrations of a continuing favourable cost-benefit ratio may help maintain or increase the flow of resources. On the other front, discussed below, managers should constantly be on the alert for ways to make the most cost-effective use of whatever resources become available.

Cost-effectiveness and strategic decision-making

In an ideal strategy, family planning services should be made as widely available as possible through multiple modes of service delivery, providing as broad a range of contraceptive options as possible. The modes of delivery would include public and private sectors, clinic- and community-based distribution networks, and social marketing schemes. Where financial resources permit, this strategy would bring about the highest possible contraceptive prevalence in the least time and ensure acceptability of services.

Where resources are tight and cannot be stretched to pursue all major modes of service delivery, hard strategic choices will have to be made. Because many countries, especially in Africa, face this situation it is urgent that data be gathered to permit reasonable judgement on the question of which modes of delivery or which modes on what scale will provide the most contraceptive protection with available resources. Unfortunately, relatively little information is available. One recent study of 63 USAID-supported projects in 10 countries suggests that contraceptive social marketing and voluntary sterilization are more cost-efficient than community-based distribution or full-service clinic programmes (see Figure I). The study covers only family planning, however, and the results might be different in programmes attempting to achieve the greatest possible coverage of all MCH services, including family planning, with limited resources. Although the methodology is less than ideal (but perhaps as rigorous as existing data bases allow) and although a non-critical reader might be led to believe that selection must be made between modes of delivery rather than between degrees of emphasis, the study exemplifies an approach to one of the several questions for which answers are urgently needed so that programmes may make optimal use of scarce resources.[46]

Figure I

COSTS OF SERVICE DELIVERY

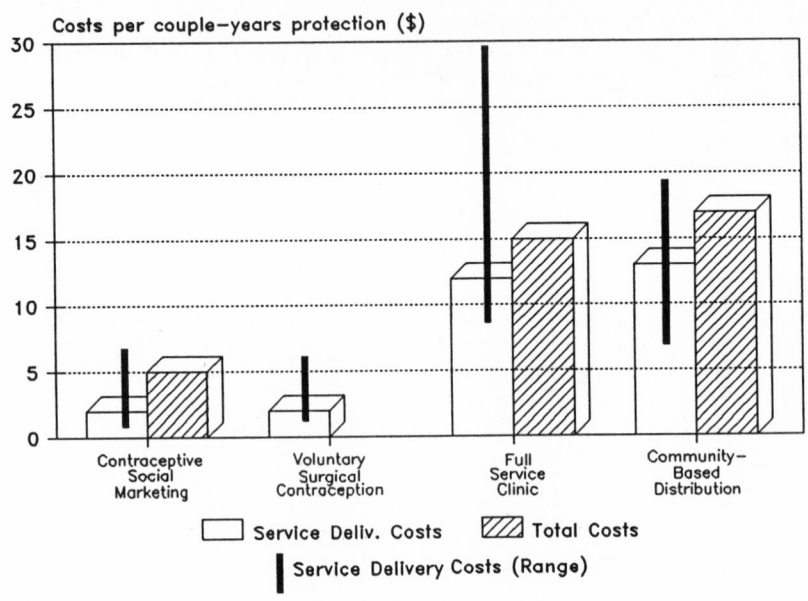

Sources: S. C. Huber and P. D. Harvey, unpublished (1988). This figure was developed as part of an article later published as "Family Planning Programs in Ten Developing Countries", *Journal of Biosocial Science*, vol. 21 (1989).

Note: The cost per birth averted and per couple-year of protection (CYP) has been calculated from 63 U.S. Agency for International Development (AID) supported projects from Africa, Latin America and Asia, encompassing 4.8 CYPs (1984 data). The calculations take use-effectiveness data (e.g., condoms 83 per cent effective), allow for wastage in distribution (e.g. 14.3 cycles of pills a year) and factor in current AID commodity costs.

One issue regarding financial resources is the extent to which public-sector costs can be abated by shifting part of the responsibility for family planning programmes to the private sector. In cases where a programme is just beginning, this aim can be achieved by developing a private-sector or social marketing alternative before, or perhaps instead of, the public mode. In the former case, a strategy of shifting some portion of the burden of public services to the regular commercial sector or to a social marketing programme--in which charging for services and cost recovery meet no political or administrative obstacles--may represent a sound option. This solution is especially applicable where public community and clinic programmes are well established and where contraceptive prevalence is so high that it may be inferred that the majority of the public is spontaneously demanding family planning. A number of Latin American and Asian programmes have already reached this stage. Under such an arrangement, public resources can then be focused on serving the last remaining unconvinced or underserved groups in the population as well as those too poor to purchase contraceptive services in the private sector. Principles of equity would, of course, dictate that the needs of the latter be so addressed. Additionally, the scaling down of government responsibility would have to be carefully timed to coincide with the extension of private-sector outlets so that availability of services would not fall below levels that have led to relatively high prevalence. Finally, precisely in those countries with the highest levels of contraceptive prevalence--Brazil, China, Colombia, Mexico and Thailand, for example-- efficient use of resources and further health and demographic impacts will require extensive efforts to pinpoint the relatively few remaining underserved populations.

For countries that are only beginning to generate and meet family planning demands, the message is less straightforward. Further examination of available data is urgently needed, along with much more experience to help guide decisions about balancing the resources devoted to social marketing and voluntary sterilization with those devoted to alternatives. Most experience with social marketing has taken place in countries where long-standing public-sector, and sometimes commercial, efforts had already accomplished much in terms of informing the population and generating demand. Thus, it remains to be seen how well social marketing will fare in environments where initial ground-breaking has not been conducted--as in most African settings. Additionally, although the social marketing costs may be relatively low for each couple-year of protection, none of these programmes contributes the majority of contraceptive prevalence in a country. Rather, they simply add another, smaller layer of "users" to those generated by other sources. Therefore, the upper limits of prevalence that can be generated by social marketing alone are unknown. Finally, the potential acceptability of sterilization, at least during early stages of family planning efforts, is not altogether certain in Africa, where cultural mores seem to favour child-spacing rather than termination of child-bearing.

113

Cost-effectiveness of micro-programme components

Financial constraints normally limit operations not only in programmes fortunate enough to operate through all modes of service delivery, perhaps employing both vertical and integrated forms of organization, but also in those obliged to select only a few alternatives. Hence, the search for more cost-effective ways of carrying out basic functions must be continuous.

Options identified for cost reduction in some programmes include the following: relegating functions (after proper training) to less expensive categories of personnel, especially allowing paramedics and village health workers to prescribe and deliver family planning methods; instituting cost recovery (charging for services); experimenting with alternatives to government compensation for outreach workers (charging for services, salaries, or in-kind income provided directly by the community); using more economical modes of transportation, shorter and less costly training techniques and less frequent and less costly supervision; and opting for "appropriate technology". Examples of such technology include using existing village buildings in lieu of new construction; employing locally made, simple examination tables, safe birth kits for TBAs and oral rehydration salts; and, under most conditions, depending on mini-laparotomy rather than laparoscopy for sterilizations.[47]

In summary, success is more likely when a programme's management is open to identifying options, analysing their cost-effectiveness and abiding by the results. Screening for cost-effectiveness, which should be integral in all management decision-making, is especially needed in incipient African programmes with scarce resources. Finally, programme managers as well as external assistance agencies should insist upon the sustainability and replicability of "models" of demand creation and service delivery.

Development of an adequate personnel base

Along with a sound financial base, the factor most often cited as crucial for MCH/FP programme success is the ability to attract and retain enough competent and motivated personnel. When relatively successful and unsuccessful programmes are compared, analysts emphasize time and again the importance of the quality of personnel in their technical preparation, openness to alternatives and desire to serve the public. The challenge of staffing programmes with such individuals is especially complicated when lack of political support results in the assignment of the best talent to other sectors. It is also complicated where public or private social service funds are insufficient to permit competing with other sources of employment (as in Egypt, Pakistan, the Philippines and Sri Lanka), or where trained personnel are extremely scarce. Through many years of external support and internal allocation of resources, many countries of Asia and Latin America and some in the Middle East have effectively dealt with scarce personnel. However, staff shortages remain a major obstacle in many sub-Saharan countries and elsewhere. The former two constraints still operate to some extent in all regions.

The need for attracting and retaining competent and motivated personnel in family planning programmes is acute at all levels. For example, to meet programme goals, managers must be capable of innovative strategy development, of careful follow-through during implementation, of accepting and applying evaluative information, of admitting mistakes and changing course and of making decisions and delegating authority. Such managers are in short supply. They are often drafted for participation in other government sectors, or subject to offers from a better-funded private sector. Too frequently, programmes are saddled at the top with political appointees with low motivation, little technical expertise and hence an inability to develop strategies appropriate for changing customs as ingrained as those relating to human reproduction. Additionally, it is common to find programmes placed under the authority of physicians who, although competent in medicine, frequently have no training in management and administration.

A second level at which the problem is acute is that of middle management. Although many programmes have attracted or been assigned excellent top-level management personnel, the limited supply of such persons, lack of resources to pay more than a few persons competitive salaries as well as unwillingness of personnel to serve outside major cities have resulted in a scarcity of solid middle management in provincial and subprovincial offices, and occasionally even at national headquarters.

At the clinic level, many programmes have also encountered barriers in attracting medical and paramedical personnel or persuading them to provide family planning services. Depending on the national context, difficulties may stem from lack of conviction among such personnel that family planning is a legitimate activity for health personnel or, for religious reasons, that it is legitimate at all. In many programmes, such personnel have been characterized as lacking a spirit of social service, which may be manifested in low productivity, denial of services that could be given, and unnecessary channelling of clients from public clinics to private practice. Again, at this level, the difficulty of persuading personnel to serve outside cities is a problem in all regions.

Finally, as suggested earlier, programmes that have advanced to the stage at which community outreach workers are required to carry motivation and service beyond clinics are often faced with the task of "creating" this cadre, not infrequently at a time when resources to pay such personnel are lacking. The selection of outreach workers can also be problematic. Although in many settings, both married and unmarried, young and old, male and female, educated and illiterate agents have performed reasonably successfully, the progress of some programmes appears to have beenretarded by the selection of agents with inappropriate characteristics. For example, sometimes males serve as agents in societies in which females are reluctant to discuss intimate

115

topics or to be examined by the opposite sex; sometimes urban residents are assigned to work in rural areas; sometimes young people with no credibility, perhaps because they are relatives of political figures, gain positions as agents. Where comparisons of the efficacy of workers have been attempted within individual programmes, the most effective agents seem to be those with a background similar to those to be served but with some claim to expertise through training. Typically, such agents are married women who have children and who use contraceptives themselves.

To deal with the above challenges "persuasive" studies of the kind already mentioned are often employed to create political will and alter financial priorities. Through this means, programmes sometimes win a greater share of human resources and more extensive training programmes for scarce managerial and service-delivery personnel. As mentioned earlier, the shortage and unaffordable expense of physician and paramedical personnel have been overcome by delegating authority for some forms of service to adequately trained, more readily available and less expensive types of personnel. Studies in Thailand and Turkey, among other countries, demonstrate that with proper training paramedical personnel can, for example, prescribe and follow up users of most contraceptive methods and insert IUDs. In some cases, the costs of outreach workers are being met through experimentation with differing incentives and compensation, including payments by the communities served.

The problems of low motivation among service delivery and outreach personnel, typically in the health sector, and lack of a service orientation (although perhaps intractable when embedded in a "demoralized system") have been approached through in-service and basic training. If the problem stems largely from the staff's lack of exposure to the health justification for family planning, this tactic is presumably productive, although there is little evidence to back this assertion. If the problem is one of low salaries, some improvement in productivity might be expected from salary increments. Once again, however, insufficient evidence is available, and programme managers rarely have much flexibility in this area. Finally, programmatic evidence also indicates that motivation is improved by a supportive supervision system.

Several programmes in different regions have attempted to win the loyalty and dedication of field-worker, medical and paramedical personnel through special incentive payments to those who deliver family planning services on either a piece-work or salary-supplement basis. Although in some cases this practice seems to have led to increased productivity, it has also led to refusal of personnel to continue services if special payments have to be reduced or eliminated. It has also led to resistance among other personnel to begin giving the services without similar payments, which may severely limit the service network if the programme is unable to offer such incentives on a wide scale. If these payments are linked to the provision of only one or several contraceptive methods available, the possibility arises that personnel may exert undue influence on the client to accept a method that bears a premium, thus infringing on free and informed choice. Thus, whenever special incentives for service providers are a part of the programme, significant efforts are required to ensure system-wide availability of the payments and to guarantee that basic client rights are respected.

In summary, available evidence suggests that motivation is best gained and retained under conditions of adequate, regular compensation (as opposed to volunteerism), which may or may not be supplemented by performance-related bonuses. Because salaries for outreach and community-based workers are beyond the financial possibilities of many Governments, creative solutions must be investigated, such as payment in-kind by the community, charging for services, and the sale of contraceptives. Accountability relating to performance is also critical; the system must be seen as fair. Supportive supervision and feedback on performance are other important ingredients in maintaining motivation.

Establishment of a planning tradition

Managers of public-sector MCH/FP programmes must occasionally operate in environments in which little tradition of long- or medium-range planning exists, and budgets tend to be unpredictable. Foresight is thus limited to relatively short political cycles at the end of which plans are discarded and personnel are disbanded. Such instability results in wasted human and financial resources--for example, training cadres that will shortly be superseded by others--and in slow progress toward extending services. Solutions seem to lie in techniques for gaining greater priority for family planning, through the creation of greater political support and, as a manifestation of such priority, for ensuring that the programme hires professional managers and provides them with job security dependent upon performance rather than upon political whim. When this moment arrives, the opportunity to shift from a management style that consists of little more than reacting to crises to one based on management by objectives and analysis of cost-effectiveness of programme options should be taken.

Management by objectives logically implies setting targets for the service points of the programme. Although some methodological difficulties remain, computer software permits translation of demographic objectives into programme targets. Similar packages are within reach for maternal and child health objectives. Such targets are unquestionably a valuable management tool for programmes at the national level. Apportionment of overall targets to the provincial, district and local levels is also potentially useful in indicating achievements that may reasonably be expected, in stimulating "healthy competition" between units, and in identifying underperforming units that need special attention. However, care must be taken to ensure that such a system is not operated in a punitive fashion and that targets are not presented as quotas. Evidence from several countries shows that under such conditions falsification of data has become common and, in extreme cases, abuses of the target population's human rights have occurred.

Many private-sector family planning agencies were initially founded by charismatic figures with relatively little planning and management experience. As these organizations grew, however, the lack of a planning and management orientation seriously hampered their progress, and in some cases continues to do so. Solutions are to be found in hiring experienced managers and in reorienting existing personnel, an approach currently being tried in the UNFPA-sponsored South Asia Management Project.

Both community-based distribution and social marketing depend upon management experience and styles that are too rarely available in health ministries, which in many countries constitute the "headquarters" of national family planning programmes. Social marketing occasionally elicits hostility among public-sector health authorities whose personal ideologies do not favour private-sector sales of anything related to health. Thus, the likelihood of success is dependent on a willingness to experiment with unfamiliar alternatives and to draw upon talent from outside the health sector.

Organizational structure

The long debate, discussed earlier, over whether the vertical or integrated form of organization is most appropriate for family planning programmes would seem to be winding down with a general acceptance of the point of view that either can be appropriate under certain circumstances and that each is especially appropriate for certain contraceptive methods. Once decisions about the form have been made, however, managers should be alert to typical operational problems. If family planning has been integrated into health services, overworked personnel may find it difficult to give it any priority, especially if the caseload of curative emergencies is high. If village health workers are assigned a long list of primary health care duties, there is no guarantee that they will give priority to family planning. Further, if the list is too extensive, the workers will be unable to perform any of the functions well.

Those more successful programmes that have opted for integration in community-based distribution programmes would appear to have ensured that personnel in health units are always (or at least at specified times) available to attend family planning cases. Programmes in which village health workers form part of the network have made efforts to guarantee that the workers begin with a readily manageable, relatively short list of activities in which family planning features prominently. After workers have demonstrated competence in delivering this package, other responsibilities are added, but with vigilance to ensure that the original package, and especially family planning, does not suffer in the process. The whole question of the size and content of the "optimum package" for delivery by village health workers--that is, the one that can be provided at greatest cost-effectiveness without sacrificing quality or coverage--is still an important topic for operations research.

Finally, whatever form of organization is selected, it is crucial that adequate facilities are available for medical back-up--through the public or private infrastructure. Such facilities should be available for those persons desirous of more extensive information, those suffering from side-effects and those wishing to "upgrade" to a method, such as sterilization or implants, that can be delivered only by medical or highly trained paramedical personnel.

Acceptability of services

Family planning and other MCH services should be adapted as much as possible to meet local customs and preferences. Because women constitute a disproportionate share of MCH/FP clients, programmes must take into account specific gender issues. Authorities both within and outside programme management have recognized the importance of these observations, and a considerable literature related to them has evolved.[48] The concept that services should be congruent with local psycho-cultural needs--with the "user perspective"--has led to concrete action, perhaps most notably the wealth of investigation into determining just what the "user perspective" may be. Ranging from survey studies of knowledge, attitudes and practice of family planning to anthropological in-depth participant observation, to marketing investigation and focus-group techniques, such research has in many countries provided valuable feedback into the design of services and IEC content.

Other efforts to tailor services to local preferences include the selection of types of service agents and contraceptive mix to be offered in accordance with cultural patterns; respect for privacy, modesty and anonymity; attempts to bring the hours in which services are offered into line with community schedules; and efforts to reduce waiting times. Occasionally, research has revealed impediments to staff-client communication (social distance and caste in Nepal, for example), and efforts would appear necessary to sensitize personnel to this problem. A major effort is also needed in many programmes to make the educational content for potential and actual MCH/FP clients reflect their concerns rather than only the views of the programme authorities. Additionally, such information should be provided in a more comprehensible form.

Acceptability of family planning encompasses other aspects in addition to cultural sensitivity and respectful treatment of clients. Some of these factors, loosely grouped under the rubric of "quality of care", refer to strict adherence to service norms and standard procedures by personnel, alertness to contra-indications and side-effects, and willingness to counsel clients adequately on contraceptive alternatives. Improvements in such dimensions of the quality of care should produce pay-offs in terms of both acceptance of the service and continuance of contraceptive use. Among the chief mechanisms for improving quality are a broadened range of available contraceptives, acquisition and timely distribution of adequate equipment and supplies, prompt and widespread dissemination of the most recent national and international information on the methods employed in the programme to all relevant staff, the updating of norms and procedures and refresher training for service personnel.

Community participation

The encouragement of community participation in MCH/FP programmes has received considerable attention. The premise is that if the community is directly involved, services are more likely to be offered in accordance with community preferences and thus to be more widely accepted. The term "community participation" is used here to refer to a broad spectrum of possibilities, ranging from simply "allowing" the community to pay for a greater proportion of service costs, through encouraging local organizations and individuals to become involved in service delivery under the direction of government or NGO personnel, to empowering the community by making it responsible for designing and operating services.

In practice, the difficulties of implementing either of the latter two variants of community participation are many. On the one hand, it is often unclear how much responsibility communities want or will accept. Community members often resist the idea of managing the services themselves, perceiving this arrangement as inferior to what the ministry of health provides more privileged groups. They may also object to bearing financial responsibility for services if they perceive that more privileged groups do not do so. On the other hand, Governments frequently feel threatened by empowerment of any group outside official structures, which themselves may be discredited in the community. Additionally, there are no universal formulae for determining who should be involved at the community level. In communities in which factions are important, the wrong choice can lead to reduced access to services for "out" groups, whereas the choice of politically well-connected individuals sometimes leaves the majority of the community mistrustful of the service. On the other hand, selecting individuals who are not politically well connected or attempting to develop community organizations outside official ones may create government resistance.[49]

Solutions to constraints in this area include analyses of existing community organizations and human resources in search of elements with willingness to participate in a sustained, honest manner and with widespread prestige and acceptability in the community. Investigations can help determine just what responsibilities the community wishes to carry out over short and extended periods. Involvement of the private sector and of social marketing can sometimes circumvent political suspiciousness. Finally, more operations research is needed on economically viable means of retaining the participation of community members, such as village health workers, who are expected to devote considerable time to the programme.

User incentives and disincentives

To accelerate the attainment of demographic goals, some countries have introduced incentives and disincentives to motivate family planning practice. Whether for reducing or increasing fertility, whether oriented to individuals, couples or communities, and whether administered by Governments or NGOs, incentives and disincentives are often perceived as controversial means for influencing fertility behaviour. However, they have been recognized for some years as playing, at least potentially, an important role in family planning programmes.

Although there are many types of incentives and disincentives, all characteristically consist of either a reward or a penalty tied to some kind of fertility behaviour. Incentives may be in cash or in kind, and encompass gifts, clothing and food; maternity leave, benefits and allowances; low-interest loans and taxation levels; priority for housing, educational and health services; employment opportunities for women and future employment priority for children; land development schemes and eligibility for participation in income-generating activities; social security benefits and old-age pensions; and special awards ranging from lottery tickets to certificates.

For acceptors, both relatively small and large payments have been used as incentives. The small-payment approach is based on the assumption that the primary purpose is to attract potential acceptors by offering them immediate compensation for lost wages, transportation and other costs incurred in accepting a family planning method. The incentive is usually a one-time cash payment given the moment a specified family planning method is adopted. The specific sum paid varies within and between countries, often depending on availability of funds and changing circumstances. The large-incentive approach assumes that couples desire numerous children, especially sons, for social and economic reasons, and that only substantial economic incentives can change desired family size by affecting the balance between costs and benefits of children to parents. Thus, the scale of the incentive must be perceived as being sufficiently large to compensate, at least partially, for the "cost" to the family of having fewer children than tradition would otherwise dictate. Rewards have included periodic payments for having not had additional births, special attention including free medical care and admission to better schools for children from smaller families, social security schemes, higher priority in housing or loan applications and savings bonds. In countries with declining populations or low fertility or both, large incentives may be used to encourage additional births through parity-related grants, family allowances, housing loans, maternity and paternity leave and other inducements.

Community, as opposed to individual, incentives are based on the assumption that communities, usually villages, are capable of perceiving the need for fertility reduction and economic development, and can be motivated to participate in family planning programmes linked to visible improvement in the quality of life. Typically, communities are rewarded for improving contraceptive prevalence rates above a base level or for reducing fertility rates in accordance with a predetermined formula. Rewards are often in the form of revolving funds, which may be tapped for loans to finance appropriate technology-oriented, income-generating activities, enhancing family and community life.

Although incentives and disincentives are becoming more common, they are not widespread. They tend to be found in countries that have relatively sophisticated infrastructures for family planning information and services, that have a relatively long history of population policies and programmes and that have perceived their population situation to be of such importance as to warrant measures beyond the mere provision of information and services. For these reasons, although examples of incentive and disincentive schemes can be found in several regions of the world, they tend to be more common in Asia and particularly in programmes aimed at reducing fertility. However, even in this region, countries without incentive or disincentive programmes outnumber those with them.

Despite several decades of experience with diverse incentives and disincentives implemented under varied administrative circumstances, the available information is insufficient for an objective assessment of their impact. In some countries, the fertility effects of incentives cannot be easily separated from the influence of concurrent societal changes and shifts in levels of rewards over time. In others, the data are either insufficient or too unreliable for rigorous analysis. Some studies suggest that a higher level of incentives leads to increased use of family planning methods; others note that couples are not motivated solely by incentives and that the success of incentives depends on their being part of a more comprehensive programme to influence desired family size. Such broader programmes often include components to improve the education and status of women, to provide opportunities for economic activity and to improve health.

Despite the relatively weak information base, certain factors may indeed improve the effectiveness of incentive and disincentive programmes. These would include the following: political and cultural acceptability, financial feasibility, a combination of several incentives or disincentives rather than a single isolated measure, and a simple design to facilitate administration. Supervisory, recording and reporting systems are needed for identifying problems and monitoring progress, and quantitative analysis should be supplemented by investigation of qualitative aspects such as client satisfaction and the effects of incentives on the quality of life.

The recurrent financial burden of incentive schemes should be carefully assessed for cost-effectiveness beforehand because, once begun, they may be difficult to withdraw without negative effects on the programme. For this reason, it may be useful to carry out carefully designed pilot studies of which rewards and constraints are effective in raising contraceptive prevalence and lowering fertility, at what cost and with what impact on the quality of services and the quality of life.[50]

Finally, the ethical and human rights issues raised by incentives and disincentives are extremely complex. Any assessment of them must take into account the socio-cultural contexts within which they operate, encompassing consideration of internationally recognized human rights, specific national value systems, community consensus, individual and national perceptions, impact on third parties (principally children), coercive or discriminatory content and the overall plan for socio-economic development. Such issues may best be settled by continuous dialogue between policy makers and the community aimed at reaching and maintaining a consensus.

Administrative issues

For maternal and child health and family planning programmes to have a reasonable chance of success a number of supportive functions must also be reinforced during the coming decade. These include the components of logistics, supervision, management information systems, research and evaluation, and training.

Logistics

Progress and supervision reports, along with special checks on service-point conditions from most programmes, reveal problems with shortages of equipment, drugs and contraceptives. Regardless of how successful a programme has been in generating demand, if it cannot maintain a continuous supply line, it will lack significant impact. Thus one of the principal operational challenges facing managers is that of establishing logistics systems that guarantee adequate material for making MCH/FP services widely accessible. The difficulty of organizing adequate logistics is multiplied as programmes incorporate relatively new modes of delivery, such as community-based distribution systems, which frequently involve a widely dispersed network of service points.

Various factors underlie the relatively poor performance of logistics systems in many countries. The most obvious, of course, has already been touched upon--financial constraints on buying what is needed for the programme, often worsened by the need to make purchases on the international market in scarce hard currency. However, even if adequate national or donor funds exist for acquiring what is needed, shortages often still occur because of inadequate inventory information or requisition systems at various programme levels; ill-defined procedures for buying and shipping, even when the information indicates the need for further supplies; inefficient warehousing practices; and lack of transport. Frequently, too, family planning supplies may become entangled in inefficient logistics systems of other services, especially in integrated health and family planning programmes. Finally, in some programmes, pilferage and, because of the opportunity for pilferage, the vested interest in not improving inventory controls constitute a serious obstacle.

Solutions have included attempts to encourage local production of equipment and supplies, where market, technological and exchange-rate conditions permit it. Other measures include developing better stock information systems and ordering and warehousing procedures. In some experiments, NGOs have been placed in charge of government logistics. A few instances have been recorded of an even more radical but potentially promising measure--turning over the responsibility for logistics in government service points to efficiently run private purveyors of such items as over-the-counter medicines or soft drinks. In programmes with integrated logistics systems, the appointment of officials charged with ensuring that family planning materials receive due priority has been seen as a possible solution. Clearly, further efforts along all these lines will be a priority in the coming decade.

Supervision

A recurring observation about MCH/FP programmes is that supervision at all levels, and especially of service providers, is too infrequent and perfunctory, contributing to abandonment of posts by volunteer workers and to demoralization, low productivity and an unacceptable quality of service among salaried personnel. Programmes emphasizing well-functioning supervisory systems, and accountability in general, have been more successful than those that do not.[51] Several factors typically constrain effective supervision. On the one hand, supervisors are generally the only source for "quality control" and medical (or paramedical) backstopping of service delivery. Yet, especially in community-based programmes, the agents they are to supervise are widely dispersed, budgets limit the ratios of supervisor to service agent, and the contact between the two is of necessity brief. On the other hand, supervisors too rarely receive training in appropriate, supportive supervisory skills and often work without a job description. Under such circumstances, supervision may be reduced to routine inventory checks and verification that service personnel are on post. As supervisory personnel are infrequently empowered to make changes in working conditions and seldom have the training to help service personnel improve technical skills, the whole exercise may be perceived as relatively unhelpful at best and as punitive at worst.

In addition to the above obstacles, some programmes find the recurring costs of personnel and transportation so burdensome that the frequency of supervision is allowed to fall to levels endangering programme effectiveness. Running out of stock at service points is also occasionally attributable to infrequent supervision. So, too, may be the inability to detect post vacancies, especially among volunteer village health workers. On the other hand, some programmes are beginning to discover that once service personnel have mastered their basic responsibilities, the frequency of supervision can be lessened with no loss in worker or programme productivity (as in Brazil).[52]

Solutions to the above challenges are emerging in the forms of special training in supervisory skills, including how to improve the technical skills of service personnel through on-the-spot instruction; delegating authority to supervisors to resolve typical problems in the working environment; attempting to develop alternative, more affordable systems for transporting supervisors to the field; and experimenting to identify the most cost-effective frequency and type (group or individual) of supervision at different levels in the programme.

Management information systems

An important obstacle to effective management in many family planning programmes around the world has been identified as the inadequate development or use of management information systems. Although in recent years significant improvements have been introduced in several countries--in Indonesia and Mexico, for example--many programme managers are still hampered by insufficient, inaccurate or outdated information on supply flows (contributing to the logistics problems discussed earlier), on existing personnel and vacancies, on training status of personnel and on service statistics. In the absence of accurate and timely information on these topics, management decision-making takes place in a vacuum.

In the case of service statistics, several deficiencies merit special attention. On the one hand, some countries lack information on even the most basic indicators--numbers, types and locations of operative and non-operative service points; new family planning acceptors; repeat visits; and contraceptives distributed. In many countries, estimates of coverage of current family planning users are rarely made and reliance is placed on the numbers of new acceptors and repeat visits, which do not constitute as sensitive a measure of programme success and of the need for further investment. Frequently, information for generating important indicators is assembled after such extensive delays and occasionally with so many inaccuracies that it is relatively useless to management. Service statistics are used at the national and occasionally regional levels in efforts to gain further funding from national and international sources and to meet certain reporting requirements. However, district- and local-level data are rarely used as a tool by supervisory personnel in identifying units requiring special attention, or by managers as indicators of different local needs for further resources. The above problems have been observed at various times in South Pacific countries, El Salvador, Liberia, Mexico, Pakistan, the Philippines and Sierra Leone, to name a few.

Attempts to improve management information systems have included efforts to simplify existing systems so that they provide accurate, timely information on a few of the most basic variables; introduction of simplified techniques, such as cluster sample interviews using portable data-entry equipment, for rapid generation of indicators such as contraceptive prevalence and immunization and pre-natal care coverage; and training for management, supervisory and service personnel in the correct production and use of information. Training courses teaching epidemiological approaches focused on coverage rates, alongside those emphasizing indicators of the volume of activities, have been valuable.

Research and evaluation

Although research and evaluation have been viewed by some authors as a part of management information systems, they are treated separately here for purposes of greater visibility. A familiar lament of both programme managers and researchers is that research and evaluation findings too rarely enter into the decision-making process in many MCH/FP programmes. The use of evaluation findings in decision-making, as the programme in Thailand demonstrates, has been positively correlated with programme success.[53]

Ideally, managers and researchers should jointly design research and evaluation plans suited to the life-cycle of programmes. Incipient programmes require baseline data on knowledge, attitudes and practices of the target populations; estimated needs and demands for services; inventories of existing service points (or points that could be so used); and inventories of available human resources for giving services and their training needs. Additionally, research on innovative approaches--for example, those aimed at adolescents or those employing paramedical personnel for the first time--can often provide the evidence to permit institutionalizing such efforts.

As programmes progress, both the quantity and the quality of services need to be monitored. In addition, investigations are needed of the "whys" of successes and failures, along with operations research on the cost-effectiveness of options open to managers. Such options include the contraceptive method mix to be offered, modalities of service delivery, length and type of training, frequency and content of supervision, mix of services to be offered by outreach workers, types of outreach workers to be hired and compensation schemes for village health workers. Clinical trials of experimental contraceptive methods are required. Research is needed to smooth the introduction of new contraceptive methods and to monitor the safety and efficacy of methods in general use. Finally, periodic assessments of whether health or demographic objectives are being achieved are necessary. If goals are not being achieved, changes in programme strategy will be required. Even when objectives are being met, other factors in addition to programme activities may be responsible, such as improved socio-economic indicators and other health improvements. Assessments of their effects vis-à-vis those of family planning programmes are still methodologically imprecise.

Among the many obstacles to such ideal research programmes are limited financial resources, which make managers reluctant to invest in research at the expense of services; scarce human resources for carrying out the research, especially in much of sub-Saharan Africa; and fear on the part of managers that research and evaluation will reflect negatively on them. Response to these constraints has come in the form of significant external support, including that of UNFPA, which currently encourages the inclusion of investigation in projects it assists, for programme research and evaluation activities and for the training of cadres of investigators.

Training

All MCH/FP programmes, whatever the stage of development and whatever the modes of service delivery, require considerable training inputs. These efforts may entail preparing medical and paramedical personnel during basic training; giving in-service staff their first exposure to family planning; developing cadres of village health workers; periodically requiring refresher courses for trained personnel; and providing special training about changes in administrative procedures or recently introduced contraceptive methods.

Despite considerable progress in a number of countries, the absence or inadequate coverage of relevant material in medical and paramedical schools still imposes a heavy in-service training burden on family planning programmes. The programmes must remedy training deficiencies wherever physicians, nurses and midwives have been insufficiently exposed to the health justifications for family planning and to the correct clinical procedures relating to the various contraceptive methods. These cohorts, who are typically expected to play key management and administrative roles in the planning, logistics and supervision of MCH/FP programmes, receive no systematic basic training in these functions. Unfortunately, in many programmes this deficiency remains inadequately addressed during in-service training. Additionally, these professionals would profit from more information than they typically receive on the importance of breast-feeding and of age at marriage.

Several other common training deficiencies have been encountered. First, in many countries the large numbers of in-service trainees to be reached make a several-tiered decentralized training strategy inevitable. Too frequently, however, greater attention is given to the quality of central-level training teams and less to provincial or district-level ones. As the "message" is passed through the decentralized links of the training chain, dilution and distortion occur. Additionally, preparation of the cohorts of trainers sometimes implies sending key individuals outside the country for training, with attendant risks of disrupting whatever functions they currently carry out and of their not returning to the programme. Second, a common tendency is to conduct both basic and in-service training in the absence of clear trainee job descriptions, or, if such descriptions do exist, to fail to base course content on them, which leads to irrelevant curricula and inadequate preparation of trainees for the tasks they will ultimately confront. Instances have also been observed in which training, and especially basic training, is not synchronized with the opening of positions in the programme, thus exposing trainees to the possibility of diminished or lost skills through lack of opportunity to practise them, as has occurred in Bangladesh and Democratic Yemen.

Another chronic problem in many programmes is the difficulty in releasing employees from their duties so as to permit adequate in-service preparation of personnel. Where medical and paramedical staff are in short supply and their absence threatens the delivery of services, superior officers are frequently reluctant to allow their staff time off for attendance. Moreover, resistance is often compounded and costs are unnecessarily elevated when all members of a cadre are assigned such training, although only a portion really need it. Whether for reasons of release-time pressures or budget constraints, many programmes tend to opt for courses that are too short to permit adequate transfer of requisite skills and knowledge and to overload attendees with general material, some of which is extraneous to actual job responsibilities. Only rarely have clear guidelines, ideally based on operations research, been produced concerning the scope of tasks and duration of training for village health workers. Finally, in smaller countries and in some larger ones with relatively low acceptance rates, a common obstacle is the lack of sufficiently large numbers of acceptors to provide trainees with necessary supervised practice in conducting sterilization, IUD insertion and, most recently, Norplant application.[54]

Further efforts will continue to be necessary to include and improve family planning content in medical and paramedical curricula, to organize regional and international courses for trainers, to develop service norms and clear job descriptions for all levels of personnel and to base training on them, to lobby for release time on the grounds of priority of MCH/FP services, to focus training on those most in need (a measure requiring an information system on the training status of personnel), to conduct research on questions of content and duration of training, and to send selected service personnel abroad for practical training in sterilization, IUDs and Norplant, until demand increases to a point permitting local training. Another promising approach for improving training is greater reliance on self-instructional materials, either written or in audio-visual cassettes. Self-instruction can be reinforced by relatively short group training sessions, and television can be employed more frequently as a medium of instruction.

Special challenges

Family planning programmes have typically focused, at least in initial stages, on married women and not infrequently on those among them at relatively high-parity levels. The needs of certain other groups have been less thoroughly addressed and sometimes neglected altogether. Given past achievements, many programmes will identify these previously marginal groups as of high priority in the 1990s. In addition, both long-standing and relatively recent health problems constitute special challenges.

Adolescents

Adolescent reproductive behaviour in most societies has great potential for controversy. For this reason and because of the magnitude of the task of delivering services to other less controversial groups, the needs of adolescents--defined here as the population of 10 to 19 years of age-- have received relatively little priority in most countries. In some, the issue has been ignored altogether; in others, it has been postponed while more pressing matters have been dealt with. During the 1970s and especially the 1980s, a number of programmes serving older women progressed to the extent that adolescents have now emerged as one of the remaining few underserved groups.

Although birth rates have been on the decline in a number of developing countries, adolescent fertility remains relatively high in many nations (see Table 16). In the countries for which data are available, 34 of 50 manifest annual age-specific fertility rates of more than 50 per 1,000 adolescents. At such levels, the probabilities that the "average" adolescent will become pregnant at some time during her teen-age years are relatively high.

Table 16

AGE SPECIFIC FERTILITY RATES
(per thousand women of age less than 20)

Country	Rate	Year
Africa		
Cape Verde	78	1985
Egypt	31	1980
Ghana	136	1977
Kenya	168	1977/78
Lesotho	76	1977
Malawi	136	1977
Mauritius	37	1985
Nigeria	173	1981/82
Rwanda	50	1978
Senegal	189	1978
Seychelles	79	1986
Sudan (north)*	77	1978/79
Tunisia	37	1980
Zimbabwe	24	1978
Latin America and Caribbean		
Argentina	82	1980
Belize	144	1984
Brazil	48	1984
Chile	61	1985
Costa Rica	96	1984
Cuba	94	1985
Ecuador	66	1981
Guatemala	126	1985
Honduras	138	1981
Jamaica	120	1982
Mexico	65	1980
Montserrat	155	1982
Panama	97	1984
Paraguay	23	1982
Saint Kitts/Nevis	104	1983
Saint Lucia	130	1984
St. Vincent and the Grenadines	145	1980
Trinidad & Tobago	84	1980
Uruguay	66	1980
Venezuela	90	1984

---

*   Data available only for northern Sudan.

131

Table 16 *(Continued)*

Country	Rate	Year
Asia		
Afghanistan	*160*	*1979*
Bahrain	*54*	*1982*
Bangladesh	*130*	*1981*
Cyprus	*34*	*1985*
Iraq	*51*	*1977*
Jordan	*79*	*1979*
Kuwait	*57*	*1984*
Malaysia	*26*	*1984*
Philippines	*46*	*1980*
Republic of Korea	*12*	*1983*
Singapore	*9*	*1986*
Sri Lanka	*38*	*1982*
Territory of Hong Kong	*9*	*1985*
Thailand	*41*	*1984*
Oceania		
Pacific Islands	*100*	*1979*
Samoa	*34*	*1977*

Source: *1986 Demographic Yearbook* (New York, United Nations, 1988)

Adolescent fertility, depending on the national context, may primarily be a problem of either married or unmarried young women. For example, in 16 of 38 developing countries for which data are available, 40 per cent or more of the women marry before their nineteenth birthday. In 32 of the 38, at least 40 per cent marry by age 20.[55] In other developing countries, however, age at marriage is higher and pregnancies, when they occur, more typically take place outside of stable unions. In the former case, because of negative consequences discussed below, a need for raising the age at marriage is manifest. In both cases, social attitudes often preclude sex/reproductive education for young girls who, as a result, are unprepared psychologically as well as physically for pregnancy.

The health implications of high adolescent pregnancy rates are that when the first pregnancy and multiple pregnancies occur too early, and especially when these take place among poor or single mothers, the

132

comparative risks of morbidity and mortality for the mother and child are unacceptably high. The probability of death among women under 20 years old who become pregnant exceeds that of women 20-24 in 14 of 18 studies, by margins ranging from 10 to over 250 per cent (see Table 17). Postponement of pregnancy to ages beyond adolescence represents, then, an important, potentially life-saving, public health measure. Essentially the same conclusions would be reached were the focus of analysis infant and child mortality or maternal, infant and child morbidity.

Table 17

RELATIVE RISKS OF MORTALITY FROM PREGNANCY-RELATED CAUSES: ADOLESCENTS VERSUS AGE GROUP 20-24 IN SELECTED

Country	*Risk**
Africa	
Algeria	*2.4*
Egypt	*1.6*
Ethiopia	*1.8*
Nigeria	*3.8*
Zaire	*0.8*
Asia	
Bangladesh	*3.5*
India	*0.7*
Indonesia	*2.3*
Philippines	*1.0*
Sri Lanka	*0.8-1.5*
Thailand	*1.2*
Latin America and Caribbean	
Brazil	*1.2*
Dominican Republic	*2.2*
Ecuador	*1.4*
Jamaica	*1.1*
Venezuela	*1.1*

Source: World Health Organization and International Planned Parenthood Federation, unpublished compilations of national or local studies 1977-1985.

---

* Relative risk is determined by dividing maternal mortality rates per 10,000 (or 100,000) live births of age group 15-19 by those of age group 20-24.

In addition to health risks, evidence is mounting that too early child-bearing disrupts female education and reduces a woman's opportunities for personal growth, thus diminishing her potential for contributing to social development. Although in highly traditional societies with a significant premium on early demonstration of fertility and extremely restricted roles for women, adolescent fertility may not have been viewed as a social problem, most societies are now in transition and find too early child-bearing disruptive for at least some portion of their female adolescent population. Concern has been voiced about this problem in all regions, most recently in a number of African countries where pregnancies among young girls who then drop out of school have become viewed as a threat to individual aspirations and societal development.

Thus far, in response to the often emotionally charged topic of adolescent reproductive behaviour, family planning advocates have pointed to the incidence of pregnancy and its negative impact. Other studies have been directed at adolescent reproductive and contraceptive knowledge and behaviour with a view to designing appropriate services. The least progress has been made in extending services to adolescents; where these have been created at all they tend to be on a modest, experimental scale in a few major urban areas. Although additional investigations are required to document the seriousness of the problem in countries where the potential for controversy remains high, the challenge is increasingly that of developing services. Given certain characteristics of adolescents observed in both developed and developing countries--tendencies towards risk-taking behaviour, beliefs in personal immortality, low receptivity to information provided by adult authority figures and high impulsivity--special approaches to this group will be required.

Only sketchy information is available on the operational issues that will likely remain important in the 1990s. Among these are whether, to win acceptance by young people, separate adolescent services must be established or whether they can somehow be reached through existing services for the general population; whether traditional agents can be used to promote services or whether special adolescent promotion/communication networks must be established; and whether unified messages and approaches will be adequate for the "adolescent population" or whether segmentation will be required to reach males and females, married and unmarried, in-school and out-of-school and employed and unemployed youth. Other issues are how to attempt to change traditional attitudes favouring early child-bearing and how to overcome ambivalence and resistance among service personnel to the provision of services to adolescents.

Males

Females often have low status and play a subordinate role in the decision-making process that frequently influences whether couples practise contraception in developing societies. A recent study in the

Sudan argues that males play a significant role in deciding whether to practise contraception, whether to stop using contraception and where and how to obtain supplies and services.[56] "Husband's objection" has been suggested as a major cause for non-practice or non-continuation. Despite a liberal trend, some countries still require spouse's (usually the husband's) consent for sterilization by legal provision or by programme regulation. In many other countries, for social reasons a wife needs her husband's permission to use even oral pills, though there is no legal or regulatory requirement. Widespread misgivings among males about vasectomy--and their perceptions equating vasectomy with castration-- limit the scope for males' sharing the responsibility for contraception.

Although male resistance has been assumed responsible for impeding acceptance of family planning, the evidence has been based largely on female responses to questions about why they do not practise contraception. Yet a significant proportion of the relatively few studies on males themselves reveals that male and female reproductive goals do not significantly differ. What seems to be lacking, then, is communication between spouses that would permit them to recognize that they both prefer to avoid unregulated fertility.

The importance of achieving male involvement in family planning has by now attained the status of doctrine. However, little programme experience is available regarding how males can be brought more directly into the family planning communication and education efforts to promote favourable attitudes. Most family planning programmes have been designed primarily on a female-to-female basis for counselling, education and services and supplies at the community as well as the clinic level.

Slow progress in involving males may be at least partially explained by lack of clarity in the desired outcome. To date, most efforts have been limited to attempts to win over male support for contraceptive use by the spouse through exposure to information and arguments about the negative impact of unregulated fertility on the health and socio-economic status of the family. Other educational interventions have emphasized the importance of responsible male behaviour; still other campaigns have been mounted in some settings to promote vasectomy and use of condoms. Where these efforts have taken place, probably a minority of programmes world-wide, evidence is scanty on their efficacy, particularly in gaining male support for female contraception. Many advocates clearly believe that something beyond mere male acquiescence--a much more active role in promoting and supporting family planning at the community and family levels--is required for success. To make real progress will require a more specific definition of what the desired outcome should be and more rigorous testing of differing strategies for bringing it about.

Abortion

Fertility-regulation goals should ideally be attained through the practice of contraception and not by abortion. The International Conference on Population in Mexico (1984) recommended, in this regard, that abortion

135

"in no case should be promoted as a method of family planning".[57] In fact, UNFPA does not support abortion programmes. Regarding the issue of legality of abortion, UNFPA does not take a position either for or against. UNFPA does not attempt to make or influence policy beyond its mandate to promote awareness in the population area and to extend assistance to countries requesting it.

Nevertheless, induced abortion has become a matter of great concern because of the serious threat it can pose to maternal health. However much it may be desired that abortion did not exist, its practice is an undeniable part of the experience of large numbers of women in both developed and developing countries. It is estimated that between 25 million and 40 million induced abortions occur annually in the latter countries, or approximately one for every three to five live births (estimates are highly inexact, however, largely because of the illegality of abortion in many settings and the consequent absence of statistics).[58]

It is estimated that 15-20 million of these procedures take place legally and under relatively safe conditions, whereas 10-20 million occur where abortion is illegal or where hygienic, affordable services are relatively inaccessible to considerable segments, if not the great majority, of the population.[59] Not surprisingly, in developing countries where safe abortion services are scarce, cases stemming from induced abortions crowd obstetric and emergency beds, often outnumbering obstetric cases. Such complications consistently figure among the leading two or three causes of maternal mortality, and conditions resulting from inadequately performed abortions are frequently responsible for 10 per cent to more than 50 per cent of maternal deaths in developing countries without accessible, safe abortion services.[60] In absolute terms, the toll in such countries may reach 100,000-150,000 maternal deaths annually from abortion-related causes.

The legal status governing abortion varies widely. As of early 1986, 76 per cent of the world's population lived in countries where abortion was legally permitted: about 39 per cent had access to abortion on request, about 24 per cent on grounds of socio-economic reasons such as inadequate income, housing or unwed status, and 13 per cent on broader health grounds. The remaining 24 per cent of the world's population resided in countries where abortion was permitted only on grounds of saving the life of the mother or where abortion was altogether prohibited.[61]

Relatively few family planning programmes in developing countries have formulated a consistent goal-oriented approach to abortion. Although nearly two thirds of developing-country women reside in countries with liberal abortion legislation, formal legal status is an imperfect indicator of availability. It cannot be assumed that countries with less restrictive policies on abortion make medically safe services accessible to their citizens. In fact, most do not, and the penalty is high-- up to 1 death per 100 interventions conducted by poorly trained providers or under unhygienic conditions. In contrast, abortion performed under hygienic conditions by adequately trained personnel entails less risk than carrying pregnancy to full term.

Clearly, a strong societal consensus against abortion will limit the response that the health and family planning community can make to it. Nevertheless, even in areas such as Latin America, where such opposition is reported to be strongest, the incidence of abortion and related complications is very high. Consequently, the weight of human suffering involved argues convincingly for the need for a more rational and systematic response than has heretofore been the case in most countries.

At the very least, countries should more vigorously promote contraception as superior to abortion as a means of fertility control. Family planning, in short, should be presented as the "first line of defense" against unwanted pregnancy. One of the highest priority groups for this message and for family planning services themselves is precisely those women who undergo abortion, to ensure that they do not continue to rely on this practice.

In countries where complications of induced abortion account for a large number of maternal deaths, suitable curative health services for treatment of septic and incomplete abortion should be made available as a maternal health intervention. It was recommended at the 1987 International Conference on Better Health for Women and Children through Family Planning that "regardless of the legal status, humane treatment of septic and incomplete abortion and post-abortion contraceptive advice and services should be made available".[62] The 1984 International Conference on Population also recommended providing "for the humane treatment and counselling of women who have had recourse to abortion".[63]

In societies where abortion is morally proscribed but where it is recognized that it will occur anyway, with disastrous effects on health unless good quality services are made available, the most delicate question in providing limited abortion services is how to attract those women who would otherwise have aborted without at the same time increasing acceptance of, and demand for, abortion. To avoid the risk of "legitimization", abortion services should be accompanied by vigorous promotion of contraception as the preferred alternative to abortion.

Wherever abortion is legal, the recommendation of the International Conference on Better Health for Women and Children through Family Planning is particularly pertinent--that "good quality abortion services should be made easily accessible to all women".[64] To save lives, services should be made accessible, most importantly, to disadvantaged segments of society who have no effective access to expensive private-sector sources. Here abortion may be actively promoted as a back-up measure in case of failure in the contraceptive first line of defense. Demand on this basis seems assured. Calculations based on the failure rates of conventional contraceptive methods indicate that the average woman depending on them would have to undergo at least one abortion during her reproductive career to achieve the lower levels of fertility (two to three children) that are becoming more widely accepted in many developing countries and that will be required to meet the demographic goals of many of their Governments.[65]

Sexually transmitted diseases, acquired immune deficiency syndrome and family planning

Acquired immune deficiency syndrome (AIDS) as well as other sexually transmitted diseases has assumed epidemic proportions in many countries, including some with the least resources in manpower, institutions and money to cope with the problem. The estimated HIV infection rate has given rise to predictions of a far greater incidence of AIDS in the future. Population programmes around the world, including those in many countries with a high HIV infection rate, have developed a network of multi-sectoral programmes for providing contraceptive methods and transmitting family life education, which can be used as a convenient channel for prevention of AIDS and other STDs.

Therefore, despite the concerns of some administrators about overburdening personnel and about diluting their dedication to their primary responsibilities, MCH/FP programmes will increasingly come under pressure to address the accelerating menace of STDs in general, and AIDS in particular. Promotional home visits, clinic educational efforts, and family life and sex education programmes--typically conducted by family planning personnel or by others supported by, or as an adjunct to, family planning programmes--present natural opportunities to educate the public on prevention of STDs.

Given the gravity of the health menace of STDs, the relatively slight risk to achievement of other objectives by taking on further responsibilities in this area seems justified. Nevertheless, care will have to be taken in training personnel, first to ensure that they are not distracted from other duties and second that the messages that they--and the mass media--disseminate do not link family planning with STDs in a negative fashion in the public mind. Although at first such a proposition may seem far-fetched, cancer screening in the context of family planning programmes led in some areas of Latin America to rumours that users of contraceptives must have increased risk of cancer since they were being tested. Further consideration of information and education issues relating to STDs and AIDS appears in Chapter 4.

Additionally, of course, provision of condoms and spermicides, a major line of defense against STDs, has been a traditional responsibility of family planning programmes and a role that may be expected to increase, particularly as the campaign against AIDS intensifies. In this context, the counselling and service provision roles of the family planning worker may become more complicated. The contraceptive methods that confer greatest protection against STDs have generally proved less effective than other alternatives in preventing pregnancy. Since a significant part of contraceptive failure attributable to condoms may be due to inconsistent use, workers will find that they have to redouble efforts to explain the importance of correct use and perhaps also to provide one method for disease protection and a second one for family planning. Given the importance of the condom in disease prevention, workers may have to deal increasingly with males in addition to their usual largely female clientele.

Finally, although family planning affords opportunities for combatting STDs, it also lends itself to the inadvertent spread of disease. All body-invasive procedures in family planning, including IUD insertions, sterilizations, injections and pelvic examinations, have the potential for spreading STDs, and particularly HIV virus, when carried out under septic conditions. Thus, managers will be faced with the task of preparing staff for adding STDs and AIDS to existing education and counselling content and for improving hygienic conditions in the provision of services. Doubtless, too, procurement and distribution of increased quantities of condoms and spermicides will require greater than previously expected financial outlays and improved logistics systems.

Infertility

Family planning has traditionally been taken to mean helping couples to achieve their desired family size. Thus, programmes have often publicly stressed that assisting couples to have children is as much a part of family planning as providing the means for postponing or avoiding pregnancies. In reality, however, few programmes have devoted a large proportion of resources to diagnosing and treating infertility, presumably because excess fertility has been viewed as a much more prevalent and socially threatening problem than subfertility. Recently, however, infertility has been discovered to reach the scale of a health threat in some areas. In parts of central and western Africa, up to 25 per cent of all couples are estimated to be infertile. Given the magnitude of the problem in that region, it is appropriate to rethink the role of family planning programmes with respect to infertility both there and in the rest of the developing world.[66]

Appropriate medical testing, treatment, provision of infertility drug therapy, and such measures as artificial insemination and embryonic implants are both labour- and cost-intensive. Additionally, with the exception of routine screening for sexual practices and venereal diseases, they require highly trained personnel and sophisticated equipment. For this reason, the services that go beyond screening and simple treatment belong in referral-level institutions. Thus, where the incidence of infertility is not unusually high, where excess fertility constitutes the predominant societal problem and where human and financial resources to meet it are limited, it is inadvisable to commit a FP programme to heavy involvement in most phases of infertility care. However, simple screening, treatment for venereal diseases and, above all, education leading to the prevention of STDs are sufficiently compatible with traditional family planning tasks. It is unlikely that those tasks would seriously disrupt work or administrative patterns and hence impair efforts to deal with problems of excess fertility. At the same time, they would contribute to reducing the incidence of infertility.

Even where infertility is unusually common, the major contribution that family planning programmes can make is again to strengthen efforts, compatible with routine family planning tasks, to prevent and treat venereal diseases. To go beyond this role would be to jeopardize relatively weak delivery systems for contraception, whereas to take this step can be highly significant because recent research shows STDs to be the most common cause of infertility in the afflicted regions.[67]

A statistically small but growing variant of infertility occurs in couples in which one partner has undergone contraceptive sterilization. Although little information is available on the potential demand for reversal of sterilization, the sheer cumulative volume of couples who have elected surgical contraception makes the probability of significant numbers of candidates for reversal rather high. Constraints on establishing reversal services are several. On the one hand, success of microsurgical techniques is uncertain: for vasectomy reversal, success rates of up to 80 per cent are now reported from developed countries, whereas for females, rates range up to 60 per cent. Also, costs are relatively high. Thus, if effective demand is on the order of, say, 2 per 100 couples sterilized at some stage after the initial intervention and if success occurs in only half of those cases, the cost-benefit ratio may simply be too low for most programmes to subsidize. Additionally, of course, some minimum "critical mass" of potential users of the service would be necessary before the start-up and subsequent costs could be justified. Thus, such a service will probably not be recommended for most small countries for the foreseeable future.

The little information that is available--principally on success rates--is derived from pilot projects in developed countries. For answers to questions about real demand, success rates and costs, it would be prudent, before initiating sterilization-reversal services on a wide scale in other countries, to await the results of the first broad-scale services in a developing country, to begin shortly in India.

Conclusions and recommendations

General

Further improvements in maternal and child health and decreases in demographic growth rates in developing countries will depend on increases in the coverage and quality of maternal and child health services in general and of family planning in particular. Such increases will have to be won largely with existing strategies and technology; no breakthroughs are foreseen for the coming decade. Additionally, they will most probably have to be achieved with less than adequate financial resources in most countries and shortages of human resources in many.

Just to maintain existing levels of contraceptive prevalence in developing countries, the number of currently protected couples will have to grow from 326 million to 420 million by the year 2000. Increasing prevalence to levels consistent with health or demographic objectives, or both, will require extension of services to as many as 167 million more couples than are currently protected. It is calculated that to achieve such expansion of services, expenditures will have to rise from current levels of $3 billion annually to between $5.6 billion and $10 billion in constant dollars by the year 2000.

At the same time that more resources are required, interest in the "population problem" in general and family planning in particular has been waning in some quarters, at least partly in reaction to successesin some countries during the 1970s and 1980s. Hence, to ensure vital financial and human resources, the need to create and rekindle political commitment will persist throughout the 1990s. Periodic demonstrations of health and demographic consequences of unregulated fertility and of the cost-benefit of investment in family planning will be required in the developing countries as well as in the countries that are assisting them.

A wide selection of contraceptive methods to ensure a reasonable "fit" with diverse individual needs will also be required for expansion of family planning. Thus, increasing public-sector investment in the search for more acceptable contraceptive methods will be necessary for increasing family planning practice, even though the pay-off may be relatively long term. The task for the future will also consist of convincing health authorities and service providers of the need to add contraceptive alternatives to the programme repertoire and introducing them in such a fashion as not to disturb programme efficiency in dealing with only a few methods. Introducing more types of contraceptives should not lead to the proliferation of brands within types (more than two or three varieties of oral contraceptives and one or two varieties of injectables), because they might confuse providers and users and unduly tax logistics systems.

IEC efforts will have to be strengthened, especially in countries where large segments of the population remain uninformed or unconvinced about the benefits of family planning and where socio-cultural factors are unfavourable to acceptance. This subject will be treated extensively in Chapter 4.

In most developing countries, considerable effort will have to be devoted to making services much more widely available. Data indicate that all modes of service delivery--clinic based, community-based, social marketing, and regular commercial channels--in both public and private sectors should be used to ensure maximum availability. However, given the relatively low probability of financial resources ever reaching optimal levels, difficult choices will be necessary in making services more widely available. The cost-effectiveness of alternative sectoral and service delivery modes will have to be evaluated to arrive at the most rational decision about which modes and which contraceptive methods to employ and how much emphasis they should be given in any efforts to expand accessibility of services. Because of resource constraints, micro-decisions about how to train, equip and supervise within sectors and for different modes of delivery should likewise be based on cost-effectiveness criteria. In sum, all decisions regarding both macro- and micro-programme strategies need to be based on cost-effectiveness analyses.

"Privatization"--encouraging the private sector to assume a greater share of responsibility for provision of services--received considerable attention in the 1980s as a strategy for expanding availability and for dealing with financial scarcity in the public sector. It will doubtless also play an important role in 1990s. Where knowledge of, and demand for, family planning is strong and contraceptive prevalence is high, Governments should consider the possibility of delegating a considerable portion of the responsibility to the private sector while focusing public resources on remaining underserved groups and on those unable to afford private-sector services. The phasing out of government services must be carefully planned and timed so as not to reduce the levels of availability associated with high contraceptive prevalence in these countries. In countries with moderate levels of prevalence and with low private-sector participation, increasing availability through greater involvement of the private sector and particularly through social-marketing approaches is often advisable.

A further requirement for cost-effectiveness in the 1990s in countries with relatively high prevalence is more precise identification of currently underserved populations to permit focusing of resources on them. Among the groups heretofore largely missed by existing services is the adolescent population, for whom unregulated fertility represents a particular threat to personal and social development. Education and services for this group will therefore be a priority. Male involvement in family planning generally has not reached optimal levels. More effective approaches will be required in the coming years.

Increased co-ordination among assistance agencies is needed to ensure more efficient use of resources. Additionally, external agencies have not consistently related assistance to programme effectiveness: to some extent, more effective programmes have been made to assume ever greater self-sufficiency while less effective programmes have been rewarded with ever greater external support. If the resource shortfall proves critical in the 1990s, agencies may consider withholding support from programmes that have proved chronically unwilling to assign priority to family planning or that have refused to use resources in a cost-effective manner. The "saved" resources could then be channelled to programmes with a high commitment to family planning and a willingness to use resources efficiently. In addition, assistance agencies and programme managers alike should ensure that all models--whether pilot or broad-scale projects--are replicable and sustainable.

The need for improved acceptability and quality of services is considerable in most programmes. Efforts should include identifying the concerns of target populations about family planning and contraceptive methods and restructuring informational content accordingly. They should offer those methods most culturally appropriate, provide a range of methods tailored to ensure "fit" with diverse individual needs, improve quality of counselling and service delivery, reduce waiting times and ensure that services are available at convenient hours, and improve personnel and client communication through sensitizing the former to the needs and concerns of the latter.

Both basic and in-service training in management, client-provider interaction, information and motivation techniques, provision of services, and introduction of new contraceptive methods will require major support throughout the 1990s. Identification of more cost-effective techniques of training should be pursued. Improvement of personnel motivation as well as skills will be crucial for success in the years ahead. In many programmes, remuneration levels are indicative of the low priority given to health objectives in general and family planning in particular. It is too common to find workers who are unaware or unconvinced of the demographic and health justifications for their work. Finally, in addition to remedying these two constraints, most programmes are in urgent need of greater accountability.

More emphasis than in the past should be placed on encouraging breast-feeding as a child-spacing technique. It has the advantage of being inexpensive, relatively effective over the short term, easy to teach, beneficial for the baby and acceptable to proponents of natural family planning. Care must be taken, of course, to ensure the timely provision of other contraceptive methods when the protection conferred by breast-feeding is most likely to cease. Organized efforts within the framework of MCH/FP programmes are needed to promote breast-feeding through educational approaches at clinical and community levels. Provisions should be made for working women to breast-feed their babies during working hours.

MCH/FP programmes must develop in the 1990s a more coherent response to the serious health problem of induced abortion under unhygienic conditions. At the least, contraception must be actively promoted in the general population as a more desirable technique for fertility regulation, and special efforts should be made to provide contraceptive methods to the high-risk population of women who have already aborted. Additionally, the toll in maternal mortality and morbidity justifies those countries that choose to make safe abortion services available to those who would otherwise seek them under dangerous conditions. Care must be taken, however, not to "legitimize" abortion unduly in those settings where it is morally questioned. Contraception, once again, should be presented as the highly preferable form of fertility regulation.

MCH/FP programmes will be called upon during the coming decade to play a more active role in combatting sexually transmitted diseases in general and AIDS in particular. Important contributions should include education on disease prevention, provision of barrier methods and strict adherence to antiseptic procedures.

Women have constituted an underused resource in primary health and family planning programmes. They should not be seen simply as the passive beneficiaries of services or as a resource suitable only for lower-level responsibilities. Rather, women must become designers and managers of programmes. Despite the substantial evidence that women can be effective agents of change in the community, policy makers and programme managers have frequently failed to take advantage of the contributions that women can make in enhancing the acceptability and quality of maternal and child health and family planning services.

Country-specific

Greater availability of contraceptives is associated with higher contraceptive prevalence and, within prevalence groups, with greater reliance on modern, relatively effective methods (see Table 18). The data further imply that, among relatively motivated populations, easy availability is conducive to the selection of modern contraceptives, whereas low availability leads to greater dependence on traditional methods.

Table 18

CONTRACEPTIVE PREVALENCE, DEPENDENCE ON TRADITIONAL METHODS AND AVAILABILITY SCORES*

Prevalence 0-20%	Prevalence 21-25%		Prevalence 36-50%		High prevalence over 50%	
	Low reliance on non-supply methods	High** reliance on non-supply methods	Low reliance on non-supply methods	High** reliance on non-supply methods	Low reliance on non-supply methods	High** reliance on non-supply methods
Africa						
5 Benin	21 Egypt	17 Botswana	20 Morocco	16 Zimbabwe	31 Mauritius	
3 Burundi			-- S. Africa			
4 Cameroon			45 Tunisia			
5 Cote D'Ivoire						
4 Ghana						
12 Kenya						
2 Lesotho						
8 Liberia						
5 Mauritania						
11 Nigeria						
3 Rwanda						
10 Senegal						
0 Sudan (north)***						
Asia and Oceania						
5 Afghanistan	36 India	41 Bangladesh	35 Fiji	41 Philippines	58 China	27 Lebanon
4 Iraq	24 Jordon		36 Indonesia		59 Rep. Korea	40 Malaysia
16 Nepal					59 Singapore	47 Sri Lanka
16 Pakistan					59 Hong Kong	22 Turkey
5 Yemen					60 Thailand	
Latin America and Caribbean						
22 Haiti	-- Grenada	2 Bolivia	-- Antigua & Barbuda	-- Guadeloupe	34 Brazil	
	30 Guatemala		-- Barbados	-- Paraguay	52 Colombia	
	25 Guyana		-- Dominica	-- Peru	34 Costa Rica	
	29 Honduras		40 Dominican Republic		45 Jamaica	
	19 Nicaragua		33 Ecuador		-- Martinique	
			46 El Salvador		45 Mexico	
			-- Saint Kitts and Nevis		-- Montserrat	
			-- Saint Vincent /Grenadines		56 Panama	
			19 Venezuela		36 Trinidad and Tobago	

* Availability scores are shown in parentheses ( ). Availability refers to male and female sterilization, oral contraceptives, intra-uterine devices, barrier methods and legal abortion. Maximum possible score is 60.

** High reliance on non-supply = more than 25% of all contraceptors using non-supply methods. Non-supply methods generally refer to traditional methods generally refer to traditional methods.

*** Data available only for northern sudan.

Table 18 *(Continued)*

	Low reliance on non-supply methods	High* reliance on non-supply methods	Low reliance on non-supply methods	High** reliance on non-supply methods	Low reliance on non-supply methods	High** reliance on non-supply methods
Prevalence 0-20%		**Prevalence 21-25%**		**Prevalence 36-50%**		**High prevalence over 50%**
Average availability		Average availability		Average availability		Average availability
7 Unweighted		24 Unweighted		31 Unweighted		44 Unweighted
11 Population weighted		35 Population weighted		36 Population weighted		64 Population weighted

Source: Contraceptive prevalence data from *Levels and Trends of Contraceptive Use as Assessed in 1988.* (United Nations publication, Sales No. E.89.XIII.4). Information on average dates from 1983. Availability data are from *Population Briefing Paper,* No. 19, October 1987. (Washington, D.C., Population Crisis Committee, 1987)

At least four groups of countries appear to have patterns of contraceptive use and availability sufficiently diverse as to warrant somewhat different strategic emphases (table 18).

Lowest contraceptive prevalence

The first group, those countries with the lowest (less than 20 per cent) levels of contraceptive prevalence, is composed of the great majority of African nations for which data are available and probably of most of those for which they are not, Afghanistan, Iraq, Nepal, Pakistan and Yemen in Asia, and Haiti in the Caribbean. This group, with several exceptions--Ghana, Haiti, Kenya, Nepal, Pakistan and the Sudan--is at the incipient stage of family planning programme development. All members received a rating of "weak" or "very weak" in terms of overall family planning programme effort and availability of services in the study conducted by W. Parker Mauldin and Robert J. Lapham and updated in 1987 by the Population Crisis Committee.[68]

For this group of countries, with few exceptions, first priority should be given to activating existing clinical, medical and paramedical networks to serve as bases for service delivery, referrals, training and supervision

---

* High reliance on non-supply = more than 25% of all contraceptors using non-supply methods. Non-supply methods generally refer to traditional methods generally refer to traditional methods.

for incipient outreach, community-based, and/or commercial systems of service delivery. Especially in Africa, shortages of staff for such functions make training of key national, provincial and district-level personnel in basic management a high priority. Another high priority is the training of instructors to conduct in-service skills preparation of personnel required to offer services in the existing health infrastructure. Given the limited geographic coverage of clinical networks and their restricted capacity for delivery of any type of health services, once they are "activated" expansion beyond them will be required in most cases to achieve significant health or demographic impacts. In these countries, however, resource constraints make almost inevitable difficult choices on the additional modes of service delivery to be employed and the degree to which they should be emphasized. Analysis of the cost-effectiveness of local options will be critical for maximizing impact with limited resources.

In all the countries of this group, considerable emphasis will have to be placed on information and motivation campaigns to convince their populations of the benefits of family planning, to make them aware of the existence of contraceptive methods and where they may be obtained and to combat erroneous notions regarding safety and efficacy. Particularly in the setting of the more traditional African and Middle Eastern countries, care will have to be taken to ensure that messages are culturally appropriate and that traditional leaders and the community are involved. Efforts to prevent erosion of current breast-feeding habits will also be important to avoid increases in fertility.

Contraceptive prevalence between 20 and 35 per cent

A second group, those with prevalence of 20-35 per cent, comprises at least 11 nations, including several--Bangladesh, Egypt and India--with large populations. These countries may be further subdivided in accordance with the degree to which the population relies on non-supply, traditional and less effective methods. High reliance is arbitrarily defined as the use of such methods by more than 25 per cent of the users of all methods. The availability scores of the entire medium-to-low prevalence group, with the exception of Bolivia, exceed those of all countries in the first group except Haiti.

All members of this group, along with Haiti, Ghana, Kenya, Nepal and Pakistan from the first group, appear to have a better foundation of basic medical and managerial backstopping resources than those of the rest of the first group. Thus, emphasis should be placed on a major, general expansion of the availability of services through extension not only of clinical but also of community-based, commercial marketing, and other private networks in accordance with the probable cost-effectiveness of local options and funding availability. Implementation issues relating to broad-scale training, logistics, information systems, supervision, etc., will be of primary importance.

This group, plus the five countries just mentioned from the first one, also contains several long-standing programmes that have been relatively

147

unsuccessful to date. The constraints lie in over-emphasis on one method (condoms in Pakistan, sterilization in India and Nepal), relatively poor quality services, low motivation of personnel, poor logistics and, despite considerable efforts, persistent inaccessibility of services. Additionally, several nations contain large populations whose culture is viewed as unreceptive to family planning. Since pilot projects show that high-quality services, sensitively offered, can win acceptance in these groups, more should be done to make the services culturally acceptable and attractive to individual clients as well as to inform and motivate the population.

Medium contraceptive prevalence

In the third group, with prevalence of between 36 and 50 per cent, services are relatively accessible in most countries (Dominican Republic, El Salvador, Fiji, Indonesia, the Philippines and Tunisia). However, availability is still below levels found in the programmes with the highest prevalence rates. Thus, a more modest extension of services than in the second group seems called for. The exception would be countries such as Paraguay, Peru and Zimbabwe, where, because of limited accessibility, an otherwise rather highly motivated population is using relatively ineffective methods. Hence, in this subgroup a major expansion is indicated. With these exceptions, extension should be focused on particular underserved groups such as adolescents, remote rural populations and pockets of marginal urban dwellers. Some additional extension of the service network will be required in accordance with growth in the numbers of fertile-aged couples. In several of these countries, although service points are relatively accessible geographically, poor logistics, poor service, inferior care and inconvenient hours discourage use. Thus, improvement in the quality of care should be a major concern.

Highest contraceptive prevalence

Finally, for the group with prevalence of more than 50 per cent, multiple delivery channels have generally been well developed. The exceptions include Brazil, where the public sector has only recently provided family planning services on a national basis through the health system. Neither development of new delivery systems nor broad expansion of existing ones would seem to be a priority, except perhaps in countries such as Turkey with very high reliance on traditional methods and relatively low accessibility scores.

A number of countries in this group and several with prevalence of 36-50 per cent are candidates for the gradual "privatization" of services, leaving to Governments the role of reaching the last underserved populations and those too economically disadvantaged to afford private-sector services. Regardless of whether privatization takes place, comparatively little emphasis on "demand creation" would seem to be required in the majority of these countries, except perhaps for specific populations such as adolescents and indigenous groups.

148

At the same time, however, in all remaining public- and private-sector programmes and in any new private ones, considerable attention could profitably be directed to improving the quality of services, especially in screening for contra-indications, monitoring for side-effects, providing a variety of contraceptive alternatives and ensuring that the methods are appropriate to the client's particular stage in the reproductive cycle.

4. Population Information, Education and Communication

Introduction

Population information, education and communication (IEC) are essential ingredients in efforts to promote awareness and understanding of population issues. Population information includes the technical and statistical information that is used to create awareness of population issues among Governments, non-governmental organizations (NGOs), communities, families and individuals. This is usually known as public information. Population education may take place either in the formal school system, where it is designed to meet the needs primarily of school-aged youths, or in the wide range of non-formal educational programmes serving people of all ages. Population communication is aimed at fostering interest, creating demand and otherwise supporting population programme activities, although it also includes efforts to increase awareness of population issues among national and international policy makers. There are clearly areas of overlap among the three types of activities. Information is basic to the other two; it presents the content. Education draws as well upon communication, for educators must communicate with learners if they are to be effective teachers.

How do information, education and communication differ from one another? Where are the dividing lines? *Information* activities, whether in the sense of dissemination of technical information, "public information" or "awareness creation", bring facts and issues to the attention of an audience, which might be the public, the scientific community or political leaders. The content is determined largely by what professionals think the audience should know, but it is not necessarily shaped or structured with a particular end in view. The primary aim is to provide the material to stimulate discussion.

The aim of *population communication* is to motivate the audience to action. The learning needs, perceptions and concerns of a target audience are studied with that end in view. At times, population communication has tended to be a "top-down" activity to promote a point of view. The current trend, however, seems to be the encouragement of participation, especially in early research and planning, so that the ultimate programme reflects the values of the target audience. This trend is further blurring the lines between communication and education.

The final component, *education*, usually exposes an individual or an audience to learning over a longer time than does a communication or information activity. Longer exposure provides the learner not only with more knowledge but also with the opportunity for thinking through the issues before making a decision. The aim of education is to foster

150

genuine understanding of problems and possible solutions. Because of the diverse programmes and projects undertaken in each of these related areas, each topic is treated separately below.

A recurring question regarding each of these fields concerns "impact evaluation". Although few people doubt the importance of IEC activities, techniques for measuring impact have yet to be perfected. To complicate matters, the difficulty of attempting such measurements is not widely understood, even in the population community. The challenge is to identify sequences of cause and effect. In the areas of population information and mass communication, the problem is one of singling out the influence of a communication or information message from that of the many other factors leading to a decision on a particular course of action. Commercial advertisers face the same sort of difficulty, but they have far greater financial resources and a somewhat less complex challenge than do population communicators: advertisers sell a product or facilitate choices between brands, whereas population communicators encourage changes in life-style that often have important psychological and cultural implications.

It is possible, however, to measure intermediate changes before assessing the impact of an educational or communication activity on population behaviour. In a school setting, for example, it is possible to measure changes in the curriculum; numbers of materials produced and distributed; numbers of teachers trained; numbers of students being taught; and changes in knowledge, as measured by standard tests or classroom quizzes. Going beyond these measurements to determine impact upon eventual migratory or fertility behaviour can be done but, typically, at great expense and with questionable validity. However, based upon experience in Bangladesh and China, new ways of making this determination are now being developed. The impact of out-of-school education, like school education, can be measured in terms of coverage and knowledge gain. In addition, although the measuring tools are imperfect, it is possible to identify certain behavioural changes, such as the adoption of family planning in workers' education projects.

The measurement of impact is only one of a number of issues related to each of the components of IEC. In most cases, when such an issue appears in any of the following four sections, it is cross-referenced to the other sections as appropriate.

Population information

Awareness of population issues has never been so high nor interest in programmes so great as it is now. Demographic information has accumulated more rapidly than ever before. Moreover, the improvements in methods of dissemination have been striking, starting with "clearing-houses" in the 1970s and progressing today towards computer-accessed data banks and electronic information networks. At the same time, awareness creation and, more broadly, communication activities have become more extensive, employing new technologies in publishing, video and satellite television, as well as the more sophisticated face-to-face, print and radio media.

Only a few decades ago, the topic of "population"--if seen as an issue at all--engendered little concerted attention. Even when the phenomenon of exponential growth of population was becoming clear to all--2 per cent every thousand years in the prehistoric past; 2 per cent every year by the mid-1950s--neither Governments nor assistance agencies had reached consensus on the causes, implications or actions to take. As a result, development strategies and assistance programmes did not take "population" into account. Developing countries were reluctant to accept the notion that rapid population growth was *not* a sign of economic health. Moreover, the motives of those advocating slower population growth were often considered suspect. The famous catch-phrase "the population explosion", followed by the proposed remedy of "population control", was criticized for concentrating on numbers of people rather than on the quality of human life. At the time of the World Population Conference in 1974, representatives from many countries still argued that development itself would solve population problems. It was then widely held that economic growth would produce the "demographic transition" to smaller families, as it had in industrialized countries. Thus, the task of the population advocates was--and to some extent continues to be--not just to introduce new ideas and information but to change entrenched positions.

Much research and interpretation of research findings have been necessary to build a comprehensive picture of population convincing to Governments and international agencies. Partly as a result of efforts in this field, the notion of a "population explosion" has now given way to a recognition of widely different population situations, with differing problems in nations and communities. Population information programmes have been the vehicle for helping Governments recognize that population policies are desirable and that family planning programmes are a legitimate component of national health and social services.

Sources of population information

Technical data and general or "public" information share the central goals of creating awareness and promoting understanding of the

152

significance of population issues among decision makers and opinion leaders in developed as well as developing countries, and acceptance among communities and individuals of the relevance of these issues to their daily lives.

Technical and statistical information

At the heart of technical population information resources are the demographic data gathered and published by the United Nations Population Division, national statistical offices and demographic research centres. As discussed in Chapter 2, these data include basic information from censuses, surveys, vital registration systems, family planning statistics and the research constituting the body of scientific and technical knowledge required to understand population phenomena. Global, regional and national rates of population growth; patterns of fertility, mortality, age distribution, spatial distribution and contraceptive prevalence; and a variety of other measures--all these are monitored and projected to assist administrators, development planners and policy makers. The whole process of planning the national infrastructure--housing, communications, transport, water, health services, schools, energy supply, waste disposal-- is highly dependent on this knowledge.

Printing remains the predominant means of communicating technical information, though television and radio have obvious advantages for awareness creation. Most printed materials have been intended primarily for the scientific and academic community and for library reference (see Box 7).

Box 7

PUBLICATIONS ON POPULATION

Many technical publishing programmes, including those of the United Nations Population Division and The Population Council, have gained international reputations. At the regional level, the information programme of the United Nations Economic and Social Commission for Asia and the Pacific (ESCAP) has spurred national publishing activity in almost every country of Asia and the Pacific. The United Nations Social and Economic Commission for Western Asia (ESCWA), the Economic Commission for Africa (ECA) and the Economic Commission for Latin America and the Caribbean (ECLAC) all issue regular and occasional population reports and country data sheets on demographic and related socio-economic conditions. In all these regions, the national member associations of the International Planned Parenthood Federation (IPPF) also contribute to the flow of population information.

Outstanding among the publications of non-governmental organizations (NGOs) are The Population Council's *Studies in Family Planning* and *Population and Development Review*; the Alan Guttmacher Institute's *Family Planning Perspectives* and *International Family Planning*

Perspectives; IPPF's journal *People,* with its *Earthwatch* and *AIDS* supplements, and the informal bulletin *Open File;* the *Population Reports* of The Johns Hopkins University's Population Information Program; the *Population Bulletin* and data sheets of the Population Reference Bureau; and Africa's French-language *Famille et Developpement.* The *Worldwatch Institute* has contributed the Worldwatch Papers series and the annual *State of the World* report as well as a magazine, *Worldwatch.* The Population Crisis Committee publishes the *Draper Fund Report,* covering various population-related themes. The Program for the Introduction and Adaptation of Contraceptive Technology (PIACT) publishes the periodical *Outlook.* The Population Reference Bureau recently launched *IMPACT,* an imaginative series of information packs for policy makers. NGOs specializing in certain aspects of population programmes--such as the Japanese Organization for International Cooperation in Family Planning, Inc. (JOICFP), the International Committee for the Management of Population Programmes (ICOMP) and organizations promoting the advancement of women--regularly publish accounts of their work.

UNFPA publishes reports, reviews and reference works, such as the *Inventory of Population Projects in Developing Countries Around the World* and the *Population Policy Compendium,* and its journal *Populi,* introduced in 1974, has found a niche as a relatively non-technical yet authoritative contribution to the periodical literature.

Catalogues of the population literature are accessible in computerized data bases established in advanced information centres.

Public information

In addition to their needs for technical information for formulating policies or designing plans, programme planners and administrators need general information about population and development to help motivate and provide the context for their work. Broad population information also serves an even larger audience of opinion leaders--representatives of the print and broadcasting media, community and religious leaders, educators and professionals from policy research institutions--who can influence decision makers and help gain public support for policy changes. Most of the information activities that constitute the "I" in IEC are of this type rather than technical information. Technical information, however, provides the foundation for the range of IEC activities.

In the 1960s, NGOs brought together demographers, health practitioners and development planners to exchange ideas about problems caused by rapid population growth. Proceedings of these conferences form an important part of the population literature, providing evidence of the steady growth in knowledge and understanding that preceded the World Population Conference of 1974. At that Conference as well as later ones, government leaders had opportunities to debate the meaning of population growth and change, define strategies and reach consensus. As the World Population Plan of Action adopted at the 1974 Conference and the recommendations of the 1984 International Conference on Population demonstrate, demographic information is a relatively small, though fundamental, part of the whole. Issues of physical resources and their relationship to human numbers are equally important. Following the World Population Conference, population issues increasingly appeared on the agendas of conferences dealing with health, food, housing, jobs, the rights and status of women and the threats to the global environment.[1] Each such meeting produced important policy and position statements from Governments, development agencies and specialists, contributing to the refinement of knowledge and the greater understanding of these issues.

In addition, many countries now have parliamentary movements for population and development, united in regional groups and a Global Committee of Parliamentarians on Population and Development. The debates and recommendations of these parliamentary groups have both added to the body of population information and helped to communicate it. The recent initiative of the Global Committee in finding ways to reach leaders of the world's major religions is a case in point.

Media coverage of population has greatly improved. Apart from news services that specialize in development reporting, many journalists and editors have increasingly covered population-related topics. The Press Foundation of Asia was one of the first in this field. The Inter-Press Service distributed from Rome gives excellent coverage of the population field; Worldwatch Features and the News/Features Service of the International Planned Parenthood Federation (IPPF) provide other examples. A notable development is the commitment of public education networks to promoting population awareness. The growing reach of the global media has itself aroused and maintained media interest in issues "behind the news," such as population. Awareness programmes and well-timed media events have produced encouraging results: in 1984, for example, a two-day "media encounter" by the United Nations helped to ensure that the large press corps in Mexico City for the International Conference on Population was well-informed, and the semi-official Conference newspaper was used extensively as a source for press reporting.

Some of the developing countries that are committed to population policies and family planning programmes have direct control of the media and have used radio and television extensively to support the programmes. Newspaper space is sometimes given free to family planning programmes. Even where newspapers are not under government control, however, as in India and Nigeria, the great increase in coverage has helped to shape the national debate on population.

The media can, however, undermine public confidence by careless and ill-informed reporting and commentary. Public confidence in contraceptive methods, for example, can be either reinforced or undermined by the attitudes of journalists and broadcasters. In many countries, the media have become watchdogs on the safety of drugs and family planning methods, and it is essential that they have all the information and support

155

necessary to play that role as authoritatively as possible. Supportive country-level communication policy is needed to improve the effectiveness of this role.

Over the years, the scope of information considered necessary for policy makers and programme administrators has broadened, partly because more information is available, partly because national programmes and projects--particularly those receiving international population assistance--need broader information on development indicators, such as health and environmental stress. Emerging issues include the characteristics and problems of aging populations, rapid urbanization accompanied by decline and neglect of rural areas, the increase in adolescent pregnancy and the spread of acquired immune deficiency syndrome (AIDS).

United Nations initiatives

The United Nations has long been involved in preparing technical information, through such bodies as the Population Commission and the Population Division of the Department of International Economic and Social Affairs. In addition, the Department of Technical Co-operation for Development (DTCD) and the United Nations Statistical Office have assisted developing countries in setting up and improving their technical information capabilities. The Food and Agriculture Organization of the United Nations (FAO), the International Labour Organisation (ILO), the United Nations Children's Fund (UNICEF), the World Health Organization (WHO), the United Nations Educational, Scientific and Cultural Organization (UNESCO) and the World Bank also helped prepare the international community to accept population activities as part of the United Nations action agenda, and all of these now engage in population information and communication activities within their special mandates. Today, various international agencies in addition to UNFPA provide important channels for the exchange of experience between countries and for new information from the United Nations and other sources.

Regional and national initiatives

Population information programmes have developed most rapidly in Asia. The United Nations Economic and Social Commission for Asia and the Pacific (ESCAP) has had a strong regional information programme for many years and has encouraged and assisted the establishment of national population information centres (see below). Extensive training has taken place in data gathering and management and in the production of information for audiences ranging from policy makers to the public. Because population policies are now established components of national development plans, they routinely attract media coverage. Many national population information activities in Asia also address information to the international community, considerably aiding the dissemination of experience (see Chapter 8).

Latin America benefits from the research and training of the Latin American Demographic Centre (CELADE) and from the economic and demographic studies centre in the Colegio de Mexico (see Chapter 9). Many eminent Latin American demographers frequently receive media and political attention. An active Inter-American Parliamentary Group on Population and Development, which includes Caribbean parliamentarians, issues regular communications on population-related matters of importance to the region.

In the Arabic-speaking countries of Western Asia and North Africa, the formation of an Association of Arab Demographers has been a promising development, complementing the population information activities of the United Nations Economic and Social Commission for Western Asia (ESCWA) and the demographic research and training centre in Cairo. High-level support from national leaders as, for example, in Tunisia and Morocco, has been useful in spreading population awareness in the region (see Chapter 7).

The Kilimanjaro Declaration on Population in 1984, endorsed by representatives of African countries, increased population awareness in sub-Saharan Africa on the eve of the International Conference on Population (see Chapter 6). However, population information is not widespread in Africa. Canada's International Development Research Centre (IDRC) has taken special interest in developing communication capacity in French-speaking African countries. NGOs have been active in disseminating information in the region and have joined with United Nations agencies in conferences on the health aspects of family planning. Information to political leaders and decision makers has been enhanced by the work of regional demographic centres and the Economic Commission for Africa (ECA). An African Parliamentary Group on Population and Development has been formed.

Non-governmental organizations' initiatives

International as well as national NGOs were in the forefront of awareness creation concerning population. Some years before UNFPA became operational, many NGOs were publicizing the need for programmes and urging industrialized countries to take the lead in providing population assistance. These efforts helped both to change government policies and to bring about the international consensus leading to the creation of the Fund. They also stimulated the development of population teaching and research programmes, considerably increasing the information base.

Non-governmental development organizations are still extremely important. In developing countries, they disseminate information through their publications and activities to local leaders and community activists whose participation can speed social change. NGOs also produce regular information on particular sectors of programme design and management for information and communication activities. For example, the Population Information Program of The Johns Hopkins University is an important resource, publishing population reports and a journal on family health topics and maintaining POPLINE, an international computerized bibliographic data base on population. In some countries NGOs act as lobbyists, keeping pressure on legislators and civil servants on behalf of population interests. For example, the Population Crisis Committee in Washington, D.C., along with many other interested groups, is part of a wider network such as the Global Tomorrow Coalition. There are also groups of interested legislators and local government officials who meet in national and international settings to discuss questions of common interest and agree on action.

Population information centres and networks

To a greater or lesser extent, population information centres now exist in almost every country. Some are small libraries supporting a demographic training or research unit within a larger context, such as a ministry, university or specialized agency of the United Nations. Others focus on a specific sector and are designed to support, for example, population education in schools, family planning programmes or national statistical data management.

One of the most important recent developments in population information services has been the growth of regional, subregional and international networks, which have vastly expanded the amount of information at the disposal of users (see Box 8). These networks include the Association for Population/Family Planning Libraries and Information Centers (APLIC), with APLIC International, the first successful population information network serving population librarians and information specialists. In 1979, a major development took place with the establishment of the United Nations Population Information Network (POPIN), which, as of 1986, had a membership of some 100 institutions engaged in population information activities. One of the largest regional networks is ESCAP, which has provided national population information centres with technical assistance, training and equipment. A subregional network, POPIN ASEAN, has been established for countries in the Association of South-East Asian Nations (ASEAN).

Box 8

INFORMATION CENTRES AND NETWORKS

All but one of the United Nations regional commissions have established population information centres. These centres collect, organize and disseminate scientific and technical information tailored to specific audiences, particularly policy makers, programme planners and managers. Regional, subregional and international networks have vastly expanded the amount of information at the disposal of users. Each information centre belonging to one or more networks can strengthen its holdings on particular topics and at the same time draw upon other specialized and general collections to meet the information needs in the multidisciplinary field of population.

In 1979, the United Nations Population Information Network (POPIN) was established to improve the flow of population information. As of 1986, POPIN had a membership of some 100 institutions engaged in population information activities. POPIN acts as the umbrella for regional and subregional networks that it has brought into existence.

One of the largest regional networks is the Economic and Social Commission for Asia and the Pacific (ESCAP). ESCAP has helped establish national population information centres, providing technical assistance, training and equipment. The information section of its Population Division helps national centres keep abreast of new literature. Through its monthly publication *ADOPT* (Asian-Pacific and Worldwide Documents on Population Topics), the Division disseminates bibliographic information. In addition, it has established in 33 countries a network of 200 correspondents who supply up-to-date information on country programmes and ongoing research in exchange for ESCAP publications. A subregional network, POPIN ASEAN, has been established for the Association of South-East Asian Nations (ASEAN) countries.

POPIN Africa links such important centres as the Cairo Demographic Centre, the Regional Institute for Population Studies (RIPS), the Sahel Institute, the Centre for African Family Studies in Nairobi and several national population information centres and family planning associations. The co-ordinating unit is within the secretariat of the Economic Commission for Africa (ECA) in Addis Ababa. At ECA, a Pan-African Documentation and Information System (PADIS) was created in 1980 as a co-operative information system for abstracting and indexing documents on socio-economic topics, including population. In Latin America, the Latin American Demographic Centre (CELADE) is helping to establish a network called PROLAP, consisting of non-govermental institutions with population interests.

Private institutions and NGOs have also established population information centres. The International Family Planning Federation (IPPF) constitutes a self-contained population information network with its member family planning associations. Its Library and Documentation Centre in London houses one of the most important collections of population literature in Europe, serving member organizations in more than 120 countries and providing a repository for member publications.

POPIN Africa is another promising regional network of information centres, libraries, universities and international agencies. At ECA, a Pan-African Documentation and Information System (PADIS) was created as a co-operative information system for abstracting and indexing documents on socio-economic topics, including population. In 1976, CELADE set up Population Documentation for Latin America (DOCPAL), a documentation system to help the countries of Latin America and the Caribbean collect, store, process and retrieve documents on population. A new network of some 50 non-governmental institutions with an interest in population, called PROLAP, is now being formed with CELADE assistance.

Each information centre belonging to one or more networks can strengthen its holdings on particular topics and at the same time draw upon other specialized and general collections to meet the information needs in the multidisciplinary field of population.

Management of information resources

As a result of tremendous growth in interest and importance of information on population and related development issues, a large body of literature now exists for which conventional systems of classification have been found inadequate. Traditionally, universal classification schemes were adapted to the specialized needs of the population field and its related disciplines. However, the need for a special language and smaller, more manageable schemes has become apparent as the breadth and complexity of the subject has grown and especially with the advent of computer technology.

Recent advances in setting international standards for the classification of population information will permit communication between information centres and hasten the establishment in developing countries of national population information centres that can quickly benefit from access to each other's bibliographic data bases (see Box 9). In general, the growth and management of population information resources are expected to change greatly in the next few years as new and less expensive computer technology spreads to developing countries.

Box 9

MANAGEMENT OF INFORMATION RESOURCES

As the breadth and complexity of the population field has grown, the need for a special language and for more manageable classification schemes has become apparent, especially with the advent of computer technology. The vocabulary for population information has been set out in the *Population Multilingual Thesaurus*, developed by the Committee for International Co-operation in National Research in Demography (CICRED) and published in English, French and Spanish under the auspices of the United Nations Population Information Network (POPIN). POPIN has also published a *Guide to the Selection of a Classification Scheme for Population Information Centres*, and a POPIN Working Group has been established to manage development of the *Thesaurus*.

Population Index, in the United States, provided the basis for the classification schemes used by Population Documentation for Latin America (DOCPAL) and the Population Information and Documentation System for Africa (PIDSA), based at the University of Ghana. The

Carolina Population Center and the Planned Parenthood Federation of America independently developed classification schemes specifically for family planning. The International Planned Parenthood Federation (IPPF) developed its own classification scheme, which has been used or adapted by many of its member associations as well as by the Centre for African Family Studies in Nairobi.

Many population library catalogues are now held on microcomputers, using various specially designed software packages tailored to the needs of population programmes and giving subject access to the collections. A recent introduction has been the Micro-ISIS bibliographic software developed by the United Nations Educational, Scientific and Cultural Organization (UNESCO) for microcomputers in developing countries. Several commercial packages are also suitable for these applications.

One of the most important international bibliographic retrieval services is POPLINE, maintained jointly by the Population Information Program of The Johns Hopkins University, the Center for Population and Family Health at Columbia University, New York, and Population Index. POPLINE provides document delivery and free searches to developing countries and is available on-line through the MEDLARS system of the United States National Library of Medicine. POPLINE now provides on disk its holdings in the social sciences related to population and associated fields, with each entry fully indexed and abstracted. The disk is updated every six months. Other international computerized data bases include Population Bibliography, available from the commercial on-line search service DIALOG; DOCPAL, which provides free searches and a document copy service; and EBIS/POPFILE, which abstracts Asian and Pacific documents and offers free searches and a document delivery service.

Computer modelling is now being used to promote awareness of population issues. The Futures Group in the U.S.A. has developed RAPID, a system of presentations showing the effects of rapid rates of population growth on development prospects and the natural resource base in different countries. Systems are also in place in academic institutions where future population programme managers are trained.

Priorities for future population information activities

The subject of population has remained controversial even though much knowledge has been accumulated and widely disseminated. Rapid population growth is, of course, a recent phenomenon, and new analyses on its implications contrast sharply with long-held notions of "strength in numbers". However, it is important to look at how population information has been presented and to ask whether everything possible has been done to reach national and local leadership. The implications of a world of 6 billion by the end of the century and a possible 8 billion by 2020 are already challenging development planners and political strategists.

161

Demands from administrators, political leaders and the public for authoritative data and interpretative comment are constantly increasing.

Improving data bases and research

The great change in population perceptions took place when countries experiencing rapid population growth and high fertility were given opportunities to study their own situations and act on them. In the past two decades, Governments have acquired the tools to collect and analyse population data and to make that information available to widening circles of decision makers, opinion leaders, media outlets and the public. As noted in the preceding two chapters, international initiatives such as the World Fertility Survey added rapidly to the store of knowledge of population trends, their causes and their implications. As more and more women accepted family planning and took up the new generation of methods of fertility control, especially the pill, studies of the safety, effectiveness and acceptability of contraceptive options became a significant aspect of population information, giving rise to vital needs for continuous monitoring. WHO publications and those of major research institutions, along with the findings and recommendations of regulatory bodies, have made important contributions to this effort.

If political commitment is to be encouraged and sustained, Governments will need improved data bases and better research and analytical capability. The importance of this task grows as the diversity between countries and subregions increases. Continued efforts will be needed to recruit and train information specialists to manage the increasingly sophisticated data bases.

Linking population to environmental and other development issues

Population information programmes, as well as overall communication and education activities, must be prepared to make clear the connections between population and other areas of development, in particular the environment, and social and economic issues linked to population, including AIDS. They will need to emphasize emerging topics of importance--aging, urbanization and international migration--in addition to growth and its consequences.

Identifying the role of women in population and development

One growth area in the immediate future will certainly be information on the relationship between the condition of women, demographic change and economic development. Changes in the traditional roles of women and in attitudes towards them will need careful monitoring, in some societies as much for negative trends as for the improvements towards which so many organizations, including the United Nations, are striving. The relation between family planning and child survival is the subject of continuing research. The roles and attitudes of men in supporting and participating in family planning programmes are not yet well documented.

Reiterating the case for family planning

It cannot be taken for granted that the case for freedom of choice in family size has now been irrevocably made. Population remains a highly sensitive area of development, dealing as it does with intimate personal decisions regarding family size and family planning. In addition, even with reliable facts and rational argument, the task of eradicating the results of misinformation and misconceptions is difficult. Though it is well documented that family planning promotes maternal and child health, family planning sometimes still meets opposition on the grounds that it interferes with the private lives of individuals, that it is dangerous, or that it is contrary to the will of God.

Maintaining media attention and political commitment

Above all, as population becomes more and more an accepted feature of the development scene, programmes must guard against losing the attention of their audience. If population messages are to make headlines or impress political leaders for the promotion and maintenance of political commitment, approaches have to be more imaginative today than they were in the 1960s. Population is often considered as a "hidden" issue, its events going unnoticed by the media. Yet population processes and their consequences, however slow to emerge, change the lives of individuals and the destiny of nations. Programmes should therefore be prepared to maintain a constant effort to attract and retain media attention.

Applying new technology to population information programmes

Thus far, the improvement in both the quantity and quality of population information has been matched by improvements in technology, so that population awareness and technical information programmes alike now have greater reach and authority than ever. Clearly, satellite monitoring of the state of the planet will produce increasing amounts of new information to add to national population strategies, and policies of population assistance will need to respond. It is impossible to anticipate all the developments in data-gathering technology. Exploration is just beginning. Population professionals will need to make it their business to develop applications of new information technology in both technical information and awareness-creation programmes.

For national programmes, these requirements imply not less but more attention to population information as awareness continues to improve. Technical information networks will improve in extent and sophistication. Public information activities will become more complex, and programme managers will need to concentrate on increasing the operational reach of programmes, expanding connections with other programme areas, and working closely with communication and education programmes to meet the needs of particular audiences.

There will be notable differences between regional audiences. Africa has many needs for content and for communications media. Though population programmes are in their early stages in most sub-Saharan countries, interest and concern are rising rapidly. Thus a steady increase in demand can be expected both for technical information networks and for the creation of awareness. Given Africa's special conditions, innovation will be required in both areas. Radio, perhaps using satellite communication, will be an important mass-communication medium, and low-cost high-technology applications such as microcomputer networks will be important for disseminating technical information. Assistance for both technology and its applications will be needed, adapted to local conditions. In Asia, given its mature population programmes and a burgeoning electronic information network for both technical and public information, assistance can be expected to concentrate on harnessing the new technology to extend the reach and effectiveness of information. In Latin America and the Caribbean, with their increasingly active population programmes, assistance can be expected to focus on improving the content of awareness-creation programmes tailored for specific audiences. In the Arab States, both technical information activities and awareness creation will continue, enhanced by the efforts of the recently created Association of Arab Demographers and the continuation of training activities in demography and related subjects at regional institutions.

Although international agencies, academic institutions and NGOs have done much to stimulate population awareness, Governments are undertaking an increasing amount of this activity, which offers many potential advantages: national media prefer information that is nationally rather than internationally generated, both for its immediacy and local relevance as well as for its domestic political content. At the international level, duplication of efforts in managing population information wastes human and financial resources, and standardization of equipment and software remains a distant possibility. A wealth of expertise is now available to government planners as well as to programme managers through training programmes and technical assistance. Approaches to programme development in one country have proved replicable in others, a valuable shortcut to progress.

The global understanding of population as an integral factor of development is growing, accompanied by flows of population assistance and the increasing involvement of Governments in developing countries in policies and programmes. A solid body of knowledge has been built up in the past two decades. The challenge of the next two decades is to improve the level of awareness, extend population information to connect with all other areas of development information, and integrate it fully into the daily activities of Governments, organizations and individuals.

Population education in the school system

Purpose and rationale

Population education is aimed at helping people understand the nature, causes and implications of population processes as they affect, and are affected by, groups or individuals. It focuses on family and individual decisions influencing population change as well as on broad demographic changes. Though sometimes linked with demography, human ecology, family life or sex education, population education is not synonymous with them. Rather, it draws its content from all these fields and others, with variations according to the setting.

Because population issues affect all aspects of life, they have to be treated as an integral part of school education, enabling children to function better and to play an active role in society. Moreover, many population issues are important national concerns, addressed in schools as part of the regular school programme. As all countries have school facilities with personnel in place, the schools are logistically and organizationally appropriate for such education, and provide a good target audience.

School systems are an important vehicle for population education for three additional reasons: first, children who spend a number of years in school are more likely than others to be the future leaders of their communities and countries. By virtue of their formal education, they will be in a better position than those without schooling to hold important private-sector and government jobs, to be in positions of influence. If they are to lead intelligently, it is important that they understand the implications of population change. Second, it has long been recognized that retention of girls in school has a bearing on the eventual size of their families. In addition, when both boys and girls are exposed to population education through the school curriculum, their knowledge, attitudes and decisions regarding other population issues can be influenced as well. Third, teachers, particularly those in rural areas, are often recognized community leaders. Their orientation towards population issues and their own fertility behaviour add another dimension to the effects of population education in school systems.

Various international conferences have affirmed the need for school population education programmes as a component of comprehensive population programmes. The World Population Plan of Action (WPPA) of the 1974 World Population Conference recommended that "educational institutions in all countries . . . include a study of population dynamics and policies, including, where appropriate, family life, responsible parenthood and the relation of population dynamics to socio-economic development and to international relations".[2]

165

The International Conference on Population, Mexico City, August 1984, voiced support for the WPPA and urged Governments to ensure that adolescents, both boys and girls, secure adequate education, including family life and sex education, and that suitable family planning information and services be made available to them, giving due consideration to the role, rights and obligations of parents and changing individual and cultural values.[3] The Conference also urged Governments to explore innovative methods for spreading awareness of demographic factors, fostering the active participation of the public in population policies and programmes, and intensifying training of national personnel engaged in IEC activities, including management and planning.[4]

Other international forums have reiterated support for both formal and non-formal population education, among them the World Conference to Review and Appraise the Achievements of the United Nations Decade for Women: Equality, Development and Peace, Nairobi, July 1985, and the International Conference on Better Health for Women and Children through Family Planning, Nairobi, October 1987.

Early development of population education programmes

One of the most rapidly growing educational innovations in the world,[5] population education began to be accepted by Governments in the late 1960s and early 1970s. At that time, however, only a few countries had introduced national population education programmes into their school systems (see Figures II, III, IV and V for regional growth patterns). By the mid-1980s, or within 15 years, about 80 countries included population education in their schools.

Among regions and countries, the goals and content of population education may differ. As a long-term policy goal, some countries aim at reducing the population growth rate. Others are concerned with improving family health or with lowering adolescent pregnancy rates. Not only can population education help achieve these ends, but the nature of these aims helps determine the selection of content and of approaches to population education. The titles of programmes--among them, family life education, sex education and quality of life education as well as population education--have generally reflected areas of greatest emphasis.

Some of the first programme efforts of the late 1960s and early 1970s were undertaken in Asia and the Pacific--India (1968), Malaysia (1973), the Philippines (1972), Singapore (1973), Sri Lanka (1973) and Thailand (1972). However, the Asia region had no sex education programmes in the 1970s, whereas by the late 1980s the Philippines, Thailand and several South Pacific countries had incorporated family life content into their population education programme. In other regions, programmes in Colombia (1971), El Salvador (1971) and Tunisia (1972) were among the first efforts.

Figure II

UNFPA SUPPORTED POPULATION EDUCATION
SCHOOL PROJECTS IN AFRICA, 1970-1988

Number of active population education school projects

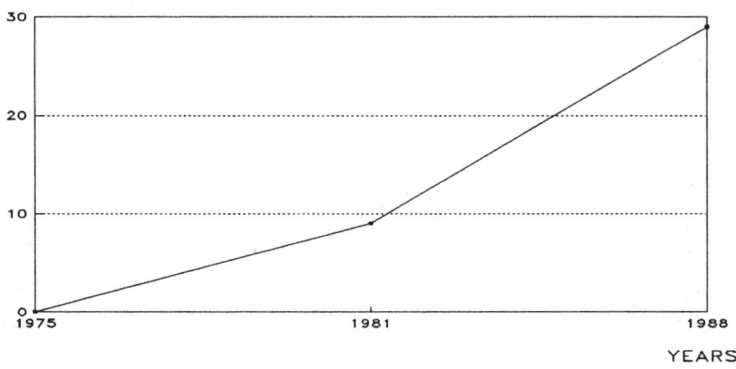

Sources: United Nations Population Fund, Technical and
Evaluation Division.

Figure III

UNFPA-SUPPORTED POPULATION EDUCATION SCHOOL PROJECTS IN THE ARAB STATES, 1970-1988

Number of active population education school projects

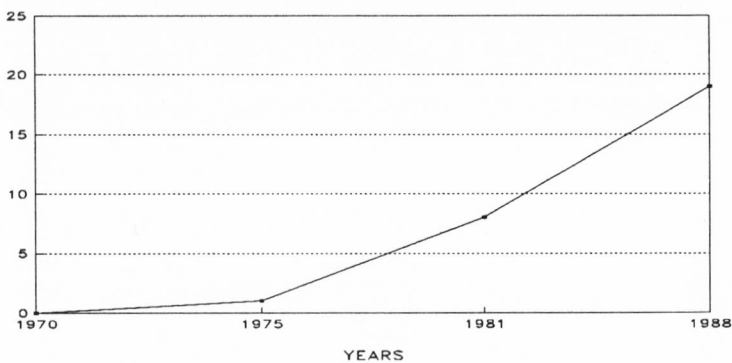

YEARS

Sources: United Nations Population Fund, Technical and Evaluation Division.

168

Figure IV

UNFPA-SUPPORTED POPULATION EDUCATION SCHOOL
PROJECTS IN ASIA AND THE PACIFIC, 1970-1988

Number of active population education school projects

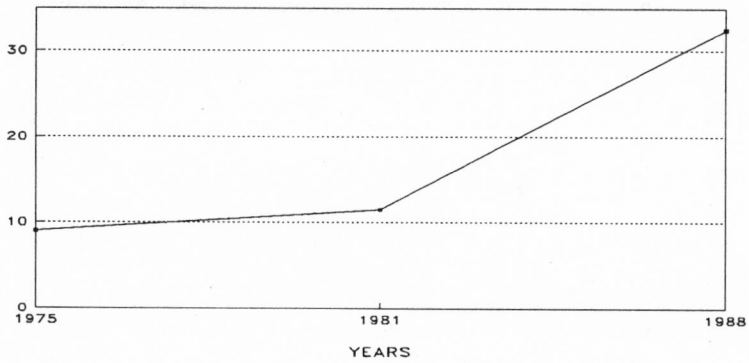

Sources: United Nations Population Fund, Technical and
Evaluation Division.

Figure V

UNFPA-SUPPORTED POPULATION EDUCATION
SCHOOL PROJECTS IN LATIN AMERICA
AND THE CARIBBEAN, 1970-1988

Number of active population education school projects

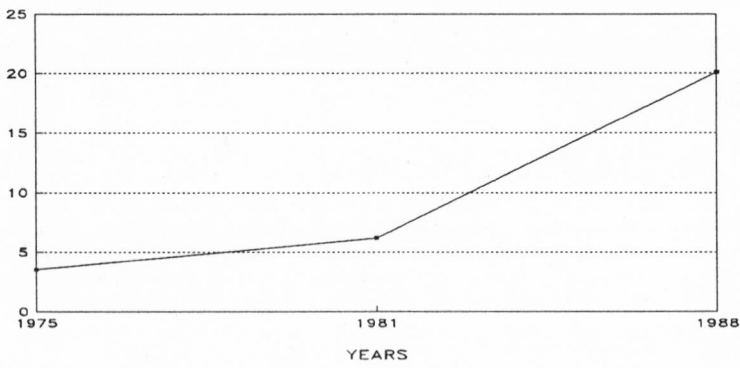

YEARS

Sources: United Nations Population Fund, Technical and
Evaluation Division.

170

In the late 1960s and early 1970s, several Latin American countries had undertaken work in sex education programmes, though ties to formal education programmes through education ministries were loose. Nevertheless, this early orientation influenced the region's approach to population education, so that balanced attention was eventually given to demographic, ecological and sex education issues. Had these early efforts in sex education not taken place, the content of current population education in this region might have focused more on broad demographic issues, possibly to the exclusion of individual and family life issues.

In sub-Saharan Africa, early concern over problems of adolescent fertility was accompanied by extremely limited programme experience in modifying adolescent behaviour. Moreover, as rapid population growth was not widely perceived as a problem, population education programmes dealt largely with education for development, environmental issues and family life education. Today, there is increasing attention to the prevention of adolescent pregnancy, rapid population growth and AIDS.

Not only do the aims of programmes vary from country to country but so, too, do the strategies for carrying them out. A programme may be designed as a large-scale nation-wide effort or as a smaller effort in a single region or district, reflecting local characteristics. New population content may be aimed at the secondary or the primary level, limited to a few grades or designed for all levels at once. The content may be incorporated into a broad educational reform in which policies are drawn up at the outset and consultation undertaken with groups in an education ministry and outside (e.g., religious and women's groups).

Options also exist in the methods of introducing population education into the curriculum, in the teaching materials, in the type of teacher training, and in administrative and managerial techniques as well as in procedures for monitoring and evaluating programmes. Lastly, population education strategies and approaches vary in the extent of co-ordination within the educational system and between in-school and out-of-school programmes.

Current regional emphases

The diversity in programmes occurs partly because individual countries are in different phases of implementing population education. In addition, fairly distinct regional differences are apparent. Asian programmes are now concentrating on institutionalization and on improvements in programme components, including the introduction of more sophisticated content and more controversial topics into the curriculum. These programmes are also developing prototype materials, refining teaching methodologies, adopting cost-effective teacher-training strategies and including monitoring and evaluation as integral elements.

In the South Pacific, population education is still in its infancy. The first regional consultation was held in 1982 and the subregion now has about 10 projects. Despite initial lack of support from high-level decision makers, projects have helped create national awareness through seminars, and some of the countries have now incorporated population issues into their school curricula.

In the Latin American and Caribbean region, current concerns are to expand national coverage, modernize population education content and design evaluation techniques. Several countries have made much progress: the Dominican Republic, El Salvador, Nicaragua, Paraguay and Peru are in various stages of institutionalizing programmes. At the regional level, prototype teaching materials have been designed, mostly by UNESCO regional advisers, with UNFPA assistance.

In the Middle East, Egypt and Tunisia have long-standing programmes that have become common sites for study tours from other countries. Some programmes, such as that in the Sudan, have made remarkable progress in little time. Others, such as that in Democratic Yemen, have progressed despite many constraints. The preparation of reference materials in Arabic has contributed much to these efforts. In sub-Saharan Africa, many countries have initiated population education, and in recent years interest has grown dramatically. However, the paucity of expertise in population education has constrained many programmes. Training, awareness creation and exchange of information are among the key issues in this region.

Lessons from formal population education programmes

The more than 100 population education projects currently under way have yielded several valuable lessons, not least that population education is a complex undertaking. It is often difficult to introduce, and it is typically a slow process; like other educational innovations, it needs time to mature. Many of the obstacles faced by these projects are common to all educational innovations: large, cumbersome and overburdened education systems; low quality of schooling; funding limitations; inadequately trained personnel; limited supply of materials; staff shortages; and resistance to change. Problems that have arisen specifically in introducing population education projects include the controversial nature of many of the topics as well as the intimate character of some of the issues (e.g., sexuality, contraception). Often educators themselves have serious concerns at the outset about how to teach such subjects. This is particularly problematic in those countries-- indeed, most of them--where opportunities for training in effective teaching methods is unavailable because of limited funds. Traditional teaching methodologies are rarely adequate for population education.

The interdisciplinary nature of many of its topics, in contrast to the usual separation of content into discrete disciplines, poses special problems for population education. Other difficulties have arisen because different groups want to emphasize different content and approaches.

172

For example, educators may want projects to focus on developing basic thinking and decision-making skills rather than on conveying specific messages, whereas family planning officials may want projects to convey specific messages on family size.

Special problems occur, too, because of the close co-ordination required among many groups and sometimes the resistance or opposition to population education among policy makers, education officials, teachers, parents--usually a result of misconceptions and misunderstandings. Population education has not undergone a long period of testing; the limited number of educational leaders with extensive experience in population education has compounded some problems. Finally, as in other areas of education, some of the results of population education occur out of the classroom, at a later time, and are thus difficult to evaluate. The particular lessons learned about population education are best grouped according to major stages or components of a programme, as detailed below.

Introducing a population education programme

Planning for the introduction of a population education programme includes defining an overall approach, strategy and type of programme and making fundamental decisions about each successive stage and about programme components--curriculum, teacher training, materials development, management and co-ordination, and evaluation. Generally, the type of programme reflects what is politically, organizationally and financially feasible in a given national context. Programme goals are usually defined on the basis of national development policy and, where they exist, national population policies. Decisions are then made about the content and grade levels, aspects that also reflect national policies and perceptions of what is needed and acceptable.

■ Source of authority and scope of programme. Notwithstanding the advantages of small-scale, pilot efforts, which have produced replicable experience in several instances, notably in China and Colombia, most population education programmes are large-scale national programmes under the direct authority of a ministry of education. This arrangement facilitates the programme's introduction because the national authority can give it priority, and the existing educational system can be relied on for its planning and implementation. Larger national population education initiatives are probably more likely than small efforts to become institutionalized, even though they require more resources and more time than smaller programmes do.

■ Level of schooling. A related basic decision needed at the planning stage is the level of schooling and the specific grade at which to introduce population education. Ideally, population education should be offered in all grades of primary and secondary education. However, introducing population education at all levels at once--as undertaken in India, the Republic of Korea and Thailand--is usually too difficult and

173

too costly, particularly in terms of teacher training and materials production.

A phased introduction has been found to be more feasible, giving the local staff experience to draw from as they expand the programme. The decision about whether to start at the primary or the secondary level has varied from one country to another. Most of the early projects started at the secondary levels and the higher grades of primary school. It was easier to persuade decision makers and teachers to start at the secondary level and it was simpler, because of the issues perceived as important, to develop secondary-level population education curricula and contents.

Today, it is as easy, and certainly as important, to start at the primary or middle-school level as it is at the secondary level. Many arguments favour beginning instruction in primary schools because of the number of children who can be reached through them. Not only does a large proportion of children drop out by grade 5, but many villages in developing countries do not even have secondary schools. Moreover, it is important to introduce population education at an early age when children's psychological development is at its most formative stage. From a long-term perspective, a strong case can also be made for beginning programmes at the middle-school level. The curriculum at this stage is more flexible than at the upper levels, and students are at an age when the content has personal relevance.[6]

Thus far, few efforts have been made to introduce population education at the pre-primary level. However, Benin and Viet Nam have demonstrated the possibility of introducing notions of planning and decision-making even at this age. The Viet Nam pre-school project, jointly undertaken by UNESCO, UNICEF and UNFPA, includes an important component of parent education, which has received increasing attention among African and Latin American educators.

At the university level, programmes have been introduced in a number of countries. A self-sustaining regional training programme is based in Venezuela, and innovative government-supported programmes are operating in El Salvador and Paraguay, having begun in response to the Governments' perceptions of the need for project staff training at the tertiary level.

■ Need for high-level support. In many countries, population education was initially promoted by small groups or organizations. Government decision makers often reacted to the idea with indifference or even opposition. Thus, in the initial stages, it was often necessary to overcome opposition and develop consensus on the desirability of population education. Several countries, among them Democratic Yemen, Peru and Somalia, successfully addressed this challenge by holding a national seminar or a series of seminars addressed to officials from all government agencies engaged in programme implementation. In such seminars, working groups were able to discuss national population issues, explain the contents and methodology of population education and thus build consensus in favour of the innovation. A complementary strategy in some countries was to sensitize the public to population issues and to the need for including these in the school curriculum. An excellent example can be found in Burkina Faso, where communities are using participatory theatre.

Seminars of religious leaders or media personnel also help build support, as do other awareness-creation activities such as newsletters or participation in national fairs, as in China and Somalia. Another interesting example of building support and defining contents is to use popular participation through community meetings, as in Nicaragua. A variety of extracurricular activities, such as poster competitions, quizzes and essay competitions at local, provincial and national levels in China, Egypt, Haiti, India and the Philippines, has helped to popularize population education among students, teachers and their communities.

To help ensure that the programme is carefully designed and that the national population education plan is sufficiently well defined, one or several national meetings, as in Nepal, for example, are valuable. Such meetings can also help planners define needs and requirements for programme components. Some countries, among them India and Zambia, employed a two-stage programme planning process: ideas were first elicited from a wide spectrum of individuals and were then refined by a ministry planning team. Yet another approach to help planners clarify initial steps and make basic programme decisions on the content, grade level, subjects and mode of instruction is through visits to other countries with experience with population education.

The process of bringing together, first, the high-level decision makers, and then programme implementors, at national and regional levels has developed commitment and helped to define careful answers to basic programme questions. It has also built general support for population issues and for their inclusion into the school programmes.

■ Curriculum and materials development. Developing population education curricula has sometimes been difficult because few people have acquired expertise in this new field. Moreover, in the early 1970s, few educators agreed on what should be part of the knowledge base for population education, i.e., the content from which curriculum developers would prepare material appropriate for different age groups. This knowledge base has had to be derived from various disciplines and from country-specific data. Not only is the content multidisciplinary, but it often touches sensitive, personal matters and needs to be developed in a non-prescriptive manner.

Because of the shortage of published data on population issues for curriculum development, many countries have successfully developed their own population education source books. In Nepal and Somalia, published and unpublished materials from various sources such as

175

ministries and national organizations have been consolidated. Studies have been carried out to fill information gaps, as in Bangladesh, the Philippines, Sierra Leone and the Sudan. In Asia, a prototype source book developed by UNESCO regional advisers and a team of consultants has been successfully adapted to local needs and conditions in national projects.

In most countries, curriculum developers and writers, particularly those working to develop population education curricula, are far less experienced than they would be under ideal conditions. One answer to this problem is to use other education ministry personnel or outside agencies, such as university faculty. It can also be addressed by training curriculum developers in the new skills. Another solution is to adapt existing materials rather than develop new ones and to co-operate with other countries, learning technical skills through regional workshops, study tours to other developing countries and other activities through technical co-operation among developing countries (TCDC). In addition, scope and sequence charts have frequently been used to help curriculum developers identify the concepts and the cumulative learning to be built into the curriculum over a period of years.

Countries have adopted diverse solutions to the common problem of how to handle controversial issues in the curriculum. For example, surveys can be conducted to learn the nature and extent of discontent, as was done in the Philippines. Often surveys reveal that opposition is much less severe than it initially appeared to be. Because preventing opposition is much easier than dealing with it once it has begun, some countries have organized massive national campaigns to forestall opposition. For example, a mass sensitization campaign on the theme of teen-age pregnancies was organized for this purpose in the Seychelles in 1979. Opposition has also been prevented by involving active or potential opponents in the preparation of the curriculum, as was done in Colombia and the Philippines. Yet another way is to clarify misconceptions through meetings with parents and community leaders, as was done in the Dominican Republic and Somalia.

Opposition can be addressed by developing support through adult programmes before introducing population education in the school curriculum (United Republic of Tanzania), or by including controversial issues in an extracurricular programme (Tunisia). When controversial issues are included, problems can be prevented if these issues are treated indirectly. For example, in India, the Sudan and Thailand some sex education themes are taught without mentioning the term "sex education". Finally, highly controversial topics may be omitted or postponed until they become more acceptable.

Another common problem with population education has been that the inclusion of such education in school curricula has resulted in a scattering of a few population concepts throughout most subjects.

The success with which the concepts are taught depends largely upon the extent to which curriculum and materials developers are trained to understand the issues. Even if a major subject area includes a specific unit on population, the topic may receive insufficient attention because teachers have to cover too many other aspects of the subject. To solve this problem, the number of subjects treating population education can be reduced, and the time devoted to it in the remaining subjects can be increased. Alternatively, students may be exposed periodically to a more intensive course or unit focusing only on population education. The latter approach was not widely accepted in the early years, but countries in Asia, Latin America and elsewhere are now experimenting with it, some offering population education as an elective, others requiring it.

Experience has shown that the most efficient way to incorporate population education contents into curricula and teaching materials is during a comprehensive curriculum revision, as has been done in Bangladesh, Nepal, Pakistan, Sierra Leone, Sri Lanka, Thailand, Viet Nam and elsewhere. Such an approach helps overcome a weakness commonly observed in the distribution of materials--that even where excellent materials have been developed, unless these materials are actually incorporated into revised textbooks, the attention to population education in the classroom tends to dissipate. In addition to incorporating population education in textbooks, a permanent national population education team maintaining high motivation and providing technical support helps sustain attention to population education.

Although population education programmes throughout the world have produced some excellent materials, they have not been widely shared. To promote greater sharing, regional population education clearing-houses and advisory teams are operating in Asia and Latin America and, to a lesser extent, in sub-Saharan Africa and the Middle East.

- Teacher training. The core team of educators plays a key role in determining programme success or failure. All programmes have started by training a core team of educators assigned responsibility for programme planning and implementation. In many instances, core team members have been sent overseas for short- or long-term training followed up by continuous in-service training, generally provided by regional advisers or through consultants. Study tours to countries with experience in population education have also been undertaken.

Generally, however, the training of teachers for population education has often fallen short. Too few teachers have been trained and the training period is seldom long enough--in some cases it has been only a few days. In addition, neither refresher training nor opportunities for follow-up training have been provided as often as needed. In Latin America, one attempted remedy was to provide classroom teachers with teaching guides and brief instructions on population education and the most salient issues. After the teachers used the guides in their

177

classrooms, a brief but intensive face-to-face follow-up session was held.

There is no clear-cut evidence as to which of the many training modalities being used in population education are consistently successful. Although face-to-face learning is generally considered the most effective, it is also expensive and time-consuming. Cost-effective approaches are being sought in all regions. Because at least one or two weeks may be needed for training, unless training is conducted during vacation periods, teachers have to be removed from their classes and substitutes provided. The length of training is less important than the quality, however. A good training programme requires much careful planning and highly skilled trainers who are free from having to handle the logistical details. To achieve this, initial project work must be sharply focused, covering only a few grades and subject areas, thereby allowing a base of positive experience to be built up before expanding the activity.

Core programme staff and trainers unable to train all teachers through face-to-face training have found several other effective methods, including various forms of distance learning to replace or, preferably, to supplement face-to-face training, as in Egypt and Guinea; self-instructional modules, as in the Philippines and Malaysia; correspondence courses, as in Pakistan; and radio and television programmes, as in India, Nepal and the Republic of Korea. Benin has developed a three-phase programme: in phase one, teachers receive one week of face-to-face training in the knowledge base; in phase two, they return to their classrooms for about six weeks; in phase three, they return to a face-to-face setting to work on teaching techniques. The pattern is somewhat similar in many Latin American countries, although less time is given to face-to-face training and more to classroom testing of the newly acquired content and methodology.

In some countries, a rapidly trained core group of master teachers continues to train other teachers face-to-face, over an extended period. Master teachers train other teachers near their places of work during vacations, weekends or off hours, which is not expensive and does not disrupt school work, a procedure employed in India, Indonesia and Sri Lanka.

Innovative participatory teaching/learning methodologies have proved far more effective in the teaching of population education than have traditional methods. These newer methods include value clarification, inquiry/discovery approach, role playing, games, theatre etc. They allow students to learn by doing, involving them in practical experiences that make them aware of their feelings, ideas and beliefs.

Various problems have been encountered. Some are common to all training: the difficulty of timing training so that it meshes with activities that follow, the failure of trained staff to return to their posts after training and the high turnover of trained staff. Other problems are specific to population education, among them the limited opportunities that exist for this specialized training and the challenge of arranging study tours that are culturally and otherwise appropriate to the needs of particular countries. For example, this is a special limitation in Africa, and more so in the French-speaking African countries. A problem common to most population education programmes has been the tendency to neglect pre-service training until several years after the start of a programme. The result is that new teachers coming into the system have not been exposed to population education through their teacher preparation courses.

Challenges in teacher training, particularly for in-service training in population education, are many. Wherever population education has been introduced at several levels and in more than one subject, many teachers had to be trained, entailing substantial financial and other resources. In addition, the process of changing traditional attitudes has often been difficult and time-consuming. Many teachers have had only limited training to start with, and both the content and the teaching/learning techniques in population education are new and more complicated than are those for traditional subjects. However, the development of new teaching skills through involvement in population education has made the job of teaching more interesting for classroom teachers (e.g., in programmes in El Salvador, India and Paraguay).

■ Programme management and related issues. Management-related problems affecting projects at various times and in various parts of the world have included poorly staffed population education units, unsuitable locations, the lack of authority of population education units, competition between various units within ministries of education, the lack of management training for population education personnel and insufficient co-ordination with organizations beyond the education ministry, to name a few.

In addition, almost all population education programmes face two particular problems. One is how to ensure that the various types of people and institutions involved with population education (programme staff, teacher training institutions, outposted education staff etc.) have adequate access to appropriate information. There is a need to ensure that new information--research results, census reports, policy changes etc.--reaches the programme rapidly. There is also a strong unmet need for better exchange of information between countries. Some of these needs have been well met through population education clearing-house services and other means, such as study tours and periodic discussions with regional advisers. In some regions, however, particularly sub-Saharan Africa and the Pacific, information exchange and distribution need to be substantially improved.

The second problem is that of co-ordination. Links between population education activities in the formal sector and the non-formal sector are especially important, and where they are lacking programmes can be seriously hampered. Co-ordination does not take place automatically;

it has to be planned and regularly followed up through meetings, seminars and workshops. Not only has co-ordination often been lacking between population education projects and other population projects in a given country, but, more importantly, it has been weak between population education projects and other educational innovations, such as major teacher training efforts.

Finally, issues related to funding have created major problems in population education, particularly because both teacher training and materials development can be extremely costly. Seldom have the funding requirements been adequately assessed nor has the planning been sufficiently careful from the start to ensure optimal use of limited resources. Only in a few instances has the gradual phasing out of external assistance been accompanied by partial or complete take-over by the Government, as in the Philippines, the Republic of Korea and Sri Lanka. Implementing a population education programme may require external funding for a longer period than previously thought necessary. Thus, external assistance is usually required for more than only one project cycle (four years).

Another problem is related to lack of diverse sources of external funding. UNFPA has been the single most important source for population education programmes in developing countries. In contrast, other external funding sources for this sector are limited. Consequently, recipient countries have been vulnerable when UNFPA has faced funding constraints, or has had to reduce its existing programme inputs. Also, because of the limits on available funding, it has not always been possible for countries to expand programmes at a pace they might wish.

■ Monitoring, evaluation and research. In the early years of population education programmes, monitoring and evaluation were given low priority. In recent years, their value has become more apparent, but even now monitoring and evaluation are used less systematically than they should.

Many projects have included monitoring to comply with requirements of an external funding agency. Although the resultant information on the evolution and history of population education projects has been used to a certain extent to revise activities, such monitoring has seldom served programme staff as a management tool. The challenge for most programmes is to ensure that monitoring and evaluation become integral to programme management. In Asia, where several countries perceive monitoring and evaluation as urgent needs, UNESCO has assisted project staff at the regional level.

A number of countries--among them India, Nepal, the Philippines, the Republic of Korea, Tunisia and Venezuela--have carried out impact evaluations focused on changes in attitudes, values and knowledge among teachers and students. However, because of the relative newness of these programmes, along with the difficulty of evaluating impact, changes in behaviour have not been evaluated.

Quantifying the effects of such school-based programmes on demographic variables does not seem feasible. Similarly, it has been difficult to design adequate evaluations without complicated and lengthy longitudinal studies of experimental and control groups. However, some solutions have been found. In Venezuela, for example, university students have carried out investigations on the impact of population education. In Tunisia, small-scale impact studies, for which national capacity exists, have been made.

Research has often been part of, and indeed is often necessary to, population education programmes. Such research may be socio-cultural and anthropological--to provide locally relevant information on specific population issues for curriculum, materials and contents--or operational research, to test new materials or activities. Often, implementation of research components has been delayed, thereby slowing down other programme activities. Sometimes new research has been initiated before making a concerted effort to locate and use already available information (as in Burkina Faso and Democratic Yemen). It has also been difficult to ensure that research results are actually used to improve the programme.

In evaluation and research, local universities and research institutes can play a helpful role. The Institute of Mass Communications at the University of the Philippines has conducted an "impact evaluation" of that country's project in 1985, for example, and universities in India have been active as well.

Institutionalizing a population education programme

Institutionalization has been achieved when population education is a regular part of the educational process. In such contexts, it receives adequate attention with little or no dependence upon sources external to the country. As the time span since the beginning of the first population education programmes has been somewhat short, however, and the introduction of population education is usually a lengthy process, it is not surprising that few countries have achieved full-scale institutionalization of population education. Where it has been reached, as in the Republic of Korea, certain problems persist in selected programme components. One such problem is that if the unit responsible for the programme is completely disbanded upon the cessation of external funding, unless some focal group is charged with follow-up, there can be a loss of monitoring, innovation and other important functions, leading in turn to a gradual loss of population content. When, for example, the school curriculum is revised, if there is no specialist with authority and adequate status overseeing the process, the population education content may be lost. If Governments cannot provide the needed financial support, continuing external support for forming such a nucleus may be needed.

Finally, sustaining awareness and support for population education has to be a continuing process. Also, linkages with other sectors, particularly with non-formal activities and with parents, in particular, have to be actively maintained. Thus, even after it is assumed that the programme is institutionalized, meetings, seminars, formal co-ordination bodies and the mass media have to be used to sustain the programme.

The key determinants of the performance in population education programmes are the following:

a) Government commitment and support which are reflected in, *inter alia*, the financial and non-financial resources necessary for implementation, and the required policy and legislative changes;

b) Creation of a central population education unit, usually within the ministry of education, with sufficient trained staff;

c) Dedication, commitment and motivation of the "core team"--the central staff assigned to introducing population education--is of central importance;

d) Availability of high-quality technical assistance and back-up, thus far largely from UNESCO as the primary source of international expertise on population education for the formal sector;

e) The tapping of local specialists via a TCDC mechanism facilitating inter-country exchanges of personnel for technical support;

f) Sensitization and awareness creation at the national level among high-level decision makers, programme implementors, and all other sectors such as parents, religious leaders, the media and the public;

g) Quality of training and of the materials produced;

h) Quality of project planning through the careful elaboration of a workable project document; and

i) The formation of relationships based on trust and mutual respect among Government, executing and funding agencies, as well as among the parties concerned at the country level; such relationships are especially important for dealing with a new, sensitive, and often controversial subject that is often misunderstood.

Accomplishments of formal population education

Population education has contributed in many ways to the overall educational process and, thereby, to development itself:

a) It has incorporated and reinforced skills that are applicable to the daily lives of teachers and students. For example, well-reasoned decision-making, development of a critical awareness and strengthening of self-esteem are three examples of population education content that affect not only demographic variables but other areas as well, providing the learner an opportunity to clarify and strengthen values;

b) Population education has provided educational systems with the kind of interdisciplinary and holistic approach to a topic that those systems often lacked, though such approaches are indispensable for the eventual resolution of world problems such as food supply, environmental deterioration and energy resources;

c) Population education has helped to improve exchanges between the school and the wider community. Projects have included consultations with parents and community leaders and institutions on the inclusion of new themes in the school curriculum. In the same manner, these projects have promoted the involvement of members of the community as teachers aides, often boosting teachers' morale and helping them improve relations with their students and communities;

d) Curriculum contents, by focusing on concrete, important individual, community and family problems, have become more pertinent to the needs of students;

e) Population education has also helped shift the emphasis in teaching from a sole focus on children's acquisition of knowledge to their active participation, thereby facilitating critical thinking, the formation of attitudes, evaluation of values and behavioural modification. Population education has thus helped change perceptions of the importance of such external factors as "fate", at the same time strengthening the learners' appreciation of their abilities, helping them feel that they can plan the future and exert control over their lives;[7] and

f) Population education has often added to the professional competence of school systems, developing skills among teachers having had little teacher training.

Beyond their educational contributions, population education programmes have also achieved remarkable success in sensitization and awareness creation at the national level through a strategy of well-planned seminars and workshops before programmes are introduced. These seminars have helped define, through a collective participatory process, the aims and approach for population education in a particular country, thereby strengthening the base of political support.

Major issues for the future of formal population education

The major issues and needs for the future in the formal sector necessarily vary according to the stage of programmes and, thus, differ considerably by region and country.

Programmes in early stages

Programmes still in the initial stages have as a major issue the securing of support and commitment to population education and the assignment of full-time core programme staff. The importance of well-trained and dedicated staff and their being able to work full-time on population education have been underscored time and again. Nevertheless, many programmes have been seriously delayed because of staffing problems. The two principal regions concerned--those with the most new projects--are the Pacific and sub-Saharan Africa. In the Pacific region, the needs are for building support at high levels for population education and ensuring the availability of full-time qualified personnel. In sub-Saharan Africa, the needs are specifically for training of trainers and increasing training opportunities within the countries and at regional level, such as study tours and the development of training capacity in existing regional institutions. Further progress is needed in identifying appropriate training sites abroad.

Many of the needs in Africa could be met through co-ordination among countries at regional level as well as through interregional exchange, on the following: information and materials; training; clarification of curriculum options in population education; development of prototype materials for adaptation at country level; and development and maintenance of a roster of persons with experience in population education in the region. These people would help fill the needs for technical manpower through consultancies and other means. In curricula and materials, the needs include developing a comprehensive, standard approach to family life issues or, at least, a number of core concepts. In societies where traditional practices predominate, the "models" used in other cultures will not suffice. "Universal" concepts, such as respect for others, may be compiled and used as a starting point.

Programmes in middle stages

The challenge for population education programmes now in middle stages is not to lose the momentum gained--often gradually and painfully--and to consolidate and build on achievements thus far. The major concerns are training, materials production and distribution, and maintaining co-ordination with all the different groups involved directly or indirectly with population education.

To prevent setbacks, sensitization and awareness-creation activities such as seminars and workshops are still necessary, particularly where Governments have not yet officially endorsed population education. Sensitization seminars will also pave the way to improving the population content of curricula and materials. In training, the focus has to be on integration of population education training into the regular pre-service teacher training programmes as well as in expanding in-service training. Multiple strategies have to be pursued for in-service training to be able to reach the large group of teachers who have not yet been trained in population education and to continue to expand the skills of those who have already had some initial training. At this time, a massive effort has to be sustained. To this end, adequate resources, human and financial, are a prerequisite. In curriculum development, the issue is to ensure that population education is included in all levels and grades, not only in selected grades. Special emphasis has to be placed on reaching primary schools, in view of their important potential impact on attitude formation.

Mature programmes

In more mature programmes--most of which are in Asia but also in Egypt, El Salvador, Morocco, Paraguay, Sierra Leone and Tunisia--the major issue is to bring about full institutionalization and to improve the quality of all programme components. Thus, to the extent possible, the conditions listed below as indicators of institutionalization need to be fulfilled:

a) Policy makers and leaders at various levels need to understand the requirement for population education and to support it by their actions;

b) A focal group should be in place with budgetary support in the national implementing agency, ministry or organization, charged with follow-up and feedback on population activities in the school system and in the community;

c) A corps of national technical specialists should be created to work on population education or to be able to contribute if the need arises;

d) The population contents and concepts for achieving project objectives should be included in the plans and programmes of study;

e) Population content reflecting those key issues should appear in textbooks;

f) Population contents should be incorporated in pre-service and in-service training programmes for teachers; and

g) Questions on population issues and concepts should be part of standard school examinations where these exist.

It is also important that the government take-over of local personnel costs be considered early, to permit sufficient lead time for adjustments to government budgets. By no means an easy task, institutionalization has to be carefully planned, and it will be all the more difficult to achieve as countries face increasing constraints in the social sectors due to their limited economic prospects.

To ensure quality, planners must prevent the population content in these mature programmes from becoming diluted and must keep the curriculum comprehensive, non-prescriptive and up to date. The population content must also be kept culturally appropriate, clearly expressed in the national language and otherwise carefully adapted to

185

local needs. Many topics that were not originally addressed because they were too controversial or not yet relevant may need to be incorporated into the programme. They include, *inter alia*, human sexuality, family planning, adolescent sexuality and pregnancy, abortion, sexually transmitted diseases (STDs) and AIDS, gender role stereotypes, roles and responsibilities regarding sexuality and parenthood, preferences regarding sex of offspring, and female circumcision.

The use of innovative participatory teaching/learning methodologies should be extended, with periodic upgrading as new methodologies are developed. This endeavour obviously contributes to the general upgrading of teachers' skills and offers useful lessons for the non-formal IEC activities, whether population-related or not.

To meet the challenges, population education programmes that are well along in institutionalization will have to include more attention to research and evaluation and to how these can be made integral to the programmes. Universities and other groups can facilitate these efforts as they have often done in the past, providing resource persons in population education seminars and preparing instructional materials as well as refining conceptualization of the field. They may also assess the appropriate treatment of content by grade and age level.

Another issue is for these programmes to increase their contribution to other countries with less advanced programmes, through more systematic exchanges of information and materials. Eventually this might become a TCDC activity financed principally by the participating countries, at least for production costs.

If they are to maintain programmes at current levels, those managing mature programmes need to pay attention to creating continuous awareness and an effective information network. In this way relevant up-to-date materials can be distributed to all personnel and particularly to all teachers. As a key element of institutionalization, the continued presence of qualified core staff for population education programmes is necessary.

Issues in all programmes

Although the principal issues for the future of population education in the formal sector vary greatly among countries and regions, it is possible to identify several common issues.

- Awareness creation and sensitization. Awareness creation and sensitization continue to be of crucial importance for all programmes. In countries where population education in schools is just starting, the need for creating awareness about population and mobilizing support for population education is obvious. In more mature programmes, because changes in support from individuals and groups in society often occur, continued sensitization activities are necessary. They are also essential for upgrading population content by, for example, adding more controversial and newer topics such as adolescent pregnancy. The involvement of women's organizations could help in sustaining activities beyond the initial programme stages.

■ Co-ordination with other groups and sectors. Co-ordination, which is closely related to awareness creation, is a strong determinant of programme success. Efforts to ensure that linkages are made with all other groups directly and indirectly concerned with population education are of utmost importance, to prevent situations, at present still too common, in which other ministries and other groups may even be unaware of population education as an action programme in their country's school system.

■ Training. Training continues to be a key issue for population education in the formal sector, both for the core programme staff and for all teachers. Staff turnover is a common problem in country projects. Adequate training of classroom teachers is a difficult and expensive task. Yet, skilled teachers are the key to successful population education. There are too few professional training facilities for population educators in all regions. Special emphasis needs to be put on training facilities that can respond to the needs of several countries. Finally, special attention is required to address the question of how to establish and institutionalize systems within countries, including training as a key element for the continuous supply of qualified core personnel. Such systems are necessary because of natural turnover in core staff managing population education programmes.

■ The conceptualization of population education. The conceptualization of population education needs to be renewed and revised. The only important effort so far made to provide a global conceptualization of population education dates back to the 1978 UNESCO study--*Population Education: A Contemporary Concern*.[8] Many current projects, based largely on approaches defined in this study, thus reflect the lessons of early experience that have become less useful in light of later experience. The important developments and redefinitions in the 1980s include the following:

(a) The relationships between population education and such fields as sex education, family life education and environmental education are more clearly understood;

(b) The objectives of population education, including those concerning fertility, mortality and migration are more precise;

(c) New content areas have been incorporated into programmes, including responsible parenthood, family planning, development of self-esteem, adolescent fertility, AIDS prevention and others;

(d) Learning experiences have been designed to eliminate stereotypes contributing to discrimination based on gender; and

187

(e)   Curriculum designs initially considered to be inconvenient or
difficult to implement have been adopted.

Once they are documented and circulated, these developments,
occurring at different paces in different parts of the world, will
undoubtedly be of great value in the planning of new projects and in
improving ongoing programmes.

■ Content. An issue closely related to conceptualization is that of how
to update the content of population education, particularly in terms of
addressing difficult or controversial issues such as human sexuality;
adolescent pregnancy, which is often accompanied by illegal abortion;
and gender roles, rights and responsibilities. Of these, perhaps the
issue of adolescent pregnancy is of greatest concern since it is
emerging as an issue in a number of countries which had not
previously identified it as a problem and, therefore, have limited
experience in developing educational approaches to deal with it. This
is a particularly complex problem in Asia, where there are many
cultural differences between countries, requiring research and different
approaches in each case. A different, but equally complex problem
exists in sub-Saharan Africa, where traditional practices extend beyond
national borders, and different family patterns and other cultural
differences often exist within the same country.

One possible approach to the prevention of adolescent pregnancy
involves the early identification of girls (and boys) with learning
difficulties and those who are difficult to reach and teach due to
discipline problems and truancy, because these children often
experience early pregnancy and drop out of school. Systematic
identification and focused attention in a positive atmosphere will be
required to guide these young people towards responsible behaviour
and to enhance their life options.

Among the most important new topics in population education is that
dealing with gender-role stereotypes and responsibilities. A few
countries have started to address the need to develop adequate
approaches, concepts and materials on gender roles and issues, and
UNESCO is doing pioneering work in this area in Latin America.
Development of population education content on gender roles will
obviously be of significant benefit to other fields now also starting to
address the issue of how best to sensitize and train staff to
incorporate gender issues into development activities.

Finally, the question of what content and concepts school systems can
afford to insert in crowded curricula needs to be carefully examined.
Materials have been developed in many countries, but they do not
always find their way into textbooks or other "permanent" or required
reading materials.

■ Student grade levels. Many countries focus population education on
secondary students because they may already be engaged in

reproductive behaviour. However, a good case can be made for devoting significant attention to the middle-school level. Moreover, to reach the majority of those who attend school in developing countries, efforts must focus on the primary level, reaching the age group most amenable to clarification of values, beliefs and prejudices. Incorporation of population education at the primary level can now be easily achieved using newly developed content, such as those dealing with self-esteem, elimination of gender stereotypes and the development of decision-making skills.

- Materials. Materials preparation and distribution as well as exchange of information and materials are issues of urgency. Prototypes that can be easily adapted at the national and local levels are needed. Materials also need to be upgraded and updated as new information and new issues emerge. Improved mechanisms are needed to facilitate information and materials exchange between countries. Furthermore, the establishment and maintenance of systems within a country to keep all teachers periodically informed on new developments in population education, as well as supplying new materials, are among key issues for the future. Innovative solutions include equipping national programmes with simple, low-cost desk-top publishing systems which, *inter alia*, may facilitate the local production of a population education newsletter that can be distributed nation-wide to all teachers.

- Evaluation and research. Evaluation and research are both needed, along with strategies to ensure that evaluation becomes an integral part of programmes and that new methodologies are developed for assessing impact. Some innovative work has started on in-depth studies of the learning experience and its impact for individual students. Research needs to be given adequate priority within country projects.

- Institutionalization. One of the major challenges facing population education today is how to institutionalize it. Three conditions seem to be important. First, population education must be included in the textbooks and other basic materials for existing courses. Most population education projects start by producing a separate set of materials and distributing them to teachers. Eventually, however, textbooks should be revised and, for this purpose, textbook writers have to be trained in population issues, as they are in El Salvador and Pakistan, or population education staff can assist textbook writers in this revision, as they have in the Dominican Republic, Nicaragua, Paraguay, Thailand and Viet Nam. Because textbook revision is complicated and expensive, some population education programmes have successfully undertaken this task in the context of a national curriculum reform, as in the Dominican Republic. Second, to ensure that population issues are given sufficient classroom time and attention, they need to be part of national or state examinations, as has been done in Bihar (India), Burkina Faso and Sierra Leone. Third, population education needs to be included in all pre-service teacher training institutions. Because many teacher training institutions are relatively independent bodies, it may be necessary to issue a governmental decree requiring the inclusion of population education in pre-service training, as has been done, for example, in Indonesia and in parts of India.

Non-formal population education

Purpose and types of activities

In view of its critical role in facilitating population decision-making, population education must rely on non-formal educational activities as well as on formal education. The non-formal channels are needed to reach, *inter alia*, the many school drop-outs and unschooled youth, particularly girls and women. Not only are these people not exposed to formal population education programmes, but, because of low levels of education, they seek early entry into the labour force, marry early and start child-bearing shortly thereafter.[9] Population education and the related fields of family welfare education and sex education are necessary for both in-school and out-of-school learners of all ages; moreover, they should be viewed as life-long education.

Non-formal population education activities are extremely diverse. Projects may be designed as a large, nation-wide effort or for a specific region or district. They may be aimed at children, out-of-school youth or adults. There are also various approaches to curriculum development, teaching and learning materials and the training of personnel. These non-formal programmes vary not only in scope, size and location but also in the auspices under which they operate.

Moreover, the number and type of institutions that might play a role in non-formal population education are many, and on-going programmes involve a wide range of audiences in countries in virtually all parts of the world. In addition, the United Nations specialized agencies and NGOs have developed various approaches to population education in keeping with their respective mandates. Non-formal population education activities have been integrated into governmental and non-governmental programmes of adult education, functional literacy, vocational training, agricultural extension, health education, special programmes for disadvantaged population groups, and the educational programmes of trade union organizations, employer and management groups, co-operatives, and women and youth organizations. Non-formal channels have also reinforced learning for people in both formal and non-formal settings. For example, educational activities in after-school youth programmes have served as a follow-up to formal education.

Steps in the development of these population education programmes generally include the following:

a) Development of awareness at the country level of the need for, and the role of, population education;

b) Establishment of practical and workable mechanisms and procedures for inter-agency and intersectoral co-ordination and collaboration at both the policy and operational levels;

c) Formulation of country strategies and programmes;

d) Determination of the locus and orientation of projects;

e) Development of human resources through training of instructors, trainees and management personnel;

f) Development and modification of curriculum and training methodologies;

g) The strengthening of theoretical and operational research as well as monitoring and evaluation capabilities;

h) Design, production and testing of education and training materials; and

i) Institutionalization of population education.

Experiences in diverse types of programmes are summarized below.

Population education in adult education and literacy programmes

Frequently, education ministries that focused first on population education in schools later became interested in going beyond the classroom to integrate or link population education to community welfare, adult education, vocational training and rural development. This has occurred in the Dominican Republic, Egypt, El Salvador, Maldives, Mauritania, Morocco, Pakistan, the Philippines, the Sudan, Tonga, Trust Territory of the Pacific Islands (Palau), Vanuatu, Venezuela and Yemen. Non-formal activities are often integrated with literacy, adult education and community development programmes, sponsored separately or jointly by government agencies and NGOs.

Individuals or couples enrolled in adult education or literacy programmes constitute an important group for population education. By enrolling, they have demonstrated their interest in improving their welfare. Population-related or family planning content designed to meet their requirements can serve as a practical tool to help them improve their situation.

Methodologies for combining population education and literacy in nonformal settings differ widely. In Afghanistan, family health and family life education have been incorporated into the functional literacy materials of the General Agency for Literacy Campaign of the Ministry of Education.[10] In India, Literacy House (an NGO) has long been active in "family-life planning education" and has developed a range of adult literacy programmes with population components. World Education, an international NGO focusing primarily on non-formal education for youth and adults, has integrated family life planning concepts into functional education, carrying out such projects in Honduras, India, Thailand and Turkey. In Nepal, World Education has worked with the adult education section of the Ministry of Education to institutionalize a programme of non-formal adult education that includes health and family planning concepts; at the same time, other efforts have been made in the country to involve women in literacy training and post-literacy income-generation activities.

An Ethiopian project employed technical assistance for its integrated family life education work. Sponsored by the Ethiopian Women's Association and funded by the United States Agency for International Development (USAID), this activity included health, nutrition, agriculture and family life education to help participants develop basic literacy and numeracy skills.[11]

Pakistan has recently implemented a project emphasizing the development of population education curricula for the training of adult education field-workers so that they can reach out-of-school youth and adult audiences. The Indonesian Ministry of Education developed a population education programme for trainees in community education, aimed at reaching adults and young people. Also in Indonesia, population education components have been integrated into education programmes for the Council of Churches, the Muhammadiyah (the religious body) and the armed forces. In the Republic of Korea, out-of-school activities for parents during summer and winter vacations have supplemented the school programme to enhance the children's exposure to consistent values.

In Latin America, the development of suitable population education materials specifically intended for illiterate, semi-illiterate, and newly literate populations has received renewed interest. Many materials were regionally developed prototypes that can be adapted for local levels. At the same time, many Asian countries, in the course of conducting literacy and other adult education programmes, have incorporated population and family planning concepts in the learning materials, thus enhancing their relevancy.

Many projects have demonstrated the possibility of incorporating population education and family life education into literacy programmes, adult education, community development activities and programmes of women's organizations and youth groups. They have also helped heighten awareness and knowledge about population among high-level decision makers and other target audiences. This heightened awareness has, in turn, helped focus attention on the urgency of expanding non-formal population education programmes to reach the many unserved youth.

Family welfare education in the organized sector

Population education components have been integrated into family welfare education and workers' education in the organized sector to help workers and employers understand population issues and their relevance to overall socio-economic development and specific labour objectives, particularly the enhancement of workers' welfare. Trade unions, personnel managers and employer organizations have channelled population education through workers' education programmes, vocational training, co-operatives and other rural institutions. Most activities in industries and on plantations are organized to include governmental as well as employers' and workers' organizations.

Within the framework of direct concerns for wages and better working and living conditions, the programmes are designed to help workers make informed decisions on family formation and reproductive behaviour, including the practice of family planning. For this reason, several non-formal education programmes described earlier, such as those in Ethiopia, Nepal and Turkey, use materials that involve the learner in decision-making on various life concerns. By reinforcing the capacity for needs analysis and decision-making through each successive learning experience, such methods make it easier for participants to reach similarly sound family planning decisions. Like other groups, workers benefit from learning about the importance of planning in their lives and from developing decision-making and planning skills.

Projects may be addressed to special audiences, such as rural women in Thailand, women factory and cottage industry workers in Mali and Nepal, and young industrial workers in the Republic of Korea. Population education units have been established in such varied structures as the Institute of Workers' Education in Somalia, the trade union organization in the Philippines and an employers' federation in Sri Lanka.

Workers in the organized sector are an appropriate target audience for population education for several reasons. Not only are they likely to be receptive to new ideas but they are often pace setters, quickly adopting new social practices,[12] and those using contraception can become important models for their neighbours. The organized sector also provides access to males, an important audience in so far as reproductive decisions are concerned.

A major achievement of projects in the organized sector has been the changing attitudes and behaviour of management personnel with regard to family planning for workers, as illustrated by the provision of time for population education classes and, in some Asian settings, of incentives for family planning acceptors. Moreover, a large cadre of trained worker-motivators can now influence fellow workers and, potentially, other community members to accept family planning. A further achievement is that, in most cases, projects have been carried out by national staff recruited and trained locally, working without the support of an international expert.

The provision of family planning services through the work-place appeals to workers and employers. Workers benefit as they can easily and conveniently obtain supplies and services that improve family health. Employers benefit as their employees are healthier and require less employer-funded care for maternity leave and pregnancy-related absenteeism. The nation benefits, for when employers pay for family planning, Governments can focus more on providing services for the jobless and those who cannot pay.

Population education in integrated rural development projects

Comprehensive rural development has been viewed as one of the most immediate and promising solutions to the problems of rapid population growth and migration.[13] Population education can play an important role in rural development, through projects that create awareness of population issues among officials and decision makers concerned with rural development. Agricultural extension and home economics education, co-operatives, 4H clubs, young farmer associations, and women's clubs and groups have all served as vehicles for the introduction of population education and the practice of family planning in rural areas.

In the Integrated Rural Development Programme in Pakistan, governmental and private agencies collaborated in providing technical assistance and training to local people. In the Philippines, in a co-operative project under the Department of Local Government and Community Development, the co-operative members have learned about the implications of population factors for the quality of life and how to make sound decisions regarding the achievement of family goals. In Malaysia, where 62 per cent of the population live in the rural areas (see Annex Table 1) and where development of arable land is an important focus of the national development programme, population education has been integrated into a training programme for the Federal Land Development Authority (FELDA), which conducts non-formal education sessions to help settlers raise their standard of living.

A project implemented by the Bangladesh Academy of Rural Development (BARD), under the Ministry of Local Government, Rural Development and Co-operatives, was designed to provide population and family welfare education for village leaders, model farmers and co-operative leaders--all influential members of the rural community--who were expected to motivate people to accept family planning in their respective villages. In Togo, a project for women extension workers focused on the integration of population education through women's co-operatives. Projects in the Programme for Better Family Living in Kenya and Swaziland represent an early "case history" for rural development planners. Although the projects did not succeed in institutionalizing population education in agricultural programmes as intended, they did lay a foundation for better co-operation between government ministries in other aspects of development. In the late 1980s, FAO initiated a major effort to help countries incorporate population education into their overall agricultural extension strategies, in support of a more comprehensive agricultural and rural development programme.

Population education in projects addressing women's needs

The women's dimension in population education activities continues to grow. Population education offers women in rural and urban areas the

195

possibility of improving their knowledge and skills in the areas of family life, family health, child spacing, nutrition and other social and economic matters. It also helps women to develop their leadership potential.

In Pakistan, Sri Lanka and the Republic of Korea, Mothers' Clubs have been established, most in rural areas, to provide women with income-generating skills and to educate and motivate them to avail themselves of MCH and family planning services. In India, an organization of rural women has incorporated population education concepts into its education programme; in Bangladesh, a women's organization has provided information on population issues and family planning along with vocational training to its members and other interested women. In Pakistan, population education is integrated with social welfare and community development activities. In Sri Lanka, a women's organization with more than 50 years of experience in promoting social welfare activities has carried out a project aimed in part at motivating village women to use governmental family health and family planning services.

In Ecuador, the emphasis has been on enhancing socio-economic conditions for women and their families in marginal areas and furthering the spatial distribution goals of the national development plan. In Guatemala, a population education programme for rural women has as one of its objectives the expansion of traditional home-making training to include family life education. Population education has stressed the development of family life skills for young women in Antigua and Barbuda and training to facilitate the involvement of women in the national population programme in Mexico. Similar education and training have occurred in all regions of the world to develop skills ranging from those important to home-making to those important for professional management.

Programmes emphasizing educational opportunities for women have been gaining in popularity around the world. One important step has been taken, but needs more attention--the reduction of opposition to women's advancement through carefully designed educational programme content for men. Thus far, most of the work in this area has been carried out in schools. There is a great opportunity for developing it further with adult audiences.

<u>Population education in projects addressing adolescent fertility</u>

A growing number of health education programmes now include the topics of human reproduction, sexuality, adolescent fertility, family planning, STDs and AIDS. In the developing countries, the proportion of young people in the population has grown enormously in recent years. In addition, the age of menarche has decreased and the mean age of marriage has increased in many countries, thus extending the period between puberty and marriage, with the consequent risk of unwanted pregnancy. Changes in traditional systems have often resulted in the decline of parental and community guidance that once governed sexual behaviour. In some countries the traditional family life education provided

196

by extended family members has been interrupted by wars, which can not only break down family structures but also frequently have a sexually liberating effect on young people participating in the hostilities.

In some countries, private organizations and government leaders acknowledge that traditional rites of passage, whereby health information and values were passed along to boys and girls upon reaching puberty, are rapidly disappearing, leaving a major and serious information void.[14] The result has been premature parenthood and high rates of maternal and child mortality and morbidity among adolescents and their children, as well as growing numbers of abortions, cases of STDs and potential dangers of infertility. In the South Pacific, unplanned adolescent pregnancies often result from drug and alcohol abuse. United Nations data show that in some countries in Africa and Asia the proportion of teen-age child-bearing that can be attributed to women below 18 years is as high as 50 per cent.[15]

Attitudes towards early sexual activity and child-bearing vary in different areas, and the social consequences may differ depending on whether a young woman is married. In all cases, however, the negative health consequences of child-bearing are compounded by poor or non-existent pre-natal care. Most adolescent women who bear children face limited educational and job opportunities, thus limiting their prospects and promoting a high degree of dependency.

Both government and voluntary agencies have developed programmes stressing education in family life and human sexuality for out-of-school youth in a variety of settings, such as multi-purpose youth centres, community centres, women's centres, work-places, churches and recreation centres. The provision of education in non-formal settings has many advantages. It brings the activities to a place where the group is comfortable and discussions may be more open than they would in a school classroom. Participation is voluntary. Young people can often help design and implement the activities, and parents can be involved. Activities gain additional acceptance in the community when carried out by traditional and respected groups.

In the Territory of Hong Kong, an effective partnership has been forged between the family planning association and the Girl Guides. Courses are provided every Saturday in Girl Guide centres to help participants understand physical hygiene, dating and marriage. In the Philippines, the Department of Social Services and Development (now the Department of Social Welfare and Development) created a programme, Population Awareness and Sex Education for Out-of-School Youth, which is carried out by a national youth agency. In Egypt, the Supreme Council for Youth and Sport has conducted a somewhat similar programme through youth centres. Grenada's family planning association works with youth organizations to reach young people with a programme that includes magazine and contraceptive distribution posts.[16]

Outreach is of special importance when the target population is difficult to attract. Programmes for young workers in the Philippines and Malaysia provide them information and counselling at their work-place. In India, the family planning association has reached out-of-school women aged 14-25 through crafts centres. Various Asian outreach programmes stress the relation of sexual education to marriage, such as the Late Marriage Movement in Bangladesh and the Marriage Law Education and Training Projects in Indonesia. In Africa, church organizations have been reaching out to youth for many years. In Ghana, Togo and Uganda, for example, churches have conducted family life programmes for youth since the 1960s. Church-sponsored population education youth programmes are also found in Kenya, Nigeria and the United Republic of Tanzania.

Reproductive health services for adolescents and youth have been slow to emerge, stirring controversy nearly everywhere. Nevertheless, some excellent programmes have been developed to meet the reproductive health needs of young people, often combining many kinds of educational, health and social services. The Philippines has three centres especially for adolescents, and educational and clinic programmes also focus on teenagers in Antigua and Barbuda, Brazil, Chile, Guatemala, Indonesia, Jamaica, Mauritius, Montserrat, Nigeria and Peru. At the Family Planning Association of Hong Kong, a youth volunteer group--Society for a New Generation--provides advice in a varied programme that includes family life education in schools and factories, a telephone hotline service and clinical services. At The Hub, a centre for teenagers in the South Bronx in New York City, where pregnancy and drug abuse are the main problems facing community youth, young people helped plan what has evolved into a peer education programme. A well-publicized model programme is The Door, also in New York City, which offers at a single site an array of services such as family planning, family living education, employment counselling, crafts instruction and recreation.

The strategy of providing multiple services to young people has been used in several Latin American settings, including the Adolescent Orientation Centres in Mexico City and neighbouring areas, started in 1978 and offering educational, medical, psychological and recreational activities to youth 11-19 years of age. Family planning services, sex information and counselling are also available and an outreach programme promoting young people's participation in local community development.

A number of programmes use youth leaders and counsellors to teach and counsel other young people. Most programmes train peer counsellors to give talks and conduct group discussions on responsible parenthood, family values, human sexuality, STDs and family planning. After training, peer counsellors work with schools, youth clubs, churches and mothers' groups. In Latin America and the Caribbean, trained peer counsellors carry out various population activities; in the Philippines, Thailand and Sri Lanka peer counsellors play a large role in projects; and in Ghana and Kenya, peer counsellors do community outreach work.

198

In Jamaica, the Women's Centre Project for Adolescent Mothers displays an innovative participatory approach to meeting young people's health education and family planning needs. It was started by the Jamaican Women's Bureau to permit continuity of education for pregnant schoolgirls (12-16 years) who, because of social censure, had withdrawn from school. The programme strongly emphasizes practical education in family life education. It also involves the putative fathers in an important programme designed to make young Jamaican men more aware of their role in the family and the responsibilities involved. A significant measure of this programme's success was the change it fostered in official school policy to allow pregnant girls to remain in school or continue at a later stage to pursue education and careers.

Many family planning associations work extensively with out-of- school youth, and in many English-speaking Caribbean countries, family life education programmes aimed at out-of-school youth have been implemented. Youth centres in Antigua and Barbuda, Barbados, Jamaica, and Saint Kitts and Nevis have offered counselling and services for youth, combining informal education and recreation with instruction in production skills. Health authorities have also recognized the need for separate clinics to supply teenagers with family planning advice and services in a congenial atmosphere.

In Chile, Guatemala, India, Jamaica, Mauritius, Mexico, Pakistan and Sri Lanka, family planning associations and other private organizations include information on human sexuality, family planning, and responsible parenthood in vocational training programmes at the work-site. The Guyana Responsible Parenthood Association conducts sex education courses in business and government offices.

Indonesia's family planning association set up a family life education centre to teach youth about sexuality and reproduction, to encourage sound attitudes towards family life, and later to offer population education for parents. In Thailand, a project of the family planning association responds to the increasing incidence of unwanted pregnancies and STDs. In Democratic Yemen, Ethiopia, Malawi and Zimbabwe, the associations are working with national youth federations to train youth leaders to educate their peers about responsible parenthood.

The challenge of reaching adolescents and youth with fertility-regulation information and services is formidable, given society's conflicting views about appropriate behaviour for young people, what information they should be given and the realities of modern life. Despite sometimes strong opposition, the array of non-formal activities of diverse groups, governments, NGOs and churches demonstrates high interest and progress in introducing fertility-regulation information and services for adolescents. Population education has helped shape community attitudes by creating an awareness of adolescent fertility and child-bearing, and by developing acceptable strategies (youth centres, peer counsellors), activities providing focal points for the discussion of sensitive issues and mechanisms for community mobilization.

Lessons from non-formal population education programmes

Though non-formal population education programmes are becoming increasingly prevalent, all experienced difficulties either initially or at a later stage in their development. Many of the lessons from these experiences may be valuable to others.

Sensitizing decision makers

Because population education is still a relatively new field, it is not uncommon to find policy makers and others in positions of influence who, having never had any exposure to this subject, lack interest and commitment or even oppose its introduction into out-of-school programmes for youth and adults. Thus an awareness-creation activity may be called for at the outset of a programme or project.

Frequently, negative reactions to population education are based on the perception that non-formal population education is one more burden on already overworked field officers. Sometimes those reactions are based on a misconception of the purpose of non-formal population education-- that it is an attempt to teach culturally unacceptable topics. Even those who support population education in principle are sometimes unclear about the scope of its content, the number of staff required, or numerous other factors requiring decisions in programme planning. This limited awareness can be especially critical because several ministries are normally involved in non-formal population education. The institutional linkages that create awareness or facilitate co-ordination of activities may be weak, seldom used or non-existent. Thus, before the basic decision to develop a non-formal education programme is made, it is necessary to institute a learning process through which the decision makers become aware of population education and understand its potential relevance for their country. This process varies. Sometimes it entails formal seminars or other meetings. At other times it can be advanced through less formal approaches.

Selecting appropriate content

The nature and depth of population content in a programme or project are determined by the broad objectives of the sector involved (literacy, labour, agriculture, health, for example), the population objectives of the country and the specific objectives of the project. The selection of content is complicated by the diverse needs and characteristics of the target audiences for out-of-school population education--marital status, degree of literacy, education and training, migratory status, occupation, socio-economic status and religion. The complexity of the task is compounded by the likelihood that the audience is voluntary--unlike schoolchildren--so the content must be pertinent and interesting lest the audience leave.

An analysis of population education curricula indicates that despite much similarity from one programme to the next, there are no ideal

200

content outlines.[17] Consensus is lacking on the selection of topics deemed controversial, such as sexuality, human reproduction, population growth, family planning, STDs and AIDS. The issue is not so much whether these topics are relevant to population education, since unquestionably they are, but how relevant they are to a particular audience and whether they might jeopardize programme acceptance. The latter is far less a problem with adult audiences than it is with youth or schoolchildren.

Given this situation, it is apparent that no uniform curriculum content can be planned for all out-of-school learners. What is appropriate for one group might not be for another. In addition, not only the content but the order in which it is presented may need to vary; a sequential curriculum similar to one developed for schools may thus be inappropriate. "Core content modules", self-contained learning packages of varying duration, have been developed for out-of-school use by UNESCO, ILO, the American Home Economics Association and others. Decisions regarding the adaptation of these modules are made by project staff.

Treating human sexuality and family life as content areas

Human sexuality depends not only on anatomical and physiological factors but especially on psychological and social factors. Personal fulfilment, self-respect, acceptance of responsibility and respect for others are important prerequisites for sexual well-being. An understanding of this and of the various roles played by men and women in the family, community and the society at large enhances the individual's ability to function as a partner or parent. It is in the interest of every society that its members have self-respect, be secure and have responsible, caring attitudes in their sexual behaviour, and thus it is in the interest of every society that its members understand their sexuality.

Education in human sexuality is important for understanding population processes and thus constitutes an important content area of population education. Sexual behaviour is traditionally regulated by customs suited to the requirements of a given society. Now, more than ever, with the grim reality of AIDS, accurate education about sexuality is needed so that learners can make responsible and informed choices that affect their own lives and the lives of others.

A topic such as human sexuality, or anything else, for that matter, may be considered controversial when there is disagreement within the society on whether it should be included in the curriculum. Policy makers are often reluctant to introduce programmes to provide sexual education, services and counselling to youth and the unmarried lest the policy makers be accused by constituents and parents of encouraging precocious sexual activity in these groups, although such a result has never been demonstrated. Further, many health and social workers and extension workers are uncomfortable with the subject matter of human sexuality and unequipped with the knowledge and skills needed to communicate on these subjects. These educators need basic training and information

201

about sexuality, information that will need to be updated periodically. They need to explore their own attitudes to see which ones stem from mistaken beliefs and which are based upon accurate information. They need to understand how their attitudes can affect their responses to learners. Educators and parents need to become comfortable with the issues and to develop skills in relating to learners with sensitivity. They need to develop the ability to see that sexuality is an important part of everyone's personality and that how it is expressed is very much a personal choice and personal responsibility. Finally, they need to understand and be able to work around the attitudes and beliefs of the people, adjusting the educational approach according to the type of resistances encountered.

Training

Because population issues and human sexuality are value-laden, often controversial and fall within an emotional sphere, educators dealing with these issues will need more than basic knowledge and skills in their particular sectors.[18] Teachers dealing with particularly sensitive issues need to be carefully selected and trained for this purpose. The success or failure of population education projects depends to a large extent on the professional competence and motivation of the project staff. There is no single setting best suited to the professional training needs of population education, particularly in view of the varied approaches taken by different ministries plus NGOs. In most regions, a range of institutions can contribute to professional preparation: teachers' colleges, universities and other post-secondary training institutions such as polytechnics, technical and training institutes and agricultural colleges. In most of the established population education programmes in Asia and to a small degree in Africa, universities and teachers' colleges have co-operated with education ministries in promoting the teaching of population education, training personnel, organizing seminars and workshops in which faculty functioned as resource persons and preparing educational materials. In all regions, however, the number of professional training facilities for population educators is inadequate.

The need for professional resources may be met in large part, and in a cost-effective manner, through the establishment of regional training centres in population education. These centres need not be separate from already established institutions; indeed, they may be units in these institutions which have been strengthened to meet the demand for a top-quality educational programme for key fellows from countries throughout the region. Such regional centres would assume responsibility for training the professional population educators up to a diploma or master's-degree level. They might also conduct research, organize seminars and workshops and prepare instructional materials. Increased involvement of the institutions of higher learning in country programmes should facilitate institutionalization of population education through the rapid build-up of national capacity for implementation. It may also heighten the awareness of both government authorities and the public about the importance of the population factors in individual, family, community and national welfare.

A major problem facing out-of-school population education programmes is the low level of knowledge about population issues on the part of the educators when they first become involved in the programmes. These educators come from a variety of fields--agriculture, health, labour, social welfare and education--and population issues as well as innovative education techniques may be new to them. To complicate matters, they usually bring to the job strongly held beliefs and, sometimes, negative attitudes about population issues and family planning.

The task of training field-workers who will be in direct contact with the target audience can be difficult and expensive, especially when they need to be trained in innovative participatory approaches rather than in traditional didactic teaching methods. They also need to learn how to integrate relevant population education concepts and principles into their own work activities. However difficult, providing adequate training for these workers is of vital importance for effective education activities.

Inexperienced project developers may consider it sufficient simply to acquaint field personnel with new information, on the assumption that they will integrate this information properly in their already heavy workload. After only a short in-service training course, however, field-workers will find it difficult to relate population education concepts to their own disciplines and to the daily lives of their clientele, unless their personal feelings are dealt with early in the training activity; the trainer knows how to identify and clarify for the learners how the concepts are important in their work and in serving the well-being of the learner's clientele; and the trainer is able to employ--and thus to demonstrate--participatory training methods in the training of field staff in ways that encourage the latter to use similar strategies in working with their clientele. Indeed, the approach for training field personnel should be similar to the one they, in turn, will use later with their clientele. If trainees are taught by didactic methods alone they cannot be expected to use more open-ended dialectic approaches in working with community members. Similarly, if sophisticated hardware is used in training field educators, but the same equipment is not available in the work setting, much of the training impact may be lost.

Dealing with adolescent fertility

Interregional and intersectoral analyses over a period of years have revealed that early pregnancy and child-bearing is an increasingly serious problem in many countries (see Box 10). The out-of-school group is of top priority in need (by virtue of the numbers involved), but most difficult to reach; the adolescent is rarely included in programme planning, and there is a shortage of personnel who are trained and equipped with the knowledge and skills needed to communicate with young people.

Box 10

ADOLESCENT FERTILITY: THE CHALLENGE TO POPULATION EDUCATION PROGRAMMES IN SCHOOLS AND OUT OF SCHOOLS

Although adolescents are seldom equipped for parenthood, emotionally or intellectually, research shows alarmingly high total fertility rates among teenagers.* Young adolescents are usually still growing when they become pregnant. A pelvis that is developing may be too small to permit normal delivery, leading to complications. In countries with sophisticated medical services, the risks are reduced, but in poor countries with limited facilities the situation is often life-threatening.

The spread of more permissive attitudes towards sex has been exacerbated in some countries by the migration of large numbers of adolescents and youths to cities, where they are often subject to exploitation and to pregnancy and child-bearing. Some young people are forced by economic hardship to abandon the children they cannot care for, who in turn must somehow find a way to survive on the streets.

Although reproductive health services for adolescents have been slow to emerge, stirring controversy nearly everywhere, some excellent programmes have been developed. Some promote young people's active involvement in the provision of health care services, such as participation in multi-purpose youth centres that provide health and family planning services and youth peer counselling. Various countries have taken both intermediate and long-term steps to promote effective action on behalf of adolescents, including intersectoral counselling workshops with key people, to sensitize them to the needs and provide them with skills; appropriate research that will help make policy makers aware of the problems; research employing the human resources and networks of national youth councils to identify realistically the needs and perceptions of the young; training of personnel; development of appropriate teaching and learning materials; and fostering co-operation among concerned agencies.

Despite the evidence, there is a dearth of country data on adolescent reproductive behaviour and of appropriate programme materials. Opposition to sex education, especially in schools, subjective biases and

---

* In large parts of Africa, in Bangladesh in Asia, and in Jamaica and Mexico in Latin America, total fertility rates among teenagers are greater than .75 of a child per woman. The rates for most other developing countries range from .25 to .75 of a child per woman, whereas in Canada and parts of Asia, North Africa and most of Europe, the rates are less than .25. See *World Population Trends and Policies, 1987 Monitoring Report* (United Nations publication, Sales No. E.88.XIII.3), pp. 338-339.

legal constraints limit provision of information and services. Thus the most frequently stated need in many countries is that the community should better understand, support and actively participate in addressing the issue of early pregnancy and child-bearing.

Each of the constraints or adverse consequences can be reduced by intermediate and long-term actions. Intersectoral counselling workshops to sensitize key people to needs and provide them with skills; appropriate research that will help sensitize and inform policy makers; research employing the human resources and networks of national youth councils to identify realistically the needs and perceptions of the young; flexible and dynamic programme designs to meet changing needs; training of personnel; development of appropriate teaching and learning materials; co-operation with other agencies; and the active participation of young people--all these steps are being taken in various countries to reduce the constraints and promote effective action.

The organized health services, as now constituted, are seldom adequate to meet the changing needs of adolescents and youth. Youth should be engaged in the planning, promotion and development of such schemes. There is a further need to review and assess adolescent and youth health and health-related problems in the context of current and emerging socio-economic circumstances.

Planning and managing non-formal population education programmes

In many instances, diverse government and voluntary organizations plan and implement non-formal population education programmes within a country, at national, district and village levels. These agencies have their own priorities in keeping with their mandates. Due to the absence of operational means of co-ordination, co-ordinated programme planning, implementation and monitoring have not always been evident. At times co-ordination may be arranged at the higher levels among senior officials of ministries or central planning offices, but not at the community level among local leaders, field-workers and other educators. The reverse may also be true when village-level service personnel collaborate or, at least, co-operate out of personal friendship. Unfortunately, this is most likely to occur on an *ad hoc* basis and, without political support from above, it may produce only limited results.

Major issues for the future of non-formal population education

The major issues and needs to be considered in the future are somewhat similar for both formal and non-formal population education. A few, however, can be identified as having particular relevance for non-formal population education programmes. Among them are the following:

a) The need to extend the present coverage of non-formal education programmes;

b) The need to make population education part of life-long education;

c) The need to institutionalize non-formal population education, accompanied by increased attention to management and co-ordination issues;

d) The need to strengthen human resources;

e) The need to ensure that project activities correspond to the problems to be solved; and

f) The need to be sensitive to cultural norms and values and differences in gender perception of population issues.

<u>Extending coverage</u>

There is a need to extend the present coverage of non-formal population education activities, because many people in the target audiences are not yet exposed to them. This is particularly important when young people are not reached by school programmes. Although it is possible to reach some of these groups through social and recreational institutions, extension programmes, farm co-operatives, women's groups, the work-place and other educational settings, as well as via the mass media, it is often difficult to achieve. In addition to the logistical problems in reaching all appropriate organized groups, ways must be found to reach those persons who are unlikely to visit community centres, clinics and training centres and those who are unemployed.

<u>Making population education part of life-long education</u>

Population education requires support from policy makers and the community if it is to become a full-fledged part of life-long education.[19] With such support, population education can provide opportunities for learning about appropriate population issues throughout the life-cycle, from pre-school age to the elderly. The types of content provided will, of course, vary according to the setting and the life stages of the participants.

<u>Institutionalizing non-formal population education</u>

To ensure that non-formal education can ultimately be self-sustaining, effective inter-agency and intersectoral co-ordination at the policy and operational levels will be required. Non-formal population education is often handled by a number of ministries and voluntary organizations. Ministerial and institutional arrangements for management, co-ordination and, especially, accountability are often absent and tend to create problems of co-ordination and coherence. Planning should envision the establishment of an inter-ministerial commission or committee to co-ordinate approaches to non-formal population education among responsible entities to ensure comprehensive treatment, so that different sectors reinforce one another's contribution. This is a first step towards institutionalization, as it means that each ministry will have to appoint an official representative to work on improving co-ordination.

Of course, institutionalization means much more. In 1987, an Inter-Agency Task Force on Project Follow-Up and Institutionalization defined institutionalization as the long-term, evolving process whereby the thrust of activities supported by the project is continued after external funding is phased out.[20] Arrangements for institutionalization and follow-up should begin with initial project formulation. They must include the creation of a legal and operational framework for the continuation of activities after external funding has ceased. Full-time national staff must be appointed and funded from local resources, and nationals must be retained after training to ensure follow through.

As an issue in the population field, institutionalization has not yet been studied enough to permit formulae to be developed. Because of the diversity of providers, the process may be more complex in non-formal education than in formal education. In most instances, institutionalization will take a great deal of time, especially in the least developed countries.

Strengthening human resources

Because specific skills are required for integrating population education into other development programmes, efforts must be made to develop cadres of local and national resource persons in each country who will be able to design, plan, manage and evaluate non-formal population education programmes, thus reducing reliance on long-term international experts. Possibilities of using these trained resource persons to assist non-formal population education programmes in neighbouring countries within the region as short-term consultants, especially in the context of TCDC, should be explored. Furthermore, if necessary, the involvement of the local private or commercial sector in specific tasks to support population education should be considered. This would constitute an additional step towards self-reliance and institutionalization.

To what extent should governmental and NGO outreach workers become involved in population programmes (as service providers, counsellors, advocates, educators and motivators conducting small group meetings)? Outreach workers of all kinds could be asked to give their tacit or overt support to family planning. As a minimum, the extension worker should be sufficiently familiar with the country's population programme through training so that he or she can make a referral for education or contraceptive services. In specific situations, extension workers may be able to offer direct support to services. Social workers may have a greater role to play, in view of their direct involvement with families. Their training would thus bear on the contribution they could make to family planning in particular, and to population programmes in general.

In principle, the social worker's approach to family planning would be the same as the approach to other client services. It would include (a) providing clients with facts about family planning services; (b) supporting efforts to obtain sustained medical care; (c) encouraging clients to express their feelings; and (d) clarifying the alternatives that are open to clients and the consequences of these alternatives.[21] Members of women's groups, if trained, can play an important role as advocates and motivators because of their day-to-day contact with all members of the household in their informal role as educators.

Designing projects to meet actual needs

Project objectives as stated in project documents do not always correspond to the problems the project is intended to address. Thus, the content may have little or no bearing on these problems.[22] This complex issue can be a serious problem, wasting time, effort and funds. The problem has several roots. Project objectives are difficult to formulate. Often they are stated, incorrectly, as activities that appear to have no underlying rationale. Organizations, institutions and individual educators may have a "package" of learning materials or a pre-set programme that does not lend itself to the changing needs of the audience. Also, real problems may be perceived by decision makers and educators as too controversial to be dealt with directly. Inadequate or improperly applied research adds another dimension to the problem of content. For example, the educator sometimes emphasizes reproductive anatomy and physiology when what the learner wants to know is how to use a contraceptive device or what side-effects to expect. If research techniques do not enable the educator to "listen" to the learner, content errors are bound to occur.

Among the major issues that have not yet been sufficiently addressed are the implications of early pregnancies; the role of education in rural-urban migration and the need for fostering better communication between parents and children and grand-children concerning family life.

Examining the health implications of early pregnancy

The health implications of early pregnancy is emerging as an issue in a number of countries that have not previously identified it as a problem, and, therefore, have limited experience in developing educational approaches to dealing with it. Age of mother has a direct bearing on the safety of the pregnancy, yet this is a particularly complex problem in countries where early marriage is traditional.

Ascertaining role of education in rural-urban migration

There is a need to clarify and further define the role of education in influencing the migration of youth from rural to urban areas, where life is envisioned as more exciting and attractive than rural life. Rural-urban migration is often encouraged by misinformation. Thus, educational efforts are needed to counteract the misrepresentation of employment opportunities and of the potential for attaining affluent life-styles. Concomitantly, employment and income-generation opportunities are needed in rural areas along with communication activities highlighting the security of rural areas in contrast to crowded conditions of the poor and unskilled migrants living in peri-urban areas.

Offering education to parents and extended families

Education programmes need to enable parents, grand-parents and the extended family to become more cognizant and responsive to the modern sexual norms of adolescents and youth and to become better sexuality educators of their children. The family members need education on population issues emphasizing enhanced communication between parent and child and facilitating parental guidance. Special topics for both generations would include developing responsible behaviour and changing stereotypical attitudes towards both males and females.

Redefining male roles in the context of improving women's status

Improving women's status implies a redefinition of the role and status of men. Gender-role analysis requires thorough discussion. Although women have progressed to some extent in this area, little has been done to help men redefine their roles. Non-formal education for men and boys is a necessary first step in dealing with this issue.

In addition to the issues cited above, the following section on population communication highlights many issues that arise also in non-formal education, among them better use of research techniques, appropriate use of language, prevention of learning gaps, loss of content in training activities, new approaches for adolescent audiences and the implications of AIDS for population education and communication.

Population Communication

Purpose and rationale

The acceptance of population concepts and services is determined not only by the availability of services but also by the degree of interest in, and demand for, those services. Population communication aims at promoting that interest and creating that demand, along with other ways of supporting population programme activities. Thus, communication activities are essential ingredients of population programmes at both national and intercountry levels. Given the vital role of communication in successful population programmes, it is imperative that activities be well conceived, well designed and carefully implemented. Communication strategies need to be feasible, culturally acceptable and financially viable, facilitating programme acceptance within a specified time frame. In addition, the results of those strategies should be measurable.

Because Governments decide on the objectives of national-level population programmes, communication activities vary according to the population policy in a given country. For example, many countries have adopted as a basic principle the right of parents to determine in a free, informed and responsible manner the number and spacing of their children. In such settings, communication complements other programme activities to ensure the availability of information and family planning services.

The reasons for employing communication methods and techniques are many, and they may be grouped under the following broad categories:

a) To identify problems among target audiences, through the application of such research techniques as focus-group discussions (discussions about a forthcoming project or activity among a small, homogeneous group of 8 to 10 people under the guidance of a trained facilitator);

b) To solve problems, using a mix of media and other communication techniques to facilitate understanding of population issues, leading to discussion and problem-solving;

c) To disseminate knowledge of innovative concepts, such as the introduction of new contraceptive technologies;

d) To bridge the gap between professional knowledge and audience understanding of population issues;

e) To motivate selected publics, including policy makers, change-agents, potential contraceptors and other target audiences; and

f) Ultimately, to bring about a desired, voluntary change in behaviour, that is, the adoption of desired practices and services, such as willingness of local residents to be interviewed by census enumerators or to use MCH/FP services.

Governments in developing countries are increasingly employing population communication to further a broad variety of objectives among diverse audiences. Among policy makers and opinion leaders, for example, the Government may aim at drawing attention to population issues as well as to the measures required to deal with them; promoting policy makers' concerns about population factors in development planning exercises; developing a national population policy with popular participation; bridging knowledge gaps on population issues and correcting false rumours about options for dealing with them; and encouraging the revision of gender-biased laws, rules and regulations governing the family or work contracts, especially as they affect employment opportunities and career choices for women.

Among the public or subgroups of the population, the Government may aim at the following:

a) To change traditional attitudes favouring male offspring;

b) To encourage healthy dialogue among young adults and couples about human sexuality and fertility;

c) To motivate young people to delay marriage and to adopt early the practice of planning or spacing pregnancies; and

d) To promote the effective use of contraceptives.

Among administrators and personnel of a population programme, the goals might be the following:

a) To test the suitability of different kinds of contraceptives;

b) To disseminate population concepts to target groups responsible for programme implementation at all levels;

c) To improve management of fertility-regulation services;

d) To motivate change-agents, administrators and managers to incorporate communication components into all population projects;

e) To support training activities, especially in the proper selection of all available and appropriate communication media, channels and technologies (including interpersonal communication); and

f) To improve programme design and management via feedback, through such mechanisms as management information systems (MIS).

Each of the audiences for population communication programmes may have a different set of needs, often requiring different approaches.

Potential participants in a national census will need one type of information. Newly-wed couples will need certain types of family planning information whereas women who have already had several children will need others. Various categories of persons in a community may become audiences requiring specific information to help them decide to support a census campaign, an in-school population education programme, a population policy or a family planning programme.

A number of theories and models regarding the process of behavioural modification guide communicators in their work. Some models outline the movement from a pre-awareness phase to acceptance of a new idea, leading to action. Others outline pre-conditions for behavioural change. These theories are well documented in the professional literature.[23] The following sections of this chapter attempt to demonstrate the experience gained from their application.

Lessons from population communication programmes

Population communication may be viewed as having more than one aim, contributing as it does to enhanced knowledge about population issues or to changing attitudes or to bringing about a voluntarily change in behaviour--or all of these together. Regardless of the particular aim, however, successful population communication is always a two-way process, with information flowing back and forth between the audience and the communication agents. All aspects of that communication entail an exchange of information and ideas. In the initial stage of the process, the target audience is defined and data are collected on the audience's needs and perceptions. Detailed planning takes into account the audience and media characteristics, socio-cultural context, population policy and programme objectives, resource availability, cost-effectiveness etc. All these form the basis of decisions about messages and media, which constitute a second stage of programming. In the second stage messages are developed to meet the needs. The lessons of experience in each of these stages have been distilled below.

Planning and strategy design

■ Roles of research, evaluation and monitoring. As a social process affecting knowledge, attitudes and behaviour, communication involves many interrelated factors. Identifying and integrating these factors in planning is essential for achieving communication impact. To do this, social science research is needed early in project design. Such research helps planners identify the target audience's beliefs, practices and social institutions, focusing on, for example, kinship patterns, religious beliefs, traditional beliefs and practices concerning nutrition and health (particularly birth-spacing), attitudes towards women, economic systems, educational and legal systems, and other cultural features, particularly as related to marriage and childbirth. Research is also essential for learning about the process of adopting family planning; developing sound communication strategies for improving acceptance levels; designing appropriate content of messages and

212

materials; and identifying the most effective way to co-ordinate mixed-media presentations for different target audiences. Communication research may also facilitate the integration of population communication with the communication activities of other development sectors, such as health, agriculture, education and environmental protection.

Like research, evaluation should begin early, in the pre-testing and field evaluation of communication materials and programme activities. These initial evaluation techniques help guide activities so that mistakes in implementation can be avoided or corrected. Pre-testing exercises using interview or focus-group discussion methods provide evidence of how intended audiences will react to messages and presentations--information that can help planners increase the effectiveness and responsiveness of their materials. Focus-group discussions help planners gain insight into the types and content of messages that will best respond to the target audience's specific perceptions and needs. In monitoring programme or project implementation, planners can use the focus-group technique to discover barriers to implementation. This qualitative technique also affords the possibility of presenting findings to research subjects and, in turn, requesting their interpretation of the data.

Such qualitative methods can help planners identify underlying causes of problems from the target group's perspective. Data gathered can also be used to create research instruments that include response categories that are likely to be more appropriate and, therefore, produce more useful results than has been the case with traditional questionnaires. In this connection, planners are giving renewed attention to the knowledge, attitude and practice (KAP) survey as a tool for both planning and evaluation, especially when complemented by other methods such as focus groups.[24]

Another aspect of evaluation concerns the impact of communication carried out in support of family planning or census programmes. The value and quality of evaluation depend greatly on the original planning of the communication components. If the communication component or project is well planned and the objectives well defined, evaluation can far more easily and reliably measure changes in attitudes and behaviour against the short- and long-term behavioural objectives. For this to happen, however, evaluation needs to be part of project design and activities planned with evaluation in mind. Evaluation of a communication component or project can be done internally, on a regular, continuing basis by the project staff, or externally, by an outside evaluation team, or by a combination of both methods. Evaluation results should be disseminated to policy makers and communication planners and, especially, to project implementors to help them keep the project on track or to reorient it, if necessary.

■ Management. Skilled management is essential in orchestrating the complex elements of population programmes, notably in assessing and

213

selecting individuals or teams for specialized training, in assigning appropriate staff to planning exercises, in co-ordinating activities with other organizations and in adhering to budgets for programmes and projects. To be effective, communication programmes require clear objectives, identification of target audiences and appropriate media. This implies the preparation of a master plan--one establishing clear guidelines for the systematic operation of communication activities. Only rarely, however, do population organizations develop such a master communication plan, even when the programme structure includes an IEC unit.

The establishment of communication objectives is an important early need in planning. The planner must do the following:

(a)   Select only those objectives that can reasonably be achieved through communication interventions with target audiences;

(b)   Consider the conditions under which activities will take place;

(c)   Determine the type of change expected; and

(d)   Decide what criteria will be used to measure success.

Communication activities should consist of more than a series of short-term campaigns; they should constitute a coherent programme with mutually supporting media, approaches and consistent messages.

If communication support is to become--as it should--an integral part of MCH/FP activities as well as of census and policy support activities, concepts need to be accepted by service providers and managers as well as by those charged with specific responsibility for communication activities. It is vital that the art of listening to an audience be introduced as a planning tool--as a prerequisite to the implementation of a successful family planning activity. Co-ordination between services and communication activities also needs to be ensured if communication is to become a useful support activity. A "mix" of approaches may be required in the MCH/FP field, just as in data collection or census projects combining mass and interpersonal communication to win both public acceptance of survey teams and public co-operation in census activities.

The complexity of designing a communication component within a project quickly becomes evident in preparations for a national census. Audiences need to be identified, census personnel require training in communication skills, and messages need to be developed to facilitate census-taking among the public--all of which calls for careful research. Once a strategy is developed for the activity, a work plan can be designed, which, for such a complex set of activities, would include the production of materials, procurement of audio-visual equipment for materials production and projection or display of materials, and the training of census takers.

The process of developing communication support for an MCH/FP project would be the same, although some target audiences would be different. The following types of MCH/FP audiences may be identified:

(a)   Policy makers (political leaders, religious leaders, health officials and project planners);

(b)   Project implementors (central, provincial, district and village officials, and field health personnel); and

(c)   Pre-adolescent children, youth, adults of child-bearing age and older citizens and other influential individuals in both rural and urban communities.

A work plan for a typical communication programme would include the following:

(a)   Segmentation and setting priorities for various target audiences and themes;

(b)   Research on the type of information each group needs;

(c)   Decisions on how to convey "messages" (choices of media, channels etc.);

(d)   Preparation of materials, including pre-testing and revision;

(e)   Training in how to use the materials;

(f)   Attention to distribution and re-supply systems; and

(g)   Provision for follow-up and supervision.

■   Initial selection of themes. An important preliminary to the design of any communication programme is research on the potential audience to ascertain not only their needs but their perceptions of what is important. Only with this knowledge can a planner design appropriate communication programmes that will be meaningful to the audience. Once this step has been carried out, the process of materials development can begin--usually with decisions on message concepts, the approach to message design and the selection of the channel for delivery, e.g., single or multiple channels, interpersonal reinforcement for group or mass audiences. Once the prototype materials have been produced, pre-testing takes place with a sample of the target audience. The materials are rated for their attention-getting power and comprehensibility. At this point communicators would also check for appropriateness of the channel selected and for possibilities of reinforcement, revising and re-testing materials as required. Production of final materials requires careful attention to any problems uncovered during the pre-testing stage.

■ <u>Training programmes</u>. Population communication training programmes have been conducted in all regions during the past 20 years as part of general MCH and family planning training to improve the skills of health and family planning personnel. Accumulated experience suggests that training must promote collaboration between communication and service personnel to ensure that "messages" sent through communication activities correspond to the reality of the service situation. Training programmes should emphasize that communication performs a support function for services, and such support can be done well only with collaborative planning and implementation.

IEC officers also need to develop skills in communication planning and strategy development, group dynamics and techniques of message analysis. Training in research would include interviewing techniques, designing cross-cultural research, pre-testing practical evaluation techniques and data interpretation.

<u>Media selection</u>

Media selection and related production of software or content are crucial elements in undertaking communication activities. Among the many possibilities for communication activities are broad-based media campaigns, using both mass and traditional or folk-media channels, for both awareness creation and programme support; more narrowly defined support activities using a variety of communication techniques and channels; or a mixture of both.

Selection of the most effective kinds of communication activities and channels depends upon the nature of the objectives, the target audience, the media within the geographical area and the local culture. Sensitivity to all of the above factors is required by communicators and programme managers alike. For example, in a campaign designed to sensitize political leaders to support their country's national MCH/FP programme, an interpersonal approach, using back-up support of audio-visual and print materials, might be employed. To reach an urban audience, the communication planner may, for example, decide upon the co-ordinated employment of radio, television, film, video presentations, popular stage productions, telephone, newspapers, posters and pamphlets and an array of interpersonal reinforcements for selected groups. In a rural setting, on the other hand, the communication planner may rely more on interpersonal techniques with community leaders and women's groups, backed by radio and folk media. The strengths and weaknesses of these media are reviewed below.

■ <u>Mass media approaches</u>. Mass media can be instrumental in promoting community participation in a population activity: they can generate and reflect public opinion, encourage dialogue between community and health providers; open channels for feedback from the community to the decision makers; and help mobilize and maintain political support for family planning programmes. When planned to support a country's

216

health and education infrastructure at the community level, the value of mass media in a population programme becomes apparent. However, it is crucial that the messages issued through the mass media be synchronized with those issued by outreach personnel. Sometimes communication programmes launched through the mass media bypass health and education personnel, especially those operating in rural settings. Not only can this create confusion and counter-productive activity, but when this happens there is no way to correct misinformation or to counter false rumours. In short, without the link between the mass media campaign and the outreach personnel, there is little opportunity for feedback to correct any flaws. To create this link, programmes must train health personnel and community education and welfare personnel and equip them with communication materials before media campaigns are begun.

The production phase includes creating inventories of raw materials, human resources, budget planning and scheduling. Pre-tests of materials and research on media usage generally determine scheduling decisions about the volume of mass production and distribution of materials as well as release dates for film, TV and live theatre performances.

Almost all family planning programmes in developing nations have used radio to reach their audiences. In some countries, because of its capacity to reach large, illiterate audiences scattered over wide geographical distances at low cost, radio is the most important mass medium. There are an estimated 1,650 million radios in the world--1 for every 4 persons.[25] In Latin America, there is 1 radio for every 3 persons; in Asia and Sub-Saharan Africa, 1 for every 10 persons. (These figures, of course, are notional, because not all sets are in working condition, and limited power supply may restrict usage to certain hours of the day.) Radio production is inexpensive compared with other media and, unlike television and film, receivers do not necessarily require external power if batteries or solar equipment are available. Radio listening is convenient: people can listen while doing other things; it is entertaining; and units can be carried everywhere.

In many developing countries, radio broadcast facilities are government-owned or controlled; thus, if policies support population programmes, radio time should be readily available, though this is not always the case because of the complexities of ministerial co-ordination.

India, the Philippines and the Republic of Korea were among the first countries to establish strong national family planning policies, and their government-owned radio stations have long been employed on behalf of the national population programmes. As early as 1964, in the Songdong area of Seoul, radio, home visits and other media were used to tell 45,000 women about contraceptive services. In the Hyderabad district of Pakistan, where radio spot announcements on family planning were broadcast daily, 64 per cent of women using family planning clinics reported having heard family planning messages on radio (see Box 11).[26]

Box 11

POPULAR MEDIA FOR POPULATION MESSAGES

In many countries, radio soap operas are being used to convey family planning messages. In radio programmes in Colombia, Costa Rica and the Dominican Republic, family planning information has been woven into the broader topic of human sexuality. The *Dialogo* programme in Costa Rica, which has been carried on the country's most popular commercial radio stations, has reached more than one fourth of the population with messages on such topics as family planning, reproduction, venereal disease, marriage, divorce, nutrition and responsible parenthood. In China, one of the most wide-reaching radio programme formats for family planning messages is the popular Chinese opera/drama.

Radio programming is flexible, permitting different audiences to be reached in different ways: through spot announcements that can be repeated often; interview programmes with health experts responding to questions from a studio audience, or via telephone or letters; panel discussions and round tables; and popular songs with family planning themes, as in Latin America, where two well-known teen-age entertainers, Tatiana and Johnny, presented a song on the theme of sexual responsibility.*

Magazines for women and teenagers have also been important channels of population information in many countries, especially in the Philippines and the Republic of Korea. Without information from knowledgeable population sources, however, articles in magazines are not invariably up to date or accurate.

Comic books have been used successfully in many countries, especially in Colombia, Costa Rica, Indonesia, Mexico, the Philippines and Thailand. They reach the literate population and attract more than children and teen-age readers. Comics help many of the newly literate, and they have become a way of maintaining literacy because their illustrations and simple text provide useful reading exercises. Agriculture, health and family planning are among the popular comic themes for the newly literate rural population. For the urban poor and youth, such topics as romance, happy family stories, affluence and fantasy are popular.**

---

* Patrick Coleman, "The power of popular music", *People*, vol. 13, No. 2 (1986), pp. 11-12.

** Everett M. Rogers, Douglas Solomon and Ronny Adhikarya, *Further Directions for USAID's Communication Policies in Population* (Palo Alto, California, Institute for Communication Research, Stanford University, 1978).

Studies and reports through the late 1970s concluded that radio was a primary source of information about family planning in Honduras and Kenya. In Colombia, Costa Rica and the Dominican Republic, radio increased contraceptive adoption rates.[27] The same studies revealed that the recall rate for family planning information communicated through radio was 69 per cent in Pakistan and 36 per cent in Nigeria.

Three major problems have been encountered in using radio.[28] First, population officials are rarely permitted to specify when their messages should be used. Most population programmes are given free access to radio, but even government-operated radio stations also accept paid advertising. Hence, stations usually air public-service announcements when the audience is smallest. The second problem is the lack of follow-up, by interpersonal communication or printed or visual materials. In general, radio can best provide information on the "what" and "where" about family planning. However, as demonstrated in India, radio forums (listeners' groups) can help motivate listeners to become acceptors. Most radio forum programmes provide their audience with feedback opportunities (as evidenced in correspondence received by the Costa Rican *Dialogo* programme, distribution of pamphlets related to the radio programme content in the Philippines and phone-in radio shows in the United States of America). The third problem is the difficulty in tailoring programme content to the needs of different socio-cultural or linguistic groups within a country.

Films are also a popular vehicle for population information. Films about family planning and population may be motivational, informational or instructional--dealing with "how to" aspects. One professionally made colour film with a population and family planning awareness message competed well in an urban commercial market, attracting a substantial paying audience.[29] However, film is not always the most appropriate medium. In 1971, the private Family Planning Council of Nigeria launched a communication programme centred around a full-length colour film designed to create awareness about family planning. Titled *My Brother's Children*, the film was made for one of Nigeria's largest tribes, the Yoruba. Drawing on Yoruba culture and played by Yoruba actors, the film tried to place family planning within the context of traditional family life attitudes. To enhance the film's effectiveness, an accompanying multimedia approach employed publicity in newspapers and on radio and a television showing of the film. Copies were provided to branches of the Council, health centres, clinics and hospitals, and screenings were often followed by a talk and open discussion. Yet, a study in an experimental and a control village concluded that viewing the film had not contributed to any significant changes in attitudes towards family planning. Failure was attributed to the villagers' unfamiliarity with film as a medium and problems with message comprehension.[30] Limited familiarity with a particular medium has been identified as an obstacle to effective communication in other cultural settings, for example, as in the early use of television in rural Egypt.

219

Moreover, content analysis has shown that many population films are overloaded with information on demographic projections and the economics of population control.[31] Content is also affected by the professional calibre of the film-makers. Another problem is that distribution channels are rarely well developed for films not produced for the commercial market, depending upon individual showings by public or private agencies with limited audience potential. Finally, film production is expensive, and showings demand an external power supply and careful maintenance.

None the less, film can be an important medium, provided the personnel involved are well trained, funds for production are sufficient, distribution channels are available and film is culturally acceptable as an educational medium. Film has aural and visual impact. In many countries--notably Bangladesh, India, Indonesia, Malaysia, Mexico and Pakistan--film as well as other audio-visual aids, such as slide-tape presentations, are shown in mobile audio-visual units. These units make regular visits to rural areas and usually combine entertainment and information. In India and Turkey, in conjunction with mobile audio-visual unit visits, medical staff provide contraceptive services. However, such units may be impractical in most countries because of the resources needed to use films properly with mobile units. For example, it has been estimated that even if each district in India had its own mobile van, it would take eight years to visit each village only once.[32]

In developing nations, television is often available only to urban dwellers. However, television may play an important role in reaching policy makers and decision makers as well as the urban public, which makes up a sizeable portion of the population in many countries. In 1987, the Nigeria Television Authority measured the impact of television on the family planning attitudes of urban Nigerians. Family planning themes on a wide range of topics, including contraceptives and health benefits of birth-spacing, had been woven into 39 episodes of an already popular television drama. During the first nine months of this project, two spot announcements per episode advertised the family planning clinic at the local university hospital. For the last four months, one of these spots was replaced by an advertisement of a new clinic opened by the Ministry of Health. A recall survey and source-of-referral monitoring scheme used by the university clinic generated data demonstrating the campaign's effectiveness. The number of new clients who attended the university clinic was significantly higher after the broadcast, and 43 per cent of the new clients named television as their source of referral.[33]

Like radio, television can avail itself of many forms of presentation--live shows, video and film--potentially any audio-visual product. A big plus is video tapes, which can be programmed rapidly, used repeatedly and kept for reference. Video tapes are also sometimes used in vehicles travelling to rural areas for awareness creation and other activities.

Video technology is also a compatible medium for use in rural development projects. Its advantages are several:

(a)   The relative ease with which a recorded video programme can be edited. In rural training, video cassettes have not only provided information and demonstrated improved farming techniques but also elicited and recorded farmers' reactions to new methods, which can then be incorporated into the original programmes and shown in other communities.

(b)   Programmes and materials can be tailor-made for each situation. Culture-specific strategies can be incorporated, thereby leading to appropriate presentations for the given audience; and

(c)   The communications skills of extension workers can be evaluated by recording and analysing the playback of the presentation.[34]

Experience has shown, however, that three ingredients are essential to successful use of video: (a) a clear idea of how it will be used, (b) a training programme for personnel using the equipment and (c) a plan for integrating it into a systematic methodology for rural training or information dissemination. FAO has refined procedures for video-based training in rural areas based on experiences in many Latin American countries, among them Brazil, Honduras, Mexico and Peru, and in several French-speaking West African countries. This training guideline emphasizes using video not as a single medium but in combination with discussion and printed materials as a complete learning package.[35]

Newspapers have the advantage of reaching a predetermined audience. Moreover, they are considered authoritative: the more literate, urban and middle-class the readership, the higher newspapers rank as a source of information.[36] Other print materials can communicate through illustrations. Although posters and billboards are useful, they require either a literate audience or the prerequisite of extensive pre-testing.

In the early stages of developing family planning programmes in many countries, newspapers were used as a communication channel to reach elites and policy makers, whose support was needed. In countries such as Egypt, Indonesia, the Philippines and the Republic of Korea newspapers have effectively contributed to policy makers' favourable attitudes towards family planning. Many believe that the press has made important contributions to the strong government support for the population programmes in these countries.

Newspapers have also been used to reach a different target audience, the literate public, in a variety of ways, such as advertisements, articles and news stories. However, the result has been generally discouraging. Analyses of newspaper articles about population indicate that much of the content is organization-oriented, such as government officials' speeches, news about adoption rates or reports of field visits. Such news is of little direct relevance to potential acceptors. Outside the outreach of an organized population programme, newspaper articles on family planning are often informative rather than motivational or persuasive; many tend to be neutral, rather than favourable, to the practice of contraception. In addition, there seems to be a tendency for newspapers to report disproportionately about side-effects or to include unfavourable stories about contraception.

However, when population project administrators and communicators have used news media, the stories about population and family planning have been integrated into treatments of broader social and economic development issues, such as unemployment, housing, education, hunger, nutrition, mother and child health and the role of women. In Asia, Depthnews, which provides service to more than three hundred newspapers in Asia with an estimated total circulation in the millions, publishes items on how population issues are affecting economic and social progress in Asian societies.[37] The news and feature network Inter Press Service provides materials on all aspects of development issues, including population, to subscribing media outlets in every region.

Magazines, pamphlets and comic books are also important channels of population information (see Box 11), and have several advantages if they are prepared with the help of the intended target audience. They can provide relevant information and, if they deal with commonly asked questions, be highly valuable, as evidenced in clients' references to such materials in discussions with health workers.

There are problems, however, in the distribution of printed materials; in many instances, IEC workers lack sufficient quantities because few programmes devote much attention to creating a system to keep field staff informed about, and supplied with, printed materials. Another problem is that many IEC materials are not thoroughly pre-tested.

Multimedia campaigns and approaches

Communication campaign strategies have probably been used more widely for family planning communication than for any other development work. One problem, however, is that often a series of campaigns are undertaken, not a coherent ongoing multimedia programme. Campaigns need to be based on coherent communication objectives among specific target audiences. The most effective media interventions are those that are co-ordinated with family planning services, as in Jamaica, Nigeria, Mexico and the Republic of Korea.

Awareness levels are enhanced when several media, rather than just one medium, are used. In Egypt, the State Information Service (SIS) in 1979 began a family planning communication project using newspapers, billboards and face-to-face contacts. Verses from the Koran and the Bible supporting family planning were stressed, especially in broadcasts to rural areas. SIS officials maintained personal contact with audiences through seminars held in local offices for social workers, nurses, health workers, midwives and religious leaders. Health workers, usually women from the village, acted as liaisons between villagers and the local offices. Results from a 1983 evaluation indicated that the SIS project had successfully achieved increased awareness of family planning.[38]

A more recent successful multimedia campaign was the 1986 effort to promote sexual responsibility among young adults in Latin America. The campaign, launched in Mexico, was based on the premise that popular music could promote the concept of sexual responsibility among the teen-age populace. Two songs with strong commercial appeal were featured in records, music videos, TV commercials and public radio spots. Colour posters, brochures, press kits with colour slides and press releases were prepared for mass media outlets. Through frequent radio airings the songs became very popular and won many awards. A 1987 evaluation showed that the target population had absorbed the messages--not to marry too young or in a hurry; not to enter into sexual relationships before both partners are ready. Although the songs alone did not achieve the goal of encouraging large numbers of people to seek sexual guidance, the public-service announcements covered these points. Overall, the campaign promoted reflection upon the wisdom of having sexual relations at an early age, and the project was judged successful at both commercial and social levels.[39] A somewhat similar UNFPA-supported UNESCO project was conducted in Mexico in 1976 with comparable results.[40]

A telephone service with information about family planning services, launched in Seoul in 1972, was designed to reach people not previously served by the national programme.[41] A majority of the callers, 59 per cent, were male--a group not adequately served by the national programme at that time. A follow-up of selected callers showed that of 530 men referred to a health centre or hospital for a vasectomy, 103 underwent the operation. Thus, there was a positive relationship between the accompanying advertising campaign, availability of the telephone service and the use of family planning services.

An innovation of the Planned Parenthood Federation of Korea (PPFK) in the Republic of Korea was the installation of some 16 Population Clock towers, which digitally monitor the nation's population growth. The clock is supported by a statue holding up the clock with outstretched arms, denoting the pressure of the growing population. The clock changes every 50.1 seconds signifying the addition of one more person to the country's population. These clocks, which were placed strategically in busy sections of the provinces, serve as constant reminders of the steady population increase and are thought to have been more influential than any other population communication message.

Today's commercial sector commands a great deal of expertise in modern communication techniques. Because family planning messages are competing with commercial advertising for the same audience's

223

attention, they need to be of the same high quality, with the same attention-getting devices. Cost-effectiveness is enhanced when family planning programmes engage the services of commercial specialists or insert messages in existing commercial advertising activities rather than duplicate audio-visual equipment and production skills. PPFK was one of the early experimenters in attracting the support of other sectors for communication activities. With government backing, PPFK held family planning seminars for top executives, middle managers and personnel directors and presented lectures for employees. As a follow-up, PPFK proposed inserting specific family planning slogans into commercial advertisements and asked the Government to send, in the name of the Minister of Health and Social Affairs, an official request for co-operation from each participating firm. As a result, pharmaceutical, cosmetics and food companies became affiliated with the Ministry of Health and Social Affairs, and incorporated family planning messages into their television commercials.

One major advantage of such an endeavour is the repetition of family planning messages, which reinforces awareness. Another advantage is the demonstration to audiences of a broad social base of support for family planning beyond the normal health channels. At the same time, the industries enhance their reputation for social responsibility. The Korean programme has demonstrated the lesson that the concerted efforts of private family planning groups, Government and industries can create a major impact on public attitudes and practices. By the end of 1985, the population growth rate, which had been at the 3 per cent level in the 1960s, had dropped to 1.2 per cent. The family planning practice rate of couples had increased from 9 per cent in the early 1960s, to 70 per cent at the end of 1985.[42] This project further demonstrates the benefits that can be derived from careful management, co-ordination and follow-up, as well as the importance of involving mass media specialists as an audience for family planning before they attempt to design messages for the public.

In Jamaica, although multimedia approaches have served to create an overall positive attitude towards family planning, about half the women of child-bearing age still do not seek contraceptive services (see Annex Table 1). In 1982, the National Family Planning Board (NFPB) of Jamaica stepped up its activities with a two-child campaign message. Multimedia advertising for radio, soap operas, television, newspapers and billboards carried the message: "two is better than too many". In 1984, another two-child theme was introduced emphasizing the economic pressures making it more and more expensive to bring up children. The emphasis was that each child is entitled to a "fair share". The 1985 campaign developed to reach teenagers used the song "You Got to Be a Woman", performed by a leading female reggae artist and promoted by a leading disc jockey to launch the campaign. Becoming an instant hit, the song was reinforced by radio and television advertisements about a young schoolgirl getting pregnant, deserted by friends and left alone with her problem.

Even more widely followed, perhaps, is the Family Planning Association's radio soap opera *Naseberry Street*, with a story line centred on a family planning clinic. Written by a successful local dramatist, this drama was first broadcast in February 1985 and is on the air three times a week for l5 minutes. An estimated 85 per cent of the adult population listen to radio, and studies have shown that *Naseberry Street* is reaching its target audience of low-income women of reproductive age. A 1984 evaluation found that awareness of family planning messages exceeded 94 per cent for the age group 15-45. Over 72 per cent were convinced that "two is better than too many", and 35 per cent said they would try to persuade others to go to family planning clinics. Still, practice remains low. A survey revealing the principal reasons--fear of side-effects and of the partner's attitude towards family planning--pinpointed a need for counselling and follow-up services. However, those needs are difficult to meet given financial constraints and strict foreign loan rules prohibiting the Government from employing additional staff.[43]

In Kenya, with one of the fastest growing populations in the world, Chogoria Hospital has been able to reduce the fertility rate in its district. A private institution founded in 1922, the hospital is now run by the Presbyterian Church of East Africa. According to the 1984 Kenya Contraceptive Prevalence Survey the fertility rate for women in Chogoria was 5.2 as compared with 7.7 for Kenya in its entirety. The results of a survey conducted by the U.S. Center for Disease Control in 1985 demonstrated that 43 per cent of married women in the Chogoria area used some form of contraception, whereas the rate was 20 per cent for the country as a whole. To achieve its goal, Chogoria employed the services of volunteer family health workers, and trained traditional birth attendants, nurses and field educators who were in constant contact with their audiences and with one another, thereby providing the feedback essential for responsive programming.[44] Also, attention was directed to couples, as opposed to women alone.

Interpersonal communication

Although the media play a major role in increasing awareness, the closing of the gap that exists between awareness of family planning and the practice of contraception remains the second major function of population communication--to bring about behavioural change. The key to behavioural change is interpersonal--that is, face-to-face-- communication in clinics and in the home. Face-to-face communication is the only way to counsel individual members of a target group, to respond to individual needs and, in so doing, to facilitate contraceptive decision-making. Interpersonal communication is thus at the heart of any family planning IEC strategy.

Good interpersonal communication calls for an understanding of the subject matter to be discussed. It also requires empathy as well as knowledge and skills in group and individual psychology and group dynamics. It demands sensitivity to the needs and views of others, listening skills and attitudes favourable to working with people as a trusted helper, rather than as an authority telling people what to do. For all these reasons, training in interpersonal communication techniques is crucial. Such training needs to include how to put the client at ease, how to ask open-ended questions, what to say about methods, how to relax when discussing sexuality and how to use educational materials appropriately.

Although interpersonal communication in clinics and in homes has few disadvantages *per se*, its use has been constrained by the high costs of recruiting, training and deploying personnel. The use of intermediaries is one means of drawing upon the strengths of this technique in cost-effective ways.

<u>Intermediaries</u>

The use of interpersonal intermediaries along with other forms of communication has been successful in countries carrying out innovative family planning work, such as Thailand and Costa Rica, where progress has been made in removing the taboos surrounding family planning and sex education. The programmes in these countries have relied extensively on using influential members of the community, outreach workers and celebrities in co-ordinated activities. In Thailand, the community-based Family Planning Services programme desensitized the topic of family planning and contraceptive devices to make communication less private, less confidential in tone and less anxiety-producing. At the same time, in a nation-wide endeavour, the programme expanded access to, and information about, contraceptive methods using each community's own personnel and resources--trained village outreach workers, mass media, market women and village distributors of contraceptives. Local schools, monks, police and district officers collaborated in making contraceptives available to people in the community and in dealing effectively with taboos and troublesome rumours.

To legitimize contraceptive supplies the local Buddhist monk's blessing was obtained for a shipment of contraceptive devices in the village. Once legitimized, the contraceptive products were treated like any other commodity and distributed through grocery shops, eating stalls, coffee shops, beauty parlours and tailors. In towns, pills and condoms were available through mail deliverers, taxi-drivers and schoolteachers. Film stars and traditional travelling entertainers were recruited as bearers of family planning messages. In one year, 370 troupes performing shadow plays incorporated family planning messages before audiences totalling some 7 million persons. The entertainers also personally distributed pills and condoms. Throughout that year, desensitizing campaigns were held in public gatherings and fairs, as well as through institutionalized channels such as factories and schools. Students in schools learned to sing family planning songs and to play a game called "snakes and ladders" based on family planning messages printed on cloth.

In Costa Rica, the experience of Centro de Orientacion Familiar (COF) offered many lessons in new strategies of integrating birth control and family planning into meaningful perspectives for people unaccustomed to discussing issues related to human sexuality. COF produced *Dialogo*, a radio programme on human sexuality broadcast throughout the country, which generated thousands of letters from listeners. The letters were analysed to form the substance of each *Dialogo* programme and personally answered by mail, thereby uniting mass and interpersonal communication. In this case the intermediary between communicators and listeners was a popular radio announcer, a trusted voice in the religious community of Costa Rica.[45]

Social and cultural organizations

Many countries have successfully used social and cultural organizations in population and family planning programmes. Indonesia established an effective health delivery infrastructure at the village level consisting of village centres operated under locally enlisted volunteers. The centres recruited and supported acceptors and distributed pills and condoms. In Bali, the *banjar* groups, which are traditional gathering points for village recreation and ceremonies, have been used for providing information and recruiting acceptors. As part of an effort to promote maternal health, Mothers' Clubs in the Republic of Korea were used as centres for population and family planning. A national survey of Mothers' Clubs revealed a great improvement in the status of women vis-à-vis family decisions on child-spacing and communications with parents-in-law.

Social marketing

Advertising for social purposes has been tried in several population programmes, especially on behalf of family planning (see Box 12). In 1961, an Indian effort supported by the Ford Foundation and developed by the Indian Institute for Management in Calcutta helped to market "Nirodh" condoms (Nirodh means "protection"). The Nirodh campaign promoted distribution in retail outlets, free distribution in family planning clinics and a rural volunteer sales programme involving a sales network of six large commercial companies. The Nirodh programme was considered highly innovative and successful because of links with widespread marketing networks and because of consultation with medical and religious leaders in naming the products to be sold to the public.

Box 12

**SOCIAL MARKETING: EXPANDING
CONTRACEPTIVE DISTRIBUTION**

Social marketing of contraceptives is one way of expanding coverage rapidly at minimal cost. Most social marketing projects in family planning supplement rather than replace the national clinic-based systems. The community-based distribution (CBD) system of Thailand uses a social marketing approach through which distributors sell pills and condoms,

227

keeping a small portion of the low price for themselves. The village distributor is integrated into the district's health care team. All acceptors of family planning are credited to the government programme.* There are social marketing programmes in India, Indonesia and Sri Lanka as well. In Africa, both Ghana and Kenya have used social marketing successfully in distributing condoms and foam. Jamaica also used this technique to recruit clinic acceptors.

World Fertility Surveys and Contraceptive Prevalence Surveys show that approximately 70 per cent of the population in many countries secure their contraceptive services and supplies from non-clinic sources. This is because shopkeepers and commercial sources serve clients directly with a minimal amount of red tape--with little waiting, at low cost and often with much free advice. To "market" the clinic services, service providers need to treat clients politely and pay attention to their needs; otherwise people will turn to other forms of promotion that are unlikely to produce long-term users.

A similar social marketing approach was developed in 1974 in Sri Lanka. This co-operative venture between the Government and IPPF was called the "Preethi" or condom campaign ("Preethi" means "joy" in the two major languages spoken in Sri Lanka). The campaign, preceded by comprehensive market research, succeeded in selling condoms as a regular household product, promoted among potential retailers through the distribution of booklets and free samples of the product. The appeal to the potential retailer pictured the salesperson as a pioneer who cared about the country's problems. By the end of the first year, some 300,000 condoms per month were being sold.[46] Besides programmes in India, Indonesia, Sri Lanka and Thailand, two African countries--Ghana and Kenya--have used social marketing successfully in distributing condoms and foam. Jamaica also used this technique to recruit clinic acceptors.

Clinic-based communication

MCH/FP clinics use communication support programmes to let their clients, or potential service users, know about available services and to provide motivation for practising family planning. Little research has been done on the use of clinics as a forum for population communication; one of the few studies found that patients in six Latin American clinics spent only 5 minutes out of 65 minutes in the clinic with the physician or nurse. Thus, the amount of information that a client could learn from a busy professional is limited. However, a great potential exists for using the waiting time educationally. The clinic milieu is well suited for the group

---

* Everett M. Rogers, Douglas Solomon and Ronny Adhikarya, *Further Directions for USAID's Communication Policies in Population* (Palo Alto, California, Institute for Communication Research, Stanford University, 1978).

media approach; that is, video, slide-tapes, film strips, audio-cassettes, overhead transparencies, flip charts and photographs. Research is essential for determining the content of these media.

In the design of clinic-based communication programmes, research using focus-group discussions was found appropriate. In Thailand, that technique was used for learning how to integrate AIDS prevention communication into the work of health clinics in rural and urban areas. The focus-group technique stimulates the expression of opinions and basic attitudes among clients. Client opinions, in turn, give insights into the type and content of the messages that should be used in a subsequent communication intervention. Most importantly, the techniques provide immediate feedback and reaction concerning identified topics.

The role of public health nurses and clinic technical staff is most crucial in communication with clients. It is, therefore, vital that the training of these personnel in how to listen to clients be made an integral part of the programme. Though it is rarely carried out, communication training can help health and family planning personnel better understand their clients and improve their communication with them. Training can help personnel identify such important factors as whether clinic hours are suited to women's schedules and how women perceive the need and existence (or non-existence) of privacy in the clinic setting. Ideally, personnel also need a certain level of skill in the production of audio-visual materials for daily use at the clinics or in the mobile teams reaching out to the villages. Practical training should permit the health and welfare personnel to design and produce their own cost-effective materials for such specific audiences as rural women, out-of-school youth and mothers' classes. Personnel also require training in using existing materials, such as flip charts.

Traditional media and communication institutions

In rural and peri-urban areas of the developing world, traditional media and channels are recommended, especially when they are integrated with the mass media.[47] Traditional media include folk theatre, puppet shows, song-and-dance performances, string configurations combined with storytelling, and symbol-laden textile arts, among others. Traditional or folk forms are age-old methods for communicating messages, and their potential is being increasingly explored in population and development programmes in many countries. The advantage of these media over the mass media is that the messages are legitimized by the familiarity of the artists, who are known within the community, and the costuming, music and dance. The messages therefore appear credible.[48]

Traditional puppet shows, folk theatre, folk opera, travelling poets, singers and story-tellers are widely used for family planning programmes in Asian countries, notably India, Indonesia and Pakistan, and in Africa and Latin America. Live theatre performances and puppet shows have also been used in census preparation campaigns. In Latin America, many theatre-for-development activities have served as rallying points for social action.

An innovative family planning project in Ogun state, Nigeria, attempts to "market" clinic services through traditional media. On the evening before market day in a particular village, a travelling mobile theatre group performs a social drama with a family planning theme. Nurses are available after the performance to answer questions, lead discussions and motivate both men and women to visit the clinics. Non-prescription contraceptives are also available for distribution.

Research is important for linking performances with the real interests and needs of the audience. Although more research is needed on traditional media and on the effectiveness of the extension of live performances into the mass media (for multiplier effect), the approach is being increasingly employed within the developing world. Training to help artists improve their performance skills and to sensitize them to population issues is an important requirement. Thousands of *dalangs* (puppeteers) of Indonesia's Wayang Kulit shadow puppet tradition receive both new and refresher training from population programme authorities.

A UNESCO conference on the integration of folk media and mass media for family planning produced valuable guidelines for folk media in family planning programmes. These guidelines emphasized the importance of selecting the most appropriate folk form for development or population communication, and of combining folk and mass media presentation.[49]

Major issues for the future of population communication

To improve the effectiveness of communication interventions programme planners need to address a number of issues touching upon all critical areas of communication activity: research methods to understand target audiences, message design and presentation, media selection, media mix and integration of media. In addition, inter-agency and intersectoral co-ordination is needed in designing messages, disseminating information, mobilizing and allocating resources, promoting public- and private-sector collaboration and fostering a phased approach to communication planning.

Qualitative research techniques

Better use of existing research techniques and the development of new techniques are needed to enhance popular participation in population activities. As a 1987 World Bank publication noted, development projects would be more effective if they incorporated the points of view of the intended beneficiaries.[50] Various innovative communication research techniques may be employed to learn these points of view. One of the problems is that qualitative methods, which enable communicators to listen to an audience before messages are designed, have been used less frequently than the more familiar quantitative methods such as surveys with close-ended questions, which are easier to measure. Too little qualitative research is being conducted, and what there is is sometimes inappropriate.

The need for getting closer to the participants and developing people-oriented approaches has occupied a prominent place in health education literature for years,[51] and continues to surface from time to time under different terminology--e.g., "user perspective", "participatory approach" and "client-responsive family planning". Even after all these years, however, the concept is still poorly understood by those who should be implementing it. Renewed emphasis has recently been placed on the need to "develop workable techniques for identifying local people's needs, problems and preferences and incorporate this information directly into the design and operation of programmes and into the evaluation of their effectiveness".[52] This is very much a "women's issue".

Operations research is especially important for developing specific, problem-solving communication strategies and plans. In the design of KAP surveys, renewed attention should be given to the target audience, to learn why messages have not been accepted. When properly conducted, KAP surveys can produce results that can be used in communication strategy development and programme planning. The survey needs to employ both quantitative methods, through sample surveys for base-line data collection, and qualitative methods. The results may uncover the reasons for negative attitudes or inappropriate practice--attitudes or behaviours that are often related to specific socio-cultural, economic or psychological factors, rather than the technology (for example, the contraceptive methods).

Focus-group discussions are one method of obtaining such qualitative information for designing strategies and activities or for designing specific messages to overcome negative attitudes. Through this technique it is possible to gain important information about how specific audiences perceive population and related issues. Insight can be gained into such variables as levels of awareness, vocabulary, cultural sanctions (especially perceptions about women) and other social and psychological characteristics that influence behaviour, motivation and learning. Because group situations alleviate much of the pressure present in other types of interviewing, individuals may feel more relaxed when they realize they are not obliged to react to every question posed and that their views are shared by others.[53] Another method is that of individual interviews, which, although conducive to confidentiality, do not yield the wide spectrum of responses available in a group situation. Interviewing is a useful follow-up to focus-group discussions for probing more deeply into individual concerns and fears. It may also be appropriate when there are too few people of homogeneous background to organize a focus group.

Two other qualititative research methods in addition to focus groups and in-depth interviews are direct observation and ethnographic profiles. The need for research to enhance people's participation and to identify local people's needs should be taken into account in project planning and implementation. Also, sufficient financial resources as well as time should be allocated for this purpose. (See also Chapter 2 concerning additional types of research and research needs.)

Participation of health educators/communication specialists

A health educator or communicator should participate from the outset of the programme planning process, so that the programme is designed on the basis of education and communication principles incorporating the target audience in project planning and implementation. Too often, education or communication personnel are consulted only to rescue a project that is not meeting its targets. Their activities are, therefore, tacked onto the core service delivery programme. Expectations for results from this kind of activity are usually unrealistically high. The communicator/educator should be called upon earlier to ensure that plans are developed for facilitating communication between administrator and staff as well as for more effective communication, including feedback, between outreach workers and the public they intend to serve.[54] This can serve to forge an important link between "top down" and "grass roots" approaches as well as the groups they represent.

Often, the failure to include education or communication specialists at the planning stage stems from their relatively low rank as compared with other technical staff, such as medical personnel, in population programmes. Furthermore, these education or communication officers are, in many instances, assigned clerical or miscellaneous tasks. Clearly, there is a need to make better, more appropriate use of their skills.

Social marketing for demand creation

There still is a need for more attention to communicating with the target audience about the availability of clinic services--that is, the location, time, cost, personnel, type of services offered and duration of treatment. World Fertility Surveys and Contraceptive Prevalence Surveys show that approximately 70 per cent of the population in many countries secure their contraceptive services and supplies from non-clinic sources. This is because shopkeepers and commercial sources serve clients directly with a minimal amount of "red tape"--with little waiting, at low cost, and often with much free advice.

Various means of communication to "market" the clinic services could be employed. In addition, more attention should be given to the clinic as a locale to conduct communication activities with clients, especially because research on family planning service delivery has shown that the personal communication skills of the family planning provider are the best way to market clinic services. If service providers treat the clients politely and pay attention to their needs, they will effectively promote the clinic and its services. Unless the health care providers in the clinic provide this kind of service and attention, other forms of promotion will be unlikely to produce long-term users. The best promotion is through a good service, with health providers who care about the welfare of their clients and show that they care in the way in which they counsel clients.[55]

232

Sensitivity to language and culturally acceptable visual images

The language used in family planning programmes can be counter-productive, for example, when top-down communication messages urging "a reduction in family size" generate popular resistance. The issue is far more complex than this macro-level injunction would imply. The challenge to communicators is to approach family planning needs from the user's perspective, which is likely to be different from the administrator's. Again, the focus-group approach may play a major role in preventing this type of problem from developing further.

One example of the importance of language and culturally acceptable images comes from the Philippines, where physicians have learned how to translate medical terms into local dialect for outreach workers who are communicating with villagers. They have learned that the key to successful communication with rural populations is to find agricultural images that run parallel to family planning concepts and methods. For birth control, the parallel image selected was that of mango farmers who limit the number of fruits to a branch by plucking defective flowers because excessive numbers would cause the branch to break; for child-spacing, the image selected was rice being transplanted from the seed-bed to the rice field, because planting too close is harmful to the plant and will give little produce; for condoms, the image selected was of bamboo fish-traps in the river, preventing the fish from going through.

Co-ordinated messages

Communication strategies and approaches have to be planned and designed in such a way that they are directly supportive of the efforts of outreach workers and clinic education programmes. This often implies, *inter alia*, close co-ordination between two "services" or structures at all levels to ensure consistency of messages.

Because the outreach workers are the "front line" personnel in a family planning project, one of the first tasks of a communication planner or administrator should be to make certain that outreach workers have the information, training and tools needed to facilitate their field-work. The feedback collected by outreach workers is an important element in ensuring the necessary consistency, as well as relevance, of the messages and material being designed. The need for IEC training of outreach and service personnel, especially in counselling techniques, cannot be over-emphasized, if acceptors are to understand the choices open to them. Counselling, or interpersonal communication, goes beyond recruitment of acceptors. Even in areas where acceptance levels are high, people are not always using contraceptives correctly or are dropping out for other reasons. Quality care and successful family planning programmes require a level of communication skills that ensures understanding on the part of the acceptors.

Approaches tailored to new target groups

New target groups are being identified in a number of countries. Each group will require approaches carefully tailored to its needs.

- **Adolescents**. New approaches to adolescents need to be designed, taking into account rural-urban and socio-cultural differences and special needs of young men and women. In many parts of the world, this group is becoming more sexually active than it has been, and adolescent fertility is now recognized as an important problem in a growing number of countries. Both formal and non-formal educational activities, supported by broader communication efforts, have a role to play in controlling this problem. Clearly, messages and materials designed for high-parity women will not appeal to nulliparous teenagers. Messages must be framed in terms appropriate to young people, helping them understand that their actions have consequences. There is also a need to develop ways to identify adolescents in greatest need of assistance.

  Because of the influence of peer pressure on adolescents, peer counselling may be effective if it includes sufficient information and personal guidance to enable clients to recognize the potential consequences of their behaviour for themselves, their families and their communities.

  Recent progress in using media and entertainers to promote sexual responsibility may be further explored and combined with interpersonal communication and appropriate service to facilitate acceptance of family planning.

- **Newly married couples**. Newly married couples need special priority in all cultural contexts. Traditionally, family planning efforts have focused on high-parity women, because their need for assistance is obvious, at the expense of low-parity or nulliparous women at risk of pregnancy. Family planning programmes, particularly those in rural areas, have often neglected newly married couples, who usually feel strong social pressure from in-laws and friends to have their first child as soon as possible after marriage. This same social pressure may also be reflected in the attitudes of health and family planning professionals. Before disregarding young couples as a primary target group, a serious attempt needs to be made to explore and develop their interest in family planning.

  Experience indicates that if the first birth to a couple is planned, all subsequent births are likely to be planned. However, if the newly-weds are not approached before the first pregnancy and have no positive experience with family planning, they may continue to have accidental pregnancies until they determine that their most recent birth(s) are "unwanted" or in excess of what they would have had, had a choice been available earlier. If family planners focus on this group, unwanted pregnancies can be reduced, child-spacing and its concomitant health benefits can reach a wider audience and the population growth rate can be moderated. In situations where evidence of fertility is a prerequisite to social acceptance, the cultural barrier may be too difficult to overcome. However, postponement of a pregnancy, even if only for a few months, can give a couple a sense of control over their desired family size, enhancing the possibility that it will become a continuing practice after "proof of fertility" has been established.

A few developing and industrialized countries, such as China, Indonesia, Mexico and the Philippines, and states in the United States of America have attempted to meet the needs of this group through widely varying approaches, such as giving the newly-weds comprehensive kits of family planning information followed up with home visits, or, when couples apply for a marriage license, giving them cards with the address of the nearest family planning clinic. The effectiveness of these approaches has not been compared, but it seems reasonable to assume that a comprehensive kit specifically designed for newly-weds, and followed up with opportunities for the couple to ask questions and receive services, would have a greater impact on their decision-making. At the least, even for those couples who have already decided to practise family planning, the learning may both reinforce decisions and contribute to more viable marriages.[56]

- **Males.** In many cultural contexts, men are the reproductive decision makers. Yet, few effective approaches have been developed to communicate with them in this role. A multifaceted approach may be required, beginning with boys in school, to modify attitudes regarding roles and responsibilities in the area of reproduction. It may be appropriate to design specific strategies to reach men in the work-place, through peers or supervisors. For example, certain large groups of men in the armed forces or police can be reached through the existing organizational structure. Male workers, such as worker-educators and agricultural extension agents, have been deployed to reach other males to complement or substitute for male health workers. Mass media can complement these efforts through the creative use of images (popular entertainers or leaders) to promote male responsibility. As with other programmes for specific target groups, a programme designed to address men should be thoroughly researched and incorporate innovative strategies and messages for their needs. (For more on this audience, see Chapter 3.)

- **Persons at risk of AIDS.** AIDS prevention is critically important in the absence of a cure. Training in materials production and distribution, interpersonal counselling and other IEC methods and techniques must be given greater emphasis as demand for programmes of prevention grows around the world. The target groups may be broken down into a variety of communities, characterized by particular sexual and/or drug-abuse behaviour that is not necessarily easy to identify, posing tremendous problems and challenges for communicators. Persons at risk of other STDs are obvious targets. Participants in family planning

235

clinics cannot be labeled "high risk", unless their partners are promiscuous, but again, identification is very difficult, complicating communication and education efforts (see Box 13).

Box 13

**IMPLICATIONS OF ACQUIRED IMMUNE
DEFICIENCY SYNDROME (AIDS) FOR
POPULATION COMMUNICATION AND EDUCATION**

To combat AIDS effectively, condom use will have to increase. However, many in the family planning community are concerned that the association of condoms with AIDS will have a negative impact on the condom's reputation as a "family" contraceptive. Some think that combining different promotional messages about one product leads to confusion, although others see the multi-purpose product image as a plus.

Another potential problem arises with the provision of AIDS counselling and services at the same site as family planning services. A related question is how to deal with the subject of AIDS and its frightening implications as part of sex education, in which sexuality is dealt with in positive terms. Research results and field experience need to be carefully documented and rapidly shared with communicators, educators, family planning specialists and AIDS workers to explore the implications of AIDS for these related areas.

■ Minorities and other groups with special cultural characteristics. In many countries, plans and materials are designed centrally, which may fail to meet the unique communication needs of distinct cultural groups in different sections of the country. The chances for successful interventions improve markedly when local images, language, concerns and perceptions are incorporated into communication approaches. Although some countries have applied this knowledge, for example in the "regionalization" approach of the Philippines population education project, other countries have not, mostly because of the expense and limited manpower. Both non-formal and formal education as well as communication programmes would benefit, however, from the localization of the design and implementation of activities.

Choice of channels

Selection of expensive, modern media hardware, such as computers and video, often takes precedence over the concern for the most effective and appropriate choice of channels for message delivery. For example, video is a leading tool with many valuable uses. But it is sometimes used inappropriately, when simpler methods would have equal or greater impact. At the same time, there is insufficient understanding among population communicators about the really innovative uses of video. This results in wasteful expenditure and missed opportunities to use media hardware appropriately. The selection of media, whether sophisticated or simple, should always take into account the desired content, audience and users, and should take place after those decisions have been made.

Potential contributions of others in the development community

A continuing issue is that of identifying how extension workers, social workers and others can include family planning among their responsibilities and what roles they can assume in family planning programmes--e.g., as service providers, family planning advocates or active family planning educators conducting small group meetings.

Role of communication in treating opposition to population activities

Because population and family planning are often considered taboo, the very act of discussing family planning activities in public and through mass media, with the support of national leaders, is in itself a major contribution towards reducing potential opposition. Opposition to family planning activities or other population activities such as sex education may come from specific organized groups. It is important that leadership of such groups be identified and reached through appropriate communication methods and channels. One such channel is person-to-person communication through credible sources, for example, arranging for religious leaders who support family planning activities to discuss their programme with religious leaders from another country who may oppose the programme on religious grounds.

In some cases, opposition will not die down immediately. Considerable controversy and public discussion may arise before people gradually shift from one position to another. This happened in Colombia, where controversy arose over the programme of the national planned parenthood organization, PROFAMILIA. Interestingly, results were positive. Over time, the more controversy that was generated, the more people heard about the programme. Now Colombia has one of the highest contraceptive prevalence levels in Latin America.

Communication about the means of preventing AIDS has substantially affected people's idea of what is appropriate to discuss in the mass media and in public communication. Opposition to condoms, for example, and to discussion of sexual practices has been diminished by the need to discuss these matters to prevent the spread of AIDS. Thus, communication about other health-related aspects of family planning and sexual behaviour can be important in overcoming opposition to discussing family planning, and thus eventually in family planning itself.[57]

237

Content loss in multiplier training

How can trainers prevent the loss of content when "multipliers" are used to train others under their supervision? Since those who receive training last are usually the most critical links in the chain--for example, the outreach workers who deal with audiences daily on a face-to-face basis--any loss of important content may have a critical adverse effect on their performance, thereby affecting the entire programme. In addition to the problem of simple loss of content, the gaps tend to be filled from the personal experience of both trainer and trainee, leading to the spread of erroneous information from credible sources. Will the use of appropriate materials such as standardized manuals help deal with this problem? Is monitoring by original trainers a solution? Can more be done?

Institutionalization of communication programmes

One important measure for the attainment of national self-reliance is the institutionalization of population communication, which in the operational sense means the following: (a) clear and specific policy formulation to include population education as one of the normal activities of concerned agencies (both governmental and non-governmental); (b) the monitoring and support of such activities during normal supervisory process of such agency; (c) continued and adequate funding of such activities as part of normal budgeting; (d) adequate training and re-training of all staff undertaking such activities; and (e) a management information system that provides for adequate feedback and follow-up for efficient management of such activities.

In 1987, an Inter-Agency Task Force on Project Follow-Up and Institutionalization defined institutionalization as follows:

> *"Institutionalization is the long-term, evolving process whereby the thrust of activities supported by the project is continued after external funding is phased out. Arrangements for institutionalization and follow-up begin with initial project formulation".*[58]

Although the task force drew up a preliminary list of indicators of institutionalization, much remains to be done to refine the concept. In the area of population communication, one important factor in securing long-term funding commitment from local and national authorities is the selection of low-cost methodologies and media, adapted to social and economic conditions in developing countries, and the visibility of the "product" (pamphlets, videos, slides, tapes, posters etc.). Once these materials have demonstrated to decision makers that they are well received by the intended audiences, funding is much more likely.[59] Provisions for institutionalization may also take into account the possibilities for income-generating services and the benefits of working with NGOs for specific activities such as surveys and production of materials.

Institutionalization is a complex process. It is an issue in developed as well as developing countries, but may require a more concerted effort and flexibility on the part of funding agencies in a developing country setting. This is particularly true where local infrastructure is weak.[60]

Technological advances

Recent advances in information and communication technology have greatly expanded the ways in which people gain access to information. The mass media, for example, are affected by the rapid proliferation of video technology, which is capable of placing programming and viewing decisions directly in the hands of local communities, thereby lessening, to some extent, the control of governmental and private-sector television producers. At the same time, an increase in the privatization of large-scale media (national television and radio networks, for example) may well change the picture of mass communication for development.

In addition, the ease of movement of computerized information and data across continents through telephone links, facsimile reproduction and satellite transmission of audio-visual programmes is forcing fundamental change upon development planners as they are challenged to develop new strategies for population communication activities.

Maintenance of acceptance levels

The responsibility of population communication activities does not end with motivating couples to visit a clinic or accept a contraceptive method. Communication activities should attempt to ensure that acceptors continue with a contraceptive method until the next planned pregnancy. Moreover, there are always new audiences or new members in established audiences, for whom awareness needs to be established and maintained.

One factor in continuation is the appropriateness of the acceptor's choice of methods. Training the service providers in counselling helps ensure their ability to help acceptors make informed choices. In this way, acceptors will be satisfied users and continue with the method until the next pregnancy is desired. The role of the media in clearly presenting relevant information at the appropriate time and place can reinforce the work of the counsellor and contribute to "informed choice".

Role of family planning in human sexuality

Communicators and service providers tend not to recognize the place of family planning in the context of human sexuality. Early research in preparation for family planning communication and services should investigate sexual behaviour patterns among target groups. To function effectively as counsellors, outreach and clinic workers need to understand and be comfortable in discussing sexual behaviour. Therefore, behavioural research findings should be incorporated into the training of communication and service personnel at all levels in a concerted effort to respond to the target group's actual characteristics and requirements.

This is not a new issue. As early as the mid-1960s, and perhaps earlier, a few organized family planning programmes acknowledged it as a need and dealt with it in their materials.[61] Some pharmaceutical companies and private physicians recognized this even earlier.[62] However, such recognition has been limited, not widespread, especially in the public sector. The advent of contraceptive methods functioning independently of sexual intercourse (oral contraceptives, intra-uterine devices and injections) has made it easy to overlook the importance of human sexuality considerations in couples' choices and decisions about contraception. The issue is surfacing again with the spread of AIDS and the need to make the condom more appealing, both as a contraceptive device and as an STD prophylactic. Efforts are under way to eroticize the condom, emphasizing the role of women in its use,[63] and to change condoms' image as, for example, being associated only with prostitutes.[64]

AIDS prevention is only one reason for resurrecting this issue. A basic understanding of human sexual behaviour (especially that a wide variety of behaviour patterns exist) is important to family planning professionals who have to ration out condoms or foams, for example. They cannot do this effectively without understanding that frequency of intercourse varies from one couple to the next. Newly-weds and new mothers, to protect their own mental and physical health, need to understand the links between sexual behaviour/functions and contraception.

Machismo is another aspect of human sexuality with important implications for the approaches taken in developing communication components of family planning programmes. For example, research findings on the nature of *machismo* in any given setting may provide clues to communicators and service providers on selection of target groups, choices of contraceptive methods, content on gender roles etc.

The list of relevant aspects of human sexuality is not a long one. In contrast, the needs for research, understanding and application of findings to family planning are great.

Family size norms

Demographers and family planning specialists have long recognized the significance of family size for both health and demographic considerations. Social, cultural and economic changes are likely to impact upon family size norms as, to a lesser degree, will IEC efforts to complement or facilitate changing norms. Typically, the weight given to changing-- usually reducing--family size norms has been so great that population communicators have sometimes converted the idea into inappropriate or ill-timed messages and slogans. When family planning communicators focus on the size of the family, their message is often interpreted as promoting sterilization rather than child-spacing. This many occur even when the messages are going to low parity or nulliparous couples as well as to those who may be more receptive to limiting family size. The results may thus be counter-productive.

If, as is likely over the next decade, new target audiences for family planning will be characterized by lower parity, more emphasis will be needed on methods and messages dealing with child-spacing. Couples already practising family planning may find such messages appropriate reminders of what they learned earlier or directly relevant to their current needs. Even in population education programmes not designed for facilitating immediate contraceptive decision-making, the topic of family size may be introduced, as the cumulative learning may indeed influence the eventual decision. Thus, more careful attention is needed to decisions on how and when to present the notions of family size in communication and education programmes.

Conclusions and recommendations

The Review and Assessment has shown that there are important issues and challenges ahead for the IEC sector as nations continue their efforts to come to terms with their population problems. The issues and their implications, mentioned elsewhere in this study, have been defined and drawn from both successes and failures.

With the statement of issues, a substantive IEC agenda is presented for the new decade and for the first uncertain steps into the next century. It remains for programme planners to establish priorities at national and intercountry levels and to define and pursue strategic planning objectives. For example, one could argue the need for strengthening the systems and structures within the IEC subsectors at all levels as well as for creating linkages with all other aspects of population programmes. The justification for such an approach is obvious. These systems and structures, together with a range of interpersonal methods of outreach, must increasingly be employed for building and maintaining awareness of population issues not only among leaders but among all strata of the population.

Population education, although it has come of age in many countries, still needs to be institutionalized if it is to be sustained over the long term in both formal and non-formal settings. In addition, new developments and recent findings are contributing to a reconceptualization of the field in many countries. These findings need to be documented and shared with countries having more limited experiences. Ways need to be found to ensure institutionalization in a manner sufficiently flexible to permit growth and adaptation while providing the structural stability needed for sustainability over the long term.

There are, as noted earlier, areas of overlap among activities within each subsector. Strategies for co-ordinated programming can help lend coherence to population programmes and ensure success over the long run. For example, population education activities in both formal and non-formal settings need continuing support from information and communication providers of up-to-date documentation, analysis of data and new and more effective audio-visual technology. At the same time, information and communication planners could learn much about awareness creation from the experience of formal and non-formal education practitioners, especially in matters concerning the introduction of innovative, sensitive and often controversial topics. From a still broader perspective, the aims of all IEC activities must be co-ordinated in an over-arching population and development strategy, embracing the MCH/FP sector as well as the policy planning processes.

242

5. Overall Issues

Any assessment of experience in the development field is likely to reveal fundamental issues, regardless of the particular policies or programmes in effect. This chapter distils nine such issues which have emerged from the Review and Assessment. In each of the three sectors covered in the preceding chapters--namely, the policy development process; maternal and child health and family planning (MCH/FP); and information, education and communication (IEC)--the analysis has pointed to the significance of these overall issues. Moreover, as the next section of this book will show, these issues have arisen in all regions of the world.

The first five issues to be introduced here are of a general nature. They refer to the importance of political commitment, national and international co-ordination, the role of non-governmental organizations (NGOs) and the private sector in general, the necessary process of institutionalization for self-sufficiency, and the role of women and gender considerations. These are followed by three issues that revolve around the significance of research, the development of human resources and the establishment of appropriate mechanisms for monitoring and evaluating programmes. A final issue is the problem of mobilizing resources at both national and international levels.

Political commitment

One of the chief lessons of the Review and Assessment is the centrality of strong political support for undertaking population programmes and policies. Indeed, without a Government's strong leadership and commensurate commitment, planners, managers and other personnel can rarely overcome the political and bureaucratic constraints that inevitably occur.

The types of constraints are several: the ideologies and outlook of those who are politically dominant or influential; the tendency of some groups to view population policies as a diversion from fundamental structural changes; hostility to policies affecting women's traditional roles; religious opposition to family planning and marriage reform laws; lack of motivation and skills of administrators for undertaking agreed-upon programmes; and competition among government ministries and departments for the scarce resources allocated to health and family planning services as against other social programmes. Moreover, population programmes often suffer from a lack of complementarity with overall development objectives and other social policies. However, even when they are consonant with other social policies, their support may be limited. Despite the evidence that programme interventions supported by

243

the social sector can produce favourable changes in population variables, the social sector receives the least priority and the smallest budgetary outlays.

Strong support by national leaders can neutralize or at least minimize these constraints. Political commitment enhances the probability of successfully developing and carrying out any policy. With such commitment, priority can be assigned to financial, technical and human resources; ministries with central and peripheral roles in programme efforts can be mobilized; and programmes and projects can be legitimized through a demonstration of the convictions of the country's leadership to the population. Political commitment also fosters support for the data collection, analysis and research that are basic to creating and putting policies as well as action programmes into effect.

As important as high-level political commitment is, however, it cannot be divorced from popular mobilization concerning population policies and programmes themselves. Political support should therefore be based on a solid assessment of the population's needs and priorities; otherwise, unilateral policies may backfire should a Government become unpopular or should political commitment be translated into policies perceived as coercive. The credibility of Governments, their genuine interest in the welfare of their peoples and their rapport with them are essential ingredients in the success of programmes.

Co-ordination of activities
and assistance

As affirmed by the World Population Plan of Action (WPPA), the principal aim of social, economic and cultural development, of which population goals and policies are part, is to improve people's living standards and quality of life. Achieving this goal requires the co-ordination of activities in the population field with activities in all socio-economic fields. Because a variety of ministries, government agencies, NGOs, private institutions and individuals will be involved, co-ordination of all their activities in population and development within countries is needed. It is also important to co-ordinate the efforts of Governments with those of the multilateral and bilateral agencies that support many of these activities.

The lack of co-ordination of project activities clearly hinders the design and fulfilment of population policies at national and local levels. This is especially the case when several government ministries or departments and voluntary organizations are executing projects, each intent on retaining its own identity and autonomy. When ministerial and institutional arrangements for management and co-ordination are absent or minimal, bureaucratic rivalries and conflicts can intensify, weakening dedication to the programme and eroding consistency and coherence. Effective co-ordination is also needed for all activities of a similar nature-

-for example, statistics, training and education--undertaken by relevant units within various ministries.

The co-ordination of international assistance efforts is critical for the success of policy development and programme functioning. It is also essential in ensuring more efficient use of resources. Country programmes have often suffered because funding requirements were underestimated or because the planning to ensure optimal use of limited resources was insufficient. When several assistance agencies are undertaking a single country programme, they sometimes compete rather than collaborate with one another, thus dissipating valuable resources. Recognizing the existence of conflict, some Governments may play one agency against another, frequently gaining better assistance terms. To circumvent this possibility, the agencies need to reach agreements on their respective roles and activities in a country or regional programme.

Frequently, population programmes require external funding for longer periods than originally projected. When external assistance is phased out, there is rarely a concomitant increase in the level of Government support as it takes over the programme. Thus far, external assistance agencies have not applied a consistent policy for deciding on continued assistance to programmes. To some extent, more effective programmes have had to assume ever greater self-sufficiency whereas the less effective programmes have sometimes been rewarded with more external support.

Co-ordination implies allocation of responsibilities to each of the agencies taking part in population and development activities. Along with responsibility, there is also the notion of accountability. Co-ordination implies orderly and systematic organization of activities to avoid wasting time, effort and resources. Hence, co-ordination presumes the existence of a mechanism by which all these responsibilities and activities can be organized, apportioned and monitored. To facilitate effective and efficient population programmes, agencies and Governments need to delineate clearly the arrangements and conditions for assistance adapted to the country's situation and resources.

Role of non-governmental organizations

National and international NGOs have been pioneers in the population and development fields at times when Governments, constrained by political, ideological or bureaucratic considerations, have been unable or unwilling to act. Because of their organization and structure, NGOs have been able to respond quickly and flexibly to expressed needs at community, national and regional levels. After experimenting to find out what works, they have urged Governments to act and provided them with workable approaches. In many instances, the planning and carrying out of population and development programmes have involved a variety of governmental and voluntary organizations, particularly women's organizations, at national, district and village levels.

In developing countries, non-governmental development organizations are extremely important sources of information through their publications and activities for local leaders and community workers, whose involvement helps speed social change. In developed countries, NGOs have engaged in research, supported national activities and acted as lobbyists, keeping pressure on legislators and civil servants on behalf of population and development interests. NGOs have also served as advocates in various countries, reminding Governments of the rights of citizens to public services. Private institutions and NGOs have also created population information centres and have provided methodological models for others. By gathering and analysing evidence from the field, the private sector has contributed substantially to a comprehensive picture of population change that has helped convince Governments and international agencies of its importance.

Institutionalization

The term "institutionalization" in the operational sense refers to the long-term process whereby project activities are continued after external funding has been phased out. In general, institutionalization has to be included as an explicit objective of each project, except in the case of temporary projects or those primarily designed for *ad hoc* activities. Institutionalization forms part of the national strategy for population activities based on a careful assessment of national needs, priorities, resources and capabilities. Arrangements for institutionalization and follow-up should be made when projects are initially formulated, with the full participation of all concerned, especially the agencies that will be co-ordinating, executing and funding the project.

Although the goal of population and development assistance is to foster self-reliance, Governments can rarely continue or expand activities in a single-phase project without external assistance. However, the work plans agreed upon in project documents are usually geared to short spans of time. Some work plans reflect an assistance agency's budgetary schedule of one or two years; others reflect the term of office of the recipient agency's or country's head, often three or four years. In either case the time periods are clearly too brief for project activities to become absorbed in national budgets. Hence, in economically strapped developing nations, the risk of project activities coming to a halt upon cessation of external funding is great.

An important step towards institutionalization of population efforts is the establishment of national population commissions or councils. Many developing countries have organized such bodies to spearhead the formulation of population policies, to co-ordinate all population-related activities in both public and private sectors, and to channel financial and technical assistance for population activities. Variations from country to country in political, economic and socio-cultural characteristics, current demographic situations and trends, and perceptions of population as a priority and of available policy options will likely influence the role, location and effectiveness of these commissions and councils. Similarly, national priorities and strategies for development planning will affect their performance.

So that progress can be measured, institutionalization requires the development of a set of procedures and the identification of specific indicators of institutionalization at the time of project design and implementation. To facilitate institutionalizing women's concerns and participation in development, for example, a mechanism should be created or identified for assessing the contribution of major project activities to improving women's roles and status. In this way, experience can be used to orient programmes.

Role of women and gender considerations

Improving the role and status of women is, by itself, an important goal of population policies and programmes. In addition, experience and research have now demonstrated the relationships between women's status and such demographic variables as fertility, maternal and infant mortality, and migration. Women's educational attainment, work patterns, income levels, access to and control of resources, and social roles--all have considerable impact on their health and the well-being of their children, in general, and on their reproductive health, practice of family planning and involvement in fertility decisions, in particular. It is not surprising, therefore, that wherever activities have been undertaken to improve the situation of women, such as education and training opportunities, women's participation in population programmes has increased. Moreover, population programmes that address women's reproductive, productive and other needs and that systematically include women as both participants and beneficiaries have been found to have a better chance of success than those that do not. Another important determinant of population programme performance is the inclusion in programme design of gender considerations--that is, considerations of the specific needs, roles and contributions of both women and men.

Despite many advances in recent years, much more remains to be done to ensure the full incorporation of gender issues into population programmes as well as other development programmes. For example, it has usually been assumed that, because MCH/FP and many IEC activities are addressed mostly to women, these activities are automatically gender-sensitive and meet the needs of women. Evaluations have shown, however, that programme quality has often been seriously wanting because the specific needs of women were not considered in project design and implementation. Among women's neglected needs are those for culturally sensitive modes of delivery, and appropriate hours and location of services, given the many household and employment demands on women's time. Women are rarely consulted or asked to participate in needs identification, programme development and management, or

247

decision-making. Although women constitute the majority of health-care providers in many societies, they seldom occupy managerial levels in the health system. Likewise, insufficient analysis of IEC and FP activities has often led to the exclusion of men from target groups. Some recent innovations have attempted to address this problem, for example, the training and use of male family motivators and the inclusion of didactic materials on gender roles and responsibilities in school-based population education programmes.

Noteworthy progress has been made in dealing with gender-specific issues in the field of data collection and analysis. However, much more needs to be done. Increased efforts are required to ensure that the collection, analysis and dissemination of data are disaggregated by gender. Accurate indicators of the actual situation of women in specific areas are urgently needed. Only with this type of information can policies and programmes that are intended to improve women's situation and increase their participation in development efforts be planned, and progress measured.

Research

Research to enhance knowledge and support programmatic activity is a continuing priority. Changing social and economic contexts within which population policies are framed and carried out as well as changing demographic conditions and new research findings themselves--all call for increased research. The relationship between population change and its determinants and consequences varies not only from country to country but also within countries, from one socio-economic, occupational or cultural group to another. To help document the role of contextual variables and the differential behaviour of groups within societies, more socio-economic research is needed. Studies should be conducted on micro-level determinants and consequences of fertility; the reasons underlying contraceptive acceptance, continued use and discontinuation; and the beliefs and practices observed in relation to disease and child-bearing and other population processes.

The WPPA lists 17 areas in which research is needed to fill gaps in knowledge. These areas range from the social, cultural and economic determinants of population variables in different developmental and political situations to social indicators reflecting the quality of life as well as the interrelationships between socio-economic and demographic phenomena. Proposals for research agendas, which abound in the literature, have usually included the important qualification that research priorities must ultimately be identified at individual country and subcountry levels by local researchers in conjunction with their own development planners and policy makers. For the most part, however, decisions about population research are made not by planners and policy makers but by individual social scientists. Their decisions about what to study rest largely on disciplinary interests, sometimes influenced by the concerns of international assistance agencies.

The last two decades have seen the accumulation of a large body of demographic knowledge--related to the causes and consequences of fertility, family planning, mortality, population distribution, and internal and international migration. Yet, the application of that knowledge to policy-making and planning remains limited. Because the research agenda has been insufficiently responsive to policy and programme requirements, not enough is known on what is needed, why and in what form. As a result, existing data are underused, inadequately disseminated and often inappropriate for population and development planning purposes. Other reasons for the inadequate use of research findings are the lack of appropriate institutional arrangements and the scarcity of qualified policy analysts and policy specialists.

At the programme and project level, too, programme managers and researchers lament the infrequent use of research and evaluation findings in decision-making for many population programmes and projects. This neglect has persisted despite the positive correlation found between such applications of evaluation findings and a programme's success. Research is an essential part of the process leading to the adoption of any innovation and to the suitable design and content of IEC support for policy development. Yet, quantitative and qualitative research methods are used too infrequently or inappropriately to obtain important information about specific audiences and their perceptions of population and development issues. In some cases, new research has been undertaken before a concerted effort has been made to locate available information. Frequently, delays in carrying out research components have slowed down other programme activities.

Ensuring that research results are actually used to improve programme activities has seldom been easy. Few attempts have been made at the local level, for example, to focus research on successful programme interventions in order to ascertain how process is related to outcome. Such efforts would yield valuable knowledge for policy formulation. In addition, much more could be done to test innovative and experimental programme interventions and to assess how population policies and programmes relate to community and family dynamics as part of the feedback into programme planning and operations.

Training

A decisive contributor to securing human well-being--the goal of all development efforts--is investment in people and knowledge. The acquired abilities of people, their education, experience, skills and health, are basic to the attainment of economic and social progress. The development of human resources contributes to their labour productivity, to their entrepreneurial ability in both farm and non-farm productivity, to household production and to moves in search of better employment opportunities and better places to live. Such abilities contribute significantly to satisfactions that are elements of present and future consumption and well-being.

To sustain development, a continuous supply of human resources at national and subnational levels has to be maintained over a long period. This requirement raises the question of long-term institutional capability to ensure the availability of skilled individuals. Although investment in people implies a continuing commitment of resources, international assistance for human resource development is usually short term, tied to the life of a project.

Both the acute shortage of well-trained professionals in research and policy analysis and the absence of institutions specializing in policy and programmatic research are making it difficult for many developing countries to undertake appropriate population programmes. Planners, development economists and demographers all require training in population and development interrelationships, whereas most training courses are addressed principally to demographic analysis, population-related data-processing, population projections etc. Some courses do include population policy formulation and elements of development planning but lack the required integrated approach to population and development. The dearth of manpower trained in a multidisciplinary, long-term courses on methods of, and approaches to, population and development remains a major constraint to integration.

Managerial training is another neglected area. Past training efforts have focused chiefly on the development of substantive or technical capability. The development of management capability implies the existence of a pool of multidisciplinary talent capable of handling managerial issues of varying degrees of complexity. The number, nature and functions of the talents required will differ, depending upon the needs of all levels of management; the goals, scope and structure of the programme; and the variety of issues being confronted.

What seems to be missing in many developing countries is a formal manpower training plan. Such a plan specifies the process of establishing in-country training activities complemented by external training. It includes the methods of creating training curricula and the methods and materials for producing the required cadre of national staff in population-related sectors. Such a plan should also include a procedure to ensure the retention of trained nationals in the country programme through such measures as career development schemes.

Without a training plan outlining training requirements along with the timing and strategies for all levels of need, programmes frequently encounter problems. Preparing cohorts of trainers sometimes entails sending key individuals abroad for training. If such steps are improperly timed, programmes may risk disrupting programme functions or losing such personnel. A widespread tendency is to train personnel without reference to clear job descriptions, leading to irrelevant curricula and insufficient preparation of trainees for the tasks assigned. In some instances, training, especially basic training, is not synchronized with the opening of positions in the programme or project. Thus, trainees risk losing their skills through lack of opportunity to practise them. Frequently, no clear guidelines have been produced regarding just how many tasks, for example, village extension workers should be prepared to handle and how long their training should last. Finally, the importance of follow-up and supervision of trainees is often overlooked.

The population field thus stands in need of a long-term strategy of human resource development. The success or failure of such a strategy will have a paramount bearing on the course of population programmes.

Monitoring and evaluation

Experience has now demonstrated the variety of policy approaches that can be effective when tailored by Governments to the particular political, social, cultural, religious and economic conditions of their countries. Yet Governments have experienced many impediments to carrying out their national population policies. One of the ways of overcoming these impediments and enhancing effectiveness is to employ monitoring and evaluation systems. These systems are important managerial tools for policy-making and programming.

Monitoring entails a continuous review of activities by management at every level to ensure that the work plan is being carried out. By providing feedback to project management at all levels, monitoring helps produce efficient and effective project performance. Plans can be improved and corrections made promptly. As an internal activity, monitoring forms part of the management information system. It needs to be conducted by those responsible for carrying out projects or programmes at every level of the management hierarchy. However, many population projects have included monitoring merely to comply with requirements of external funding agencies and not as a management tool.

Evaluation is the analysis of the extent to which goals have been met and of the appropriateness of programme design. It entails systematically and objectively weighing the relevance, efficiency and effectiveness of projects while they are under way or gauging their impact when completed. Evaluation can be undertaken internally or externally. It should enable management both to improve ongoing activities and to incorporate valuable information into future planning, programming and decision-making. In actuality, however, evaluations seldom address the difficult issue of impact, because many factors in addition to a single project or programme may be responsible for influencing change.

The usefulness and quality of monitoring and evaluation depend greatly on the original planning of the project. In well-planned projects with well-defined objectives, evaluations can reliably measure progress towards immediate and long-range objectives. Evaluations can also help planners ascertain the effectiveness and impact of programmes and their continued responsiveness to community needs. Furthermore, through evaluations, planners can gauge the extent to which women have participated in, and

251

benefited from, programmes. For these benefits to accrue, however, evaluation plans need to be part of project design. In general, monitoring and evaluation have been used less systematically than they should.

Resource mobilization

Because the population field is multifaceted and multidisciplinary, it requires a variety of resources--administrative and technical as well as financial. Technical and administrative staff capacity is the most critical need, because of the widespread shortage of trained staff in developing countries. However, staff development as well as other programme needs is dependent on the availability of financial resources, both internal and external.

The resources available for assistance in population more than doubled in nominal terms between 1974 and 1984. Yet this increase did not keep pace with demand, which increased dramatically. Nor did it sufficiently compensate for inflation. Despite the allocations by developing countries of increasing shares of development expenditures for population programmes, the need for assistance in this field continues to grow. Meanwhile, the international economic crisis has impeded developing countries' overall social and economic development and the undertaking of effective measures to deal with population trends over the past 15-20 years. In the majority of the developing countries, economic events have crippled Governments' capacities for action. Recession and inflation have hurt particularly those economies dependent on the importation of foodstuffs, manufactures or oil. Faced with dwindling resources, many Governments have been compelled to restrict public expenditures.

The following case illustrates the urgent need for generating resources: Merely to meet national demographic and health goals of developing countries, contraceptive prevalence levels would have to rise from about 48 per cent in 1987 to 58 per cent in the year 2000. This implies extending contraceptive protection from the 326 million couples covered in 1987 to 535 million by century's end. Although the task is immense, such a goal seems achievable provided the necessary political and financial support is applied. On the basis of current estimates, to cover 535 million couples by the year 2000 would imply an amount varying from $5.3 billion to $6.5 billion in that year alone, taking into account only direct costs of delivering family planning services. If the costs of other primary health care or maternal and child health care services, which are often linked with those of family planning in multi-purpose delivery systems, are included, the estimates are staggering. These calculations underscore the formidable challenge to the national and international community to muster the essential resources for family planning services and other population programmes.

Given the economic and political realities, there is a critical need for convincing Governments and assistance agencies to provide the needed resources, by demonstrating the cost-benefit value of investments in population and social programmes. The second major need is to use whatever resources become available in the most efficient ways, through the development and application of cost-effective strategies.

In the chapters that follow on regional perspectives, the issues discussed here will be seen to arise with varying emphases, depending on what stage the region has reached in the consideration of its population problems. Notwithstanding those variations, these issues remain significant challenges to those in the population field world-wide.

Part Two:

Regional Perspectives

6. Population Policies and Programmes in sub-Saharan Africa

Trends in national population policies and programmes

Before the 1974 World Population Conference in Bucharest, many planners and policy makers were unaware of the seriousness of the population situation in Africa and its consequences for socio-economic development. The official view in several sub-Saharan African countries was that rapid population growth did not constitute a major problem for development. Agricultural land was abundant, human resources were underused and most of sub-Saharan Africa was underpopulated. Because of the lack of analysed population data, few Governments had reliable information on population distribution, growth, structures, trends etc. and the resultant impact on national development. For example, at the time of the first round of the African Census Programme (1965-1974), 15 African countries had never had a complete census of their population. Moreover, before 1974, only three sub-Saharan countries--Ghana, Kenya and Mauritius--had explicit population policies. Even those political leaders who were convinced of the need for action preferred remedies in development, education, employment opportunities, higher income, industrialization etc. as vehicles for moderating the rate of population growth. At the Bucharest Conference, Africa's position was almost unanimous that the region was not ready for population policies--that "development was the best contraceptive".

Today, however, partly as a result of the adverse economic situation after the depression of the late 1970s and early 1980s, and of desertification and sporadic drought, population issues--especially those of growth, distribution and migration--are at the forefront of concern.

Perceptions of growth rates

In the decade between 1974 and 1984, and perhaps even more so since then, perceptions about population issues in African countries changed markedly. In contrast to the pro-natalist views expressed at Bucharest, the representatives of 44 African countries at the Second African Population Conference in Arusha (January 1984) acknowledged population as a major component in planning for social and economic development and declared that family planning was a health and human rights measure (see Box 14). In all, the Conference made 93 recommendations covering all aspects of population and its relation to social and economic development. The recommendations in the African Population Programme--known as the Kilimanjaro Programme of Action for African Population and Self-Reliant Development--were endorsed by the Economic Commission for Africa (ECA) Conference of Ministers in Addis

Ababa, Ethiopia, in May 1984, and by the African Heads of State and Government at the Organization of African Unity (OAU) meeting in 1985.

Box 14

KILIMANJARO PROGRAMME OF ACTION FOR AFRICAN POPULATION AND SELF-RELIANT DEVELOPMENT

Representatives of 44 African nations at the Second African Population Conference, held in Arusha, the United Republic of Tanzania, 9-13 January 1984, adopted the Kilimanjaro Programme of Action for African Population and Self-Reliant Development. Recommendations were made on a broad spectrum of population issues, including population and development strategy and policy; fertility and family planning; morbidity and mortality; urbanization and migration; the changing role of women in the development process; children and youth; population data collection, analysis, training and research; population information; and community involvement and the role of private and non-governmental organizations. The goals include undertaking programmes to reduce high levels of fertility and mortality, to achieve growth rates compatible with the goals of economic and social development; improving living conditions in rural areas; and developing urbanization policies and programmes.

The Kilimanjaro Programme notes that "countries should recognize that a substantial decline in infant and childhood mortality is a pre-requisite for fertility decline" and that family planning and child-spacing positively affect family stability and well-being. The recommendations urge countries to incorporate family planning services into the maternal and child health services and to give special attention to "educating and motivating the population at grass-roots level on the health, social and demographic values of family planning". Governments are also to ensure the availability and accessibility of family planning services to all couples or individuals seeking such services freely or at subsidized prices.

Source: *United Nations Economic and Social Council Document No. E/ECA/POP/10,* 13 January 1984, in *Annual Review of Population Law, 1984* (United Nations Fund for Population Activities and Harvard Law School Library), vol. 11, pp. 580-588.

As of 1986, 26 sub-Saharan countries perceived their current rates of population growth as too high; 3 countries perceived their growth rates as too low; and 16 countries considered their growth rates satisfactory (see Annex Table 2). Two countries that considered their growth rates satisfactory (Côte d'Ivoire and Mauritania) would like to raise them.[1]

Nature and content of population policies

Fertility

Before the Bucharest Conference, only a few African countries even accepted the need for family planning. However, some Governments supported family planning initiatives for the health and welfare of mothers and children. Moreover, as of 1971, eight countries--the Gambia, Ghana, Liberia, Kenya, Mauritius, Nigeria, Sierra Leone and the United Republic of Tanzania--had become affiliated with the International Planned Parenthood Federation's (IPPF's) Africa Regional Council.

By 1984, at least 10 sub-Saharan countries--Botswana, Burkina Faso, Ethiopia, the Gambia, Kenya, Liberia, Senegal, the United Republic of Tanzania, Zaire and Zimbabwe--had public-sector family planning services. Since the Second African Population Conference in Arusha (1984), a number of countries have given increased attention to the promotion of family planning services through the national, non-governmental, and private-sector networks. In addition, more and more countries, among them Kenya, Nigeria and Zimbabwe, have emphasized the demographic rationale for family planning in addition to the traditional justification of family planning for health reasons. Several sub-Saharan Governments have been carrying out explicit policies to modify fertility levels (see Annex Table 2) in line with development policies and goals.[2] In at least 20 sub-Saharan countries, the total fertility rate (TFR) in 1985 was between 5.8 and 8.5 (see Table 6 in Chapter 3).

To complement family planning services, many countries have now initiated related projects in other sectors--for example, population information, education and communication (IEC) and training in demography. Furthermore, in recognition of the need for multi-sectoral approaches to addressing population and development problems, by 1984 about 13 countries had included demographic factors in their national development plans.

Contraceptive prevalence

In most of Africa's rural areas, demand for modern family planning methods and commodities is potentially high, but at present unmet. As shown in Table 6 in Chapter 3, in 1983 the contraceptive prevalence rate was 10 per cent or less in several sub-Saharan countries. Effective means of assessing and meeting the demand are needed, as are means of influencing socio-cultural attitudes towards family size. IEC support to family planning services has contributed to increased contraceptive prevalence rates in a number of countries, although the potential of IEC projects for promoting family planning programmes has yet to be fully exploited.

Mortality and morbidity

Although health conditions in rural areas of many African countries are poor, the health trends have been marked by gradual reductions in infant mortality and increases in life expectancy. In 1950-1955, for example, the infant mortality rate for Africa was 187 per 1,000 live births. By 1980-1985, it had declined to 116 per 1,000 live births and was projected to fall to 88 by 1995-2000. Life expectancy rose from 38 years in l950-l955 to 50 years in 1980-1985, and was projected to increase to 56 years by 1995-2000.[3] (For data on individual countries, see Annex Table 1.)

All sub-Saharan Governments have endorsed the universally adopted objectives of "Health for All by the Year 2000". Primary health care has become the major channel for attaining these objectives, with maternal and child health care and family planning (MCH/FP) as an essential component. In all countries of the region, special attention is now given to the health of mothers and children through antenatal, delivery and post-natal services. Within MCH, the emphasis on infants and children in such programmes as oral rehydration therapy (ORT) and the expanded programme on immunization (EPI) has often outweighed attention to maternal health. The problem has been compounded by the lack of data on maternal mortality. However, maternal death rates are known to be generally very high--1 in 21 in Africa, in contrast to 1 in 90 in Latin America or 1 in 2,089 in Europe.[4]

Spatial distribution

Many African planners regard population distribution rather than the rapid rate of population growth or high fertility as their main population problem. Until recently, a number of Governments in the region held that the demographic obstacle to development was not excessive growth but the "irrational" distribution of their national populations. Most African countries have small, sparsely distributed populations and low levels--but very high rates--of urbanization. These factors have combined to produce policy problems not found in other developing regions.

Results of the 1987 United Nations Monitoring Survey show that, as of 1986, not a single country in the region considered its pattern of population distribution satisfactory; 17 countries reported that their population distribution patterns were partially appropriate; and about two dozen considered that their patterns required major spatial restructuring. A total of 26 countries proposed policies to decelerate the basic trends in internal migration; 6 countries desired to reverse internal migration trends; and 10 countries proposed no direct intervention measures.[5]

Although inappropriate distribution of population is viewed as a major policy challenge in the region, few countries have adopted vigorous policies to modify trends. Policies aimed at readjusting the spatial distribution of population are often components of broader development goals and programmes. Some of these policies are explicit. Others are

259

implicit in such regional planning goals as integrated rural development, promotion of growth centres, incentives and disincentives for industrial location, and administrative decentralization. Programmes aimed at retaining migrants in rural areas or redirecting them to smaller urban places or accommodating them in the towns are most often introduced for non-demographic reasons.

Contributors to changing perceptions

Awareness creation

One stimulus to rapid change in governmental perceptions and actions in the field of population was a series of major sensitization and awareness-creation programmes. Conferences, seminars and workshops have generated awareness of the interrelationship between population issues and development processes among political cadres, policy makers and key opinion leaders. The Second African Population Conference in Arusha (1984) and the preparations within each country for delegations to the International Conference on Population in Mexico City (1984) revealed intensified interest in population issues. Shortly before and especially after the International Conference, seminars for national leaders reinforced attention to population concerns. These included the Seminar on Population and Development for Parliamentarians in the United Republic of Tanzania (May 1984), the Workshop on Population Growth and Socio-Economic Development in Uganda (June 1984) and the National Leaders' Seminar on Population and Development in Kenya (July 1984). Political support for population activities in the region was fast growing.

At the 1984 International Conference on Population, policy makers, parliamentarians and other public figures were encouraged to promote solutions to population and development problems by increasing public awareness and working towards the formulation, implementation and co-ordination of national population policies and programmes. One result of the interest generated by the Mexico Conference was the All-African Parliamentary Conference on Population and Development held in Harare, Zimbabwe, in May 1986. In addition, the World Conference to Review and Appraise the Achievements of the United Nations Decade for Women: Equality, Development and Peace, held in Nairobi in July 1985, provided a forum for reviewing progress in enhancing the role and status of women. The Nairobi Forward-looking Strategies for the Advancement of Women is one of the meeting's significant outcomes. In addition, the Safe Motherhood initiatives have also increased awareness of the importance of maternal and child health. All these efforts have helped to broaden regional leaders' attitudes towards population issues.

The levels of awareness of population issues in Africa have also been heightened by the increased availability of data on various facets of countries' population situations and the impact on Governments' development efforts. The 1970 and 1980 census rounds, the World Fertility Surveys, Demographic and Health Surveys and other specialized surveys--all have revealed the startling facts of Africa's population profile:

the rapidly growing young population, high and increasing fertility rates, and high overall mortality rates, especially for infants and mothers. In addition, their economic situations, with the associated structural adjustment programmes that many countries have had to undertake, are intensifying the Governments' appreciation of the need to monitor their population growth rates in keeping with national resources. At the family level, such factors as improvements in health care service, higher costs of child upbringing, the need for education etc. have themselves contributed to awareness of the need to manage family size.

Institutional arrangements

Another contributor to changes in the region's approach to population and development issues has been the strengthening of national institutions in population and development fields. For example, by strengthening the national offices responsible for generating demographic data, many countries have been able to provide the necessary analysed data to assist planners in population policy-making and programme design.

A key aspect of institution-building has been the setting up of national population commissions and planning units. These bodies are serving as the focal points for the formulation and co-ordination of overall population policies and programmes. The scope of responsibilities of population commissions and units may differ from one country to another. Also, their effectiveness has been found to be highly influenced by their location in the national structure. For example, in Kenya, the National Council for Population and Development, which is located in the Ministry for Home Affairs, is responsible for co-ordinating all population activities in the country. In contrast, Nigeria's National Population Commission is charged with the conduct of census, surveys and vital registration rather than with implementation of the population policy, which responsibility rests with the Department of Population Activities, located in the Federal Ministry of Health.

Other policy formulation efforts

The institutionalization of population activities has often been accompanied--sometimes preceded--by a variety of efforts to formulate population policies in an array of structures. In Benin, awareness of population matters grew among top-level policy makers with the dissemination of the results of the 1979 census and the demographic and fertility surveys of 1981-1987. The Government has now given priority to formulating a population policy. In Botswana, following the recommendations of a conference on population and development for senior public officials in June 1986, work started on the draft of a population policy. In Senegal, the Interministerial Committee on Population outlined a population policy that was adopted by the Government in April 1988. In Togo, after a week-long conference on population in 1987, an appointed national committee drafted a population policy which is under review by the Government.

Political support

To the extent that political representation in Government and financial subventions to different regions of a country are often linked to population size, Governments have long tended to view population as a political issue. In recent years, however, Governments have been making efforts to depoliticize population issues. Increased availability of demographic data and higher awareness of population issues have helped increase political leaders' appreciation of population problems and their interest in adopting appropriate strategies to address those problems. Even in countries with much arable land and abundant natural resources, where population issues and particularly population growth were formerly considered matters of little concern, political leaders at the highest levels now recognize the importance of population to their countries as a whole and have taken steps to manage the overall impact of population on development.

Resources for population programmes

As African countries are today increasingly formulating population policies, they need the resources to translate policies into programmes. Government contribution to programmes has usually been in the form of providing institutional and infrastructural support, assigning technical and administrative support staff and mobilizing necessary political support and local concessions. However, the current economic crisis--characterized by heavy external debt, devalued currency and a variety of negative social consequences associated with structural adjustment programmes--has continued to weaken the ability of most African countries to mobilize local resources for implementation of population policies and programmes.

UNFPA, the largest multilateral source of population assistance for several countries, has supported activities throughout the region and has designated 30 sub-Saharan countries as those in special need of population assistance. Other multilateral sources of population-related assistance include the Food and Agriculture Organization of the United Nations (FAO), the International Labour Organisation (ILO), the United Nations Children's Fund (UNICEF), the United Nations Educational, Scientific and Cultural Organization (UNESCO), the World Bank, the World Food Programme and the World Health Organization (WHO). Bilateral assistance--based on such criteria as historical links, economic and political ties, and geographic areas--has also played a role in support of population programmes.

The regional setting: Constraints and favourable aspects

The implementation of population programmes in sub-Saharan Africa has encountered many constraints in the technical, economic, religious and socio-cultural context. This context includes deep-rooted traditional beliefs about family size; political factors, including weak support; inadequate national infrastructure and resources; and insufficient technical expertise. There are, however, favourable elements in the sub-Saharan environment, including the influence of traditional community leaders, the local community structures, and the potential role of grass-roots organizations and women's groups in enhancing awareness of population issues and motivating the practice of family planning.

Religious and cultural context

Religious and cultural constraints to the successful implementation of family planning programmes are pervasive. For example, in Zaire, which is officially a secular state, 70 per cent of the population are Christians (40 per cent Catholics, 30 per cent Protestants), and about 60 per cent of all health facilities are run by church groups that also control the educational institutions.[6] The Catholic church still opposes the use of modern forms of contraception, and its influence is strong in several African countries. The religious influence is also strong in countries that are predominantly Muslim. However, the religious basis for opposition to family planning has weakened somewhat because of the series of sensitization seminars and workshops for Muslims and Protestant religious leaders.

Because of high rates of infant mortality and the economic value associated with children, preferences for large family sizes have been deep-rooted. The social system in many countries still places great importance on male children, which itself contributes to large family sizes. In addition, polygyny is still practised in some countries, and the social status of women tends to be linked to the number of children they have. However, with urbanization and other modern developments, there has been a move from traditional to modern family planning methods. In addition, better health care and technological advancements may now be contributing to a decline in the preference for large families. In Zimbabwe, for example, where the TFR ranged between 7.2 and 7.5 from 1950-1955 to 1970-1975, the TFR is projected to decline to 5.79 by 1985-1990 (see Annex Table 1). Zimbabwe's infant mortality rate is projected to decline by half between 1960-1965 and 2000-2005, dropping from 106 to 50 per 1,000 live births.[7] Similar patterns may be found in many other sub-Saharan countries.

None the less, many hindrances still exist to contraceptive acceptance and use, among them inadequate information, lack of access to services, weakness in the quality of service delivery, and insufficient or irregular supplies of contraceptives. Most service points are still in urban rather than rural areas. For rural women, long travel time to clinics tends to influence their decisions on which contraceptive methods to use. Increasingly, they prefer methods that require only occasional check-ups, such as the intra-uterine device (IUD) or injectables. Such methods also free them from daily usage and the problems that process entails.

Historical legacy

The performance of family planning programmes in Africa has been influenced to some extent by the historical legacy in these countries. Although traditional family planning has long been part of African cultures, the introduction of modern methods in the early 1970s generated resistance from certain sub-Saharan Governments. Some were skeptical about the promotion of methods that, in some cases, had not been accepted in Western countries. Moreover, those initially promoting family planning were perceived to be emphasizing its role as the solution, in and of itself, to development problems, rather than as one of a number of strategies. In addition, because the region lacked the trained personnel needed for programme implementation, few nationals took part in the development and implementation of family planning projects. This reinforced the perception of family planning projects--and, indeed, population projects--as being exogenous. In some countries, too, nationals believed that the former colonial powers indiscriminately promoted family planning among indigenous populations to keep the latter's population size down. This perception has continued to evoke resistance to modern family planning.

Other obstacles to family planning arose from the legal environment, inherited from colonial days. Some countries retained laws and statutes that prohibited the sale of, or publicity about, contraceptives. These laws have only recently been changed. In addition, in many countries, non-medical professionals, such as paramedicals and traditional birth attendants (TBAs), were not permitted to deliver family planning services. These regulations are, however, under review.

One additional constraint is that countries with high levels of infertility have, despite their low growth rates, been approached in the same way as countries with high growth rates. There is not one "population situation" in sub-Saharan Africa, but rather a diverse array of problems and issues requiring specific responses to particular local situations.

Existence of a planning tradition

Since independence, several sub-Saharan African countries have outlined basic development objectives in five-year development plans. Goals include the eradication of illiteracy, attainment of equal opportunities for all citizens, equitable distribution of income and the promotion of employment opportunities. Countries that lacked the highly skilled manpower required for planning and implementing development programmes pursued educational expansion and the training of nationals with vigour. Today, as a result, national cadres fill the key positions in central planning ministries, sectoral ministries and parastatal organizations. The possible exceptions are countries in southern Africa, which to some extent still rely largely on non-national personnel.

The ministry of planning is the central agency that provides guidelines for national plans, co-ordinates sectoral plans and monitors implementation in line with national goals and objectives. Because development planning is perceived mainly as economic planning, government ministries responsible for such affairs are usually staffed by economists and a few regional planners. At independence, few countries had demographers. Those that did have them employed these scarce skills in their central statistical offices, especially in census bureaux. Even there, demographers were often at odds with statisticians because their roles were confined to censuses.

In the not-too-distant past, population was seldom mentioned in the development plans of most African countries. Population was treated as an exogenous variable by economists who tended to dominate the planning machinery, whereas population programmes were conceived of mainly as population control measures. One of the major points at the Bucharest Conference, reiterated at the Second African Population Conference (1984) and at the All-African Parliamentarian Conference on Population and Development in Harare (1986), was the emphasis on the integration of population policies into other development policies. The increasing awareness of the need to relate population matters to other socio-economic phenomena and to integrate population into the planning process legitimized, as it were, the role of demographers and population experts in central-level planning ministries and in sectoral ministries. Partly as a result of the greater involvement of population specialists in the planning process and of Governments' increased appreciation of the population-development interrelationship, a rethinking of the role of population in development planning has occurred.

The extent to which population issues are reflected in development plans varies from country to country. For example, Zambia's Fourth National Development Plan (1989-1992) not only devotes a separate chapter to population issues but reflects on population variables in other chapters as well. Generally, however, population issues have been treated as distinct aspects rather than being integrated into other sectoral programmes like employment, education, housing, agriculture and health. Moreover, the lack of national expertise and the absence of clearly defined policy have also constrained the integration of population elements into development planning. Integration of population in development is a specialized task that requires technical expertise and analysed data. Its importance has, however, been recognized, and appreciable initiatives have been taken towards its implementation (see Chapter 2 for more details on the problems surrounding the integration of population variables into development plans).

265

Health interventions

Progress towards better health has been hindered by illiteracy, poverty and poor sanitation; the scarcity of health personnel; shortages of equipment and drugs; and inadequate health infrastructure. An additional obstacle is the maldistribution of health services and trained staff vis-à-vis population distribution--70 per cent or more of health institutions and personnel are located in urban areas, where no more than 25 per cent of the region's population live.[8] These difficulties have been compounded by the inability of national economies to expand health services to meet the needs of rapidly growing populations.

However, most countries in the region have now integrated family planning services into their MCH programmes, which has increased awareness and outreach of family planning services. In addition, non-governmental organizations (NGOs) provide services in many countries.

Administrative and management infrastructures

The formulation of appropriate population programmes and their successful implementation and institutionalization depend upon a number of elements, including political will, technical expertise, supportive institutional framework and local infrastructural facilities (see Chapter 5). In many sub-Saharan African countries, these elements are weak and need strengthening. As a result of these weaknesses, the Governments do not have the capacity to make full use of available technical assistance for strengthening their institutional infrastructure and technical capabilities. In some cases, national project personnel, although given responsibility for a wide variety of tasks, have received little management training.

Some of the problems associated with technical assistance projects have been (a) overambitious objectives, (b) inadequate technical expertise on the part of project personnel, (c) failure to meet legal and institutional prerequisites and (d) inadequate attention to management and administrative aspects of proposed programmes. These problems are further compounded by, among others, the tendency in some countries to deploy the few population-trained nationals in areas outside their specialization. As emphasis increases on the integration of population variables in development planning, the need for specialists in population and development will grow. It will become increasingly important to deploy such personnel appropriately, so that the fullest use can be made of their training and expertise.

Community participation and grass-roots organizations

The basic constraints to intervention are linked to Africa's diversity in culture, ethnicity, religion, politics and economy. This heterogeneous situation would suggest the value of approaches that rely on local perceptions, skills and resources (the "bottom-up" approach) rather than on programmes imposed on the local community by a higher authority (the

266

"top-down" approach). A "bottom-up" approach would afford due assessment of needs and recognition for the roles and resources of all sections of society--household, community, bureaucracy etc. The strategy of initiating programmes at the village level and of obtaining grass-roots participation in the decision and implementation process of political and socio-economic activities can be adopted for population programmes. Some African Governments are already making attempts to integrate population matters into their district-level development planning and also to involve grass-roots communities in overall planning of population policies and programmes. To further this process, more attention is needed concerning the rural populations generally and disadvantaged groups particularly. Similarly, there is a clear need for gender-specific approaches, with priority given to special groups of women--female heads of households and female migrants and refugees concentrated in the rural areas.

Status of women

The status of women in sub-Saharan Africa has traditionally been linked to their roles as mothers and their other domestic functions. High fertility has been fostered by early and near-universal marriage, pressure from kin groups to perpetuate the family name through the male child, the low level of education for women and the occupations they engage in. In addition, the social network often cushioned some of the strains and stresses of child-rearing. To these contributors to high fertility must be added the fear of infant deaths.

Teen-age pregnancies in Africa constitute a sizeable proportion of the total fertility rates (see Chapter 3 for discussion of the health risks and Table 16, which shows age-specific fertility rates for women under 20 years). As noted in the UNFPA Annual Report for 1988, "Africa has the highest rate of births to very young mothers: 40 percent of teenage births are to women aged 17 or under. . .".[9] Early pregnancies severely impair the health, education and employment status of girls and the future of their children. In addition, compared with other age groups teen-age mothers face even greater risks of maternal mortality, which is already extremely high in Africa (mainly as a result of haemorrhage, eclampsia, infection or obstructed labour).[10] In addition, the health of women and children is jeopardized by certain traditional practices, dietary habits, and customs during pregnancy. Early child-bearing, closely spaced births, and pregnancies among older women have led to serious health problems among many African women.

Overall, 80 per cent of all African women live in the rural areas under conditions that support and sustain high fertility. Hence, it is not sufficient to create awareness on the potential contribution of women in the development process. Efforts should be made to promote women's activities concretely through education and out-of-home employment. It is now recognized that enhancing the status of women can reduce infant and maternal mortality, encourage the practice of family planning and permit women to participate more actively in the society and economy.

267

Historically, although women performed important productive roles in the family and the economy, they have not been adequately recognized. For example, in some sub-Saharan countries women are still legally considered minors, although they occupy high positions in Government and serve as *de facto* heads of households. In addition, the lack of reliable data on women's situation has constrained the ability of Governments to design and implement appropriate policies and programmes for improving the extent to which women participate in, and benefit from, national development programmes. The situation is gradually changing, however, as more and more Governments are taking special action to address these anomalies. For example, a number of countries have undertaken field surveys to permit analyses of the situation of women. The results will be used in the formulation of pilot projects and to set up data banks. Legal constraints to women's situation are also being addressed. In Zimbabwe, for example, the Legal Age of Majority Act 1982 gives women over 18 years old essentially the same rights as men in such matters as divorce and the holding of marital property.[11]

Many African countries have recently created the institutional framework for promoting women's concerns and for integrating these into overall development plans. For example, the Central African Republic established a Directorate for the Advancement of Women, and Senegal drew up a Plan for Action for Women, to ensure women's progress in economic, social and cultural areas.

Assessment of country programmes and projects

Data collection, research and training

Under the aegis of the 1970 African Census Programme, 19 national population census projects were assisted, and another 30 such projects received support for the 1980 round of censuses in sub-Saharan Africa. Activities are now under way throughout the region for the 1990 census round (see Chapter 2 for discussion of censuses and other data collection and analysis). In addition, several African countries have undertaken demographic surveys designed to provide detailed information on fertility, mortality and migration. More than a dozen sub-Saharan countries--including Burundi, Gabon and Zaire--have undertaken pilot vital registration projects. In addition, a number of countries benefited from the World Fertility Survey.

To meet the needs for demographers and other social scientists in great demand in the planning ministries, statistical offices and parastatal organizations, several African countries are establishing or strengthening training centres that offer courses in population in their universities. Sub-Saharan countries that have initiated such projects include Benin, Botswana, Côte d'Ivoire, Ethiopia, Lesotho, Malawi, Mauritania, Mozambique, Swaziland, Togo, Uganda, the United Republic of Tanzania, Zaire, Zambia and Zimbabwe. A key part of these training programmes has been improvement in the capability for demographic research to generate data for policy and programme formulation. Increasing emphasis has been given to the training of national planners and policy makers in the integration of population into the development process.

Supplementing the national efforts are the UNFPA-supported regional and global research and training programmes. Thus, training in demography and in population and development are offered at the Cairo Demographic Centre in Egypt, the Regional Institute for Population Studies (RIPS) in Accra, Ghana; the Institut de Formation et de Recherche Demographiques (IFORD) in Yaounde, Cameroon; and the African Institute for Economic Development and Planning (IDEP) in Dakar, Senegal. Other training is provided through the nine-month Global Programme of Training in Population and Development at Louvain-la-Neuve, Belgium; the Institute of Social Sciences, The Hague, Netherlands; and the Centre of Development Studies, Trivandrum, India (see Box 15).

Box 15

GLOBAL PROGRAMME OF TRAINING IN
POPULATION AND DEVELOPMENT

The Global Programme of Training in Population and Development has been designed to help professionals in the population field integrate population factors into development planning and processes. Participants range from staff members of national planning commissions or ministries of health or social development to population programme officers with field-level responsibilities. Supported by the United Nations Population Fund, the Programme has been undertaken in conjunction with the Governments of the host countries and participating institutes.

The Global Programme offers training for French-speaking participants from developing countries at the Catholic University of Louvain in Louvain-la-Neuve, Belgium, and for English-speaking participants from developing countries at the Centre of Development Studies, Trivandrum, Kerala State, India, and at the Institute of Social Studies in co-operation with the Netherlands Interuniversity Demographic Institute at The Hague, the Netherlands. The courses review theories of population in relation to development and present methods of analysing population dynamics and development processes, with supplementary training in support skills, such as statistics, mathematics and computers, as needed. Those completing the training course are awarded a post-graduate diploma in population and development.

In addition, several countries have undertaken studies on the relationship between law and population for the purpose of developing appropriate policies and programmes.

Policy development

As noted earlier, African Governments have increasingly recognized the need for strengthening or creating institutions for formulating and co-ordinating population policies. Since mid-1987, at least 16 countries have established population planning bodies aimed at integrating population into national development plans, and another 10 have set up or are planning to set up population commissions for formulating and co-ordinating population policy.

The creation of population planning units constitutes a significant indicator of sub-Saharan Governments' recognition of the need to implement population policies as an integral part of overall development programmes. However, the effectiveness of the planning units has been found to be associated with the priority assigned by the Government to population issues, the professional prestige of the staff and the director's political influence. All these elements largely determine the extent to which a unit can interrelate with and co-ordinate other sectoral ministries' population programmes. The unit should be located in an arm of the Government that has core responsibility for formulating and monitoring national development plans and that, as a result, has the mandate to interact with other parts of the Government, NGOs and the private sector. Where population units are located in statistical offices, their functions tend to be narrower and are sometimes confined to collecting, analysing and disseminating basic demographic information required by sectoral ministries, including the ministry of planning.

Maternal and child health and family planning programmes

Because of weak health infrastructures in sub-Saharan Africa, MCH service units, where they exist, are overextended. Usually, coverage of MCH services is itself low. In Sierra Leone, for example, only 30 per cent of the population has access to MCH facilities.[12] Hence, the additional responsibility of providing family planning services is in most cases undertaken at the expense of efficiency in the provision of MCH services. However, throughout most of the region, family planning has now become part of MCH and primary health care programmes. Significantly, the promotion of family planning through MCH services has contributed to its increased acceptance.

The effectiveness of integrated MCH and FP services is influenced by a wide array of factors (see Chapter 3), including institutional arrangements and degree of co-ordination, staff structure, and location of service outlets. Even in countries where MCH services have achieved wide coverage, the family planning component may be lagging. In one country, the Government located health posts within easy distance of the population; clinical and health posts offered a wide range of medical services including family planning; and the programme promoted primary health care and permitted nurses to carry out duties formerly carried out only by physicians. At the same time, however, family planning services were de-emphasized. In another country with adequate geographical distribution of MCH/FP clinics, the planned integration of MCH and FP services had been only partially achieved. In still another country where MCH/FP services were widely distributed, the family planning component had been judged weaker than others within primary heath care, although more recently, family planning services have been substantially extended. (For details on the topic of vertical versus integrated MCH/FP services and other administrative and structural issues, see Chapter 3.)

Problems in the provision of FP services include the lack of privacy in some settings. In Kenya, for example, the MCH/FP programme was integrated into the Rural Health Family Planning Services in 1982. Between 1980 and 1982, although child welfare attendance had increased by more than 80 per cent and antenatal attendance by 70 per cent, family planning attendance had declined by 10 per cent. The different MCH/FP services were provided in separate rooms, and it was found that the lack

271

of privacy in the clinical areas adversely affected family planning clients' attendance.[13]

Information, education and communication

An increasing number of countries have, with UNFPA support, embarked upon projects aimed at promoting knowledge and awareness of population issues to enhance responsible parenthood and to increase appreciation for the multifaceted roles of population in achieving development aims. These efforts have taken two major forms: the integration of population education into the curriculum of the formal school system and the introduction of population IEC into non-formal informational/educational programmes. During 1987 and 1988 alone, population education was introduced into school systems in more than two dozen African countries. By mid-1989, another nine countries were anticipating the introduction of population education on a pilot basis. In addition, eight countries had launched projects to introduce population education into the training of professionals through the curricula of, for example, agricultural and teacher training colleges, journalism schools, research institutions and institutes of public administration.

The number of non-formal population education projects has also recently increased--to more than three dozen in the 1987-1988 period. In at least six sub-Saharan countries, population education has been introduced into adult literacy programmes, agricultural extension, labour and trade union, and other non-formal programmes. Communication support for population-related activities covers a wide range of sectors, including family planning, censuses and civil registration, and policy formulation. (See Chapter 4 for discussion of each facet of IEC activities in the region and world-wide.)

Women's programmes

Increasingly, women's programmes and projects have received attention and support from the Fund in the areas of training, research, seminars, IEC, policy formulation, and action programmes. To ensure more concrete attention to women's issues and more effective integration of women into the mainstream of economic development, a new strategy is contained in a proposed "Plan of action: The UNFPA strategy for women, population and development in sub-Saharan Africa (1988-1991)".

272

Future directions

Programme issues in the region

The serious economic problems facing many African countries are exacerbating the difficulties of undertaking population activities--an enterprise that requires material and financial resources--skilled staff, facilities, equipment and supplies. The constraints to effective programming in sub-Saharan Africa that are posed by the inadequacy of demographic data, shortages of trained personnel and generally insufficient institutional infrastructure have been compounded by procedural problems in executing agencies. These include delays in project approvals, recruitment of experts, and equipment deliveries. Insufficient backstopping and administrative support, as well as the problem of staff turnover, have also hindered successful project implementation. The possibility of active participation of local expertise has sometimes been overlooked, despite the advantages that such participation would offer in lowering expenses and in enhancing acceptability. In addition, the capacities of Governments to sustain project activities have sometimes been unrealistically assessed. Greater involvement of national personnel and institutions in project design and formulation would help planners better gauge the extent to which local resources are available and likely to be committed to a programme.

Data collection, policy-relevant research and training needs

The need for improved data collection is perhaps as urgent now as it was in the early 1970s. There is still the need to improve aggregate data through surveys, vital registration systems and routine economic-demographic surveys such as the household capability surveys, the demographic and health surveys and migration surveys (see Chapter 2). Information on mortality--and especially on maternal mortality--remains scanty. Countries that participated in the 1970 and 1980 census rounds need to institutionalize decennial censuses and inter-censal surveys as regular activities--activities that have been constrained by shortages of human and financial resources. Cadres still have to be trained in all facets of census organization: planning, cartography, data collection, processing, analysis and publication.

In addition, more micro-level data as well as gender-sensitive and specific policy-oriented data are needed. Policy-relevant research to inform decisions on population policies will require much more attention over the next decade. As more African Governments set up their population programmes and attempt to integrate population into the development process, research should be geared to investigating the effects of specific population programmes on development as well as, ideally, the effects of development activities on population. Hence, efforts to improve the data base and institutionalize the data-collection machinery and procedures should increasingly focus on data for planning. Special efforts should be made to promote studies of socio-economic and demographic interrelationships by incorporating demographic questions into ongoing agricultural, health, housing, employment and related surveys to generate data for planning and evaluations. The need for studies that will help in the formulation and monitoring of population policies and programmes is urgent. Moreover, if the data are to be used for planning, timely processing and analysis of study findings are essential.

The training of a critical mass of national personnel in articulation of population policies and programmes as well as in all other sectors of population programmes is of paramount importance. This goal is in keeping with the overall objective of achieving self-reliance in formulating and implementing population policies and programmes, as set out in the Strategy for UNFPA Assistance to sub-Saharan Africa. Increased support should thus be given to regional and national training institutions in this effort. Such training programmes should draw upon available facilities at RIPS, IFORD, IDEP and the Global Training Programme in Louvain-la-Neuve, The Hague and Trivandrum among others. The substantive content of all training programmes should be strengthened to cover women's concerns and, to the extent possible, more women should benefit from these training programmes.

Finally, a research team composed of African nationals should be constituted to define, conduct, review and refine research on regional issues that would serve as a foundation for a future regional strategy for Africa.

Maternal and child heath and family planning

African Governments have consistently expressed the view that the current demographic crisis encompasses a variety of issues: the problem of population growth and high fertility; high mortality; rapid urbanization; population maldistribution; and teen-age pregnancies. The consensus expressed at the Second African Population Conference in Arusha (1984) is that child-spacing is a means of improving family welfare. Hence, programme efforts and resource allocation should reflect this view. Since African Governments have expressed concern over infant and child mortality and, more recently, maternal mortality, technical assistance projects should give more focus to these problems as well as to programmes that have direct and indirect impacts on population redistribution, tailored to the needs of specific countries.

Results of the World Fertility Survey show that in some African countries, even where fertility was already very high, many women desired more children than they were actually having. In Senegal, for instance, desired family size was as high as 8.8. Findings like these are particularly disturbing when related to numerous cases of illegal abortion and alarmingly high rates of adolescent pregnancy. Because contraceptive use rates are exceedingly low among African women, one critical task in the years ahead is the formulation of strategies for stimulating and meeting increased demand for family planning among women in general and especially among those at risk.

Research has shown that current programme efforts at child-spacing and family planning can also reduce infant mortality: both goals--the reduction of mortality and the promotion of family planning--should be vigorously pursued. Increased efforts must also be made to promote knowledge and acceptance of family planning practice among male groups in the society. Messages should be firmly rooted in the reality of every-day African life, acknowledging the importance of kin relations, the media of popular music, folk, drama etc. Results of anthropological-cultural surveys will indicate the most appropriate messages and approaches in diverse cultural settings.

The expansion of training programmes in family planning management and service delivery has become crucial in order to meet the increasing needs of sub-Saharan African Governments for trained family planning staff and improved management. This calls for increased support to various institutions in the region which undertake training in aspects of family planning. In addition, evaluation of the impact of projects should no longer be viewed solely as periodic events: continuous in-built evaluation mechanisms should form part of the strategies for project execution.

In view of the pervasive high maternal and infant mortality, Governments and the international community need to support the extension of MCH/FP services to hitherto unreached groups in remote rural areas and urban slums. Services, primarily available to motivated or easily reached groups, need to be extended to the population at risk--the four fifths of the population who are living in widely dispersed rural areas. Achieving this urgent goal will be difficult and will require effective integrated planning. Moreover, in a situation of scarce and dwindling health resources as is the case in several sub-Saharan countries, the participation of large numbers of health workers, backed by appropriate referral, follow-up and supervision systems, would be desirable.

With improvements in Government support, as well as management and monitoring, community-based distribution (CBD) of contraceptives could complement clinic-based services in reaching rural communities. NGOs have already employed innovative community-based approaches in which TBAs and traditional healers have been trained as agents to distribute non-prescription contraceptives--condoms and foaming tablets--as well as to treat common ailments. The potential roles of TBAs, traditional healers and others as workers in rural health care services and as channels for distribution of contraceptives should be further explored. In several rural areas, these are the only available "health" personnel and they are respected by the local communities. (See Chapter 4 on communication efforts as part of CBD.)

Of special importance herein are women's organizations at the local level which could serve as viable channels for reaching identified target groups. Market women's associations, thrift societies, women's religious groups and, in recent times, Rural Women in Development associations should be effectively mobilized for MCH/FP programmes and for immunization of children. Women's key roles in maintaining family health need to be better recognized and utilized for effective planning and implementation of primary health care and child welfare programmes. As mothers, they are responsible for sanitation and nutrition. African women also provide about 60 per cent of the food, which they process and market for cash income.[14] Finally, women are currently the prime recipients of family planning services.

Information, education and communication

Until recently the prevailing climate in several African countries was unfavourably disposed to population programmes, and there still exist pockets of resistance to public acceptance of population programmes. Evidence from various parts of Africa reveals the need to sensitize all sectors of the population, including political leaders, planners and policy makers, traditional and community leaders, and special groups, such as men, youths and newly-weds who will soon become parents, on the importance of population issues to family health and welfare, and to community and national development. Appropriate awareness efforts should also be aimed at the youths and teenagers who will constitute future cadres in the bureaucracy. (See Chapter 4 on IEC efforts and particularly on efforts to reach young people in non-formal educational settings.) All technical assistance projects should have a built-in research and evaluation component, as well as provisions for application of the findings, for enhancing acceptance of population programmes.

Women's role

Women should participate increasingly in decision-making, especially in formulating policy and in designing and implementing programmes that affect their lives. Projects that increase their capacity and skills to plan and manage such programmes should be actively supported along with explicit sectoral strategies to integrate women into the mainstream of economic development. UNFPA now requires all projects to show the extent to which women will benefit from the proposed activities. Thus, in addition to specific women-oriented projects, women's concerns are being built into all UNFPA-supported projects and programmes. Increasing attention is also being directed to assisting Governments in improving the data base on women and in developing appropriate women-in-development policies and programmes.

Role of international assistance

Today, more than 20 multilateral and bilateral assistance agencies support population programmes in sub-Saharan Africa. These different sources of assistance need to be adequately co-ordinated. At the same time, many sub-Saharan African Governments lack succinct policy goals and have limited absorptive capacities. Hence, they are unable to make full use of the assistance. It is thus imperative for the Governments to clearly define their policies, goals, programmes and priorities and then use these to guide them in directing available technical assistance to the priority needs. To achieve this, international agencies should provide more assistance to strengthening Governments' national and local machinery responsible for planning and co-ordinating population policies and programmes.

Governments receiving assistance from several multilateral and bilateral agencies should establish or strengthen central co-ordinating units within their administrative structures. The staffs of these units should be adequately trained to plan, design, manage and evaluate population programme sectors. Co-ordination of the external assistance agencies' inputs vis-à-vis countries' policies and priorities would be essential. In addition, technical assistance projects must show increased sensitivity to the special needs of sub-Saharan Africa in the field of population and development. This should be reflected in the nature, level and types of technical expertise brought to programme design in the region.

To ensure that population assistance is consonant with the needs of African countries, Governments, bilateral and multilateral agencies and experts from within and possibly outside Africa should continue to meet regularly to discuss substantive programme issues. Similar meetings among international agencies could also promote more joint programming and provide forums for the sharing of experience.

7. Population Policies and Programmes in the Arab States

The Arab region, consisting of 21 states and the Palestinian people, is unique in that its populations, despite great variation in wealth, share common social, cultural, linguistic and demographic features. Furthermore, though they live in independent political entities or states, the Arabs like to be considered as one nation. Socially and demographically, most countries of the region are similar. They all have high rates of population growth, a young population structure, high rates of marriage, a predominantly young age at marriage and high fertility rates with large family size norms. In addition, although most have recently displayed high rates of urbanization, the Arab States tend to have an agrarian, rural-oriented community life.

Along with the similarities, there are differences. Gross national product per capita (in 1987 dollars) ranged from $290 in Somalia to $15,680 in the United Arab Emirates (see Annex Table 1). Population size, according to United Nations estimates for 1988, varied from less than 0.5 million in Qatar to more than 50 million in Egypt (see Annex Table 1).

Demographic trends and their ramifications

During the late 1940s, mortality started to decline incrementally in several countries in the region--Algeria, Bahrain, Egypt, Jordan, Lebanon, Morocco, the Syrian Arab Republic and Tunisia. By the mid-1950s, several other countries, including the Gulf States, Iraq and Saudi Arabia, also experienced mortality declines. With fertility at high levels or actually increasing in the early 1950s due, in particular, to improved health conditions, the population growth rates increased substantially. In a third group of countries, those with more limited economic resources at the time--Democratic Yemen, Djibouti, Mauritania, Oman, Somalia, the Sudan and Yemen--mortality declines were delayed until the 1960s. Hence their rates of natural increase did not grow significantly until more recent years, which is why this group of countries showed relatively little concern about over-population during earlier decades.

Currently, all countries have high rates of population growth (see Annex Table 1). The region has a population growth rate of approximately 3 per cent annually, compared with 2 per cent annually for the developing world as a whole. Growing at this rate, the region will double its population in about 23 years. Fertility has been extremely high. Women in this region are likely to bear six, seven or eight children during their reproductive span, in contrast to two children per woman in more developed regions and four children per woman as a global average. High fertility stems from early age at marriage, the universality of marriage, pro-natalist cultural attitudes and the high correlation between a woman's fertility and her family's prestige in the community. Children are still regarded as assets rather than as liabilities. Contraception is not yet widely accepted (see Annex Table 1 for contraceptive prevalence rates for individual countries); neither is it liberally available from public sources in all countries.

Growth patterns in specific countries

Both the growth rate and the pressures it exerts vary from one country to another. In this regard, countries in the region can be grouped into four categories, only the first of which has adequate resources. The groups are characterized by the following:

(a)   Rapid population growth with adequate resources, the pattern in the oil-rich countries: Bahrain, Iraq, Kuwait, the Libyan Arab Jamahiriya, Qatar, Saudi Arabia and the United Arab Emirates;

(b)   Rapid population growth with moderate resources, the pattern in Jordan and the Syrian Arab Republic;

(c)   Rapid but declining population growth, the pattern in Algeria, Egypt, Lebanon, Morocco and Tunisia; and

(d)   High and still increasing population growth with limited resources; where, until the 1960s, the growth rate was prevented from climbing by high death rates. With further declines in mortality, however, over-population problems will worsen in Democratic Yemen, Djibouti, Mauritania, Oman, Somalia, the Sudan and Yemen.

In addition to excessive population growth in countries with limited resources, there are serious problems related to uneven population distribution; unplanned urbanization and explosive growth of the major cities; and poor distribution and unco-ordinated movements of manpower. In addition, some countries view themselves as underpopulated. With the exception of the Gulf States, countries in the region have high rates of childhood and maternal mortality. These problems have been building over many years, certainly long before the 1974 World Population Conference in Bucharest. The dislocations attendant on such trends--the pressure to provide for the health, housing, educational and employment needs of growing populations; the burden on urban infrastructures; and the economic and social imbalances associated with migration, particularly international migration--all pose serious problems for Governments in the region.

Relationship between population and resources

The relationship between population and resources in most Arab countries is becoming increasingly complex on both sides of the equation. On the population side, the excessive growth of 5 million or more people a year has been accompanied by increasing rates of consumption and rising social expectations. On the resources side, problems are contingent upon difficulties of expanding the cultivable area to keep pace with population growth; the need to import staple food, thereby increasing dependence on foreign aid and loans; rising rates of inflation; uneven distribution of wealth; and deterioration in public services. A few of these issues are discussed below, using Egypt as an example.

Increasing per capita consumption exerts pressure on resources. If, by the year 2000, the population of Egypt were to reach 70 million and if the rate of per capita consumption were to double, the pressure on resources in the year 2000 would be the equivalent of 140 million people at the current rate of consumption. If the per capita consumption rate were to increase by just 50 per cent, the pressure would be equal to that of 105 million people.[1] As oversimplified as this illustration may be, rapid population growth and increased consumption rates have already had severe effects on government expenditures in Egypt, as noted in a 1976 report by Prime Minister M. Salem, who remarked on the great increase in consumption rates over those of 1965-1975 and the shortfalls in production to meet those consumption rates.[2] Rising social standards and expectations intensify the pressure on resources. The result is increased demands for schooling, public services, communications systems, modern household and farming equipment, hospitals, clinics, housing projects, co-operatives, roads, transportation, imported food and

280

clothing, and so on. And, typically, it is the Government that is held responsible for providing socio-economic environments necessary for standards of living to rise, in both urban and rural areas.

Inflation, compounded by the uneven distribution of wealth, is straining still further the availability of resources. Thus, many resources are now beyond the means of the poor, the majority of the population in rural areas and in urban slums. Inflation also wipes out a sizeable proportion of the rising per capita income.

The seriousness of rapid population growth in Egypt stems from the nation's limited habitable area. The cultivated area increased from 4,758,000 feddans (1 feddan = 1.038 acres) in 1882 to 6,300,000 feddans in 1974, a modest increase over 90 years. The cropped area almost doubled, from 5,754,000 feddans in 1882 to about 11,250,000 feddans in 1980. Because of population growth, however, the per capita cropped area declined 50 per cent, to a meagre 0.27 feddans per person in 1980.[3] This decline is serious in a country still dependent on agriculture, with almost half the labour force engaged in agriculture. At best, the land contributed by mega-projects such as the High Dam can accommodate another 4 to 5 million people. However, it takes only four or five years to produce yet another 4 to 5 million. Thus, rapid population growth tends to nullify the land or job-creation benefits of huge development projects, which can hardly be duplicated every five years.

Policy development

Trends in perceptions of population issues

Countries of the region vary greatly in their perceptions of their population problems and of population policies to solve or mitigate these problems. Before 1974, only two countries, Egypt and Tunisia, perceived rapid population growth to be a serious problem and adopted policies to reduce fertility and slow the rate of natural increase. Several countries-- Democratic Yemen, Djibouti, Mauritania, Somalia, the Sudan and Yemen-- were concerned about their economic problems, not about population issues. Furthermore, the high death rates at the time kept their rates of natural increase down. Three countries--Jordan, Morocco and the Syrian Arab Republic--though aware of rapid population growth, did not perceive a need for intervention. The balance of countries--the Gulf States, Iraq, the Libyan Arab Jamahiriya, Oman and Saudi Arabia--welcomed their rapid population growth.

After the Bucharest Conference, however, almost all countries became aware of their high population growth rates. Yet, the perception of high growth as a serious population problem has continued to vary among countries. More countries have become aware of the effects of unregulated population growth on the economy and the well-being of their citizenry, particularly the impact of high fertility on maternal and child health. Relatively greater acceptance, or at least tolerance, of family planning has been followed in some countries by movements towards policies to reduce fertility for demographic or health reasons. Political support for these programmes has been increasing, although slowly and sporadically. All Governments are aware of problems related to population distribution, migration and uneven manpower distribution. The pro-natalist countries have not changed their stand, although some have made statements favouring the integration of population factors in development. The data base for demographic, social and economic planning is becoming available for more countries than ever before. Furthermore, in some countries, the media have been giving more attention to population issues, along with the introduction of population subjects into curricula. All of this is encouraging but will require gigantic efforts to be translated into operational solutions to population problems.

Population growth policies

The countries of the region can be classified into four groups according to policy direction. Annex Table 2 shows the countries' views on their fertility rates and population growth rates.

Four countries in the region have explicit population policies. All view their fertility levels as high and seek to lower them. They also view their population growth rates as dangerously high, and needing to be slowed through appropriate interventions. Two of the four countries in this group, Egypt and Tunisia, have had policies since the mid-1960s to attain the explicit demographic goal of slowing population growth. The other two countries, Algeria and Morocco, have recently expressed similar intentions to reduce fertility through family planning, with a view to slowing the population growth rate.

Six countries in the region--Democratic Yemen, Jordan, Lebanon, the Syrian Arab Republic, the Sudan and Yemen--do not have explicit population policies but have to varying extents accommodated family planning within maternal and child health (MCH) services or through private family planning associations. All view both their fertility rates and their population growth rates as high. Until recently, however, only two countries, Democratic Yemen and Yemen, had expressed a desire to lower their fertility rates, though they did not aim at a similar reduction in the growth rate. The other four countries did not plan to intervene. Jordan, the Sudan and the Syrian Arab Republic, have recently shifted their positions from no intervention to a desire to lower both fertility and population growth rates. The Sudan and the Syrian Arab Republic have been preparing the blueprints for a population policy (1988 field information). Lebanon has intervened through a successful family planning association and liberal access to contraception. Moreover, Lebanon has for some time had a fertility level lower than that of other countries in the region. Lebanon's birth rate in 1985-1990 was 29 per 1,000 and its population growth rate was 2 per cent annually (see Annex Table 1).

Three countries in the region--Djibouti, Mauritania and Somalia--do not have an explicit population policy and are not likely to have one soon because their main concern is economic development. They have maintained a stand of no intervention with respect to fertility rates.

The balance of countries in the region are pro-natalist, explicitly or implicitly. These include Bahrain, Iraq, Kuwait, the Libyan Arab Jamahiriya, Oman, Qatar, Saudi Arabia and the United Arab Emirates. Bahrain, however, has started to allow family planning in MCH centres.

Spatial distribution policy

Most countries are aware of the uneven distribution of their population and of erratic urban expansion, with unprecedented, explosive growth. These problems are common to all countries, rich and poor, and are compounding the overall problem of rapid population growth. Several countries want also to decelerate internal migration.[4] Nevertheless, little has been done to rectify the maldistribution of the population or to plan further urban expansion. Attempts have been made to build new cities to attract internal migration from the principal cities. Several of these city projects were started in Egypt near Cairo--for example, the 10th of Ramadan City. In Yemen, a second-cities project has been designed to create new nodes of human settlement. In Saudi Arabia, a multi-billion-dollar project has been undertaken to build at least two major cities.

International migration policies

International migration is active in the Arab region, where strong pull or push factors induce cohorts of professional, skilled and unskilled workers to seek opportunities in other countries. Governments have a great stake in the size and direction of such migratory movements. Countries that view themselves as underpopulated or lacking manpower resources have been doing everything possible to attract human resources. Most of these countries are oil-rich, formerly drawing their migrant manpower largely from the Arab region but now diversifying their recruitment elsewhere. In addition, there are migration movements towards southern Europe, especially to France, for French-speaking migrants from Algeria, Morocco and Tunisia, as well as towards England and the United States of America.

Some countries view international migration as undesirable. When professionals seek permanent residence in the West, they create a "brain drain", which affects many countries in the region. On the other hand, a number of countries (e.g., Egypt, the Sudan, Yemen and, to a lesser extent, the North African countries) encourage migration of professionals and skilled workers and labourers to the oil-rich countries in the region because of the sizeable remittances from emigrants. Remittances constitute a principal source of hard currency and national income in Egypt, for example. In addition, the sending countries can use the newly acquired skills of the returning emigrants. However, neither the size nor the temporary nature of migration is enough to relieve over-population in the sending countries. Morever, the sending countries have incurred one risk. As they become increasingly dependent on remittances from emigrants, their economies can be adversely affected by changes in the policy or the economic strength of the receiving countries.

The countries of the region may be classified into three groups:

(a) <u>The sending countries</u>: primarily Algeria, Eygyt, Lebanon, Morocco and Tunisia;

(b) <u>The receiving countries</u>: primarily the oil-rich countries, to which the bulk of migration is temporary, as a matter of policy; and

(c) <u>The sending and receiving countries</u>: primarily Democratic Yemen, Jordan, Somalia, the Sudan and Yemen.

Co-ordination between the sending and receiving countries is still limited. Both sets of countries would realize benefits from greater co-ordination, while enhancing the welfare of the migrants in the receiving country as well as in the sending country after they return.

Policies on maternal and child mortality and morbidity

The population-related health problems relevant to policy development include infant mortality and child survival; maternal mortality and safe motherhood; morbidity in relation to unregulated fertility, including teen-age pregnancy; and family planning as a health influence. These health problems are directly or indirectly influenced by the following sets of four factors:

(a) Demographic factors, particularly repeated pregnancies, teen-age pregnancies and closely spaced pregnancies;

(b) Social and environmental factors, particularly housing, environmental sanitation, nutrition and education of mothers;

(c) Health care factors, particularly the level of medical care, attendance at labour and childbirth, and child care; and

(d) The family planning factor.

Infant mortality and child survival

Infant and child mortality has undergone substantial change over the last 40 years, and particularly during the last 15-20 years. About the time of the 1974 Bucharest Conference, 17 countries in the region, including 4 oil-rich countries, had infant mortality rates of 90 per 1,000 live births or more. Only one country in the region, Kuwait, had a rate of less than 50 per 1,000. By 1988, a relative decline had occurred in all countries, with only 7 countries still having rates of more than 90; a total of 7 had rates under 50 (see Annex Table 1).

The greatest change was registered for the oil-rich countries, which have been able to manipulate social and environmental factors as well as health care factors, not only because of their sheer wealth but also because of their small, manageable population sizes, health policies, sound programming and political commitment. Countries with moderate or poor resources, that is, those that cannot afford extensive health care systems, have to depend heavily on family planning to reduce infant and child mortality. Thus, the risks attendant on pregnancies that are too early, too late, too many or too close, depicted in Figure VI, should be avoided.

285

Figure VI

HEALTH RISKS FOR MOTHERS AND CHILDREN
ASSOCIATED WITH PATTERN OF FAMILY FORMATION

*Number of children higher risks
for first, fourth and over
Safest: two or three*

*Pregnancy spacing higher risks
for under two years and over five
Safest: two to four years*

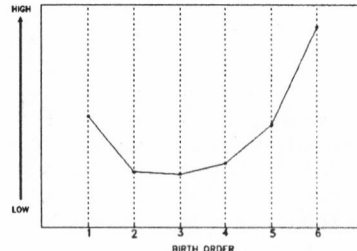
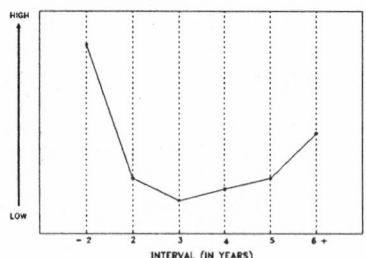

Sources: Adapted from Abdel R. Omran, "Health benefits of
family planning for mother and child", *World Health*
(January 1974), p.11.

Maternal mortality and safe motherhood

There is no accurate estimate of maternal mortality in the region; a conservative estimate of the average rate is 340-500 per 100,000 live births.[5] (See Annex Table 1 for estimates in individual countries of the maternal mortality rate and the lifetime chance of maternal death.) Concern about maternal mortality was expressed at the Regional Safe Motherhood Conference in Amman (1988) and at a national conference in Egypt (1988), where delegates from most countries of the region expressed acceptance of family planning as a measure for safe motherhood. The safe motherhood concept may thus become an effective vehicle for family planning, especially in areas opposed to the concept of population control.

Pregnancy-related morbidity

As discussed in Chapter 3, certain patterns of human reproduction and family formation can result in serious health hazards and increased mortality for children and mothers. They can also affect children's physical growth and intellectual development. These patterns occur when fertility is unplanned or unregulated, especially when pregnancies are too frequent (too many children per woman, or high parity), too close together (at short birth intervals with no adequate spacing), occurring too early in a woman's reproductive life (under 20 years) or too late (over 35 years). These hazards have been confirmed by scientific epidemiological studies, which, until recently, came principally from the more developed countries because of their early interest in maternal and child health. Recent information from the region points in the same direction, as indicated in a study sponsored by the World Health Organization (WHO) in 10 countries including three Arab nations, Egypt, Lebanon and the Syrian Arab Republic.[6] The results of this and many other studies indicate a variety of risks, which are depicted diagrammatically in Figure VI.

Family planning as a health influence

It is logical to assume from Figure VI that the planning of pregnancies to avoid risks would benefit mother and child alike.[7] In addition, studies attempting to quantify the health benefits of family planning have reported that almost one third of infant mortality could be prevented through family planning;[8] likewise the percentage of risks that could be avoided under specified family planning measures are reported to be high. If women who say they want no more children used effective contraception, maternal mortality would be reduced by about one fourth in the region. If, in addition, no births occurred after age 35, maternal mortality would be reduced by almost one half. Thus, the life of one of every two women at risk of death would be saved.[9]

Population policy approaches

In the policy and programming areas, the Arab region adopted demographic, health or human rights rationales for population and family planning policies, as discussed below. In addition, some countries introduced family planning within a development context.

The demographic rationale

Family planning to serve demographic goals is not universally accepted in the Arab region. Only four countries--Egypt, Morocco, Tunisia and, more recently, Algeria--have developed programmes to lower fertility and slow down the population growth rate, sometimes with specific demographic targets. In these countries, family planning is hardly separated from population growth issues; the media produce messages about the disastrous consequences of over-population for the family and the community, and planners and politicians sometimes emphasize the linkages. The demographic approach is typically rejected by the pro-natalist rich countries, because they can afford and would welcome higher population growth rates. In the remaining countries, including Democratic Yemen, Jordan, the Sudan, the Syrian Arab Republic and Yemen, talk about demographic policies was formerly almost a taboo. Proponents of family planning tried to dissociate the practice from the demographic implications. Only recently have these countries started to recognize the linkages.

The health rationale

Family planning to prevent calculated health risks to mothers and children is the most universally acceptable motivation for family planning in the region. There is no political or cultural sensitivity attached to this approach. On the contrary, Islamic doctrine endorses the protection of the health of mothers and children. If family planning can achieve that goal, it is religiously sanctioned, if not mandated.[10] The only problem that has surfaced is whether the health risks associated with reproduction are real or imported notions. Data from England, Europe and the United States of America documenting these risks have been summarily rejected as "imported" information that is irrelevant to the region. This was one of the reasons for the WHO study and others collecting indigenous data on family formation and health from several developing countries, including three Arab countries.[11] The results have been used in conferences and in information, education and communication (IEC) messages to enhance acceptance of family planning. The health rationale has also been publicly promoted in the 1988 Safe Motherhood meetings in Amman and Cairo.

Family planning within health services--MCH and primary health care--and for health improvement seems to be popular in the region. Eight countries--Algeria, Bahrain, Egypt, Jordan, Morocco, the Sudan, the Syrian Arab Republic and Yemen--are using this approach, which has paved the way for the development of population policies.

The human rights rationale

Governments in the region have accepted the basic human rights rationale for family planning as set forth in the World Population Plan of Action (WPPA), adopted at the World Population Conference in Bucharest in 1974 and reiterated at the International Conference on Population in Mexico City in 1984. At these meetings, Governments were called upon to ensure that their citizens have access to family planning information, education and services, so that they may effectively exercise this right. However, acceptance of the human rights rationale should not be construed to mean that these Governments are about to adopt population policies or provide family planning services regardless of their stand on the issue of population. Except in countries with official policies and programmes, the concept of family planning as a human right rarely surfaces as a rationale for family planning. However, all countries in the region are in agreement on leaving the choice of family planning to individuals, with no attempt to impose demographic targets (of decrease or increase) at the family level.

The development approach

The development approach holds that problems caused by population growth will be solved through faster rates of economic development and that family planning will be ineffective until certain thresholds of development are reached.[12] This idea was the subject of considerable debate at the Bucharest Conference. Interest in this approach in the region stems from the experiences of Egypt from 1972 to 1983 and, until recently, those of Algeria. The lack of enthusiasm for family planning in Democratic Yemen, Jordan and the Syrian Arab Republic may also reflect this notion. Many leaders continue to believe that funds for family planning would be better spent on development.

Although the Bucharest debate did not characterize the development approach and the family planning approach as an either-or situation, advocates of the former promoted the concept so forcefully that an either-or choice resulted. Many family planning proponents suspected that the development approach was intended to do away with family planning as a national concern. If the threshold hypothesis in the development approach is true, they argued, then until these thresholds are achieved, family planning will be ineffective, and once they have been achieved, family planning will become unnecessary.

Institutional arrangements

Two types of institutional arrangements were adopted in the Arab region: population commissions or councils and population units. The planning and implementing bodies in the region vary in name, structure and mandate. Some councils assume many of the functions of the population units established elsewhere.

National population councils

In Egypt, a Supreme Council for Family Planning was established in 1965 to moderate the rate of population growth, which had been identified by the National Charter in 1962 as the most serious obstacle to the development of the country. In February 1966, a National Family Planning Programme was launched using the health infrastructure as service outlets and, in 1973, a population policy was adopted. A manifestation of the "development approach", the policy stressed interrelated factors in socio-economic development, including mechanization of agriculture, improvement of the status of women and social security, better education, lowered infant mortality and the provision of family planning services. The policy also delineated the roles of ministries and national agencies implementing the policy. The name of the Council was changed to the Supreme Council for Population and Family Planning, with a secretariat or board carrying the same name. The board devoted a large share of its attention and resources to the Population and Development Project (PDP), which attempted to alert individuals and communities to the need for fertility reduction. For reasons that are not entirely clear, some of which are unrelated to the programme itself, the programme did not have a major impact on fertility.

In 1985, the National Population Council (NPC) was formed to replace the Supreme Council, with the President as chairman. Recently the chairmanship was given to the Prime Minister. The mandate of the new NPC covers family planning, women's programmes, child health and illiteracy. NPC has promoted an increase in the role of the media and emphasized population education in the schools. The current goal is to reach a contraceptive prevalence of 60 per cent by 2000. Programmes are being planned to increase age at marriage and provide employment for women.[13] Although there is no explicit policy to modify the inappropriate distribution of Egypt's population, efforts are being made to ease population congestion in urban and metropolitan centres through the establishment of new urban centres. Other measures include the expansion of industries in rural areas to improve the standard of living there.

In Tunisia, after initial family planning activities during the 1960s and early 1970s, a National Office for Population and Family Planning, with regional family planning offices and councils, was established in 1973. Though financially autonomous and staffed with its own personnel, the Council is linked to the Ministry of Health. The Council's mandate is to implement the population policy of reducing rates of fertility and population growth. The programme receives the support of not only the Ministry of Health but also the Ministry of Planning, which co-ordinates policy, and the Ministry of Education, which is responsible for population education in schools. In addition, new legislation has been enacted prohibiting polygamy and limiting the number of children eligible as income-tax deductions. Moreover, the social status of women has been improving.[14]

In Morocco, after limited activities in family planning delivery as part of health services, a National Commission on Family Planning within the Ministry of Health was proposed in 1980. In 1985, the Ministry of Planning expressed the desire of the Government to include a comprehensive population policy in the 1987-1991 development plan.[15]

Population units

A population unit is intended as a special unit, located in the Ministry of Planning, to handle population issues within the central planning units. The unit, ideally staffed by a core group of professionals consisting of demographers, economists, sociologists and urban planners, would be responsible for ensuring that population variables are effectively integrated into the planning process. It should be accorded sufficient authority and status to undertake the following:

(a)   Collate, synthesize and make available existing bodies of demographic knowledge in an understandable manner to policy makers as well as using such knowledge in awareness creation;

(b)   Advise policy makers on how to use the available knowledge for population policy formulation;

(c)   Draft or contribute to the drafting of population policy proposals;

(d)   Co-ordinate sectoral programmes for their integration into development plans; and

(e)   Assist in monitoring and evaluating the policy.

In the Arab States, as practice reveals, the functions of a population unit considerably overlap those of a national population council. The NPCs have had more prestige and political clout than have units placed in planning ministries, staffed by junior demographers or economists. Even if such a unit has a special status, it still reports to a division chief or an under-secretary and rarely to a minister. Thus, it lacks authority in relation to other ministries or sectors. Furthermore, the ministry of planning in the region is itself not a policy-making body; rather, it co-ordinates plans developed by individual ministries. Additionally, most such units have been placed in a manpower division--as Egypt, Morocco and the Syrian Arab Republic, for example--or in a statistics department, as in Yemen. With such a location in a department or division possessing no authority for formulating development plans or for monitoring other ministries, the population unit cannot monitor or co-ordinate activities of other ministries; this task has been assigned to the national population council. In Yemen, for example, the Population Unit in the Department of Statistics experienced difficulty in the promotion of population policy formulation because the Department itself was seen as a provider of statistical services, with no policy- or decision-making functions. Wherever the population unit was located in manpower divisions--in Egypt, for example--its functions were dispersed among those of the division; the functions of policy formulation and intersectoral monitoring were left to the national population council, which had been given the political power to undertake them.

Realistically, the roles of the population unit need the combined efforts of several institutions for their implementation. In Egypt, for example, the NPC's technical secretariat formulates policy and is responsible for co-ordination, the Central Agency for Public Mobilization and Statistics (CAPMAS) is responsible for data collection and analysis, the Ministry of Information is responsible for awareness creation and the Ministry of Planning is responsible for integrating population into development planning. In the Syrian Arab Republic, the Central Bureau of Statistics carries out research, data collection and analysis, whereas the Population

Unit in the Manpower Division of the Ministry of Planning undertakes the integration in development planning. Thus, the strategy of using population units as the initial step to achieve integration, as envisaged by initial UNFPA projects, does not fit neatly with the planning experience in the Arab region. Apparently, the concept of a population unit within a planning ministry was introduced at a stage when the planning process differed from what it is today.

Political support

Because of the sensitivity of population issues in the region, political support has played a crucial role in the introduction and successful implementation of population policies and programmes. The most prominent example in the Arab region was the consistent support given by President Habib Bourguiba from the inception of population activities in Tunisia. He used the media extensively for this purpose, never letting a public opportunity with relevance to the family and population go by without endorsing family planning.[16] In addition to noting the demands created by rapid population growth, President Bourguiba was also a force in raising the status of women and in incorporating population matters into development planning.

In Egypt, the initiative of President Gamal Abdel Nasser, through the National Charter in 1962,[17] led to a national family planning programme and to the adoption of a population policy. To give the highest endorsement to the population programme, the President became the chairman of the Supreme Council. However, this policy led to a shortcoming in implementation because, given the President's other pressing priorities, the Council could not meet as frequently as it should have. The National Population Council, which replaced the Supreme Council in 1985, was initially chaired by President Hosni Mubarak. It is now headed by the Prime Minister, who can delegate one of the involved ministers to chair the meeting in his absence. President Mubarak has repeatedly called upon the Egyptian people to take population problems seriously by adopting family planning. Other examples include the political support of the President of Algeria, the Queen and the Minister of Health of Jordan and the King of Morocco. In contrast, the lack of political support in some countries of the region has been constraining the family planning effort.

Extent of change

Since the 1974 Bucharest Conference, a dramatic change in perception of the population issues has occurred in the region, with increasing numbers of countries viewing their population growth rates or their fertility rates or both as excessive. Moreover, population subject areas, including family planning, are now more frequently and openly discussed in national, regional and international seminars and workshops in several parts of the region. A decade ago in Jordan, for example, family planning was rarely ever mentioned in public discussions, certainly not as a planning concern. In recent years, however, with the support of the new Minister of Health, family planning became a legitimate subject, especially within the Ministry. This new visibility was apparent in the discussions at the 1988 Regional Safe Motherhood Conference in Amman.

As a consequence, the number of countries adopting explicit or implicit policies to allow family planning--for health, demographic or other reasons--increased from only two before 1974 to four afterwards (including Algeria and Morocco). Two more, the Sudan and the Syrian Arab Republic, are drawing up blueprints for policy; and three more, Jordan, Somalia and Yemen, are providing family planning within MCH programmes.[18] There are also attempts at regional collaboration and co-ordination, with a possibility of developing a regional population strategy where interests coincide.

The family planning programme effort, as depicted in Table 15 (see Chapter 3), shows that some countries, particularly Algeria, Egypt, Morocco and Tunisia, are moving up the scale in relation to other countries in the region. Since the time of that evaluation--1977-1983-- contraceptive prevalence has increased by 5 to 10 percentage points in several Arab countries: for example, to 41 per cent in Tunisia and 30 per cent in Egypt. If both the social setting and the programme effort are considered, Tunisia may be characterized as having a "moderate" programme effort, and Algeria, Egypt, Morocco and probably Lebanon are moving from "weak" to "moderate". Even in the countries with "weak", "very weak" or no programme efforts, improvements have taken place.

Despite the achievements, the changes in perception and political support have fluctuated and in some areas have yet to be translated into action. Religious pronouncements of support for family planning are not absolute or universal in the region. Some theologians as well as politicians still view family planning as an attempt to reduce the size of the Arab population, and great effort is needed to convince them otherwise.

Problems associated with high population growth are today being compounded by increasing rates of consumption, high inflation and maldistribution of wealth among and within countries. Because progress has been slow and sporadic, each delay in action means that the number of births to be averted over time will become greater. Despite all the effort in the region, the demand for family planning is still low and, with one or two exceptions, the programme efforts are weak or non-existent. Moreover, population issues have not been sufficiently incorporated into development plans. Finally, although the countries view themselves as one nation, and there are vast areas that could accommodate larger populations, it is inconceivable that the surplus from over-populated areas would be permanently accommodated in the low-density areas.

Prospects for policies and programmes

The Arab people are pro-natalist by tradition. High fertility is a source of prestige and is perceived as proof of a woman's fecundity and of a man's virility. This attitude has been reinforced by high rates of child loss, which called for maximal procreation. To shift from this centuries-old pattern to one that condones curtailing fertility requires social, economic and political transformations. Even then, the impact is not instantaneous. Social change involving deep-rooted traditions is slow and uncertain. Over the last 50 years, such changes have somehow been setting in. In 1937, a group of Egyptian physicians concerned about the consequences of repeated pregnancies sought the opinion of the Grand Mufti of Egypt, Sheikh Abdel Majeed Salim, regarding the permissibility of family planning in Islam. The answer was affirmative and paved the way for a family planning movement in Egypt pre-dating the national family planning programme by 30 years. The notion of family planning spread to other countries, and thus the concept of family planning in the Arab region is unequivocally indigenous. The diffusion of the concept has been uneven, however. As discussed below, the factors influencing the success or failure of family planning are social, economic, political and cultural.

Facilitating factors

One of the factors facilitating changing perceptions of population issues is the unending debate about population in the newspapers, on radio and television, and in conferences, meetings, mosques, churches, parliaments and classrooms. The topics receiving media coverage are not restricted to family planning but extend to resource development, subsidies, manpower, emigration, "brain drains", new contraceptive methods, religious attitudes and many others. Although many of these debates are in opposition to family planning, they keep the issue alive in people's minds and may possibly be sensitizing them or at least removing the taboo of discussing that issue.

The introduction of population education in institutions of higher learning and universities is a further step in expanding the interest in population issues. Population education has been introduced, for example, in the Faculties of Economics at Al Azhar, Cairo, Aleppo and Damascus Universities, the Faculty of Arts at San'aa University in Yemen, the Faculty of Social Science at El-Jesira University in the Sudan, the Departments of Community Medicine in the Universities of Baghdad, Egypt, Morocco and Tunisia and the Institutes of Statistics at Cairo and Morocco. Population education in primary and secondary schools is scheduled to follow and has actually been introduced in some countries.

Statements by political leaders voicing concern about population problems or endorsing family planning have special influence in shaping the views of the populace and of policy makers and planners. Increasing visibility through the media of the consequences of population pressures may also change people's attitudes. These consequences include, for example, housing shortages, unemployment and underemployment, food shortages, a limited number of places in universities and institutions, and declining coverage by public services.

The emergence of the health rationale has had great impact on the acceptability of family planning. All countries have accepted planning as the means to achieve development goals, attitudes that may foster eventual acceptance of family planning.

The countries in the region have, over the years, developed considerable institutional infrastructure in the population field, including national population commissions and councils, population units and centres in statistical departments, planning ministries, ministries of health and other governmental bodies. There are also many training and research institutions, including some that are regional or international. All in all, the region now has a "brain trust" for population activities.

The region has also developed service delivery infrastructures that could be used for the provision of family planning services. In 1966, Egypt's national family planning programme was able in a short time to equip more than 2,000 health units to deliver contraceptive services--now more than 4,300 centres. Family planning associations and other non-governmental organizations (NGOs) have been providing services in 14 countries--including Bahrain, Egypt, Lebanon, the Sudan and the Syrian Arab Republic--some having no explicit policy.

Last, financial and technical resources have been made available to countries from national, bilateral and multilateral agencies. Population has thus been placed on the agenda for consideration by planners, policy makers, political leaders, educators and media specialists.

Constraints

Encouraging as the above factors may seem, several constraints are reducing the impact of these changes, although the result varies from one country to another and, in the same country, from one period to another.

The first constraint is the great sensitivity of population issues in the Arab States, based on social, cultural or political orientations. All the prominent remedies for population problems are controversial, including family planning, raising the age of marriage, effective population redistribution and relocation, restriction of internal migration and promotion of external migration. Still another remedy is increased gainful employment of women, which is not universally acceptable.

One lingering tradition in the region is the equation of numbers with power. There is also a nationalistic belief in some countries--Iraq, the Libyan Arab Jamahiriya, Saudi Arabia, the Sudan and the Syrian Arab Republic--that a larger population could be supported. Moreover, the ethnic composition in some countries has led to communal conflicts and rivalries to increase numbers. Such "demographic wars" are manifest where the size of the ethnic group brings with it access to power and prestige.

Pronouncements favouring family planning have been forthcoming from both Muslim and Christian theologians in the region. Because there has been debate in Islamic circles regarding the position of Islam vis-a-vis family planning, this topic will be given special attention. Since the Fatwa (legal Islamic opinion) given by the Grand Mufti of Egypt in 1937, several other opinions sanctioning family planning have been given over the last 50 years in different countries. Examples include opinions of the following: the Fatwa Committee of Al-Azhar (1953), Sheikh Shaltout, the former rector of Al-Azhar (1959); Sheikh Qalqily of Jordan (1964); Sheikh Nasiri of Morocco (1974); Sheikh Abdallah of the Sudan (1974), Sheikh Al-Boutti of the Syrian Arab Republic (1974); Sheikh Jadel-Haq, the Grand Imam of Al-Azhar (1980); Sheikh Qaradawi of Qatar (1980); Sheikh Sha'rawi (I980); and, most recently, Sheikh Tantawi of Egypt (1988).

However, some influential theologians have held opposing views, such as those of Sheikh Abu Zahra, Professor of Shari'ah Law at Cairo University, voiced in 1970. Opponents admit that practising contraception is not, in itself, against religion, but there is suspicion of the motives behind the family planning movement. For example, family planning has frequently been sponsored by countries that do not advocate the same practices for their own citizenry. Moreover, having maintained high fertility throughout history, Muslims cannot understand why they are suddenly called upon to curtail their fertility. Their experience with high infant and child mortality makes them insecure. What would happen if women reduced the number of their children and then some or all these offspring died? Children are the built-in social security for ailing or aging parents. Rumours about the dangerous side-effects of modern contraceptive methods are another constraint. There is also the background influence of religious faith in shaping a fatalistic attitude towards life. This attitude inherently conflicts with the basic philosophy of planning family size, which appears to be an important factor influencing fertility behaviour.

The planning environment

Despite what their name suggests, many planning ministries function more as co-ordinating than as policy-making bodies. Development plans are usually prepared by the individual ministries or departments. Algeria and the Syrian Arab Republic have more centralized planning, however. Egypt, after its 1952 revolution, and Tunisia, after independence in 1956, were the earliest countries to consider development planning. Initial attempts at planning were followed by successive multi-year development plans, a practice that spread through the region. These multi-year plans concentrated on social and economic prospects of existing and future population. With the exception of Tunisia's plan, however, the initial plans made no mention of population planning. After 1974, the approval of the World Population Plan of Action stimulated thinking about population and its possible integration into development planning. Pro-natalist countries have been more likely to incorporate population increase and spatial distribution into their development plans than have countries with family planning programmes.

In countries with programmes to reduce population growth rates, the budgetary allocation of national resources is concentrated more on satisfying population needs than on supporting family planning. The largest share of the family planning budget comes from bilateral and multilateral sources.

In Egypt, despite a longer tradition of development planning, population has not yet been integrated into development plans. Population is mentioned only vaguely and not even the latest population targets, set by the National Population Council, have been incorporated in the recent plan, although NPC intends to incorporate targets into annual plans. In Iraq, where economic planning has existed since 1959, attempts to integrate population issues into development planning became apparent in 1968, reflecting a pro-natalist policy with emphasis also on spatial distribution and agricultural reform. A Demography and Manpower Statistics Department was established in 1969 within the Ministry of Planning. This was followed in 1972 by the establishment of a National Committee for Population Policies, which is responsible for the national programme in development. Because emphasis was placed on data collection and analysis, a Central Agency for Demographic Studies for those functions was established within the Central Statistics Office. In Saudi Arabia, the orientation of development planning, which started in 1965, was to offset the limited population size and to maximize the use of revenue. A Central Planning Organization was established in 1965 to attempt the co-ordination of all facets of development planning, and comprehensive five-year development plans followed.

History of health interventions

The Arab countries have been more responsive and genuinely motivated to undertake health interventions than to undertake population interventions. The region's long history of health intervention started in Egypt in 1833, when a Sanitary Board was set up for quarantine measures and international hygiene. Six years earlier, the first and oldest medical school in the region was established. Progress in health agency development culminated in the establishment of an independent Ministry of Health in 1936. Because of foreign domination, other countries in the region did not immediately adopt this tradition of health intervention and organization. After the Second World War, however, with the advent of antibiotics and insecticides, much progress took place. All countries, occasionally with the help of WHO and other international organizations, launched programmes of disease control and eradication. These include immunization programmes, tuberculosis and malaria control programmes, oral rehydration to control child diarrhoea, nutrition programmes and

297

school health programmes. All countries have accepted the WHO target of Health for All in the Year 2000.

The features of the health system of the Arab countries that are relevant to MCH/FP delivery include the following:

(a) In all countries health care is the primary responsibility of the Government and is often provided free of charge. This is also expected in family planning services;

(b) In each country, a ministry of health is the central body co-ordinating and administering the country's health care services. Regardless of their population policies, all countries have witnessed the recent emphasis on MCH and primary health care. Many countries have added family planning to the functions of MCH centres;

(c) Health ministries are also experienced in health education, experience that can be used by family planning organizations;

(d) Other governmental bodies and ministries may also be responsible for specific health services. For example, ministries of education provide school health programmes, and in some countries they conduct population education; ministries of labour are responsible for the health of workers and can provide workers with family planning education and services; ministries of social affairs, which are sometimes joined with ministries of labour, provide health services for special groups and are responsible for the voluntary family planning associations in many countries, whereas the military is responsible for the health care of the families of the armed forces and hence can be an avenue for family planning services and education;

(e) Pharmacists are a significant component of the health system in the Arab world. Not only do they fill prescriptions, but they provide counselling and care for common ailments. Because of their direct proximity to the public, including women, a project was started in Alexandria, Egypt, to train pharmacists in contraceptive methods and the provision of related counselling. This approach is gaining popularity in Egypt and the region;

(f) The private sector--that is, private practitioners--is actively providing care. Although the prices are much higher than those of official institutions, the public has more confidence in the private services than in the public clinic or hospital services. In many countries, the private sector is a more trusted source of family planning counselling and services than the public clinics, but it is accessible only to those who can afford its services;

(g) The health infrastructure, which can be used by family planning programmes, is a network of local, district and central services (clinics, centres, hospitals and programmes). Shortcomings of the health system include the lack of long-term planning, lack of a system of priorities, inadequacy of services in countries with modest or strained resources, the predominance of curative services, poor training and motivation of personnel, weak referral systems, poor recording and inefficient data systems, and insufficient linkage of health service systems with other components of family care. All these factors should be considered in planning to use the health system for family planning delivery.

Extensive discussion usually precedes decisions about which infrastructure to use for family planning service delivery. (See detailed treatment of this issue in Chapter 3.) The most common practice is to use the health infrastructure as a matter of convenience, especially MCH and primary health care centres. In Egypt, for example, once the decision was made to provide family planning services to the public, it was immediately possible to do so by using the health infrastructure. The drawback of such an approach is that family planning counselling is more private and less pressing than treating diarrhoea, for example. Special training of personnel in IEC and tactful handling of clients are needed. Another drawback is that the health system's coverage of the population is less than what is needed in family planning.

An alternative is to build up another special infrastructure for family planning, which takes the form, in many countries, of special clinics run by the voluntary family planning associations. Lebanon is the most prominent example, where the association is the major provider of contraceptive services. In most Arab countries, such associations provide services but on a more limited basis.

Administrative and management infrastructures

The administrative infrastructure is perhaps one of the weakest links in the process of formulating, implementing and managing population projects in the region. There are several reasons for this situation. Top managers are usually political appointees who are seldom well-versed in up-to-date management technology. Rapid changes in management and administrative technology have fostered dependence on foreign experts, some of whom may not teach their local counterparts sufficiently. The few trained nationals are shared by many projects and their contribution to each individual project may be less than adequate. Nationals sent abroad for long-term training seldom return before the end of the three- to five-year project that originally sponsored them.

Other problems are that political decisions may supersede technical counselling, even after considerable investment locally or help from an outside expert. In addition, family planning and population programmes are difficult to manage because of their multidisciplinary nature. Moreover, administrators with multidisciplinary training are not easy to find. For all these reasons, repeated training is needed, along with adaptation of concepts to fit the administrative culture of the region.

Community participation

Community participation in the region as a whole is somewhat weak. This is in part a reflection of an administrative culture in which official organizations are expected to make decisions and implement policies. Yet, as mentioned above, the first move to institutionalize family planning in the region by seeking religious blessing came from a community group in Egypt. Most of the groups who participate in community decisions and activities come predominantly from the elite urbanites, women's groups, organized labour, professional associations and the religious hierarchy. The rural areas should not, however, be counted out because they are difficult to reach. There are traditional leaders in villages--village politicians, school principals and traditional birth attendants (TBAs)--who, if properly recruited, can play crucial roles in increasing acceptance of family planning. Even before the adoption of policy, NGOs--mostly in the form of voluntary organizations--were active in most countries, paving the way for population policy. They continue to do the same in other countries.

Role and status of women

The region has recently been witnessing revolutionary changes towards improving the status of women, a condition fundamental to their free choice of the kind of family to have. Some of the changes have evolved slowly within societies, but several are the result of legislation.

Legislation

Most countries have new legislation that amends the old personal status laws, recognizing the equal rights of women in giving their consent to marriage. Several countries have raised the age at marriage (to 17 in Tunisia, to 16 in Eygpt, Yemen and many other countries) and permitted women to have the right to vote and participate in political life (Democratic Yemen, Egypt, the Syrian Arab Republic and Tunisia). Laws regulating the process of divorce have made it available to both sexes in Algeria and Tunisia. Democratic Yemen and Tunisia abolished polygamy; other countries chose to restrict polygamy to actual need, provided the first wife is told of it (Egypt) or with court permission (Iraq).

Women's organizations

Women's organizations, associations and unions are now found in most of the Arab States. Their strength varies from one country to another, but they all constitute a major ally of family planning. The driving forces of many of the family planning associations in the Arab world are highly motivated women volunteers.

300

Assessment of country programmes and projects

Stages of awareness and action

Governments of the Arab States have developed different approaches to addressing their population problems. The greatest variance is between those in the Organization of Petroleum Exporting Countries (OPEC), which aimed at increasing their populations, and those in the family planning group, which aimed at reducing population growth.

Countries in the family planning group were not always so. For a long time, these countries also were pro-natalist. They expressed, first, awareness of the high rate of population growth but cultural reluctance to reduce fertility. Censuses and demographic surveys provided bench-mark data that helped foster greater awareness. Slowly, a stage characterized by fragmented and unco-ordinated effort began. These beginnings sometimes included the provision of limited family planning counselling and contraceptive supply in a few clinics, usually those run by voluntary NGOs. Media attention to population issues was limited, with cautious mention of family planning, mostly for health reasons. In this stage, occasional conferences or seminars on population were coupled with advice from international experts, usually sponsored by external agencies. Political leadership had become more alert to population issues but was reluctant to make forceful pronouncements.

This beginning stage was followed by increasing awareness and apprehension about the potentially adverse consequences of continued high rates of population growth--a stage of policy formulation. During this stage, a population commission or unit was usually set up to study problems and make recommendations to the Government. It sometimes took a long time before such a commission's recommendations were heeded by the Government. During this time, the use of contraception increased slowly through the efforts of voluntary associations, women's groups and the private sector. Some Governments also started to provide family planning services in MCH or primary health care centres, leading to an implicit or explicit population policy to reduce fertility. In many countries, a family planning programme was implemented, and a national population council was usually established for the purpose. This stage of policy formulation was sometimes followed by, or associated with, a stage of integration of population into development plans.

Initial undertakings: The Jordan experience

In countries currently in the beginning stage and moving towards policy formulation, the scenario may take the following shape, with Jordan as an example.

In 1970, a population adviser attached to the Jordanian Prime Minister's office as well as a number of consultants in various sectors were supported through external assistance to produce studies on the relationships between population and education, health, employment, water supply, housing etc. After two years of this effort and the preparation of nine sectoral papers, a national symposium was held for the discussion of those papers. As a result, the Government increased its appreciation of the importance of addressing the population issue and analysing its impact on different sectors. A programme was designed to conduct the first exhaustive population census to avail the Government of bench-mark data on the Jordanian population and its composition.

To train nationals in demographic and development aspects, two programmes were created. One was short-term training activity with two years of attachment to the Ministry of Planning's Central Office of Statistics for middle-management personnel from various ministries. They received training in population matters and the relationship of population to their own specializations, such as education, labour, health and housing. To meet the long-term demand for personnel sensitive to population issues, a project was started in the University of Jordan for teaching demography. It began with an inter-faculty committee and then matured to become the first Population Research and Study Centre in the Middle East, which now offers bachelor's and master's degrees in Population Studies. With these and other activities, the perception of population issues has been changing in Jordan, along with an increase in MCH/FP services. A recent decree from the Minister of Health specified that all Ministry clinics and centres should be ready to respond to family planning on request by the citizens.[19]

Basic data collection

Countries that had no population censuses--e.g., Democratic Yemen, Djibouti, Mauritania, Somalia and the Sudan--were encouraged to conduct one. For those who had census experience, UNFPA assisted them in modernizing their infrastructure and supplying the most modern computer equipment and training their staff in its use. Once adequate population data had been generated from censuses or demographic surveys, population planning units were established in many cases, usually within the ministries of planning to assist Governments in formulating population policies.

Maternal and child health and family planning activities

To enhance the capabilities of Egypt and Tunisia for undertaking nation-wide programmes for delivery of family planning services, external assistance was directed to equip their networks of health centres and to intensify the training of health personnel. In other countries, the main focus was to assist in strengthening services for MCH, with the declared objective of reducing infant and maternal mortality. Cases in point are Democratic Yemen, Jordan, Somalia, the Sudan, the Syrian Arab Republic and Yemen. Some of these programmes did not initially include the provision of any contraceptive method. As these programmes matured, and as citizens realized the importance of the smaller family norm, demand for family planning services was generated. It became incumbent on ministries of health to provide such services. In the areas of population education and information, Governments were encouraged to incorporate population concepts into the curricula of primary and secondary schools and to provide population messages through non-formal educational programmes, such as adult literacy activities. Simultaneously, intensive teacher-training programmes were launched, producing manuals to assist teachers in including population concepts within various subjects, such as civics, biology, mathematics and history.

Migration and labour force

For the Gulf States, the chief population concerns centred on their manpower needs as well as the need for accurate bench-mark data. UNFPA supported through technical assistance the organization and modernization of population censuses in Kuwait, Qatar, Saudi Arabia and the United Arab Emirates and through the International Labour Organisation (ILO) a regional study entitled "Towards a Planned Migration of Skilled Labour".

Regional activities

Several regional activities have taken place, including regional conferences, training and the establishment of a Population Unit in the League of Arab States.

Effects of programmes and projects

Considerable efforts have been undertaken in the population field for relieving population pressures at the national level, improving the social and economic welfare of the communities and, at the family level, safeguarding the health of mothers and children and lightening the economic strains on the family. This huge undertaking has been shared by the Arab States themselves, by bilateral agencies and by multilateral agencies. Even well-to-do countries have had multilateral assistance, largely in the form of technical assistance, conferences and seminars, training workshops and publications. Though it is relatively easy to measure the inputs in dollars or in the form of in-kind contribution, it is extremely difficult, except for isolated projects, to quantify the output and to determine which change is due exclusively to which source of support. There has been undeniable progress in many countries. For example, the percentage of married women of reproductive age using contraception in recent years is 53 per cent in Lebanon, 41 per cent in Tunisia, 36 per cent in Morocco, 30 per cent in Egypt, 26 per cent in Jordan and 20 per cent in the Syrian Arab Republic (see Annex Table 1). It is generally agreed that the size of the input has been much larger than the size of output, whatever measures are used. None the less, achievements must be assessed against the background of the region and with the recognition that most of the countries were unaware of, or indifferent to, demographic trends 20 years ago.

There have been improvements in the perception of population issues, awareness of the associated problems and, especially, a clearer understanding of the health consequences of unregulated fertility. What is still lacking is better articulation of the significance to programming of the data from the region. The data base in the region has unquestionably improved. Census taking has occurred for the first time in some countries; others have improved census methods and analysis and have gathered considerable amounts of data from population dynamics surveys, KAP studies and health surveys. Still unsatisfactory, however, are policy-relevant research and health service research in reproduction and family planning. Also lacking are regional studies with unified methodology and standard design. Another area of deficiency is the clarification of the relevance of the research efforts and dissemination of research results to policy makers.

There has been progress in policy formulation, with the help of advisers. The drawback is the inclination among some advisers towards adopting pet approaches to policy formulation and programme implementation, rather than undertaking the more difficult job of working with existing approaches.

Tremendous resources have been assigned to training projects for all types of personnel, ranging from TBAs to professionals in various fields and to top administrators and co-ordinators of projects. Deficiencies exist, however, in management training and the training of theologians in demographic concepts and situations in the region.

Development of a regional strategy

Programme issues in the region

Experience with population issues in the Arab world over the last 40 years has revealed several programmatic issues, some of which are specific to the region. Such issues deserve the attention of planners and policy makers as well as of the external assistance agencies and their experts. Prominent among these are the following examples:

(a) Programmes that involve social change, especially those involving change in family norms, are suspect in the region because such change is often perceived as leading to population decline. Hence, programmes should be culture-sensitive, and their potential benefits to the society and the family should be articulated carefully and tactfully. Community leaders are the best suited to undertake that task, provided that they themselves are convinced and motivated;

(b) Programmes involving social change, such as population projects, are also known to be slow in evolution. Rushing such programmes would give the impression that they are being imposed upon people;

(c) Political commitment by leaders can contribute much to changing negative perceptions of population issues and to articulating a country's need for population programmes. Securing this commitment will require convincing the leaders themselves;

(d) Religious support for population programmes is crucial, and religious leaders need to be made aware of the relevant demographic, social and health issues. A technical error is to take for granted the support of religious leaders, on the assumption, for example, that Islam supports family planning;

(e) External support for population programmes is sometimes suspect, especially when it comes through bilateral agreements. Multilateral support, particularly from United Nations agencies, is more acceptable. Furthermore, the final decision on directions and approaches should be that of the country itself.

(f) Because of the notion of Arab unity, the region is prone to adopting regional strategies based on commonality of certain issues, without precluding stratification based upon the goals of individual countries or groups of countries. The concept of regional strategies originated in the region itself, for example, in the Amman Declaration of 1984. This approach does require further nurturing and programming;

(g)   Countries in the Arab region have been more inclined to put the central authority for formulating population policy and co-ordinating population activities in national population councils than in population units. In Arabic, the term *Wihdah* or "unit" means a subordinate institution. There is also an inclination to put a top official (sometimes the President, the Prime Minister or a key minister) as the head of the Population Council;

(h)   The media have become an authority not only to reckon with (the press is described in the region as the Fourth Authority) but also to involve as an equal partner in IEC regarding population issues and programmes. All population information should, of course, be culturally responsive.

(i)   The role of international experts, once technical assistance has been well articulated, becomes prominent. Not only do experts provide counselling and direction, but they have a catalytic role in population programmes, and their participation is associated with improved and more creative performance by national consultants;

(j)   Integrated programmes of family planning, as part of MCH and primary health care, are more culturally acceptable in the region than are independent family planning clinics, provided the health rationale for family planning is articulated. Programmatically, however, the experience in the region is that family planning is the weaker partner in an integrated approach, whether integrated with health or with development. For this reason, some mechanism should be developed--in the form of a population council, a population unit, NGOs and other pressure groups--to speak out for population and help strengthen the role of family planning in the integrated programme. In addition to the MCH/FP approach, other outlets for service delivery should be used.

Future directions

The diversity of the population problems in the region should be recognized in population policy development or programming. A working framework, simplistic as it may seem, of what a population problem implies may be formulated in such a way that pro-natalist countries would feel they have a share therein. Such a framework may define a population problem as one that is related to population growth (being high or low), distribution, composition, characteristics, migration (internal and external), including the untoward consequences of population dynamics at the national level and the health consequences of unregulated fertility at the family level. Such population problems require the enactment of implicit or explicit policy for their management.

A related issue is that family planning is not exclusively envisaged for countries with over-population and limited resources. The rich pro-natalist countries should allow child-spacing, pregnancy timing and maternal health as reasons for pregnancy planning. Breast-feeding is another practice to be widely promoted. In addition, countries can go a long way towards improving child survival, which, if properly publicized, would eliminate one of the most deep-rooted motivations for excessive fertility.

The management of population programmes continues to demand recruitment of good managers and the development of managerial skills through well-planned training. The aim is to maintain and expand a critical mass of high-level administrators of population activities.

Evaluation of population activities should not be left to the end of projects. More interim evaluations should be conducted to supply feedback and permit corrections during a project's implementation rather than after its termination. Evaluation and management efforts will also benefit from improvements in the data base.

The infrastructure in the health and population fields requires considerable strengthening, expansion and reorientation. In addition, the motivation of the service providers has been insufficient for realizing objectives. In-service training and other means of handling this problem are required.

The turnover in population programmes is frequent and un-coordinated with policy objectives. When turnover takes place at the highest level, policy may be changed or the strength of the programmes may be affected. In Egypt, for example, with successive directors of the family planning programme, the emphasis in the population effort moved from a traditional, medically oriented family planning approach in the 1960s to a development approach in the 1970s, and then to a complex approach, including health and social development components, in the 1980s.

The range of target groups for population programmes for IEC should extend beyond the women in reproductive age groups to husbands, mothers-in-law, newly-weds, youth, community and religious leaders and policy makers.

A system of priorities is needed not only for the national programmes but also for external assistance agencies, which would increase the cost-efficiency of population activities and reduce unnecessary duplication.

Improving the status of women within the cultural norms of the region and with due respect to existing legislation will have a positive impact on population and family planning. Women's organizations can be energized and their role in population and family planning can be maximized if their involvement is stipulated in programme activities.

Because of the homogeneity of culture and social character, and also because they view themselves as one nation living within separate political boundaries, the Arab countries meet most conveniently the qualification for regional strategies. Several steps towards a regional population policy have taken place in recent years, including the Amman Declaration of 1984, the Regional Safe Motherhood Initiative of 1988, the activities of the Arab Council of Health Ministers and the formation of the Regional Arab Union of Fertility Care. The challenge to formulating a regional strategy in population is that some countries have diametrically opposed views on population growth and the need for family planning.

Amman Declaration

A regional conference on population held in 1984 prepared the Amman Declaration, which deals with the importance of the population issues in the Arab countries and endorses family planning as a human right. It also endorses, in principle, a regional strategy for population, provided that the variation in policy direction in various countries be accommodated and with the expectation that the policies would eventually become more homogeneous "within one Arab comprehensive conceptual frame".[20]

Amman Safe Motherhood Initiative of 1988

During the Regional Safe Motherhood Conference in Amman, 1988, an initiative was developed calling for, among other things, a unified regional strategy to reduce maternal mortality by 50 per cent in the region by the year 2000. The initiative also calls for regional studies using unified strategy and methodology for data collection and analysis.[21]

Arab Council of Health Ministers

The Arab Council of Health Ministers was formed in the 1970s to harmonize approaches and strategies to health problems in the region. The Council has an executive secretariat in Kuwait and is headed by the Kuwaiti Minister of Health. Although the Council has not yet addressed population issues, it was asked in the Safe Motherhood Initiative of 1988 to schedule safe motherhood on the agenda of its meetings.

Regional Arab Union of Fertility Care

The Regional Arab Union of Fertility Care is a pan-Arab society of professionals and policy makers involved in fertility care, including both contraception and infertility control. The secretariat of the Union is in the Sudan. The Union in 1986 convened an expert group to draw up a regional strategy for introducing fertility care services into the medical curricula in the Arab region.[22]

Co-ordination of external assistance

With so many population activities and so many sources of external assistance, co-ordination has become crucial to maximize cost-efficiency in using resources and to minimize duplication and wastage. It is incumbent on the Governments to co-ordinate external assistance through the governmental body in charge of foreign aid--the ministry of planning or the ministry of foreign affairs. Some countries have established a special office in one of the ministries to co-ordinate external assistance. The external assistance agencies themselves are, and should be, keen to maximize the results from their assistance through co-ordination.

8. Population Policies and Programmes in Asia and the Pacific

Stretching over nine time zones, from the Islamic Republic of Iran in the west to Samoa in the east, the region of Asia and the Pacific includes the earth's highest mountains and deepest seas, great deserts and fertile rice and grain fields. Asia is home to more than half the world's population and more than two thirds of those living in developing countries. Many millions reside in areas that are the world's most densely populated, and several millions in barren lands that are the least populated.

The region also contains most of the world's poorest and some of its richest people. Of 33 developing countries and territories of the region, 13 had a gross national product (GNP) per capita in the range of $80-$400 in 1987, and another 11 had GNPs of less than $1,000; in contrast, 4 had GNPs ranging from $1,800 (Malaysia) to $7,940 (Singapore) (see Annex Table 1).

The crude birth rate in Asia--28 per 1,000 population--is close to the world average (27 per 1,000, 1985-1990), as is the crude death rate (9 per 1,000, compared with 10 per 1,000 as the world average). The population growth rate is the lowest among the developing regions, except for Oceania; it declined from 2.44 per cent in 1965-1970 to about 1.85 per cent in 1985-1990.[1] Despite its moderate growth rate, more than half the world's annual population increase takes place in Asia. Of the world's 10 most populous countries, 6 are in Asia. (For birth, death and growth rates of individual countries in 1985-1990, see Annex Table 1.)

Much of the recent reduction of the Asian growth rate occurred because of the dramatic reduction in China's growth rate, from a peak of 2.61 per cent in 1965-1970 to 1.39 per cent in 1985-1990 (see Annex Table 1). Nevertheless, because of its population base of more than 1 billion people, one in every eight of the world's births occurs in China.[2]

Trends in national population
policies and programmes

Early efforts

The countries of Asia led the way in formulating and implementing population policies. In the years after the Second World War, public health measures coupled with the use of modern medicines brought about a dramatic reduction in the death rates in many Asian countries. Fertility rates did not, however, decline in parallel, and consequently, population growth rates reached unprecedented levels. By the late 1950s and early 1960s, Governments in several Asian countries--notably India, Pakistan and the Republic of Korea--realized that rapid rates of population growth were undercutting their prospects for achieving socio-economic objectives.

The importance of Asian countries in the history of population programmes was emphasized by Rafael M. Salas, the first UNFPA Executive Director. His statement to the Second Asian Population Conference in Tokyo in 1972 recalled the context for the first Conference in 1963:

> *"[The decision to hold the first Conference] came at a time when the international community was deeply divided on population questions. During the 1950's and early 1960's, the majority of Member States of the United Nations were reluctant to face up to the implications of rapid population growth. It was the Asian countries which kept population issues alive in international forums and which began an international laboratory for the formulation and implementation of strategies to deal with population problems".[3]*

By the time Governments of major developed countries fully recognized that high population growth rates were threatening their efforts to assist in the economic development of poorer countries, some of Asia's larger countries had already attempted to modify reproductive behaviour. India adopted family planning as a national policy in the 1950s, as did Malaysia and Pakistan, which then included Bangladesh, by the mid-1960s. By 1974, when the World Population Conference was held in Bucharest, 17 Asian countries had adopted population policies and almost all countries had family planning programmes.

Perceptions of growth rates

Policies and programmes differed from country to country, according to economic and political situations and perceptions of a country's demographic future.[4] They also differed over time, as did Governments' perceptions concerning whether population size was too high, acceptable, or too low. Despite changing perceptions, however, most people in the region "still live in countries whose Governments perceive the rate of growth as too high" (see Annex Table 2).[5] In response to the United Nations Fifth Population Inquiry among 35 countries in Asia and the Pacific, the Governments of 16 countries consider their growth rates too high and have intervened to lower them. This group includes Bangladesh, China, India, Indonesia and Pakistan--all with populations exceeding 100 million, plus Fiji, Kiribati, Nepal, Papua New Guinea, the Philippines, the Republic of Korea, Samoa, Sri Lanka, Tonga, Tuvalu and Viet Nam.[6]

The second largest group of Asian and Pacific countries responding to the Inquiry comprises those countries in which Governments consider their population growth rates as too low and are intervening to raise them: Democratic Kampuchea, the Democratic People's Republic of Korea, the Lao People's Democratic Republic, Mongolia, Nauru and Singapore.

The third largest group consists of countries in which Governments consider the growth rates satisfactory and are making no interventions: Brunei Darussalam, the Islamic Republic of Iran, Japan, Maldives, Myanmar (formerly Burma), New Zealand and Vanuatu.

The perception of population growth rates as too high or too low does not necessarily prompt government intervention. For example, Afghanistan and the Solomon Islands consider their rates too high but report no direct interventions to reduce them.[7] Bhutan considers its growth rate as too low but reports no direct intervention to increase it. In contrast, Thailand, which considers its rate satisfactory, is intervening to reduce it further.

The Government of Malaysia in 1984 revised its policy. Though still committed to reducing the current population growth rate, the Government adopted a strategy of gradually decelerating the rate of decline in population growth by encouraging earlier age at marriage and child-bearing. The rationale was that a substantially larger population would serve as an expanded base of consumers, with increased purchasing power to generate and support industrial growth through productive exploitation of national resources. Although family planning programmes continue to be available, the Government is attempting to influence the fertility rate by offering special benefits to those having more children--the aim being to reach a population of 70 million by the year 2100.[8]

For the most part, however, Asian Governments are firmly committed to intervening to reduce population growth: such policies are part of most Governments' development plans and it is widely accepted that reduction of growth rates is vital to socio-economic development and improved standards of living. Among the Governments that wish to increase their population sizes, several have intervened not to increase growth rates but, rather, to modify the spatial distribution of the population or to encourage or discourage international migration.

Nature and content of population policies

Population growth

In 1987 the Economic and Social Commission for Asia and the Pacific (ESCAP) collected statements of policies towards population growth at its Seminar on Population Policies for Top-level Policy Makers and Programme Managers, held in Phuket, Thailand. The policies of 10 countries, most of which are set forth in development plans, reveal the range of current concerns. These are presented in capsule form below.

Bangladesh. Having recognized population growth as its number one development-related problem, the Government has launched a multi-sectoral population programme emphasizing domiciliary delivery of maternal and child health and family planning (MCH/FP) services with community participation. The goal is to provide for health and family welfare and to improve the chance of child survival, so as to make the small-family norm more acceptable. The Government projects a population of 115 million people by the year 2000 and 175 million by the middle of the twenty-first century. The plan for 1985-1990 has set targets for an increase of couples practising family planning from 4.5 million in 1984 to 10.5 million by 1990, to achieve replacement-level fertility before the end of the century.

China. China's family planning programme aims at the postponement of marriage and the promotion of the one-child family so as to reduce the rate of natural increase from 1.2 per cent in 1978 to 0 by the year 2000, when the total population is expected to be approximately 1.2 billion.

India. Aiming at replacement-level fertility by the year 2000 and at establishing a two-child family norm, India's plan for 1986-1990 has set goals of obtaining, by 1990, 62.5 million users of conventional contraceptives, 31 million sterilizations and 21.3 million insertions of intra-uterine devices (IUDs).

Indonesia. The Government's population policy has as its primary aims reducing the population growth rate, achieving population redistribution, improving the economy and creating prosperous families. Since 1978, priority has been given to family planning for lowering fertility. To reduce the annual population growth rate to 1.9 per cent by 1994, the Government has adopted tax disincentives, income-generating activities for acceptors of family planning, a minimum marriage-age law and efforts to improve the status of women. To achieve more equitable population distribution and to control rural-urban migration, it was anticipated that by the end of 1987 approximately 2.5 million people from the islands of Java and Bali would have been resettled on other islands.

313

<u>Malaysia</u>. In addition to decelerating the declining rate of population growth, the Government has restated that it will provide family planning services as part of the family health programme to enable couples to exercise their right to decide on the number and timing of births, and to protect their health and well-being. Under the Fifth Malaysia Plan (1986-1990), the target for the number of new family planning acceptors during the period is 600,000.

<u>Nepal</u>. Since 1983 the Government has implemented its population policy through enhanced family planning services, the integration of population components into socio-economic development programmes and improvements in the status of women. The goal is to reach replacement-level fertility by the year 2000.

<u>Pakistan</u>. As set forth in the seventh plan, the Government's goal is to reduce the growth rate and to increase the country's capacity to save and invest, while improving per capita availability of goods and social services. The Government has adopted a multi-sectoral approach to family planning, with a comprehensive programme focusing on family health, responsible parenthood, individual well-being and family planning, with community involvement. The support of community leaders and others is enlisted for the social marketing of contraceptives on a commission basis. Mass media are being used to popularize contraceptive use.

<u>Philippines</u>. Under the 1987-1992 development plan, the population programme will continue to promote family planning to achieve a net reproduction rate of one by the year 2010 and as a means of promoting family well-being and responsible parenthood. Family planning will be provided as part of primary health care.

<u>Republic of Korea</u>. The Government's demographic targets for the sixth-plan period (1987-1991) call for a reduction in population growth rate to 1.0 per cent by 1993.

<u>Thailand</u>. To attain a goal of reducing the population growth rate to 1.3 per cent by 1992, approximately 6.6 million new acceptors of family planning will need to be recruited over the period of the sixth plan (1987-1991). In addition, approximately 5.7 million continuing acceptors will need to be retained. Measures to achieve these goals include expanded services, improved capability of paramedical personnel, increased IEC efforts, research on population formulation and management, and improved co-ordination between public and private sectors.

<u>Fertility</u>

Fertility levels have generally declined throughout the region over the past two decades. In East Asia, the rate declined in almost all countries, the most significant declines occurring in China, the Democratic People's Republic of Korea and the Republic of Korea.

In the Eastern and Middle South Asia regions, Malaysia, Singapore, Thailand and, to a lesser extent, Democratic Kampuchea, India, Indonesia and Sri Lanka experienced significant declines. In the remaining countries the rates were only marginally reduced or remained relatively unchanged. In the Oceania subregion, Australia and New Zealand experienced marginal declines.[9]

Because most countries of the region have been concerned about their fertility levels, both direct and indirect measures to modify those levels are in evidence. By the 1970s modern methods of contraception, such as the IUD, pills and sterilization as well as condoms and foam tablets, were being provided, generally through hospitals and health centres. Condoms and foam tablets were also available in many countries through mail distribution, home delivery, subsidized sales and village organizations and co-operatives.

Bangladesh, China, India, Pakistan, the Republic of Korea, Singapore and Sri Lanka have relied more heavily on sterilization than have other countries in the region. In China, for example, male and female sterilization were reported to account for about 47.8 per cent of family planning users in 1986.[10] Of these sterilizations, 25 per cent were vasectomies. In some countries specific laws permitting sterilization are in effect. Others permit sterilizations even though there is no official legal provision. Those countries in which new laws were instituted, or old ones amended, to permit sterilization in the 1970s include the Republic of Korea in 1973, Singapore in 1974, Bangladesh and the Philippines in 1976, and New Zealand in 1977. India in 1977 explicitly eliminated compulsion for sterilization or any other contraceptive practice. Countries in which voluntary sterilization continued to be illegal were Afghanistan, the Democratic People's Republic of Korea, Mongolia and Myanmar.

Though there was a trend towards the liberalization of access to abortion in the 1970s, today the only countries or areas where abortion is permitted on request are China, Singapore and the Northern Territory of Australia. In most other countries, abortion is allowed on specific socio-economic, medical, eugenic or juridical grounds. In Afghanistan, Bangladesh, Indonesia, Kiribati, Lao People's Democratic Republic, Mongolia, Myanmar, Nauru, Pakistan, the Philippines, Sri Lanka, and Tonga, abortion is permitted only to save the life of the mother, with a variety of penalties for breaking the law.

To encourage increased contraceptive use, during the late 1960s and early 1970s a few countries offered monetary incentives to acceptors. The first Governments to do so were India, Pakistan and the Republic of Korea, which gave cash grants to individuals to compensate them for loss of earnings resulting from a vasectomy operation or the side-effects of other methods. India also gave monetary awards and gifts to acceptors and referral agents.

315

Among countries seeking to lower the growth rate, the leading type of incentive is provision of free or subsidized contraceptives or services. Sterilization, IUDs, pills, condoms, and other methods are provided free of cost in most cases. In Singapore, all the services are subsidized. In Fiji, Malaysia, Pakistan, the Republic of Korea and Sri Lanka, pills are subsidized; sterilizations, where permitted, are entirely free except in Singapore and Thailand, where they are subsidized. In the Republic of Korea, families with a limit of two children receive priority in obtaining government housing, and, since 1982, low-income couples who are sterilized after having two or fewer children have been given a special allowance. As of 1988, free IUD insertion services have been available to all acceptors, regardless of the number of children they have or their financial situations. Since 1983, heavier residential taxes have been levied upon families having more than three children. The family law has been carefully amended to provide equal rights for women.

The Indian Government offers additional retirement benefits for families having a limited number of children. Some other Governments, especially in countries that have recently attained greater development, have introduced a variety of disincentives. Essentially these measures aim at financially and socially penalizing families that do not conform, through measures such as imposition of an extra tax, limiting paid maternity leave or adjusting priority in housing or employment. In the Philippines, maternity leave is granted only for the first four children; the Republic of Korea permits tax exemptions only for the first two children; in Nepal also, according to a 1975 law, tax exemptions are based on the number of children. China's "one-child family" policy has received great attention as it is the most stringent government effort to reduce fertility. Couples obtaining a "one-child family" certificate receive substantial benefits in health care, housing, cash payments, educational opportunities and professional advancement.

Ever since the concern with population growth and fertility issues arose, Governments have fixed targets for desirable rates of growth and fertility levels. From time to time, in response to social, economic or political changes in a country, they have also revised targets. For instance, India and Pakistan have revised some of their targets upwards, whereas Indonesia achieved its targets ahead of schedule.

Aside from the various policies for directly regulating fertility, other population policies have less specific effects upon individuals but anticipated long-term effects on fertility. These include policies expanding educational opportunities, raising the status of women and creating more equitable income distribution while lessening poverty. India, the Philippines, the Republic of Korea, Sri Lanka and Thailand have embraced these aims. Most of these countries also attempt to integrate family planning with other development programmes.

Mortality and morbidity

Over the past two decades levels of mortality in Asia have continued their downward trend. Almost all countries of the region showed improvement in life expectancy at birth and declines in the infant mortality rate (see Annex Table 1 for 1985-1990 levels).

Governments have generally expressed great concern about mortality rates, although specific concerns vary from country to country and over time. The eradication of certain diseases such as smallpox is no longer a priority in most countries. Interest has increased in a more equitable distribution of health care services and facilities, particularly to reduce urban and rural disparities, male-female differentials, and age differentials in mortality.

Many developing countries inherited their health systems from former colonial governments. Health care was primarily curative, and services were offered at hospitals and health centres, usually in urban and metropolitan areas. After independence, most Governments continued this pattern until its inadequacies became all too apparent. Among the first attempts to change the systems were the nation-wide campaigns to eradicate certain diseases-malaria, smallpox and tuberculosis among them. Temporary mobile teams fanned out from urban to rural areas as part of these campaigns, yet the health infrastructure in rural areas, where the great majority of the population lived, remained minimal. To develop this infrastructure, decentralization and co-ordination were later emphasized. In recent years interest increased in promoting integrated primary health care, including family planning, and in engaging community health workers to reach populations in remote and poor regions.

Today, all countries in the Asia region have policies aimed at reducing morbidity and mortality rates. Most have formal health plans, which are usually a component of the national development plans, although the share of the budget and priority given to health in the national plans have seldom been high.

Migration

Policies towards international migration have changed over the past decades, particularly in response to the changing economic climate. In the 1950s and the 1960s, little migration took place between Asian countries. Countries that had previously attracted migrants imposed restrictions on further immigration and, in some cases, minority groups that had formed as a result of immigrations were repatriated. The major movements within Asia at this time were refugee movements. Among continents, there was increasing emigration from many countries of the region towards the more industrialized parts of the world. During these decades, major movements were from China, the Philippines, the Republic of Korea and the Territory of Hong Kong to the United Kingdom and, to a lesser but increasing extent, to the United States of America. Other countries that sent fewer, though not negligible, numbers of migrants

317

outside Asia included Malaysia, Singapore and Sri Lanka. Many Asian emigrants also moved to Canada, Australia and, to a lesser extent, Brazil, the Federal Republic of Germany and New Zealand. Noteworthy migration took place among the islands of Oceania, from the smaller islands to New Zealand, and between Australia and New Zealand.

In the 1970s, the nature of international movements changed significantly. The recession faced by Western Europe reduced emigration in that direction, while the oil boom and resulting economic expansion in the Middle East greatly increased immigration into that area. Many migrants to the Arab countries were from Asian countries, mostly from India and Pakistan and in smaller numbers from the Philippines, the Republic of Korea and Thailand. Migration to other regions, such as North America and Australia, continued through the 1970s.

At present, a large majority of the countries are satisfied with the level of emigration, perceiving it as demographically insignificant. However, an increasing number of countries consider their own situations as unsatisfactory: the Republic of Korea sees its level as too low and would like to increase it; Afghanistan, Cook Islands, Fiji and New Zealand perceive their emigration levels as too high and would like to reduce them. As to immigration, only Australia perceives its level as too low and would like to increase it.

Spatial distribution

In the past few decades, Governments have given increasing attention to the distribution of population in the national territory, especially to the problems caused by increasing urbanization. Highly urbanized countries in the region have been the more developed ones, but countries that remain predominantly rural have come to appreciate the problems inherent in the megacities that exist today or that are fast approaching. Governments have adopted policies to meet demands for employment, housing and other services in the urban areas, and to ease pressures on large cities through partial redistribution of industrial activities and social services among cities of smaller sizes. They have also undertaken measures to slow down or reduce the exodus from rural areas. In the mid-1980s, these policies continued with increasing emphasis on rural development and technological modernization. Many countries have pursued the development of mid-size towns as industrial centres, with small-scale industries. The means of promoting these policies are familiar: incentive payments, free land, relocation or the building of transportation systems. More emphasis on regional development policies is likely as their demographic impacts become better understood.

Resources of population programmes

Accurate data on governmental expenditures on population activities are difficult to collect, as population activities now embrace censuses, resettlement and transmigration schemes, research in planning ministries on integration of population factors, and women's programmes as well as action programmes in MCH/family planning. However, most Asian countries have had for many years regular censuses, vital registration systems, research centres, family planning delivery systems and the routine budgetary processes necessary to fund these governmental activities.

While acknowledging the difficulties both in defining the limit of "family planning activities" and in correlating the data, The Population Council has gathered useful data on the resources budgeted for family planning programmes in 18 countries, 9 of which are in the Asia region. The analysis finds that in many Asian countries more than half the funding for such programmes is domestic, and in several--among them China, India, Malaysia, the Republic of Korea, Singapore and Thailand--the Government's expenditure for family planning constitutes from 66 to 100 per cent of the total.[11]

Bilateral agencies have also contributed, though population assistance has always been a small share of total assistance, usually less than 2 per cent of total foreign aid. However, such assistance plays a strategic role because it comes in the form of hard currency, permitting the purchase of equipment and contraceptives not otherwise available. It also brings urgently needed technical assistance. Multilateral assistance for population activities in the Asia and Pacific region has come primarily from the World Bank, the Asian Development Bank and UNFPA. Several non-governmental organizations (NGOs), including the International Planned Parenthood Federation (IPPF), have made substantial contributions, especially in the early 1970s, when they led the way in focusing attention on population issues.

The regional setting:
constraints and favourable aspects

Socio-economic and cultural context

The majority of the people in the developing countries of the ESCAP region are members of large, dense, rapidly growing low-income rural populations. Approximately 90 per cent of the total population of the region live in the low- or lower middle-income countries, which include the three most populous-China, India and Indonesia. Moreover, with the exception of the Philippines, more than 70 per cent of the population of each of the low-income and lower middle-income countries reside in rural areas (see Annex Table 1). National strategies designed to deal with problems of poverty and deprivation and the demographic problem of rapid population growth must direct their efforts at these rural populations.

For the majority of the countries in the low-income group, indicators of basic socio-economic needs of health, education, food and nutrition reveal great deprivation. For example, between 1965 and 1985, daily calorie supply per capita declined in Afghanistan, Bangladesh, Bhutan and Democratic Kampuchea, while in India it increased by only 26 calories per day. In China, over those 20 years, the daily calorie supply increased from 2,034 to 2,620 or 29 per cent.[12] Although all the middle-income countries start with a higher level of well-being and greater resources, they, too, suffer shortages of health services, housing and education. Because of unequal income distribution these problems are most serious among the lowest 40 per cent of the population.

Low adult literacy rates are linked with high birth rates and low life expectancy. To improve these conditions, the education of children is vital. Between 1965 and 1985 the ratio of pupils to the population of school-age children increased substantially. In many of the poorer countries, however, substantial proportions of children, especially girls, were not enrolled.[13]

In most countries of the region, religion has not presented serious obstacles to the introduction of family planning programmes over the last 30 years. Almost every Government has a population policy. The religious faiths with the most adherents in Asia are Hinduism, Buddhism, Confucianism, Taoism, Islam and, to a lesser extent, Christianity. Hindu teachings on the whole have a strong pro-natalist orientation: the begetting of a son is regarded as a prime religious duty, as a means not only of continuing the family line and serving the caste law but also of providing salvation for the father and his ancestors. Islam is also pro-natalist, an orientation stemming from the belief that children are among the richest blessings of Allah. Roman Catholicism, the religion of the majority of Christians in Asia, holds procreation to be an obligation for those who choose to marry. Buddhism lacks the injunctions to marry and procreate found in other major religions. Pro-natalist influences in Buddhist cultures appear to come mainly from folk mores.

Societal views towards contraception may be shaped by fatalistic beliefs, such as those associated with *karma* and *kismet*, more than formal religious tenets. Neither Hinduism nor Buddhism has explicit teachings bearing on family planning in the contemporary sense. Though Moslem opinion may be divided on the morality of efforts to regulate fertility, the weight of Islamic scholarship holds that temporary measures to prevent conception do not contravene Islamic law, and various Islamic principles provide the basis for sanctioning contraception.[14] In Catholicism, periodic abstinence is the only acceptable "method" of family planning. However, in the Philippines, where the influence of the Catholic church is strong, the Government in 1987 adopted a policy that permits couples to choose voluntarily whatever means they wish for determining family size; both governmental and non-governmental programmes provide family planning services.

Even though major religious figures in the country may support the practice of family planning, many villagers in Moslem, Hindu and Buddhist countries assume that their religion prohibits family planning. To overcome this lag in attitudes, family planning programmes are increasingly turning to traditional health providers and community leaders for the delivery of rural services. They are also designing programmes to be compatible with specific religious and cultural mores.[15]

Other societal and cultural constraints affecting attitudes towards fertility and contraception are found in varying degrees throughout the region. These include the low status of women in patriarchal societies, discussed later in this section, dependence on children--especially sons--as insurance against old age and infirmity, the labour value of children to the family, continuing preference for sons, and low ages of marriage for women. Information and education programmes as well as programmes to increase health care and well-being of the population are addressing these attitudes with varying degrees of success.

Political ideology and commitment

If the pace of economic development is to increase--if politicians truly mean to lead their people to better lives--they must devote more of their energies and attention to population problems.

The continuing commitments of Asian Governments to population programmes over the past quarter-century would seem to demonstrate considerable political will to solve national population problems. Another indication of strong political support for population programmes is the "Statements by World Leaders", prepared for the 1984 International Conference on Population in Mexico City.[16] Yet these manifestations of support must be reviewed against actual governmental actions. The strongest political will is unavailing when a Government lacks the domestic resources or foreign assistance necessary for carrying out its programme. Many Asian and Pacific countries are attempting to cope with urbanization--with all its attendant problems of housing, transportation and maintaining a livable environment--while simultaneously attempting, with more or less success, to deliver health care, education, better agricultural practices, and sometimes even land reform, to the rural areas where most of their populations live. Several countries are facing internal rebellions of ethnic or religious or political minorities. In such contexts, long-term population programmes may seem to lack the urgency commanded by floods, uprisings or threats of invasion.

One evidence of strong support, however, is the establishment of the Asian Forum of Parliamentarians on Population and Development. The First Conference of the Forum was held in New Delhi in 1984, the second in Beijing in 1987. Parliamentarians from 23 countries attended the Second Conference, issuing a declaration on population and development that could serve as an outline for action in the region for years to come (see Box 16).

Box 16

ASIAN FORUM BEIJING DECLARATION

Following are selected passages from the Declaration of the Second Conference of the Asian Forum of Parliamentarians on Population and Development. Held in Beijing, China, 23-25 September 1987, the Conference was attended by Parliamentarians from 23 Asian countries to address population and development issues.

"PREAMBLE":

1. We, the Parliamentarians from 23 countries of Asia attending the Second Conference of the ASIAN FORUM of Parliamentarians on Population and Development . . . in addressing ourselves to the issues related to population and development:

   ■ Note with satisfaction the continued commitment of Asian Parliamentarians to initiate and pursue action to achieve effective integration of population into development policies and programmes and to work out a sound solution to the problems of population and development;

   ■ Recognize the progress made towards the reduction of fertility and infant mortality rates through organized family planning programmes and general socio-economic development activities in Asian countries, taking special note in this regard of the inextricable link between population, resources and environment in the efforts to resolve the issues of poverty and development;

- Strongly reaffirm the commitment to help achieve one of the key recommendations of the Beijing and Delhi Declarations: to attain a 1 per cent annual population growth rate for the Asian region by the year 2000;

- Recognize that further reduction of maternal and infant mortality, strengthening of maternal and child welfare programmes and acceleration of family planning acceptance are urgently needed;

- Emphasize the crucial role of the family as the basic unit of the society in the solution of population and development problems;

- Recognize the changing position of women in Asian society and fully support measures aimed at providing women equal access along with men to opportunities which will enable them to discharge new and enlarged roles in the family and the society;

- Reiterate the need to establish effective measures to achieve patterns of population distribution appropriate for each country's overall level of socio-economic development.

PROGRAMME OF ACTION

Population Growth Rate Reduction:

The following action needs to be initiated and supported by parliamentarians in order to achieve the desired rate of growth:

- Incorporation of comprehensive population policies in all development plans;

- Rapid expansion of easily accessible family planning information and services to all segments of the population throughout the region;

- Immediate, and continuous, improvement in both the delivery of primary health care and services to the entire population and the linkage of these services with family planning services;

- Acceleration of efforts to attain universal literacy, especially among women and youth;

- Abrogation or removal of laws, rules, regulations, customs and practices that discriminate against women or limit their access on an equal basis with men to opportunities in health, education and employment;

- Strengthening of family planning programmes through improved management, expanded training of personnel, and development of information, education and communication programmes appropriate to different groups within the

323

population, especially young men and women, who constitute nearly 60 per cent of the Asian population;

■ Establishment of public information programmes and other programmes to promote responsible parenthood including family planning for both men and women and sharing of responsibilities between them in child rearing and household work;

■ Removal of all bureaucratic obstacles to participation in family planning programmes".

Source: *Report: Second Conference of Asian Forum of Parliamentarians on Population and Development*, 23-25 September 1987, Beijing, China (New York, UNFPA, n.d.), chap. I, pp. 1-4.

In many countries, however, political commitment must be renewed if the Governments are to be able to deal effectively with population issues. The very poor--of whom there are so many--have little time or strength to devote to ideologies, leaving politics to the powerful elites that have ruled for many years. There is a tradition of respect for the ruler, but few countries have the links from villages to the central government--or even to the state or province--that would bring the information, direction and financing necessary to carry out the Government's development plans effectively.

For effective programmes, the ability to reach people with information and a broad range of contraceptive services is more important than ideological stance. China, Indonesia, the Republic of Korea and Thailand--with very different political ideologies--have implemented their family planning policies successfully because they have devised means of reaching the men and women who make the decisions and use contraceptive measures to limit their family's size. Regardless of the channels, when information and services are continually available to couples, family planning programmes have succeeded in reducing fertility.

Institutional arrangements: existence of a planning tradition

A great advantage for Asian and Pacific Governments in dealing with population problems is that a planning tradition exists in almost all the countries of the region. Whether it emerged from a history of colonial rule, from the necessity for order after a revolution, or from ideological commitment to socialist economic principles, the concept of intervention to improve economic and social life is fully accepted by Governments. One effect of the concern with growing populations has been to establish long-term planning even more firmly as a governmental task. If populations were stable, planning for future needs would assume far less urgency, even in the poorest countries. The awareness of growth rates derived from recent censuses and statistical analyses has given greater force to rationales for comprehensive planning.

The World Population Plan of Action, adopted by the 1974 Bucharest Conference, emphasizes the need for policies that recognize the relationship between population and development issues. To implement the agreement reached at Bucharest, many Governments incorporated population policies into their national development plans. The formal system of development planning at the national level that many developing countries had initiated in the 1950s and 1960s became more detailed and comprehensive as experience with planned development grew. Today, Governments often include population policies and programmes in their plans, usually in the form of estimates of population size and growth, projections, major problems, basic policy to solve them and detailed measures aimed at changing the current situation.

Yet the extent to which population planning has been integrated into development plans varies a great deal in the region. Development plans of several countries mention a wide range of problems linked to population growth, and some emphasize rapid growth as the primary obstacle to achieving plan targets. In a number of countries, e.g., Indonesia, Malaysia and Thailand, an increasing sophistication in dealing with population-development relationships is evident from one plan to the next. As discussed in Chapter 2 on policy development, however, much remains to be done to ensure sufficient attention to the often negative demographic impact of economic policies.

The major population policy concern of Governments of the region has been with problems of over-population and high fertility levels. Many countries have established institutions that are responsible for formulating and implementing population policy. Some Governments have institutions concerned only with a special sector of the population policy, such as family planning, as in Bangladesh, China and Malaysia; others, like Indonesia, have more than one institution equally responsible for implementing population policies. In China, the responsible institution is the State Family Planning Commission; in Indonesia, the responsible institutions are the State Ministry for Population and Environment, the Ministry of Transmigration, and the National Family Planning Co-ordinating Board; in Pakistan, the institutions are the National Council on Population and the Population Welfare Division; in the Philippines, the institution is the Commission on Population; in the Republic of Korea, the institution is the Economic Planning Board (Population Policy Co-ordination Committee); and in Sri Lanka, the institution is the Ministry of Policy, Planning and Implementation.

As more attention has been paid in recent years to interventions beyond family planning, most countries have adopted policies to improve the status of women, establishing institutions to implement these policies. If the increasing concern with spatial distribution and international

325

migration persists, one can expect to see new institutions established within Governments to implement policies affecting these areas.

Population units have sometimes been established within national planning agencies, but in the competition for trained staff in the overall planning effort population planning has not performed notably well. Some national planning agencies operate as if, once a population policy to limit growth has been adopted and a programme of family planning installed under another agency, there is little more to be done in the national plan. Although university research and *ad hoc* committees can be valuable in assessing the population aspects of the national plan, they are no substitute for a qualified population staff continually working within a planning agency itself.

Administrative and management infrastructure

Because of their early adoption of population policies, and especially policies to reduce fertility, the larger countries of the region today have better placed administrative and managerial infrastructure than have most countries in other regions. Many Governments have population planning and co-ordinating units, with experienced, high-ranking civil servants frequently responsible for implementing the Government's population policies. Experts in demography, family planning management, logistics, contraceptive technology and the many other professions of the population field are frequently recruited from Asian countries to provide their skills to programmes in developed and developing countries and to international organizations. Population institutes and centres for study and research have been established in many countries, especially in China and India, and universities that offer population or demographic studies are found in almost every major country. Because of the nature of their transition from the colonial period, the Governments of the sub-continent in particular have a tradition of professional civil servants and adequate budgetary mechanisms at the central level of administration.

There is, however, room for improvement in the administration and management of population programmes. One problem cited by every observer of programmes in the sub-continent is that, while professional civil servants abound, many of the men and women employed in family planning programmes are not members of the civil service and have none of the protections of pay scales and tenure that make such service attractive. Although many reasons for this can be advanced, the final conclusion must be that Governments have not yet given population programmes the continuing priority that is necessary to attract and keep the best qualified staff available for government posts. When Governments are uncertain as to how best to carry out family planning programmes, they are unwilling to commit themselves to establishing trained permanent cadres of family planning workers. Field-workers are trained and assigned responsibilities, often at the insistence of an external assistance agency, but when the agency's attention shifts to other programmes or when extra-budgetary funds are unavailable for any reason, cadres are dismissed or reassigned to other work.

The very fact of the enormous populations of the largest countries of Asia means that Governments with the most severe problems of over-centralization and difficulties of communication with rural populations are those that should do most to design and implement effective family planning programmes. If the family planning programme is too centralized, the great size of the governmental subunits, such as states and districts, can be a handicap to operationalizing large programmes.

The Indian Family Welfare Programme, which has shown substantial progress in recent years, may serve as an example of some of the administrative and management problems afflicting some programmes in the region. It is a centrally organized and funded programme located within the Ministry of Health and Family Welfare. State governments are responsible for implementation of programme activities. The Indian programme's orientation towards attainment of demographic objectives, emphasizing sterilization as a certain one-step intervention to reduce fertility rates, has resulted in target-setting for the numbers of sterilizations and the generation of innumerable reports upward from rural areas to Delhi. This approach has the benefit of relative simplicity of administration, though no programme covering all-India can be simple. However, it underestimates the emerging understanding that men and women do not welcome sterilization until they are certain that they have achieved their desired family size. Acceptance of sterilization is thus likely to occur towards the end of their reproductive lives.

The Government of India has announced the desirability of expanding the use of reversible methods, with the expectation that this will increase the contraceptive prevalence rate. Although a wider choice of contraceptives may make the programme acceptable to more people, this shift of emphasis will bring more problems of administration and management. A "peoples' programme" will require a different approach from a centrally directed programme.[17]

National administration of a programme like India's requires a recognition of variations among subunits in terms of population density, availability of transport and communications, or contraceptives. An overly rigid comparison of results by subunit will rule out experimentation with new means of reaching people. Increasing the flow of information to programme managers rather than to the state and central levels would be helpful. Increased use should be made of India's management research and training institutions for the programme, as should the highly developed Indian communications industry. The programmes of the many NGOs in the field should be examined for applicability to the national programme.

UNFPA has recently evaluated training in maternal and child care/family planning services in several regions. Its report on six countries in Asia-- Bangladesh, India, Indonesia, the Philippines, Sri Lanka and Thailand--

points out several managerial or administrative deficiencies. For example, no country had adequate data on the capacity of training institutions upon which to base plans for training sufficient manpower. Improved administration of fellowships is also desirable. Though in some countries training fellowships were well used, with trainees continuing in their posts, in others, the trainees had moved on, their training wasted for the health service. In some, the available fellowships went unused.[18]

Community participation and grass-roots organizations

Asia has many examples of the merging of self-help traditions with modernization and development, and the approach to development has begun to shift from top-down to bottom-up. Many NGOs with firm roots in communities have successfully assisted family planning programmes. More than 21 Asian countries have national family planning associations (FPAs) that are members of IPPF, which in 1987 contributed about $10 million to the Asian members' programmes.

The Governments of Indonesia and the Republic of Korea have helped organize and finance Mothers' Clubs, which provide advice on health and nutrition as well as family planning. Bangladesh has many voluntary organizations concerned with birth-spacing. The Government has sponsored a Family Planning Council of Voluntary Organizations and a Family Planning Services and Training Centre to co-ordinate NGO activities and provide technical support and training to local institutions. In Pakistan, the Shadab project illustrates the value of tripartite co-operation among the national Government, a local institution and NGOs. Covering an area of 47 villages, the project seeks to improve agricultural production and living conditions through community development, agricultural education and assistance, banking and credit schemes, adult and child education and family planning. The Pakistan FPA provides the family planning component through the training of all project staff--agricultural development assistants, volunteers and provincial government officials.[19]

Most NGOs are voluntary organizations. They usually lack the necessary human and financial resources to provide services on a national scale. They can, however, contribute significantly to testing programmes, stimulating members in the community to join in family planning efforts and duplicating successful programmes in new areas of the country. The approach of the Japanese Organization for International Cooperation in Family Planning, Inc. (JOICFP), demonstrates this NGO function. Experience in post-war Japan indicated that family planning was more acceptable when services were provided along with other measures--such as parasite control and nutrition education--that had an immediate and visible effect on the health and quality of life of the people of the community.

Role and status of women

The traditional attitude towards women in most of the countries of the Asia and Pacific region has kept them subordinate and dependent. Their social role has been defined almost exclusively in terms of motherhood. Women in the region generally lag behind men in participation in political affairs, education, health and employment. The attitudes and cultural definitions of women's roles in society have continued to prevent women's full participation in development.

With the increasing economic development of most of the countries in Asia, there is a clearer acknowledgement of the need for improving the status of women, so that they can contribute to, and share the benefits of, the development process. At the Asian Regional Conference on Women, Population and Development, held in Beijing in 1985, participants agreed on several major areas of concern that could improve women's participation in the development of their countries. These were literacy, training and education, employment, legal rights, social and cultural factors, institutionalization, NGOs, and health and family planning.[20]

Conference participants reported that their countries had attempted to improve literacy levels. Yet in some countries literacy remained low, women had lower literacy levels than those of men, and literacy was lower among rural women than among urban women. Most women in most countries are economically active outside their homes. Whether they are paid depends on the sector in which they work, and that depends on the level of economic development. In low-income countries, women contribute to the economy mainly as agricultural workers--usually as unpaid workers on subsistence farms. In middle-income countries, women work both in agriculture and in the urban wage sector as teachers and service and production workers. In high-income countries, most women are employed in clerical and service work or as teachers and nurses. Unemployment levels are higher among women than among men, and income levels are lower, reflecting the lower status of their occupations.

Several countries have enacted legislation requiring equal pay for work of equal value. However, these laws usually apply only to the public sector, and even there subtle forms of discrimination prevail. Most of this legislation does not apply to the small-scale industries in which women are predominantly employed, and even when it does, enforcement is lacking.

Almost every Asian country has some form of maternal and child health services, and most Governments have policies aimed at achieving a balance between population growth and economic growth. These policies are acknowledged as contributing to the improvement of the status of women by relieving them from unwanted child-bearing and freeing them to seek employment.

Many Governments of the region have established ministries or special departments concerned with improving the status of women by developing and monitoring policies related to women. Afghanistan, China, Fiji, Indonesia, the Islamic Republic of Iran, the Philippines and Thailand have national-level women's organizations; Bangladesh, India, the Republic of Korea and Papua New Guinea have representation for women's issues at the ministerial level; many other countries have special offices or units dealing with women's issues. However, these departments are not always adequately staffed and funded.

ESCAP has a Programme on Women in Development, which includes research, training, the development of innovative approaches and pilot projects, information dissemination, the provision of advisory services and the organization of meetings. UNFPA-supported projects directed at women's concerns in Asia include, for example, the training of Muslim women and university women in Indonesia, the training of women extension workers in Nepal and Sri Lanka, and the organization of courses and women's councils in the Solomon Islands. Research projects have examined the role of women related to the family planning programmes in the Republic of Korea and rural fertility and women's economic activity in Bangladesh. Projects have been funded to increase women's income-generation in Nepal and Sri Lanka and to support Mothers' Clubs in Nepal, Sri Lanka and countries of the South Pacific. In 1987 funds were allocated for a clearing-house for information on women in development in Malaysia and for a regional meeting on better life for women in Asia. Several large comprehensive projects of external assistance agencies have included women's concerns. In the USAID-funded Integrated Family Planning-Nutrition-Credit Project in East Java, credits were given to villages for small loans to women for small businesses, handicrafts, trading, agriculture and livestock-raising. The World Bank included a research component on women's activities in villages in the Gujarat Medium Irrigation Project.

Characteristics of country
programmes and projects

In the Asia and Pacific region, family planning programmes today rely on a mixture of approaches consistent with national policy goals and with the availability of human and financial resources to implement them.

Variety of organizational approaches to family planning programmes

Programmes may concentrate on only a few contraceptive methods or include them all, and give more or less attention to creating demand, typically through information efforts while also making contraceptives readily available. Some encourage supplementary efforts through private medical and commercial channels and social marketing schemes. They may also provide special inducements in the form of incentives or disincentives, including free or subsidized supplies and services. They may be single-purpose or multi-purpose programmes integrated into other health or social service or economic development programmes. They may be administered through one or more delivery systems, such as fixed or mobile clinics, post-partum programmes, full-time or part-time field-workers, local community agents, auxiliary health workers, household distribution, private physicians, sterilization camps, special drives, and incorporation into broader systems of maternal and child health. Finally, they may cover, or intend to cover, the whole of a country--as in a national family planning programme--or only the urban centres where the medical infrastructure is more nearly adequate, or only a small pilot area.[21]

Most Asian countries have gone beyond simply improving access to contraceptives and have worked vigorously to increase popular demand for contraceptives through information and education programmes. As discussed in Chapter 4 on IEC, such programmes have employed every form of modern and ancient communication--from television soap operas and vans equipped with audio-visual equipment to puppet shows and folk art--to carry the message of the benefits of smaller families. In addition, many groups have been enlisted to educate or influence mothers, farmers, soldiers, factory workers and schoolchildren in understanding and accepting family planning.

For many years, and certainly since bilateral and multilateral assistance agencies focused their attention on population problems, family planning experts have debated whether fertility could best be controlled by undertaking so-called vertical programmes planned and administered by government entities organized for that specific purpose or by integrating fertility control into existing or improved health care programmes or other social or economic development programmes.

A vertical organizational approach was often the first system tried by Asian Governments in the 1960s, when they took action on the "population problem", with substantial assistance from external agencies that were anxious to concentrate funding on fertility control in developing countries. Family planning services were provided through the public health systems or through separate agencies reporting to a high-level co-ordinating board, as in Indonesia and the Philippines. These vertical programmes had a separate administrative staff for family planning. Their service staffs were either wholly engaged in family planning or were regular health service staff devoting specific service areas or hours to family planning. In extreme cases, an entirely separate and often better-paid family planning service was set up to duplicate the regular health staff network.

In the last 10 years, a consensus has emerged that specialized population efforts have their useful place, but that involvement of health administration and services with family planning is important to the success of a programme of fertility control. In some countries, oral contraceptives can be prescribed and IUDs inserted by paramedical personnel, but where these are important methods in a programme, medical back-up is required to maintain clients' confidence. Most countries still require medical supervision for the provision of Depo-provera and Norplant, though paramedics in Bangladesh, Indonesia and Thailand sometimes provide these two contraceptives.

ESCAP has examined experience with integrated family planning programmes. Though the programmes of the Asia and Pacific region vary widely in content and organizational patterns and their histories show a good deal of experimentation, a common feature of all these programmes is some form of integration in the sense of linking specialized activities to one another. This linkage has been accomplished in many ways and under many organizational designs. The most common forms of administrative integration in the ESCAP region are those programmes in which family planning is an integral part of maternal and health care programmes or of primary health care services, especially in rural areas. India, Singapore, Thailand and, more recently, a portion of the Malaysian programme provide good examples. Sometimes integration at the implementation level has been tried with special regional and rural development programmes, such as the New Community Movement in the Republic of Korea, the Integrated Rural Development Programme of the Philippines, the Small Area Package Programme of Nepal, the various special area development programmes of India and the Federal Land Development Authority scheme of Malaysia. (See Chapter 3 for a detailed discussion of the vertical versus integrated approaches.)

Non-clinical distribution programmes have been used in many Asian countries to deliver contraceptive services outside the medical and clinical systems. These programmes are intended to make modern contraceptives widely available to the many people who have little access to doctors or medical facilities. Distribution points are located where clinics are unavailable, as in many rural areas or urban squatter settlements. The programmes have been variously called "community-based distribution (CBD) projects", "village or alternative delivery systems", "inundation or household distribution programmes", "subsidized commercial programmes" and "social marketing programmes". Contraceptives in these programmes are usually limited to oral contraceptives, condoms and spermicides. Women with side-effects from oral contraceptives are referred to medical consultation, and in some programmes the referrals are made for IUDs or sterilizations. Because these schemes need a constant flow of supplies, the contraceptive distributors, usually lay villagers with brief training, are important to the programme.

CBD and household distribution schemes are staffed by volunteers or low-paid local people. The programmes offer contraceptives free of charge or at nominal amounts, and sometimes include an educational programme, which usually enhances success. Distribution points may be in homes, markets, shops, post offices or police stations, wherever convenient to the community. Medical histories of acceptors are dispensed with and few records are kept, other than the client's name and address and the supplies given. Indonesia and Thailand have had national CBD programmes reaching hundreds of thousands of acceptors. In other Asian countries, Governments or voluntary organizations have sponsored CBD projects.

Subsidized commercial or social marketing schemes rely upon the network of small shops or stalls selling consumer goods such as toothpaste, tobacco, soap or candy. These shops, which extend into the remotest areas, sell contraceptives supplied by the Government or an external agency at a subsidized price to make them affordable by couples with limited incomes. In countries like India, Bangladesh, and Nepal, when supplies have been maintained, these schemes have effectively distributed contraceptives to people with no other access to them.

To gain acceptors and keep up continuity of contraceptive use many countries have employed a variety of incentives and disincentives. The advantages and disadvantages of such schemes are discussed in detail in Chapter 3 on maternal and child health and family planning.

Research

Countries in the Asia region may be ahead of developing countries elsewhere in their ability to carry out population programmes, but, for this very reason, population research is important. Applied and operational research is needed on the interrelationships between population trends and social and economic factors, on human reproduction and epidemiological factors, on the organizational and administrative aspects of family planning programmes under different administrative systems and on policy implications of population, environment and resource variables. Many countries need demographic studies on the determinants of fertility, mortality, migration, population growth, urbanization and population distribution.

Because of the importance of analysis and policy studies for formulating population policies and programmes, external agencies have supported population research in censuses, vital registration, population dynamics, family planning, population education, communication, information, and contraceptive research and development. Many of these projects are carried out in collaboration with research programmes of United Nations specialized agencies or ESCAP. Others, like the massive World Fertility Study organized by the International Statistics Institute, were conducted by international NGOs.

Information, education and communication

Modern communication techniques are important in every aspect of population programmes designed to reach large numbers of people, whether for family planning or censuses or to create awareness of population policies. Availability of television is growing rapidly in Asia, and several Governments have used this medium to carry population messages to large audiences. Television dramas designed to modify traditional preferences for sons and to promote small families have proved popular in India, the Republic of Korea and Viet Nam. Messages on family planning have been broadcast by the government-owned radio stations of India, the Philippines and the Republic of Korea. Telephone services to provide information on family planning and contraception have been organized in more urbanized countries like the Republic of Korea.

Because of the region's youthful age structure, the education of future generations of parents in the socio-economic implications of population growth, in responsible parenthood, and in community participation in population activities is most important in Asia and the Pacific. Population education may include population studies, family life, sex education and family planning education. It may take place in formal schools and universities as well as in non-formal settings. These subjects have been integrated with more comprehensive education programmes such as adult literacy, agricultural extension, labour and trade union education, community development, vocational training, home economics and rural development. To avoid dilution of content and ensure focus, a regional workshop organized by the United Nations Educational, Scientific and Cultural Organization (UNESCO) Regional Office in 1984 proposed that the population education programmes of the Asian and Pacific countries adapt five core messages, concerning family size and family welfare, delayed marriage, responsible parenthood, population change and resource development, and population-related beliefs and values.

In Afghanistan, the Government's functional literacy materials have included family health and family life education. China's training materials for agricultural extension workers now include population education materials, and China's population education programme is being expanded from its experimental stage. India is preparing a national source book on population education for all educators in their activities and will soon launch an All-India Quiz Competition on Population Education.

In Nepal, the adult education section of the Ministry of Education, working with World Education, is institutionalizing a programme of non-formal education that includes health and family planning concepts. Pakistan completed a project to develop population education curricula to train adult education field-workers to reach out-of-school youth and adults; in the formal schools Pakistan's pre-service teacher training programmes will include population education. The Philippines is developing a national plan for population education. Viet Nam, having completed its pilot phase in population education in five provinces and cities, is now expanding the programme to other provinces and cities, offering teacher training, family life and sex education, and a Parent Education Programme for parents with young children. Thailand is introducing education about acquired immune deficiency syndrome (AIDS) into schools to provide students with knowledge to protect themselves.

Population education activities are also taking place in the Cook Islands, the Federated State of Micronesia, Fiji, Kiribati, the Marshall Islands, Palau, Papua New Guinea, the Solomon Islands and Vanuatu, all assisted by the UNESCO Regional Office for the Pacific. (See Chapter 4 for more details on education programmes in the region.)

Assessment of country programmes and projects

Viewed as a whole, and surely in comparison with developing countries in other regions of the world, Asian countries have followed effective approaches to fertility regulation. Most of the region's Governments are fully aware of their demographic problems and have adopted policies designed to solve them. If one lesson has been learned by the Governments, it is that successful family planning programmes must respond to the people's concerns. Education and information programmes can shape and change people's views. They may even lead to acceptance of long-term goals over short-term preferences. But government plans will fail if they do not accurately assess the state of mind of the multitude.

Responsiveness

China and India have both learned lessons from their attempts to control fertility. China has succeeded in dramatically reducing fertility, but at some cost in discontent among its people and criticism in the world community. India, after the excesses of the sterilization campaigns of the late 1970s, which set back the entire population programme, is shifting towards a more popular programme with greater attention to promoting family welfare than to limiting births.

Indonesia and Thailand have instituted strong and effective family planning programmes, differing in some ways, but appropriately adapted to the characters of their peoples and the structures of their communities. Bangladesh and Pakistan still have much to do in educating their people if their programmes are to gain acceptance. The people of the Philippines are ready for family planning if their elected officials at the highest level can lead the way.

Population educators have learned much from experience with different approaches. In the 1970s, perhaps under the same urgent influences that created the free-standing family planning programme, some ambitious population education programmes sought to introduce the subject in all school levels at once, as a mass education effort. This was unsuccessful, partly because too few trained teachers were available, partly because appropriate curricula had not been prepared, and partly because of cultural opposition to, or misunderstanding of, the subject matter. Much more sophisticated approaches have been introduced as the capacity of education ministries has improved over the years, and a list of all such educational activities would be extensive. From the most tentative approaches in the past, often limited to the study of population size and growth in various countries, population education has come to include consideration of human sexuality, physical and emotional maturing, adolescent fertility, contraceptive practice, and AIDS. Whether more widespread population education would influence fertility has not been firmly established. It would be useful to fund sufficient research on its effectiveness to guide population educators.

Degree of institutionalization

Population programmes have been firmly established by all but a few of the Governments of Asia. The infrastructure to assess and respond to population pressure is in place: the apparatus for census-taking is adequate, population policies are accepted as national policies, development planners are appreciative of the need to integrate population variables into national planning, population education is increasingly being incorporated into all kinds of training, research in population dynamics and contraceptive technology is continuing, and family planning programmes are being more carefully designed to reach and serve the people. Having responded comprehensively to population issues, Asian Governments can be expected to continue and improve their efforts towards solutions.

In addition to these national institutions, those United Nations specialized agencies with mandates that include some facet of population activities have institutionalized their programmes. ESCAP, the best source for demographic data about the region, provides advisory and training services through its Population Division. It also organizes meetings to assist Governments and regional institutions concerned with population issues in expanding their capabilities in such fields as the collection and evaluation of basic demographic data; planning, design and analysis of demographic research; studies and research in family planning; and the establishment and strengthening of national clearing-houses on population. The International Labour Organisation (ILO), the Food and Agriculture Organization of the United Nations (FAO), the World Health Organization (WHO) and UNESCO all have regional offices staffed with persons who are involved in population activities, and all provide regional advisers in population.

A review of the latest UNFPA *Inventory of Population Projects in Developing Countries Around the World* finds that today more than 50 independent organizations, institutions, centres or forums in the region are concerned with population activities. They contribute importantly to national programmes through their research, their exchanges of information and their funding and advice to national agencies.

Development of a regional strategy

Programme issues in the region

The Beijing Declaration of the Asian Forum of Parliamentarians, September 1987, identifies the broad concerns that must be addressed by Governments: (a) reducing the rates of population growth; (b) reducing mortality, especially infant and early child mortality; (c) achieving more balanced population distribution; (d) strengthening security for the aged; (e) improving the position of women in society; and (f) strengthening health care and family planning.

In the context of these priorities, improvements need to be pursued for several facets of existing population programmes.

Meeting contraceptive needs

The introduction of newly developed contraceptives into programmes should be sponsored--with modern IUDs, Depo-provera and Norplant made available wherever appropriate and feasible--and research for better contraceptives should be promoted. Every family planning programme should be enabled to forecast its future contraceptive needs, and all large countries should be encouraged to become self-sufficient in producing their most widely used contraceptives. Projects to provide modern equipment and technology for the manufacture and packaging of contraceptives should be proposed to Governments.

Developing human resources

Staff training in every area of population activities should be emphasized to remedy a persistent deficiency in all programmes, whether in family planning or data collection or development planning or IEC work--the lack of well-trained and motivated staff. It is up to Governments to supply the motivation, which will require equitable compensation for all staff, job security, and other usual benefits that will permit population agencies to compete with other governmental bodies for good staff. External assistance agencies can help provide advisory services, local training costs and equipment.

Governments and external agencies should enlist more community members--local leaders and committed individuals--into family planning programmes. Inducements for communities to welcome family planning can be devised. Local development or agricultural projects can easily include population education: it is a step forward, for example, if an an inexpensively produced pamphlet to teach better fish-farming also shows an illiterate person how fewer fish can feed a smaller family. Countries that have many physicians in private practice should find ways to involve them in family planning efforts and should offer training in new methods of contraception. Governments might subsidize the costs of private family planning counselling and care.

Drawing upon non-governmental organizations

In many countries, such as India and Pakistan and several in the South Pacific, the original impetus for family planning came from private voluntary organizations. Though Governments may now have established their own programmes, they should not overlook the considerable experience of these organizations. Family planning associations may well be more skilled than the Government in reaching certain groups, such as the urban or rural poor.

Family planning associations and other NGOs should recognize that funds received from private voluntary sources will never be sufficient for their needs. They should prepare careful financial projections, showing both their likely receipts and their inevitable annual shortfalls against their plans, and they should try to convince Governments to include provisions for these shortfalls in their annual budgets if they are to benefit fully from NGO capabilities. Governments should endeavour to use NGOs in a co-operative, not a competitive, way.

Improving logistics

External agencies and Governments should encourage experimentation with schemes for improving logistics systems. Distribution of contraceptives or other supplies is frequently an obstacle to good service delivery. Yet cigarettes, cooking oil and Coca Cola seem to reach the farthest villages. Governments should consider using private transport or other commercial means to deliver supplies to its clinics.

Emphasizing management

Management of family planning programmes, already difficult in many countries, is often made more so by the complete lack of managerial training. Governments in the region manage railways, irrigation works, electrical grids and fertilizer distribution--often very well. Although family planning may not have the public acceptance or the immediately foreseeable benefits that these enterprises enjoy, the actual management of a service delivery system does not present insuperable obstacles in today's world. Many a state enterprise operates a first-rate motor pool and a good supply distribution system. The capacity to manage and administer nation-wide government programmes of many kinds certainly exists in India, Indonesia, Malaysia, Sri Lanka and Thailand, and in the army medical services of several countries. This expertise is transferable to management of family planning programmes. The demand for better family planning management offers a great opportunity to demonstrate successful technical co-operation among developing countries (TCDC) within the region.

Continuing support

Many Governments have organized their population programmes well, and much has been learned about how programmes should be structured and how the problems encountered can be resolved. The causes of failure of some national programmes can usually be readily identified. No dramatic or innovative methods for data collection or family planning delivery systems or communication or education programmes are being considered today. In addition, unless the perfect contraceptive is soon discovered, much of the next decade's effort in population activities in the Asia and the Pacific region will be more of the same, with gradual improvements year by year. This pace is inherent in the nature of social programmes that must reach so many individuals.

No one should conclude, however, that because family planning programmes are institutionalized in most Asian countries they no longer require the continued support of external agencies and the unflagging efforts of Governments. Further study of population and development is required of ways to increase employment opportunities in rural areas to remedy the imbalance between population distribution and resources. Moreover, when population policies succeed, the consequences for the aged must be foreseen. National policies, as part of broad population policies, should deal with support of the aged who are not supported by their small families. This may require social security, health care and housing programmes for the aged, as well as retraining some of them for work.

The Parliamentarians also noted the importance of adequate funding for research, public education and preventive measures relating to AIDS. All of the measures to be taken that are listed in the Beijing Declaration have an effect upon population growth, or will themselves be influenced by population growth. Some research may be needed to demonstrate the connection between these areas of concern and population growth or fertility. This research or data collection or analysis will point the way for Governments' decisions on policies.

Recent political events in Asia, riots, student strikes and clashes between young people and police forces should alert Governments to the readily foreseeable consequences of the present massive majority of the young in Asia who need education, jobs and housing. A regional effort to reinforce the understanding of this phenomenon could have an important effect on a wide range of policies and would be of great value to population planners in their work with development plans.

Future directions

Despite the great accomplishments of the past 20 years, it would be erroneous to conclude that population policies and programmes in Asia and the Pacific region, with the one exception of China, are guaranteed the strong and continuous political backing required to succeed. They simply do not enjoy the priorities of leadership, attention and financing that are necessary. Stronger political backing will not appear overnight, but Governments should make greater efforts to give population policy and programmes the priority they deserve. Government leaders, parliamentarians, programme administrators, academics, physicians, community leaders and all individuals aware of, and concerned with, the problems their countries face if population growth continues at present rates should strive to improve the performance of their Governments in educating people about population issues and in providing health and family planning services. Support should thus continue for the excellent information services in the region, and for the Asian Forum of Parliamentarians, whose members can do so much to increase the political support for population programmes.

The Asia and the Pacific region is in the forefront of all regions of the developing world in its population programmes. Thus, other countries can learn much from the Asian and Pacific experience, which can be a source of technical and managerial advice on population activities throughout the world. The region has the skilled manpower able to conceptualize new approaches to family planning, to fertility research, to new contraceptives, and to policies to deal with the problems of its enormous population.

For country programmes in Asia and the Pacific, the greatest amount of funding should continue to flow to family planning programmes, especially for training of managers and field-workers of all kinds. Training for family planning programme managers should include familiarization with up-to-date management information systems and this in turn will give rise to requests for computerization. If directed to the field level, assistance can stimulate better management at service delivery points. Self-sufficiency in contraceptive production should have a high priority for those countries potentially able to manufacture modern contraceptives. Because projects for contraceptive production almost always require imported technology and equipment, funds from external assistance agencies should be used for these projects in preference to allocating them for local programme costs such as salaries. Success with local production will diminish the Governments' needs for foreign exchange.

Programmes to ameliorate the situation of women in Asia will have enormous impact if they can succeed in improving women's roles in family life and in preparing them to participate equally with men in rapidly modernizing economies. Projects to gather data on women's roles and pilot projects to demonstrate the benefits of educating girls and women for a modern society should be funded.

More emphasis should be given to research than in the past. Funds for research are modest compared to the expenditures on government programmes, and knowledge is needed on such emerging problems as external migration, housing, urbanization, aging, youth and employment, and adolescent fertility. Expertise for this research is available in the region, and small expenditures now might be of enormous value in the next decade as the region experiences the effects of both a larger, younger population and smaller family norms.

341

9. Population Policies and Programmes in Latin America and the Caribbean

Latin America and the Caribbean in transition

Latin America and the Caribbean have gone through tremendous demographic, social and economic changes over the last 40 years. The region is experiencing a demographic transition basically similar to the one previously experienced by the currently developed countries. An important corollary of this observation is that Latin American countries are not locked into a pattern of immobility as regards their near demographic future.

The demographic history of Latin America and the Caribbean can be divided into three major periods. During the first period, the American continent was settled by human groups--a process that started when the land bridge between Asia and North America facilitated the transfer of populations from Asia to the Americas. The second key period was the tremendous demographic upheaval initiated at the end of the fifteenth century by the arrival of Europeans and, in their tracks, other racial and ethnic groups in the American continent. This upheaval set the stage for the third key demographic period--the "demographic transition" that is currently taking place.

Within the current period, the demographic transition of North America, as defined by the United States of America and Canada, is sharply differentiated from that of the remainder of the American continent. Further in the future, however, these two demographic transitions will seem to be basically one and the same process, although with their own particularities. The most distinctive characteristic of Latin America's transition compared with that of North America is that Latin America's transition has been marked by efforts to modify demographic behaviour with the help of specific programmes.

Demographic characteristics of the region's current transition

The region's demographic transition consists of three major elements: (a) the mortality and health transition; (b) the fertility and contraceptive transition; and (c) the transition in the rate of population growth. At any given moment, there is wide variety in the extent and pace of the transitions for different Latin American and Caribbean countries. The timing of their onset has differed all over the region. Some countries, such as Chile, Costa Rica, Cuba and Panama, have almost completed these transitions. Others, such as Brazil, Colombia and Mexico, have

342

gone a long way. Others, such as Ecuador and Peru, have started but need to make substantially more headway. Finally, Bolivia, Haiti and some Central American countries are still in the initial stages of their demographic transitions.

Within countries, the extent to which these transitions have affected various geographic areas and socio-economic groups of the population differs greatly. The differences between the underdeveloped rural northeast and the developed industrial south in Brazil are widely covered in the development literature. Less well known but no less important are the differences between the highly urbanized coastal areas of Peru and Ecuador and poor regions of the Andean sierra. There are also important differences according to social class and educational level. Even within the same metropolitan area, the level and range of demographic and social indicators can vary greatly.

Health and mortality transition

If average life expectancy and other measures of mortality and health are used as an indicator of progress, Latin America has made substantial strides on the road to development. At the beginning of the 1950s, life expectancy in Latin America was about 51 years. It is now more than 10 years higher in almost every country in the region (see Annex Table 1 for 1985-1990 levels). Infant mortality over the same period declined from a rate of 126 per 1,000 live births to 56 (1985-1990).[1]

As mortality has declined, its causes have changed. For example, the relative importance of diarrhoea, of acute respiratory diseases and of diseases that can be prevented by immunization has been reduced as causes of infant mortality.[2] In many countries of Latin America, more than half the children have been immunized against measles. Although still low, the number of diarrhoea cases treated with oral rehydration therapy is increasing.[3]

Although mortality in general has been declining, the rate of decline has been slower than it would have been had political will been uniformly strong throughout Latin America to formulate and execute adequate public health programmes. It is now doubtful whether the region can attain the internationally accepted goal of reaching a life expectancy of 70 years by the year 2000. The risk of maternal mortality remains too high. In Latin America, illegal abortion together with its consequences account for almost one third of maternal mortality.[4]

Fertility and contraceptive transition

Fertility is well below the high mark for the Latin American region. The total fertility rate has decreased from a level of almost 6 in the beginning of the 1950s to less than 4 (see Annex Table 1 for the 1985-1990 rates in individual countries).[5] As usually happens initially with fertility declines, the reduction of fertility has been the most marked for women above age 30. Increasingly larger proportions of Latin

343

American populations are reducing the size of their families with more efficient contraceptive use. In Brazil, Colombia, Costa Rica and Cuba, more than 40 per cent of married women of reproductive age are currently using modern contraceptive methods.[6]

In Western Europe, a neat distinction can be made in many cases between the fertility transition and the contraceptive transition. Fertility transition refers to extraordinary declines in fertility, which were obtained originally through the use of traditional family planning methods, such as coitus interruptus. The contraceptive revolution, announced by large-scale acceptance of modern contraceptives, came much later. In most countries of Latin American and the Caribbean, the fertility transition and the contraceptive transition coincide.

Transition in the rate of population growth

Because of the rapid decrease in fertility rates, the rate of population growth in the region is slowing down. It probably reached its maximum, at almost 3 per cent, in the 1960s.[7] By the late 1980s, it was approaching 2 per cent (see Annex Table 1 for 1985-1990 rates in individual countries).[8]

Socio-economic characteristics

Vast and important changes are now taking place in the social and economic fabric of Latin American and Caribbean society. Many of these changes have helped bring about demographic changes. However, the demographic changes have themselves contributed to the social and economic changes in ways not yet completely understood. Demographic transitions are not just the passive consequences of social and economic changes, but active ingredients in these changes. Among the host of social and economic changes affecting the region at present, three are crucial: the urban transition, the educational transition and the transition in the status of women.

Urban transition

One of the most significant changes has been the relative decline in the proportion of rural populations. In the 1950s, the majority of the Latin American population was rural, but by the mid-1980s--scarcely 30 years later--it was predominantly urban.[9] The movement of people out of agriculture has been extraordinarily rapid. In 1950, in countries like Brazil, Colombia and Mexico, about 60 per cent of the labour force were occupied in agriculture; now the proportion is less than 30 per cent. In a few countries, the agricultural population has already started to decline in absolute numbers.

The urban transition, despite many misunderstandings of the process, should be perceived basically as a positive phenomenon. However, this is not to deny that unjustified policies resulting in "urban bias" have unduly accelerated the process. Urban bias coupled with high natural growth rates in rural areas has also been partly responsible for huge rural-urban migration streams and for the appearance of megacities on a scale not necessarily conforming to general welfare. Today, some of the largest metropolitan areas in the world can be found in Latin America.

<u>Educational transition</u>

The educational transition and the urban transition are probably the two single most important processes that have changed Latin American society. In 1950, many Latin American countries had illiteracy rates of more than 50 per cent. Now, with the exception of Haiti, no country in Latin America or the Caribbean has more than half of its population 15 years and over illiterate. In most countries of the region, less than 30 per cent are illiterate. For those 6 to 11 years old, school enrolment ratios in many Latin American countries have also risen to more than 80 per cent of the age group.[10]

Both the urban and the educational transitions have played an enormous role in the creation of a Latin American middle class, with important implications for political aspirations, consumption patterns and demographic behaviour. The reduction in fertility goes hand in hand with the appearance of this middle class.

<u>Transition in the status of women</u>

Less well documented are the tremendous changes in the status of women taking place in Latin America and the Caribbean. The changes range from profound shifts in values and psychological interactions at the level of the couple to those in macro-social and macro-economic variables, such as the participation of women in the labour force. Activities of many women's groups are promoting improvement of the status of women in all segments of social life. Changes in the status of women, according to abundant research evidence, are potentially important causative factors in the acceptance of new demographic behaviour, resulting in lower childhood mortality and lower fertility. These demographic changes also affect women's status in ways that are less clear and need more investigation. Among the macro-economic changes affecting women's status in Latin America and the Caribbean, one needs to be singled out--the school enrolment of young women. The gaps between males and females have increasingly narrowed. In some Latin American countries, more women than men are now enrolled in secondary and even in higher education.[11]

Distinctive cultural and economic features

Latin America and the Caribbean share many characteristics with other developing regions in the world. In many ways, though, the region differs markedly. Three distinctive characteristics are especially relevant for population issues: Latin America's cultural and linguistic homogeneity, unequal income distribution and the effects of the debt crisis. The first characteristic is a permanent one. The second characteristic--not

345

necessarily a permanent one--is, nevertheless, deeply embedded in the region's social and economic structure. The third characteristic, though more temporary, will plague the continent for the remainder of the century. Distinguishing the region from other regions should not obscure the important social, economic and political differences that exist among subregions and countries. Demographic differences are especially important in this regard.

Cultural and linguistic homogeneity and its implications

The cultural and linguistic homogeneity of Latin America has allowed, more so than in other regions, the development of common population activities and programmes. It has allowed, for example:

(a) The development of networks, such as the Programme of Social Research on Population in Latin America (PISPAL) for the social sciences and population policy research, or institutional arrangements serving the whole region, such as the Latin American Centre of Perinatology and Human Development (CLAP);

(b) Comparative research on a scale not seen in other developing regions, such as the comparative urban and rural fertility surveys and the comparative abortion surveys undertaken by the Latin American Demographic Centre (CELADE) and the comparative studies on childhood and infant mortality undertaken by the Pan American Health Organization (PAHO) and others;

(c) Well-organized training courses for the whole of Latin America, such as those organized by CELADE, PAHO and the Panamerican Federation of Faculties of Medicine; and

(d) The possibility of developing regional programmes, such as the UNFPA Regional Programme for Population Education, resulting in the establishment of journals and other publications directed to specific audiences of the region. For example, the journal *Nexo* is published for professionals who participated in training activities provided by the Regional Programme for Population Education.

However, the possibilities afforded by this cultural and linguistic homogeneity have not been exploited to the fullest. Internally, for example, Latin America does not yet have an association of population scientists and practitioners. Nor is there a Latin American population review that presents a forum for the exchange of new ideas on population activities and programmes. Externally, the advantage of a common language could have been instrumental in making the world more aware of interesting developments in Latin American thinking and action on population. This has not yet happened to the degree expected.

346

Unequal income distribution

Although per capita income is higher than that of other developing regions, the region is characterized by the persistence of higher degrees of income inequality than other regions, whether more developed or less developed than Latin America. According to a study of development patterns in Latin America, "the income share of the lowest 20 per cent in Latin America is less than half as high as in . . . other developing regions".[12] The shape of income distribution may have important implications for some demographic variables. Costa Rica and Cuba, for example, have among the lowest levels of income inequality in the region. These countries also have among the lowest infant mortality rates. In contrast, Brazil, with an income level of the same order as that of Costa Rica, has a childhood mortality rate about three times higher than that of Costa Rica.[13]

Debt crisis

The severe debt crisis affecting many Latin American countries, although a phenomenon of economic conjuncture, is rooted in more profound causes and will affect demographic trends in complex ways that have yet to be unravelled. The complementary perspective--the ways in which population dynamics affect the debt crisis--has seldom if ever received attention. Although the status of information about the impact of the debt crisis on demographic trends is unsatisfactory, the following hypotheses seem increasingly likely:

(a) The debt crisis has had a serious impact on internal migration patterns, intercountry migration patterns and migration patterns between Latin America and the United States, Canada and other developed countries;

(b) The unequal impact of the debt crisis has created serious problems of undernutrition and malnutrition, resulting in greater morbidity and possibly in higher infant mortality and other mortality indices among some social groups; and

(c) The debt crisis may also, as some suspect, have led to lowered fertility levels, especially in urban areas, though more research is needed to ascertain the dimensions of this effect.

Effects of population activities and programmes

Population assistance and programmes have helped to make population issues an important concern in Latin America and the Caribbean. These activities and programmes have also had an impact on some demographic changes, specifically on declines in fertility and mortality.

Population activities and programmes include a variety of projects such as data gathering, research, communication, education and action programmes. "Population activity" is used here broadly to include any of these activities. The term "population programme" implies the planning and preparation of several population activities, which are often formally evaluated as a means of assessing overall programme effectiveness.

Development of a hospitable institutional framework

Population programmes have contributed to making population issues a matter of concern and to influencing certain demographic trends, a result of the combined initiatives and decisions of many organizations. Some are from the international sector; others are national or local in character. Some are public; others are private. The experience of these agencies over the last three decades permits some generalizations about their role in the genesis and execution of population activities and programmes.

Private-sector assistance agencies

Private agencies providing assistance for population activities have played a critical role in three ways: as initiators, as innovators and as strengtheners of population activities. They initiated support for population activities at a time when such activities were often the subject of incomprehension, controversy and even hostility. The Ford Foundation, for example, played an important role in stimulating research and training on the social and biological aspects of population. Some of its programmes were direct; others were undertaken indirectly through The Population Council of New York. The International Planned Parenthood Federation (IPPF)-Western Hemisphere also played a major part. Through its respect of national autonomy and encouragement of local initiatives, it often provided the only viable institutional framework and necessary resources at a time when family planning in some Latin American circles was associated with impropriety.

The private-sector agencies, through in-house scientific expertise and adaptable technical assistance, also helped introduce new approaches, test experimental programmes and establish networks enhancing co-ordination and comparison. Two such networks were PISPAL, for population and the social sciences, and the Latin American Programme of Research in Human Reproduction (PLAMIRH), for the study of human reproduction. PISPAL linked several Latin American social research

348

centres into a network for the design and execution of social-science population research relevant to policy-making. PLAMIRH aimed at the development of capabilities for research in human reproduction and particularly the stimulation of such research attuned to the Latin American situation.

Finally, once population programmes became more widely accepted, private agencies provided critical resources, such as technical expertise and fellowship assistance, strengthening large-scale projects financed by multilateral and bilateral agencies.

Executing agencies

Without agencies in the private non-profit sector, the population scene in Latin America would be almost barren. In some cases, they were private universities, such as Cayetano Heredia University in Lima, Peru, for maternal and child health and family planning, and Los Andes University in Bogota, Colombia, for population and development studies. In other cases, they were institutes established specifically for dealing with population issues, such as the Regional Population Corporation in Bogota and the Centre for Population Studies and Responsible Parenthood in Quito, with activities covering the economic aspects of population dynamics and issues of family planning and reproductive behaviour. Private social-science research institutes, such as the Brazilian Centre for Analysis and Planning, were frequently important greenhouses for research on the social-science aspects of population. There were also hybrid organizations, such as the Latin American Council for the Social Sciences, which helped promote population research among social scientists, and the Colombian Association of Faculties of Medicine, which led the way for the establishment of population and family planning programmes in Colombia.

Two examples from Peru are briefly reviewed to give a concrete picture of the importance of private agencies, although they are not the only private Peruvian agencies to have played an important role in the promotion of population activities. Set up about a decade ago, the institutes are the Multidisciplinary Association for Population Training and Research (AMIDEP) and the Andean Institute for Population and Development Studies (INANDEP). The aim of AMIDEP is to disseminate population research and training throughout Peru; INANDEP is basically a research organization.

Even their supporters underestimated the importance and productivity of these two institutes for population activities in Peru. Their achievements are attributable to several characteristics in their mode of operation. Neither organization exists in an ivory tower. Both have selected and organized activities in response to the nation's pressing needs, and they have pursued the wide dissemination of their findings to the Peruvian population. In addition, both institutes have contributed greatly, through manpower and other support, to the work of the National

Population Council and subsequently to the Presidential Population Commission of Peru.

During periods in which, for a variety of reasons, the Government's interest in population research waned, these institutes not only provided a hospitable environment for population researchers but became indispensable structures for the continued existence of scientific attention to population issues in Peru. Both institutes have been able to attract funds from a relatively large number of external agencies. Both institutes have maintained a balance among the different sectors of population research, giving studies on human reproduction and family planning their due attention. Activities of both institutes have also reflected awareness that Peru's different regions vary widely in ecological and socio-cultural characteristics. AMIDEP has organized a series of regional meetings to interest local universities and governments in population activities. Through its research competition programmes, it has stimulated population research in many parts of Peru. The regional concerns of INANDEP have been evident, for example, in its organization of a seminar on Amazon development, in its efforts to construct regional demographic indices for Peru and in its research to unravel the complex influences on population within a regional framework.

In addition to research activities in private institutes, private agencies have played an important role in direct action programmes. For example, PROFAMILIA in Colombia, the local IPPF affiliate, has become the most important promoter of family planning in the nation. Thanks to able leadership and a strategy of educational campaigns, combined with a system of contraceptive distribution second to none in Colombia, PROFAMILIA merited the annual population prize of the United Nations, awarded in 1988.

Two public-sector organizations also played key roles: CELADE, during the 1960s and early 1970s in the field of demographic research and training, and the School of Public Health of the University of Chile, until just before the military take-over, in the field of public health and family planning. These agencies are in many ways similar to the private agencies. They are relatively autonomous; they have flexibility, strong leadership and well-qualified and committed staff; and they have built upon a psychological ferment that turned all those ingredients into a critical mass.

CELADE, due to its relatively flexible and autonomous status within the United Nations system, its leadership and the quality of its staff, helped put population issues on the intellectual map of Latin America. It was responsible for the first fertility survey (1959) in continental Latin America (in Santiago, Chile), and it organized and co-ordinated the Comparative Urban Fertility Surveys and the Comparative Rural Surveys. The findings from these surveys destroyed many myths concerning reproductive behaviour in Latin America. The surveys were the inspiration for a host of fertility surveys undertaken independently of CELADE and were a partial model for the World Fertility Survey (WFS) programme. In addition,

CELADE promoted and organized research dealing with such topics as abortion, family planning evaluation, migration, urbanization, labour force dynamics, and population and development. Through its regular training programmes in Chile and Costa Rica, CELADE also educated a whole generation of demographers who subsequently became a pressure group for improvements in demographic data and research in each of the Latin American countries.

The initiatives and activities of the University of Chile's School of Public Health in family planning make it clear that the introduction of family planning in Latin America was not a purely exogenous affair. Staff members of the School of Public Health were the first to draw attention to the incidence of illegal abortion in Chile, with its negative effects on the health of mothers and children, and to organize systematic research on the topic. One of their staff members was later responsible for a comparative survey on abortion in various Latin American countries under the auspices of CELADE. Staff of the School also contributed to the organization of the nation's family planning (FP) programmes. They and members of the University's Faculty of Medicine were involved in the first systematic testing of new contraceptives in the Latin American context. The School was also responsible for the region's first generation of physicians and public health specialists trained in family planning.

Trained personnel

Although exact figures on the existing manpower for population activities are unavailable, many signs indicate substantial improvement. Only a few national statistical offices in Latin America do not have a least one or two persons trained in demography. Their presence has resulted in the improvement of the quality of basic demographic data, in the compilation of multiple demographic indices from incomplete data and in methodological development especially adapted to Latin America. More and more universities have at least one population course in their curricula, and several have special programmes in population studies. Public officials and others can now select from a wide variety of short-term training courses on different aspects of population. In addition, many family planning organizations have one or more persons with training in population studies on their staffs. As a result, these organizations are now publishing documents that are more scientifically sound than was the case in the past.

It is now possible to have in-depth demographic profiles for almost all countries of the region. These profiles are based on a variety of activities, including basic data collection, special demographic surveys and socio-economic studies of population dynamics. The total number of books and articles on Latin American population issues, as attested by the bibliographic work of the Population Documentation for Latin America (DOCPAL) group in CELADE, has risen phenomenally. Thirty years ago, one person could still easily read the annual output of population publications; today, this is impossible. Regular periodical publications dedicated to population include *Notas de Poblacion* and *Boletin*

351

Demographico, published by CELADE, and the journal of the Brazilian Population Studies Association. In Mexico, the publication of *Demos*, an annual journal reviewing Mexican population matters, has just been initiated. In Central America, a journal has been planned on the specialized topic of child survival.

Five Latin American institutes are among the 25 institutes collaborating with the World Health Organization's (WHO) Special Programme of Research, Development and Research Training in Human Reproduction. Research topics that receive special attention are the development of new contraceptives, contraceptive efficiency and safety, infertility, the psycho-social aspects of family planning and the organization of services.[14]

The training contributions of universities have been uneven. However, the programme at the Colegio de Mexico has attracted many Latin American students. Another well-known programme is at the University of Minais Gerais in Belo Horizonte, Brazil. Faculties of Medicine now also usually include some training in population and family planning.

Community of interest

The existence of a community of interest is indispensable for the unfolding of successful population programmes. As long as population activities remain restricted to the efforts of a few isolated groups--however necessary such efforts--there is no critical mass, which is needed for a continuous long-term development of well-articulated programmes on various aspects of population. Once this critical mass is attained, the doors open for a wide variety of population activities and programmes and for the eventual entrance of the Government into population programmes. Such a community of interest now exists in Colombia, Costa Rica, Mexico, Panama, Peru and elsewhere; it formerly existed in Chile; and it is coming to maturity in Brazil. It does not yet fully exist in Bolivia, Ecuador, Haiti and other countries.

A community of interest in population issues is characterized by the existence of a group of people from different work environments--private and government sectors, action organizations and the academic world, educational and communication sectors--with a deep interest in, though not necessarily the same views on, population issues. Both formal and informal networks will exist among persons with an interest in population issues. Professional associations such as the Brazilian Population Studies Association, considered one of the most successful professional population associations in Latin America, will be set up. There needs to be productive exchange and collaboration between medical practitioners, family planning proponents and social scientists with an interest in population. The group brings intelligent discussion of population issues to the foreground. Though irrational interventions in the country under consideration may still take place, thanks to the community of interest these will no longer occupy centre stage. The existence of a community of interest does not require that the Government be already formally engaged in population programmes. However, it does require that there be a sizeable number of persons in various sectors of the Government with a strong interest in population matters.

United Nations role

Because some population activities in Latin America were initially supported by agencies from outside the region, especially from the United States of America, population programmes were in some quarters erroneously perceived as the product of outside influences. Thus, United Nations auspices presented an ideal framework in Latin America and the Caribbean for a major step towards the acceptance of a variety of population programmes, including efforts to reduce fertility. The Economic Commission for Latin America and the Caribbean (ECLAC) had been positively identified with a concern for, and an understanding of, the region's development problems. By the time UNFPA began operations, CELADE, itself a creation of the United Nations system, had already completed several years of influential population activities and had thus prepared the way for additional initiatives.

Building on these favourable foundations, UNFPA developed official contacts with most of the Governments of Latin America, helped develop several networks and comparative projects and organized important "population happenings" in Latin America, such as the Conference on Small and Intermediate Cities in Mexico City (1986) and the Conference on Women, Population and Development in Latin America in Montevideo (1986). Other conferences were organized for a world audience, such as the International Conference on Population (1984) and the International Forum on Population Policies and Development Planning (1987), both in Mexico City. Such meetings have always had a catalytic effect because Latin American Governments and experts were closely associated with their organization. Furthermore, in the case of international meetings, Latin Americans had the opportunity to observe the degree to which population programmes had become a concern of the world community.

Government involvement

Thirty years ago few, if any, could have imagined the current degree of involvement of Latin American Governments in population activities and their widespread interest in population policies attuned to the social goals of development. As the President of Mexico said in 1987 at the inauguration of the International Forum on Population Policies in Development Planning:

> "Population policies are a part of every nation's project, a matter of national sovereignty, the basis of development and an essential factor in overcoming inequalities and increasing existing opportunities. In short their main objective is to upgrade people's quality of life".[15]

Almost all Governments in the region undertake the formulation of policies and the implementation of population programmes. A major aspect of the change during the last 30 years is the governmental institutionalization of population concerns, discussed later in this chapter.

Birth and growth of population consciousness

Population and family planning concerns have now become part of the discussion about development, welfare and health issues in every Latin American and Caribbean nation. The rise of "population consciousness" is one of the most important features of the population scene in the region. The term "population consciousness", as used here, refers to a wide variety of phenomena. It covers the collective awareness of population problems as reflected in public opinion and in government decisions. It also covers private decisions to reduce family size and to use family planning, whether as an expression of awareness of population problems or, as is usually the case, as a personal preference. The use of a single term to refer to the multiple and interrelated facets of population and family planning concerns in society and among individuals brings to the foreground the many linkages between these phenomena.

Increased public awareness

In contrast to the mass media's almost complete neglect of these topics in the past, the discussion of population and family planning issues, contraceptives and sexuality has now become a prominent and regular feature of the region's mass media. At the same time, the treatment of these topics has become more positive. In the Peruvian press, for example, the influential weekly *Caretas* published an article on the occasion of the five billionth baby, strongly emphasizing the need to reduce population growth in Peru (July 6, 1987). Some weeks earlier (May 15, 1987), *Comercio,* an important daily, printed a full-page article on population issues, stressing the need for responsible parenthood.

Information, education and communication (IEC) activities and programmes have played an important role in heightening awareness of population issues. A recent report on population communication from the Population Information Program of The Johns Hopkins University describes the many innovative Latin American IEC efforts, with examples ranging from audio-cassettes with family planning messages mixed with comments from bus drivers for the entertainment of passengers to plans for national educational campaigns on acquired immune deficiency syndrome (AIDS).[16]

Since their introduction, IEC programmes have undergone conceptual changes and their contents have been enriched. During the 1970s, efforts to change individual reproductive behaviour were based primarily on a model that focused on the determinants of population growth and on their interrelationships with social and economic development. This model was usually accompanied by components related to sexual and family education. These programmes were always developed in a framework that emphasized respect for human rights, promotion of social justice and indigenous development. Since 1983, population education programmes, while maintaining the same fundamental values, have pursued two basic orientations. One orientation aims at transmitting clear ideas on the nature of population problems and their relationships with development. Based on concepts and principles from formal and social demography and from human ecology, this orientation emphasizes the intelligent participation of citizens in formulating population policies and executing action plans and programmes. The other orientation is concerned with direct action on specific demographic variables at the root of problems threatening the quality of personal, family and community life. Examples are high fertility, including high-risk pregnancies, high infant and childhood mortality and problems resulting from migration.[17]

More demographic information

Thirty years ago, there was a dearth of population data for Latin America and the Caribbean. Since then, the situation has changed radically, both quantitatively and qualitatively. The quantitative changes reflect the increase in the number of censuses, national and regional demographic surveys and special-purpose surveys on various aspects of population dynamics. Thirty years ago, some Latin American countries had not organized a census in more than a half-century. At present, there is no Latin American country without a relatively recent census. When the first fertility surveys were organized, many precautions were taken to avoid problems; now, in contrast, Governments usually treat the conduct of a fertility survey as routine.

The qualitative improvements have ranged from the application of well-adapted sampling frames to the critical analysis of concepts used in census questions. Examples are the following:

(a)   Most national statistical offices in Latin America have at least one person with in-house sampling expertise, and some have a full-fledged department for sample surveys. Although the experience seems uneven, several countries of Latin America are combining sampling designs with their national censuses;

(b)   The view is now widely accepted that censuses and other demographic data are generally incomplete and need updating, evaluation and methodological improvement;

(c)   Some Latin American countries have now had several rounds of the same type of survey, such as contraceptive prevalence, allowing more systematic study of the dynamics of fertility and contraceptive use;

(d)   More persons are aware that a multitude of influences can produce misleading impressions that fertility is declining; through changes in survey methodology and the use of more appropriate

concepts, it is possible to obtain better estimates of actual
fertility levels; and

(e)   A series of efforts has been made to improve the quality of
population data on women and their incorporation in the labour
force, including their role in the non-formal sector of the labour
market.

Growing awareness of the interrelatedness of population and other problems

There is much more awareness now of the importance of population
dynamics for a full understanding of a variety of social, economic and
health problems. For example, a study of employment problems in Latin
America sponsored by the Regional Employment Programme for Latin
America and the Caribbean (PREALC) emphasizes the relevance of
population growth and other population issues to certain employment
problems in Latin America, including persistent underemployment.[18] A
1986 book dealing with ecology and development in Latin America
dedicates an entire chapter to population.[19] A 1987 book dealing with
corruption in the Amazonian border regions of Colombia links population
problems in Brazil's north-east to migration streams to the Amazonian
regions and Brazilian settlements beyond the border, which have created
ecological and other problems for neighbouring countries.[20]

Waning importance of ideology in population debates

Ideological considerations, such as religious objections, have frequently
hindered the development of population programmes in Latin America.
Those who raise such objections are often likely to see no problems in the
region's rapid population growth. This tendency is frequently associated
with conservative positions on religion and on other social issues, such as
divorce and women's role.

Another ideological direction is rooted in development perspectives that
place major responsibility for socio-economic problems on external factors,
often combined with social-class analysis. Opposition to explanations of
the role of population factors in development problems often extends to
objections to the promotion of FP programmes, even if the programmes
are based purely on health considerations. This tendency is often
associated with leftist ideologies and was once especially popular among
some Latin American Marxists. More sophisticated treatment of
population issues is now evident, however. The examples of China,
where the reduction of fertility is seen as an essential component of its
development strategy, and Cuba, where family planning is treated as a
important element of maternal and child health (MCH) programmes, along
with the emphasis on family planning as a basic human right and the
growing attention to women's issues--all have led to a broadening of
views on population.

Increased recognition of the importance of women's status

Few organizations now active in the population field do not give prominence to women's issues. Among assistance agencies, The Population Council, Pathfinder Fund, Ford Foundation, and the United States Agency for International Development (USAID) have all given strong support to programmes specifically directed to women's issues. UNFPA has taken major steps in Latin America and the Caribbean to bring attention to women's issues to the foreground in population programmes. One expression of this concern was the 1986 Conference on Women, Population and Development, organized under the sponsorship of UNFPA and the Ministry of Education and Culture in Montevideo.

More focused attention to women's issues has uncovered problems that specifically affect Latin American and Caribbean women and that are the direct result of high fertility. Such problems include high rates of induced abortion and the attendant risks for women's health; low labour-force participation rates among Latin American women; labour-force participation patterns that continue to freeze women in traditional occupations, with lower incomes and limited opportunities for advancement; the need for thorough reform of labour legislation, taking women's issues more fully into consideration; the condition of women in the rural economy and the need for increasing their access to land; and the many pervasive psychological and cultural obstacles that will require substantial efforts to overcome.

Wider acceptance of family planning

In the 1950s, Latin America was essentially a high fertility region. There were interesting exceptions, such as Argentina and Uruguay, which had experienced the same demographic transition as had Western Europe. Other cases, such as Cuba and Chile, showed more ambiguous patterns but nevertheless had fertility levels lower than those in other Latin American countries.

In recent years, strong evidence indicates that fertility has started to decline substantially as a consequence of greater contraceptive use in several countries, including Brazil, Colombia, Costa Rica and Panama.[21] There is no doubt that some Latin American and Caribbean countries are now experiencing the fertility declines deemed to be characteristic of the demographic transition. The decline of fertility in the region, as in other parts of the world, is a complex process in which many factors have intervened. Some of these factors are the consequence of structural and institutional changes. Population policy measures might be counted among those factors.

MCH programmes have played an important role in these developments. PAHO, in its 1988 report, states that the majority of Latin American countries have now established MCH units and programmes. The same report mentions that supervision, training and evaluation are more likely to be integral to these programmes; that there is more

357

emphasis on the accurate delimitation of the specific groups at risk, both for local programming as well as for appropriate referrals of patients; and that more and more countries have adopted the perinatal clinical history form.[22]

Current population education programmes have also contributed to modifications of fertility behaviour. They have attempted to change gender stereotypes associated with *machismo* and male dominance. They have promoted intracouple and intergenerational communication, emphasizing greater knowledge of the human body and reacting against superstitious beliefs that often hinder acceptance of modern methods or result in inadequate use. They have also emphasized self-esteem and oppose fatalistic attitudes that create obstacles to the perception of family formation as a process over which the couple should have autonomy.[23]

Development of a population research tradition

Few Latin Americans were involved in population research 30 or 40 years ago. Partly as a consequence of the role of CELADE, partly as a consequence of internal developments and partly as a consequence of the action of external agencies, population research became accepted as an important research branch in academic programmes, government sectors and private research centres. This acceptance was not without controversy. The legitimacy of population research frequently became an issue in ideological debates that deflected attention from the permanent value of well-selected population research for an understanding of Latin American society and its development. The complete inventory and assessment of research findings pertinent to population issues would require a study by itself. Therefore, only a few examples of important findings are presented below.

When the first fertility survey on the Latin American continent was organized, no questions on contraceptive use were included because it was thought that they would interfere with the survey. Questions on contraceptive knowledge were already considered controversial enough to make the survey problematic. However, the researchers found that women who were questioned on contraceptive knowledge talked spontaneously about contraceptive use. From then on, questions on family planning were included as part of fertility surveys. Moreover, because fertility research had showed that people were much less inhibited in talking about sex, human reproduction and the use of contraceptives than had been expected, such issues could be touched upon in IEC programmes. Initially, too, it was feared that the existence of the cultural phenomenon of *machismo* would present a formidable obstacle to family planning on the part of males. *Machismo*, as the ideology of the strong man, so the argument went, was shared by many males in Latin America. One of its manifestations was a strong sexuality, reflected in a large number of children. This connection has proved to be false.

Other research with practical implications has shown that medical practitioners, especially at public institutions in countries with population programmes, can play an important role in the process of contraceptive acceptance.[24] Research has also demonstrated that large differentials in infant and childhood mortality exist among social and regional groups in Latin American countries and that these differentials can be lessened through special measures. Research on settlement possibilities of frontier regions, such as the Amazon region, has shown that subregions cannot provide a solution to population and other problems. Moreover, unregulated settlement may cause significant ecological problems with ramifications for long-term welfare of the country.

Latin American population scientists have developed theoretical frameworks for the integration of population dynamics into theories attuned to the development realities of the region. Three orientations, not necessarily mutually exclusive, can be distinguished. One develops a population theory on foundations that borrow directly from Marxist social and economic theory. Within this framework, efforts are made to link geographic and temporal differences in mortality, fertility and migration patterns to differences in the modes of production. The modes of production create different class systems, which influence family structure and demographic behaviours. The second orientation follows closely the road designed by the "dependency school". Demographic trends are directly linked to Latin America's location on the periphery of the world system. The specific demographic situation of the region then results from the ways in which major actors in the world system are able to influence demographic trends for their own benefit, based on the ready availability of cheap labour. The third and most successful orientation emphasizes the styles of development. The styles of development--the ways in which a country organizes its social and economic developments and the attention given to health and social welfare--will have important implications for population trends in Latin America.

Institutional arrangements

Governmental institutionalization of population issues is especially visible in the following: (a) establishment of national population commissions, national population councils and population units in national planning offices; (b) inclusion of population matters in development plans, other important government documents and legislation, and publication of guidelines for population programmes; and (c) establishment of sectoral programmes under ministries and other governmental units.

Establishment of population commissions, councils and units

A variety of government bodies for dealing with population issues has been set up in many Latin American countries. The exact nature of these bodies differs from country to country, and their responsibilities may vary over time. Population commissions may be temporary or permanent. Their objective is usually the review of major population issues with recommendations for policies and programmes. They may initiate the

359

establishment of national population councils and population units in national planning offices. In other cases, they may be the result of the activities of modest population units in national planning offices.

Two positive developments can be traced to the establishment of these population bodies. First, the existence of such an entity usually changes the context of debate on population issues in the country. Public officials are confronted with the question of how to deal with population issues, and officials with interests in those issues have more confidence in doing something about them. Second, the sheer presence of these population entities represents a start at linking population programmes more closely to development programmes.

Examples of Bolivia and Panama are given in the following paragraphs, although these two examples are not necessarily the most successful. The initial expectations based on the proposed plans for Bolivia have not yet been met. However, Bolivia's efforts to set up a National Population Council have been inspired by an approach that represents the thinking of many Latin American countries. In Panama, the institutional framework for the integration of population and development is more firmly embedded in the overall government structure and, as a result, some collaboration has been evident in population activities. The extent to which population behaviour has been effectively influenced by governmental policies in Panama remains a moot question.

Bolivia's establishment of the National Population Council (CONAPO) was the culmination of many efforts of the Population Unit in the Ministry of Planning. Given a broad mandate, CONAPO could, in principle, execute a wide variety of activities in all important population areas to achieve important socio-economic objectives. It was intended that CONAPO would promote, provide norms for, co-ordinate, integrate and control the adoption and execution of population policies; be responsible for demographic planning and the inclusion of population variables in social and economic planning; and undertake the evaluation of all such activities. It was intended that CONAPO would set desirable targets for population growth and propose measures for the reduction of infant mortality and measures affecting population distribution and international migration, executing its activities through the nation's educational, communication, health, social security and labour protection systems. Its mandate was to organize activities nationally, regionally, locally and by sector, ultimately relating its activities to a series of important socio-economic objectives. These objectives include general social and economic development, improved standards of living, full employment, welfare coverage for the needy and improvement in the status of women.

In Panama, the population unit of the National Planning Office, called the Department of Population, is located in the Ministry of Planning and Economic Policy. It grew out of a Technical Population Unit in the same ministry. Originally, the Ministry of Health was responsible for population, but it was later realized that population issues required a multi-sectoral approach. Therefore, population matters were transferred to the Ministry of Planning and Economic Policy.

The Department of Population ensures co-ordination through a Technical Population Committee (not to be confused with the aforementioned Technical Population Unit). The Committee, which meets bimonthly, includes representatives of the Ministries of Planning and Economic Policy, Labour and Social Welfare, Housing, Education, Government and Justice, Health, Agricultural Development, and the Migration Office of the Ministry of Defense. Also included are representatives of the Controleria General de la Republica, Social Security, Institute for the Development and Training of Human Resources and the Legislative Assembly. This Committee is the technical support for the National Commission for Population Policies and the core of interinstitutional communication and co-ordination of population matters in Panama. Through its subcommission on population projections it ensures consistency and co-ordination of all population projections, including those for the labour force. It is represented on other commissions dealing with population-related issues, such as the National Commission of the Family. This group has also strengthened Panama's presence at international meetings dealing with population.

Compared with other such arrangements in Latin America, the Panamanian structure has several favourable features, the result of four key factors:

(a) Strategic location of the Department of Population in the government administration and the existence of appropriate mechanisms for multiple interrelationships with other government units;

(b) Well-trained personnel in the Department of Population and the presence of persons with population training in other government units, resulting in improved communication and collaboration and high productivity;

(c) A tradition of basic data collection, evaluation and application, which compares favourably with such activities elsewhere in Latin America; and

(d) Good physical facilities, intensive use of computers and a well-organized documentation unit.

Inclusion of population matters in development plans,
other documents and legislation

One of the major preoccupations of population bodies, as mentioned above, has been the incorporation of demographic variables into social and economic planning. As an initial step, some bodies made sure that explicit attention was given to population variables in the national development plan. Other bodies were able at least to get guidelines for some population activities published in government documents, such as those of ministries of health or labour. In some countries, population bodies were instrumental in the adoption of special laws dealing with population issues. One example from Bolivia is the volume *National Development Strategy and the Four-Year Plan 1985-1988* (1984) of the Ministry of Planning. References to population variables are made in the sections on public health, regional development and future perspectives. More important, a special subchapter in the chapter on social aspects of population gives a concise, clear and balanced view of Bolivia's current population situation, together with implications for the future. It draws attention to five important population problems; (a) high infant and childhood mortality; (b) need for access to family planning services for the urban poor, who often resort to abortion, which is illegal; (c) possible problems resulting from too rapid population growth, in regard to living standards, land availability, housing, nutrition, employment and education, especially if substantial advances in mortality reduction are made; (d) problems of population distribution and regional development; and (e) problems of urban growth and structure. In addition, the subchapter contains a general discussion of population policy objectives and instruments to remedy the situation.

One example of legislation dealing directly with population is Peru's Population Law of 1985, the result of several important policy studies undertaken by the National Population Council. The Population Law, which covers fertility, mortality and migration, states explicitly that family planning is a basic right and that it is the Government's responsibility to promote family planning. The Government of Peru also established a Presidential Population Commission to advise the President on population policies.

Establishment of sectoral programmes under ministries and other governmental units

In most Latin American countries, concern with population issues started not at the top but in specific ministries or entities of the Government. It would require a special study to document fully the processes by which various sectors of the Government became involved in population issues. With the results of such a study, typologies could be devised and evaluated to enhance the speed of acceptance of population policies and the efficiency and stability of the country's population programmes.

Such a typology might conceivably include the following categories: (a) initiation of population programmes as a result of "demographic alarm clocks". This has been the case when national statistical offices, as a consequence of their responsibilities for the collection and analysis of demographic data, sound the alarm about high population growth rates; or (b) initiation of population programmes as a result of activities of problem watchers. Ministries monitor certain problems pertaining to their particular sectors, such as employment problems for a ministry of labour, housing problems for a ministry of housing or investment problems for a ministry of capital development.   In the course of looking at these problems, the ministries may recognize that population growth is an important contributor to the problem and then they often become the pioneers within the Government for population programmes; or (c) initiation of population programmes as a result of the activities of "doers". Particular segments of the Government sometimes initiate some type of direct action programme. For example, the ministry of health, the social security system or the army health services may, without formal policies, become involved in the distribution of contraceptives or in other family planning activities.

Population education offers one example of governmental institutionalization in a particular sector. Population education activities are increasingly being supported by the Governments of the region. All countries that have formulated a population policy now have a special chapter on population education in the document outlining their population policies.   Population education has become more and more institutionalized in public education systems. The education budgets in several Latin American countries now include provisions for specialists in population education. Structures set up in ministries of education give legitimacy to population education and provide for the creation of facilities for conducting population education programmes. In addition, more and more persons at higher levels in ministries of education participate in the formulation, execution and evaluation of population education projects. In 1988, for example, a meeting in San Jose, Costa Rica, brought together Central American Vice-Ministers of Education to make recommendations for a regional project on population education.

Constraints to population activities and programmes

The scope and quality of population activities in Latin America and the Caribbean are impressive. However, the structure has deficiencies. In many cases, though by no means all, fragility characterizes the penetration of population concerns into Latin American society.´ The upheavals caused by political changes and religious or ideological incursions have had disturbing effects on population concerns. Meanwhile, weaknesses continue in the institutional structure for population activities and programmes, in population awareness and in research on population issues. These topics are briefly reviewed below, along with considerable attention to the weaknesses in efforts to integrate population into development policies and planning. Putting the weaknesses in strong focus is meant to facilitate the search for solutions.

Institutional structures for action and research programmes

Although population activities have been institutionalized in Latin America, important weaknesses remain: lack of strong organizational frameworks for MCH and FP activities, lack of efficient monitoring systems for action programmes, lack of permanent academic population programmes and lack of permanent networks of population scientists and practitioners for the whole region.

Weak organizational frameworks for maternal and child health and family planning activities

Although Latin American Governments generally accept the desirability of strong MCH programmes, the organization and execution of national MCH programmes suffer from serious institutional weaknesses. Government FP programmes share some of the same weaknesses affecting MCH programmes. In many countries, MCH and FP programmes remain vastly underfunded because of the lack of strong political support. The interests of groups that would benefit from these programmes are seldom represented in the political parties active on the national scene. Pressure groups representing these interests, such as women's groups, public health practitioners and family planning associations, have to learn appropriate tactics to ensure better representation of these interests in political party platforms.

Government-sponsored MCH and FP programmes have also been lagging in developing effective institutional arrangements because they have neglected the search for imaginative ways to collaborate with private-sector agencies that have acquired in-depth experience in maternal and child health and family planning.

Despite substantial progress in public health training, the situation is far from satisfactory. The public health perspective remains woefully inadequate in many medical training programmes. Furthermore, the technical contents of training programmes, primarily oriented towards public health, are often weak. This training seldom provides the technical and administrative knowledge necessary for efficient management of MCH and FP programmes. One manifestation of this situation is the lack of effective monitoring systems for government MCH and FP programmes, as discussed below.

One of the most important institutional weaknesses of MCH and FP programmes in the public sector in Latin America is the lack of power for intermediate levels of the bureaucracy of these programmes. Central authorities often try to deal directly with the lowest levels. The intermediate levels have neither decision-making powers over funds nor effective command and communication channels with the lower levels. As a consequence, national programmes are frequently conducted without any consideration for local cultural and social variations, making it less likely that imaginative programmes will rise up from the bottom. The programmes, becoming rigid, are difficult to evaluate and even more difficult to adapt quickly to new conditions in some regions of a country.

The use of family planning, the decline in mortality and the distribution of MCH and FP programmes remain uneven across Latin America and the Caribbean. Important segments of the population have been excluded from the aforementioned demographic and social transitions--the educational transition and the transition in the status of women. Programmes will have to make more concerted efforts to identify these groups and to develop programmes especially suited to their needs and to the context in which they live. Reinforcement and development of the local systems of health as promoted by PAHO can be useful in this regard. However, to be really efficient such efforts need to be accompanied by identification of the optimal local level at which different health and family planning services need to be dispensed. Further, specific measures are required to ensure continuous involvement of the local community.

Inadequate monitoring systems for action programmes

Few large-scale MCH and FP programmes, especially those in the public sector, are adequately monitored. Monitoring would enable administrators to know how their programmes are currently operating and to make timely adjustments to changing conditions or unexpected developments. Yet, there is little awareness in many bureaucracies of the need for monitoring and evaluation systems. The overall weakness of public administration in many countries creates a difficult context for the introduction and efficient use of such systems. Moreover, the quality of data collected by public administration for health purposes remains vastly inadequate. For example, some studies have found that maternal mortality is underestimated by more than half.[25] Even when data are available, they are seldom used to establish priorities or to pinpoint the social groups needing special attention. Aware of these weaknesses, PAHO created in 1985 the Programme for the Analysis of the Health Situation and its Tendencies.[26]

PAHO is also supporting efforts to improve attention to the collection of data on health, mortality and fertility and to emphasize the importance of their use for evaluation and monitoring systems in the training of public health practitioners. In collaboration with the Statistical Office of the United Nations, the Inter-American Children's Institute and the International Institute for the Registration of Vital Events and Statistics, PAHO is giving renewed attention to providing future physicians with the requisite knowledge and motivation to fill out birth and death certificates and to become familiar with the use of health, mortality and fertility statistics in health planning and monitoring.[27]

Lack of permanent academic population programmes

The introduction of population studies in Latin American universities cannot be considered a complete success. The number of universities with well-rounded and stable programmes remains too small for such a large region. In addition, training on the relationships between population and health is almost non-existent. Population sciences also remain conspicuously absent from many social-science programmes. Moreover, many programmes are functioning within an environment that continually threatens their stability--and that has actually killed some promising programmes in population and the social sciences as well as academic programmes in population and public health. Much of this situation is a result of the general conditions of Latin American universities, especially public ones.

Another problem is that many participants in training courses do not subsequently have the opportunity to work in the field for which they were prepared. UNFPA, in evaluating training programmes in four countries (Brazil, Honduras, Mexico and Panama) found that neither the training institutes nor the institutes engaging the persons who had received training had prepared human resources development plans. The same evaluation found an urgent need to redirect the training of personnel for services towards knowledge and practical training, with more emphasis on the quality of the services.[28]

Lack of permanent professional networks

Although many regional programmes and networks dealing with population in the social sciences or in human reproduction and family planning have been set up, no stable and permanent network has resulted from these efforts. As a consequence, population scientists and practitioners have no regional organ as a forum for the exchange of ideas and for the promotion of a continuing well-informed debate on population issues and policies for Latin America and the Caribbean.

Population consciousness

The birth and growth of a population consciousness in the region are undoubtedly the most important results of all the population activities and programmes organized over the last 30 years in Latin America and the Caribbean. However, weaknesses remain, including insufficient attention to population variables; ideological backlash; polarized attitudes towards family planning policies; the need for better quality, coverage and responsiveness in family planning activities and programmes; the need for IEC programmes; and threats to women's programmes.

Insufficient attention to population variables

Despite growing awareness of population issues among social scientists and the public, this concern is often underdeveloped. For example, a detailed and otherwise valuable study of environmental problems in six Latin American cities, with active participation of a centre dedicated to population studies, contains few references to demographic variables, except for infant mortality, and then only as part of an index of environmental quality. Yet, these variables are part of the matrix influencing environmental problems in the metropolises of Latin America. Moreover, no effort is made to develop a conceptual scheme in which population variables play a more important role.[29]

Ideological backlash

Although controversies over population issues have lost some of their stridency, recurrent ideological backlash interferes with the conduct of population programmes. Sometimes, population policies are depicted as offending national sovereignty, and population agencies are still considered suspect in some quarters.

Polarized attitudes towards family planning policies

Attitudes towards fertility reduction as a policy matter are often polarized. Some depict family planning as a purely controlling (*controlista*) policy replacing proper development policies. Hence, they dismiss it as a policy option. Others consider family planning as a basic human right enabling couples to choose the number of children they really want and fostering health for mothers and children. A comprehensive position--in which family planning is considered not only a basic human right and a means towards better health but also an important though partial element of a integral policy for social and economic development--is seldom sufficiently developed or does not emerge as a clear policy option.

Need for better quality, coverage and responsiveness in family planning activities and programmes

Increasingly larger segments of Latin American populations have accepted family planning. Yet, the quality of FP programmes remains uneven. Some populations are still unserved and in need of services, and urgent new problems need innovative responses. According to a Briefing Paper of the Population Crisis Committee, 6 programmes in 21 countries can be considered as good, 7 as regular, 7 as deficient and 1 as very limited.[30] Furthermore, many MCH services to which many FP programmes are attached have serious organizational problems, among the most important of which are weaknesses in programming norms and procedures. For example, a PAHO evaluation found that 85 per cent of 425 services evaluated had to be considered unsatisfactory, whereas only 15 per cent were acceptable.[31]

Sterilization is an important family planning method in several Latin American countries.[32] As practised in Latin America, sterilization is basically female sterilization. When practised on a large scale and when undergone at younger ages and at lower parities, as is now happening in some Latin American countries, sterilization may create problems in the future for societies that feel that fertility is declining too fast or that the decline may bring about too rapid changes in the age distribution.

Substantial proportions of women are still having unwanted pregnancies, particularly women with lower income and education levels.[33] Most of these women can be described as in need of services. Among many other groups needing family planning services in the region are those in which the desire for a large number of children remains powerful. A major responsibility for FP programmes will be to identify underserved populations and develop appropriate strategies to increase their acceptance of family planning.

Family planning and MCH services are often slow to respond to new trends and problems requiring special attention and innovations. Two instances are the increase in sexual activity among adolescents, frequently accompanied by an increase in teen-age pregnancies, and the spread of AIDS. Having found that many programmes directed to adolescents are isolated and inefficient, PAHO advocates an integral revision of all adolescent health activities, aimed at better educational and preventive approaches.[34] The threat of AIDS will require more in-depth studies of its prevalence and a more accurate identification of the high-risk groups. As discussed in Chapter 4 on IEC programmes, it will also require changes of emphasis in FP programmes and suitable educational campaigns.

Need for information, education and communication programmes

Persistent misconceptions about population issues have lingered among the general population. According to a recent report on IEC strategies for the region, many people continue to associate population programmes with compulsory sterilization and with abortion.[35] The same report notes that many more efforts are needed to reflect the real ingredients of population issues.

Social scientists need to be more involved in IEC programmes to ensure that programmes are continually adapted to changes in the cultural and social environment, to changes in the media and their role in particular societies and to changes to the content and messages of IEC programmes. In addition, closer contacts are needed between those in the field of population education and information, on the one hand, and those who produce population research, on the other hand. Population researchers need to be able to transform their insights into a format useful in IEC programmes.

Threats to women's programmes

The emphasis on women's importance in population programmes has a sound foundation in scientific research. However, there are dangers of misplaced emphasis which, in the long run, could threaten these programmes. Some people support programmes for women because it is the thing to do, the fashion of the day. Ritual support of women's programmes will result in sterile thinking and ultimately to programmes lacking in imagination and originality. Other people, convinced of the importance of women's programmes, promote them in a way that makes them lose connection with other programmes or with other components of population programmes. In the final analysis, such support will do little for the authentic promotion of women's interests. The danger is that women's programmes will become isolated rather than connected to the fundamental objective, which is the enhancement of women's role in society on a base of equality and of consideration for the specific interests of women.

Research

Weaknesses in Latin American population research can be found in theoretical frameworks that are applied too simplistically and that remain incomplete. In addition, certain research areas remain underdeveloped, as discussed below.

Weaknesses in theoretical frameworks

Theoretical frameworks for the study of population are often applied simplistically. Sometimes, simple direct relationships are assumed to exist between particular modes of production and fertility or migration behaviour. No allowance is made for the empirical evidence that similar modes of production can be accompanied by a variety of family structures or that social systems based on different modes of production can be characterized by identical fertility behaviour. Thus, some studies have explained the fertility behaviour of different social classes as uniquely determined by the interests of the dominant classes. Studies using the existing style of development as an explanatory framework are often too general, neglecting similarities in the levels of infant mortality among countries with quite different social systems and policies, such as Chile, Costa Rica, Cuba and Jamaica.

In addition, theoretical frameworks often over-emphasize the macro-level at the expense of the micro-level. In the absence of efforts to explain how modes of production, dependency relations or development styles influence individual behaviour, concrete hypotheses are lacking for designing practical programmes or for deepening understanding of the dynamics of human reproduction and migration, for example. Moreover, researchers applying these frameworks to demographic variables are often unaware of the significant modifications that these general theories have undergone. Many of these theoretical frameworks tend to look at demographic variables as passive players pushed by macro-social variables towards ineluctable outcomes. The possibility of demographic variables having an autonomous influence on social and economic structures, on family and social class, is seldom considered.[36]

Underdeveloped research areas

More knowledge of abortion patterns is needed for a better understanding of fertility dynamics and for the design of special programmes with emphasis on the use of family planning. More study is also needed on the interrelationships between population dynamics and environmental problems. This topic has been neglected because of the attitude that solving costly environmental problems is a luxury that developing countries cannot afford or that population dynamics are only indirectly related to environmental problems. Another reason is that few persons have the skills to do sound research on this issue, which receives little attention in the training of population and environmental scientists.

Despite numerous studies of population dynamics among rural populations, many unknowns remain. For example, there is insufficient information on how fertility and health decisions are made in rural areas. Operationally, a strong demand continues for programmes specifically attuned to the rural areas of Latin America and the Caribbean. More research is also needed on the impact on population dynamics of economic and social policies not specifically aimed at population variables. Such policies range from exchange-rate policies to social security programmes. More research is also needed on the impact of large development projects.

Population units of national planning offices

Among all population projects, the establishment of population units created probably the most enthusiasm. This activity corresponded well to the prevailing perspective in Latin America that, for successful programmes, population had to be integrated into comprehensive development strategies. However, despite the assertion that the establishment of population units in national planning offices has been a positive step, it cannot be denied that their influence has failed to live up to expectations. One basic reason for this unsatisfactory situation is the fragile status of many population units within the government bureaucracy and within the country itself; another reason is their seeming inability to develop effective programmes integrating population and development.

Status of population units

Political instability has threatened the stability of many policies, programmes and organizations dedicated to the execution of population policies and programmes. Even normal governmental changes in Latin America imply more discontinuity and more shake-ups in administrative structures and in the location of specific government units than occur in more developed countries. Moreover, the population units of many national planning offices were usually established years after the founding of those offices. They were thus newcomers in an environment that had often been apathetic if not hostile towards any population programmes. The units often had to spend more time on bureaucratic infighting to legitimize their role within the national planning office than on building up their own activities and programmes. They were often staffed by persons who had little preparation for the work and frequently had to be trained on the job. In some cases, motivation was lacking.

The two aforementioned problems, political and administrative instability and inferior status within the government bureaucracy, were often the result of inadequate staffing and poor leadership. In turn, they often bred personnel turnover on a scale unfamiliar to persons acquainted with more stable bureaucracies. Because of this high degree of personnel turnover, contacts and communication links with other sectors inside and outside the Government had to be rebuilt over and over again. Turnover also affected the unit's personnel, who had to work in an atmosphere of permanent insecurity. One result of the problems of finding well-trained manpower and of coping with personnel turnover was that it took much longer to set up viable units and agendas for their work than had been anticipated by external assistance agencies. In the meantime, agreements had been structured on the assumption of adequate staffing. In many cases, initial project documents had to be substantially revised for more realistic programming.

Problems also arose when, as often happened, it was assumed that a project could be executed successfully without outside technical assistance. When technical assistance was provided, it was often sporadic and inadequate or too purely demographic to be helpful. One example involves assistance for making population projections, a necessary tool for the work of a population unit in a planning office. Technical assistance in this regard was often limited to training these units to make population projections, which often had already been compiled elsewhere in the Government, without instruction on how to apply such projections to obtain estimates of future needs for housing, education and employment. Few population units received the type of technical assistance needed for the identification of realistic policy measures and operational programmes that could be introduced and subsequently evaluated in a particular context.

Because of their relatively inferior status in the pecking order of the national planning bureaucracy, many population units have yet to develop a strong network of internal and external relations. Within the national planning office, they have often reinforced the walls that already existed between the unit and other branches of the office. Externally, they have forged only weak linkages--and sometimes none at all--with the public sector and the private sector.

371

A variety of population activities usually preceded the establishment of a population unit. For example, private-sector organizations had often already taken many initiatives in the population field: some managed action programmes in population education and communication or in family planning; others had conducted studies often pertinent to the responsibilities of the population unit. The pre-existing situation reinforced the unit's sense of inferiority, which was sometimes translated into apathy, inaction, unproductive criticism and even the desire to control all existing population projects and to have the power to approve all population projects in both public and private sectors.

Integration of population and development

The scientific development of the integration of population and development remains incomplete, lacking appropriate methodology despite the sophistication of many planning models. Moreover, the theoretical frameworks employed are often rigid and unimaginative. Still, population units could do more. Much more attention is needed to analyse how population variables are affecting, and are affected by, socio-economic factors. The fragmented efforts of population units are one result of the lack of a common approach and framework. As one evaluation report notes: "The general failure to progress beyond the descriptive level can be traced to both the design and the execution of the work plan . . . . No analytic framework . . . was elaborated".[37]

Econometric and other quantitative models are useful adjuncts of planning and indispensable instruments for a better understanding of the interaction of population and socio-economic dynamics. However, many population units have considered the construction of new models or the adaptation of existing quantitative models as their primary function. What should have been only a part of their work has become in some cases the principal activity.

Too often the analytic work of population units in planning offices has been limited to descriptive exercises or, at best, to the economic and social analysis of demographic patterns without any operational considerations concerning how to influence these patterns. Whenever there is a desire to influence a demographic pattern, such as migration, detailed attention will have to be given to what measures and programmes can be introduced, strengthened or reoriented to obtain more desirable patterns. In the case of migration, for example, these measures would entail investment policies, urban policies, rural development etc. The same observation is applicable to fertility and health policies. Much more effort will have to be directed towards the search for instruments to execute population policies. As yet, there are no efficient channels for communication among persons working in this field in Latin America and the Caribbean. Many planning offices might benefit from greater knowledge of population and development projects in other countries within and outside Latin America and the Caribbean.

372

Part Three:

Agenda for the Future

10. International Co-operation in the Field of Population

The previous chapters have shown that international co-operation has played an important role in the development of population programmes. Given the large and increasing needs and the economic situation prevailing in much of the developing world, it has also become clear that the international community will have to continue to provide financial and technical support. What, then, are the specific characteristics of international assistance? What has been learned from the implementation of assistance that will be useful for planning? This chapter attempts to answer some of these questions.

Resources

International assistance for population programmes was pioneered by non-governmental organizations (NGOs), especially the International Planned Parenthood Federation (IPPF), as early as the 1950s. The first bilateral support--from Sweden to Sri Lanka (then Ceylon)--came in 1958. In the 1960s, a few other bilateral agencies and the United Nations system followed suit. By then, several developing countries had already initiated their own population programmes, usually family planning programmes. Nevertheless, both in the 1960s and later, international assistance in many countries provided an incentive for Governments to become more active in the population sector.

By the end of the 1960s, almost a dozen Governments were providing international population assistance; UNFPA had been set up to lead the United Nations system in channelling some of these funds; certain United Nations specialized agencies had mandates to work in this field; and many NGOs and private foundations were active, although most of them on a small scale. The number of countries with national population programmes was still small, however. Today, in contrast, support for some kind of population activities is almost universal. Moreover, the resources provided by the developing countries themselves have increased greatly. Although reliable estimates are lacking, in part due to the difficulties of separating population activities from other development efforts, it is clear that most countries use more from their own budgets than they receive in international assistance. In India and China, the contribution of the Government is many times that of the international community.

At the same time, the number of those providing assistance, in particular Governments, has multiplied. Due to difficulties of statistical reporting, the discussion below focuses on population assistance in grant form. There are also loans, such as those provided by the World Bank, which amounted to $750 million during 1982-1987. Today, almost all Governments in developed countries contribute to population assistance. The total amounts provided have increased sixfold, from a little less than $100 million in 1969 to just under $600 million in 1988. However, a closer look at the numbers reveals that the picture is not uniformly positive.

First, the amounts provided today are far from sufficient. As discussed in Chapter 5, the demand for family planning services alone exceeds by far the financial resources available from national and international resources. Comprehensive population programmes will require much larger infusions of resources.

Second, the increase in resources has varied over the years, resulting partly from the shifting value of the U.S. dollar and partly from the changing priorities of the major sources of aid. During the 1970s, although funding activity tripled at current prices, there was actually a slight decline in real terms (adjusted for inflation). During the first half of the 1980s, there was growth both in absolute dollar amounts and in real terms. In addition, the growth in funding from 1980 to 1985 was more rapid than the growth in developing country populations, implying a rise in commitments in the developing world from 1.1 to 1.4 U.S. cents per capita. Since the mid-1980s, however, both the rate of increase and per capita commitments have declined.

Third, the same small number of countries provides the bulk of the assistance today as in 1969. In 1988, only 10 Governments provided more than $10 million annually. The United States of America remains the principal source of assistance, but its share decreased from 56 per cent in 1985 to less than 42 per cent in 1988. Japan, the second largest source of assistance today, consistently provided about 9 per cent of the total during the 1980s. These two are followed by a cluster of countries, including Canada, Denmark, the Federal Republic of Germany, Finland, the Netherlands, Norway, Sweden and the United Kingdom of Great Britain and Northern Ireland.

Fourth, despite overall increases in the contribution of leading sources of assistance, population assistance as a share of the total official development assistance is still modest--approximately 1.3 per cent, and it has decreased from a near 2 per cent level in the early 1970s. The Scandinavian countries retain a leading position here, with the highest level--5 per cent of official development assistance--being reached by Norway. The United States is also above the average, whereas Japan has recently fallen slightly below the average, and the Federal Republic of Germany is well below.

Fifth, population concerns are usually overlooked in development assistance programmes outside the population sector. This neglect has been a detriment to both population and development activities. The lack of attention to the role of population in development is particularly notable within the United Nations system--despite mandates covering certain aspects of population and despite occasional high-level statements indicating political commitment to the population sector. In 1987, less than 8 per cent of multilateral population assistance--again, excluding that of the lending institutions--came from the regular budgets of United Nations organizations other than UNFPA. Notwithstanding some improvement in recent years, there is little evidence in the content of their activities to suggest that other United Nations agencies are incorporating population concerns into their regular programmes. This is true even in areas where the expression of population concerns would be expected--for example, in development planning efforts or in health programmes. The situation is similar among the Governments providing bilateral assistance.

Sixth, and this is not necessarily negative, the three major assistance channels are used more or less evenly. That is, about one third of population assistance is provided bilaterally, one third multilaterally and one third through NGOs. Almost all of the funds originate from Governments, although a small part is generated by NGOs and foundations and, as mentioned, a small part comes from regular United Nations budgets. A few Governments provide direct bilateral assistance in addition to supporting both multilateral (for example, UNFPA) and NGO (for example, IPPF) activities. Some others provide all their support through one or both of the latter.

There are obvious advantages in having several different channels of assistance. For example, multilateral organizations may serve as a neutral channel in sensitive areas and may relieve a bilateral organization of some administrative tasks; NGOs may have better contacts than other organizations with grass-roots groups in the countries. However, the multitude of channels makes it extremely difficult to trace funds and analyse their use. Furthermore, the intermediaries may add to administrative costs.

Recipients

In 1969, about 30 countries, most of them in Asia, had requested and received some kind of population assistance, almost exclusively for family planning programmes. Over the years, and partly as a result of the international community's efforts, almost all developing countries have joined the group requesting such international co-operation. The largest portion still goes to the most populous region--Asia. With the earliest population programmes, this region has the most mature institutional infrastructure, resulting in high absorptive capacity. Although the total amounts have grown absolutely, the percentage share going to Asia has decreased recently, from a high of around 60 per cent in the late 1970s to less than 50 per cent of the total since 1986. There has been a corresponding increase in the share going to Africa--28 per cent in 1988, more than double the level in 1982. Latin America and the Middle East have remained at almost the same level during the 1980s--20 per cent

376

and 10 per cent, respectively. The increase in Africa is attributable both to a shift in priorities among the assistance agencies and to a change in attitude towards population policies in the African countries themselves.

Some resources are also provided to activities at regional or interregional levels. Such activities--providing training, developing research methodologies, and analysing and disseminating lessons learned--aim at benefiting individual countries but are more efficiently undertaken at the intercountry level.

Assistance priorities

There are vast needs for assistance, but not all population activities have an equal chance of support because various sources of assistance have different priorities. As a result, certain countries and sectors have an overconcentration of limited resources, while others are neglected.

The bilateral agencies concentrate on recipient countries that are selected on the basis of both political and economic criteria. Often, many agencies favour the same countries. In contrast, the United Nations organizations and many NGOs work with any developing country that requests their support. However, they also concentrate on a certain number of priority countries, which receive the largest portion of their resources. For example, UNFPA provides up to 75 per cent of its country programme resources to 56 countries, which have been designated as priority countries based on demographic and socio-economic criteria. Agencies that can work with all countries, such as UNFPA, should ensure that no urgent country needs are left unattended. At present, in the absence of any objective methods of assessing relative needs, this task is difficult. Nevertheless, efforts have to be made to avoid obvious duplication or neglect.

It is also unclear which agencies can provide support to intercountry activities. All agencies seem to favour country over intercountry activities, but some also support certain kinds of activities that can be better undertaken at the regional or global level. However, there is even less co-ordination of support at regional or global levels than at the country level. A few striking exceptions include support to the human reproduction research programme and to the periodic fertility surveys.

Assistance agencies also support different population sectors and different target groups (for example, women, local NGOs or central Governments). Some agencies assist only family planning programmes, whereas others support censuses and still others co-operate in population policy projects. A few have wide mandates that can include a variety of population sectors. The co-ordination of their support to a country is a task for the Government. To facilitate governmental co-ordination, however, the international community needs to harmonize and make the various sectoral priorities better known. In addition, assistance agencies need to ensure that Governments are aware of the different sources of funding and can make best use of them.

Finally, there are also differences in the kinds of resources agencies offer. Here again, clearer information on the various priorities would facilitate improved government planning. Some agencies can provide only experts and equipment from their own country, whereas others permit the purchase of services and supplies world-wide, and some even support local costs.

Programme quality

The international community has been complacent about ensuring that its support is based on appropriate assessments of past experiences and country needs. Support has often been provided to individual projects rather than to comprehensive programmes with measurable objectives and clear plans. There has also been a tendency to transplant project approaches from one country to another without tailoring them to each country's particular situation. Moreover, few efforts have been made to measure the effectiveness and impact of the population programmes and the contributions made by the assistance to these programmes. Such deficiencies in programme design and evaluation are surely not limited to the population sector, but the consequences may be more serious in this sector. This is a relatively new area, in which learning from experience is especially important.

A related problem is the limited exchange of information among assistance agencies about which approaches--substantive as well as operational--do or do not work. There has been a general reluctance to work together to find common solutions to problems. This may reflect, among other things, an inherent resistance to change. However, there have recently been some initiatives to at least harmonize procedures for support to country programmes.

Procedures for planning and implementing assistance programmes vary considerably. This variety of approaches creates complications for the Governments, as they must follow the prescribed procedures, even those that are contradictory or inefficient. Some agencies, notwithstanding lengthy preparations for funding decisions, do not sufficiently take into account the Government's priorities and capacity, nor the lessons learned from past programme experience. Some organizations have decentralized decision-making to the field offices, whereas others are highly centralized. Although the trend is towards decentralization, the fact that it is not uniform hinders possibilities for co-ordination at the country level. Recent initiatives to harmonize and improve procedures for development assistance in the Development Assistance Committee (DAC) for bilateral agencies and in the Joint Consultative Group on Policy (JCGP) for the United Nations funding agencies are welcome. Yet, they are still insufficient to solve the procedural problems, let alone the need for harmonization of priorities.

In addition to country programme priorities and procedures, there is also a need to address the issue of which intercountry activities work best in which circumstances and how to co-ordinate support for them to maximize their usefulness for the country activities.

Co-ordination

The above discussion has shown that there are several gaps in the knowledge about assistance and a lack of co-ordination of international assistance, both at national and international levels. Additional issues referred to in previous chapters warrant attention. Among them are policies for continuing assistance, once a country has been selected--that is, issues of government contributions and the promotion of self-reliance. Another such issue is the relative advantage of each of the various assistance channels in a given country situation.

Several organizations--bilateral, multilateral and non-governmental--have attempted to collect information about aspects of the assistance provided. Some data banks have information on the amounts that different agencies provide to various countries, in particular for family planning. However, no systematic effort has been made to collect and analyse more comprehensive information on policies, strategies and procedures of the assistance agencies.

Furthermore, efforts to co-ordinate assistance have been insufficient. At the country level, although some Governments have taken an active interest in such co-ordination, others have been passive or have preferred to play one agency against another. At the international level, some efforts at harmonization of procedures have taken place, but each of them has been confined to only one group of assistance agencies, that is, to bilateral or to multilateral agencies, not to both.

At present, there is no agreement among agencies as to which organization should collect information, what types of information are needed, and how and by whom it should be analysed. Nor is there a forum in which these and other issues related to the co-ordination of population assistance can be discussed. The following chapter includes suggestions for how to deal with these and other international co-operation issues.

11. Programmatic Implications and Conclusions

The main task of the Review and Assessment exercise has been to identify the most salient factors in the success of national population programmes along with the continuing constraints to implementing these programmes. The sectoral assessments have sought to identify emerging needs and unresolved issues in the policy development process, in the design and implementation of maternal and child health and family planning programmes, and in information, education and communication programmes. Chapter 5 has summarized the major issues common to each of these sectors, in programmes everywhere. The regional analyses have sought to identify constraints and issues specific to each developing region. This chapter deals with the implications for population programmes.

Although population problems seem rather similar in many developing countries, the determinants of such problems are not. The ultimate influences on demographic variables are mainly socio-cultural and behavioural. Many programmes fail because planners neglect the unique influence of socio-cultural and behavioural factors in programme design and implementation. The lack of appropriate data, information and knowledge on these and other aspects, and the inadequate analyses and dissemination of whatever data do exist continue to be a problem.

Another problem is that population programmes seldom fit neatly with overall development objectives and other social policies. Even when they do, the social sector, and population programmes within it, receive the least priority and smallest outlays. For instance, the importance of the role, status and participation of women in population and other development activities has now been acknowledged. Yet, effective legislation and other legal measures, as well as economic and social instruments in support of women, are still lacking. This gap is a persistent and major constraint to achieving programme success.

Still another constraint is over-reliance upon the government sector. As discussed later in this chapter, population programmes succeed only when they have the active and direct support of the people. Regardless of the type of population programme--whether it deals with censuses, vital registration, or family planning service delivery--bottle-necks are likely without the support of community organizations and other grass-roots, non-governmental institutions.

To meet the challenges raised by the issues, needs and constraints covered in this book, strategies need to be modified in many ways. Programmatic changes will be required within each sector of population activity: policy development; maternal and child health and family planning; and information, education and communication. In addition, changes will be required in programming at both the national level and the international level.

380

Modifications by sectors

Policy development

If the policy development process is--as it ought to be--based upon scientific data, research and analysis, progress will depend first and foremost upon strong political commitment, institutional support, human resources provisions, budgetary commitment and a willingness to use the findings. Next, the quality and content of research and analysis should be improved, with the development of a research agenda for population issues. Such an agenda would include critical unresolved research issues with programmatic underpinnings. In addition, the contribution of data and research to policy and planning activities in developing countries should be periodically assessed. Formulating population policies should become a solid endeavour, with the participation of individuals, grass-root organizations, religious institutions and political leaders. Training activities need to be closely re-examined, and a cost-effective strategy designed for training specialists to undertake policy development. Finally, Governments, international and bilateral organizations, and NGOs should support, in co-ordinated fashion, institutional development for data collection, research, analysis, planning and policy formulation. Because developing countries possess varying institutional capacities, technical co-operation should be tailored to meeting each country's particular needs in institutional development.

Maternal and child health and family planning

The principal challenges in the MCH/FP field are essentially those of making services more accessible, of improving their quality and of reaching previously underserved populations with them. Meeting these challenges will require widespread application of several approaches already under way in some countries. Provision of services through as many modes of delivery as possible, with emphasis on outreach approaches in both public and private sectors, would appear advisable. However, given limited resources, the number and relative merit of the various modes that might be employed in a given national situation shoud be assessed using methods of cost-effectiveness analyses. To gain maximum benefit from available funds, cost-effectiveness analyses should also be consistently applied to the "micro" programmatic options that present themselves within modes of service delivery--for example, duration of training, frequency of supervision, means of transporting supplies. Increasing the provision of services through the private sector may be an important way of maintaining programme viability, because it will permit public resources to be focused on remaining underserved, unconvinced, and economically disadvantaged and rural groups. Finally, providing the widest possible selection of contraceptives will help ensure that all couples have an opportunity to assess and meet their needs in the best way.

To accomplish the above, continuing efforts to gain political commitment and the resulting allocation of national, financial and human resources will be required. Additionally, management information systems will have to be improved. Managers themselves need further training in the use of data for decision-making and in the more efficient organization of training, supervisory, logistical and other support systems. The motivation and skill of service personnel should also be addressed. These personnel will benefit from training in the health rationale for family planning as well as in standards for providing services. Such standards include the implications of introducing contraceptive methods that were previously unavailable, counselling, and special requirements for dealing with males, adolescents and other previously underserved groups. Productivity will be increased by holding staff accountable for reasonable, but specific, standards of performance. Training must be reinforced by supportive supervision and by logistical systems ensuring timely availability of adequate supplies. Most importantly, programmes should be sensitive to institutional settings and reflect the socio-cultural characteristics of individual countries.

Information, education and communication

The programmatic implications of the IEC issues identified are many. In addition, because of their range and complexity, the issues cannot be resolved with vertical sets of activities; strategic planning will be required to help forge suitable frameworks for action. Among the implications is the need for further investment in a variety of training and research activities, with great care given to improving the effectiveness of training and to ensuring the appropriateness of research and its application. Qualitative research on audience perceptions and knowledge is especially important. Messages can then be tailored to specific needs, which would be ascertained largely through audience participation and thus reflect views of the audiences themselves. Segmenting audiences into groups with distinctive characteristics and needs will help ensure that underserved groups--such as youth, newly-weds and men--receive the attention that is pertinent to them.

A comprehensive IEC strategy will take into account the needs of political decision makers as well as those of the underserved groups referred to above. To ensure effective outreach, it is advisable to bring communication and education personnel into the planning process so that the resulting programme will reflect important communication principles. For IEC and other activities to be most effective, co-ordination of efforts within Governments and among external assistance agencies will be needed. This goal will require sufficient political will to override the tendency towards intersectoral and interinstitutional rivalries sometimes evident in development work.

Modifications of population programming at the national level

The modifications to population programming at the national level should centre around the following: (a) obtaining needed political support, (b) introducing strategic planning and programming, (c) diversifying the agents for demographic change and (d) strengthening resource mobilization.

Obtaining political support

Typically, many factors, substantive and other, are responsible for lack of political support. For this reason, overcoming lack of support requires an interrelated set of activities aimed at the following:

(a)   Generating popular support to programmes;

(b)   Including all important actors--politicians, policy makers, planners, Parliamentarians, community and religious leaders and others;

(c)   Undertaking research on socio-cultural and behavioural aspects of population and making the findings available in useful formats for programme design and implementation;

(d)   Formulating a strong IEC programme that takes into account religious and cultural values and that presents messages appropriate to the social setting; and

(e)   Forging institutional development at all levels and in different fields, including research, training, policy formulation and management.

Introducing strategic planning and programming

Introducing strategic planning and programming is indeed the most important programme modification. Strategic planning may be defined as the art of mobilizing all the political, economic, social and other resources of a nation to achieve the objectives of a population policy and programme. It entails at least four activities: (a) adoption of a long-term time horizon, (b) selection of critical points for intervention, (c) co-ordination of programme efforts and (d) careful programme design and planning.

The first step in strategic planning is the formulation of a comprehensive population policy, covering not only fertility and population growth but also mortality, migration, integration and population structure. Such a policy should be made a component of both the short-to-medium

383

term planning scenarios. The population sector should be supported by all sectors, particularly the social sector, and both population and the social sectors should enjoy the same priority attention as the economic sector in the planning process.

The Review and Assessment exercise has identified several factors of strategic importance in the success of programmes. It has found, for instance, that even where institutional support for meeting family planning demand is weak, the quality of family planning services plays a positive role in contraceptive practice (for example, the Matlab experience in Bangladesh). Similarly, wherever IEC programmes have been specially adapted to particular social and cultural settings, as in Burkina Faso and Indonesia, they have led to better programme performance. The improvement of the role and status of women is another element of strategic significance to the success or failure of population programmes. Wherever programmes have taken this factor into account, as in India's Kerala State and in Indonesia, the impact on society in both demographic and health terms has been substantial. In addition, where effective policy planning units are in place, as in Mexico and Thailand, policy formulation has been successfully co-ordinated with development planning. Likewise, wherever good quality data and capabilities for analysis are present, as in Indonesia and Tunisia, assessments of programme impact and success have been facilitated. It is essential, therefore, that such contributors to programme success be integrated into the process of strategic programming.

A companion to strategic planning is strategic programming. Such programming seeks to identify priorities for programmatic action, including the following:

(a) Ascertaining the critical mix of programme components and identifying the appropriate formulating and executing agencies (Government, United Nations Agencies and organizations, NGOs, private sector);

(b) Selecting the target groups for programme intervention (the poor, landless, underdeveloped regions, high-risk groups, etc.);

(c) Determining the various inputs to the programme;

(d) Specifying the operational thrust--whether, for instance, to improve quality of service or extend programme coverage, or whether to initiate new programmes or strengthen existing programmes where success is most likely;

(e) Establishing the degree to which population programmes should be harmonized with social and economic sectors; and

(f) Identifying the types of women's concerns that should be part of population objectives.

One basic requirement for such a strategic approach would be to expand rapidly the national capacity to manage the programme effectively and efficiently. This would entail strengthening capabilities in the following areas, among others: translation of policy goals into programmatic measures; elaboration of programme requirements in both financial and human resource terms; development of a management plan to bring into concert inputs, outputs and sequencing of activities; institutionalization of monitoring and evaluation; and co-ordination of programme activities. The national plan, which incorporates strategic planning and programming, should also serve as a framework for collaboration and co-ordination of activities supported by external assistance agencies, both multilateral and bilateral, as well as by national government sectors, the private sector and other sources.

Diversifying agents of demographic change

Studies reveal that population programmes are more successful when they are supported by individuals and communities. Reliance on the government sector as the sole agent of demographic and social change thus has to be reduced. For both substantive and programmatic reasons, the involvement of other groups as agents of such change is essential. Experience shows that NGOs, community organizations, socio-cultural and religious groups, women's groups and influential individuals can and do play an important role in influencing the attitudes and behaviour of people. The national plan should, therefore, take into account the basic make-up and outlook of such groups and organizations, and involve them along with the intended beneficiaries when designing and implementing the national programme.

Strengthening resource mobilization

In the final analysis, the availability and effective use of resources will determine the scale, character and impact of population interventions. In this regard, resources refer not only to finances but also to institutional and human capacities. The existence of a strategic plan will greatly aid the assessment of resources needed as well as their effective mobilization. Most estimates indicate that close to $9 billion to $10 billion will be required for population activities in the year 2000. National Governments, international assistance agencies, private organizations and others should all increase their responsibilities in meeting this challenge. In addition, they need to complement financial allocations with institutional and human resource commitments (see Box 17).

385

Box 17

"A BETTER LIFE FOR FUTURE GENERATIONS" --THE AMSTERDAM DECLARATION

The Amsterdam Declaration was adopted by consensus by delegates from 79 countries at the International Forum on Population in the Twenty-First Century. Organized by UNFPA in co-operation with the Government of the Netherlands, the Forum was held in Amsterdam, 6-9 November 1989. In addition to Ministers and senior government officials from 79 countries, representatives of 20 United Nations agencies and organizations, 6 inter-governmental organizations, 32 non-governmental organizations and 16 academic and training institutions attended the Forum. Following are excerpts from the Declaration.

"The Forum Participants . . . call on:

All countries

■　　To increase their political commitment to population programmes and policies in consonance with national priorities and aspirations and taking into account the principles of the World Population Plan of Action of 1974, as confirmed and expanded upon at the International Conference on Population in Mexico City in 1984;

■　　To contribute to the development of comprehensive population goals and objectives, involving both the public and the private sector and taking into account the findings of the wide-ranging review and assessment population experience conducted by UNFPA upon which the recommendations of this declaration are based;

■　　To adopt integrated population, environmental and natural resource management policies, including those which address population movement and distribution with the objective of minimizing their negative consequences.

■　　To make every effort to provide the financial resources necessary to reach the medium variant population projection by the year 2000, viz. a total of almost US$ 9 billion a year for core population activities;

■　　To strive to improve the role and status of women throughout all spheres of life and to ensure that women actively participate in and benefit from all population and development activities;

■　　To ensure that population programmes provide education, counselling and services for young people and promote their participation in all development activities;

■　　To ensure that all couples and individuals are guaranteed the basic human right to decide freely and responsibly the number and spacing of their children and have the information, education and

386

means to do so, in accordance with the World Population Plan of Action;

■ To ensure that the results and follow-up of this Forum are duly taken into account in the formulation of the international development strategy for the fourth United Nations Development Decade as well as in the preparations for and the deliberations of the 1992 United Nations Conference on Environment and Development and the proposed United Nations International Population Meeting in 1994;

■ To support research for new, safe and effective means of family planning, and to expedite adequate production and distribution of existing methods which have been proven safe by international research.

In adopting this Declaration, we the participants of the International Forum on Population in the Twenty-first Century commit and dedicate ourselves to bringing about higher levels of advocacy and attention to the crucial importance of population trends for the well-being and quality of life of future generations and to setting a firm course of action towards sustainable development and the protection of the environment of our planet.

Modifications of population programming at the international level

The previous chapter on international co-operation discussed constraints to international population assistance and the need for enhancing both the quality and the quantity of assistance. Implications of those constraints are twofold: first, strategic programming is needed at the international level; second, the roles of major members of the international community need to be modified.

Employing strategic programming

Ensuring that resources are put to the best use is a challenging assignment. A major obstacle to successful and sustainable population programmes has been a lack of strategic thinking. As a result, population activities are often unfocused, unco-ordinated, *ad hoc* and without follow-up. A framework for population assistance is needed, based on strategic planning at the international level, for which the population assistance community must take responsibility. To establish an international strategy, several actions are required: agreement must be reached on the overall population objectives and their relation to general development goals; fund-raising targets for the international community must be specified; and, at the programme level, priorities have to be determined, procedures harmonized and the roles of the various agencies delineated.

Priorities and procedures

The precise role of the various external assistance agencies in each country will have to be determined within the context of each government programme. However, as mentioned in the previous chapter, agencies are constrained by their mandates and general policies and priorities. These limitations on the population activities of the various parties are not well known and must be clarified. There are, in addition, many agencies that, though not active participants in the population field, nevertheless support, or could support, programmes that influence population. General health programmes, development planning projects and activities involving women fall into this category. Therefore, better analysis is needed of the influence of population variables on different development sectors and vice versa, to maximize the benefits of overall development programmes. Further efforts to streamline, simplify and introduce flexibility, including decentralization, into the procedures are necessary. Because these kinds of procedures apply to all types of programmes of a particular agency, the issue cannot be resolved by the population assistance community alone. It must be handled in a larger context. However, the international population community can bring the issue up in international and national development forums and suggest improvements.

Mechanism

It may be impossible in the short run to arrive at a comprehensive and detailed international strategy. None the less, certain principles can be established, information exchanged, and programmes and procedures harmonized. A mechanism capable of accommodating the totality of the assistance programme--bilateral, multilateral and NGO--is required. At present, only parts of such a mechanism exist: the Development Assistance Committee (DAC) analyses bilateral assistance; UNFPA reviews multilateral assistance; and the roundtable discussions of the United Nations Development Programme (UNDP), consultations of the World Bank, and inter-agency meetings in the United Nations all address specific issues.

To devise a mechanism for developing an international strategy, it is necessary to establish a system for gathering information and holding regular forums for discussion among all parties concerned. For the former, assistance agencies must create an inventory of data banks and gather and analyse information on agency policies, programme experience and future country needs. Gaps in information have to be identified and ways found to fill them. The selection of a particular agency to fill the gaps will depend on the mandate and capacity of the various organizations concerned. Given the complexity of the task, it is likely that several parties will have to take part. To facilitate this task, the agencies will have to establish a focal point to co-ordinate activities and undertake the overall analysis. The focal point will also be responsible for organizing regular forums in which representatives from the three agency groups and from developing countries can discuss pertinent issues and take action.

Modifying roles

For certain tasks, all parties involved must take responsibility. These include advocacy of critical issues, such as the importance of considering population as an integral part of development, the urgency of intensifying population interventions and the importance of improving the status of women. The advocacy function must also include efforts to increase resources available for population programmes. Moreover, to arrive at a more efficient international assistance programme, all parties must actively participate in the development of the framework or strategy for population assistance.

Certain tasks are, however, more suited to one body than to another. Some of these tasks are already being performed; others remain to be undertaken. Some can be performed within existing technical and administrative configurations; others may require additional capacities in the organizations concerned. Pressing tasks to be performed by the different parties are presented below.

Developing countries

The Governments of developing countries have the main responsibility for programme co-ordination at the national level and for mobilizing resources with the aim of establishing self-sustaining sources of funding. Support from the international community should supplement the Government's contribution rather than serve as the major source of the programme's funding. Governments also must strive to ensure that international forums dealing with development as well as those of the governing bodies of international organizations place increased emphasis on population whenever development issues are considered. Most important, developing countries should have the responsibility for strategic planning in population, which includes policy-making and planning.

Developed countries

Developed countries must continue to provide the bulk of international assistance funds in the population sector, channelled through bilateral as well as multilateral programmes. To facilitate population advances in the developing countries, financial support must increase substantially in the coming decade. The co-ordination efforts within the DAC group should continue, not in isolation, but in collaboration with other groups.

The United Nations' Resident Co-ordinator

The Resident Co-ordinator has an especially important role to play in promoting population as an integral component of the United Nations development assistance programmes in the country. At the same time, the Co-ordinator must ensure that programmes supported by the United Nations are complementary rather than compartmentalized, as is often the case. The Resident Co-ordinator must also assume a major role in assisting the Government in its efforts to co-ordinate development programmes.

United Nations Development Programme

UNDP has a unique role in developing countries as both a primary funder and an adviser on development programme issues. It must use this position to ensure that population issues are dealt with appropriately in the country programmes it supports and that, where feasible, priority is given to those development projects that are likely to have a positive impact on the population situation of the country. As far as possible, UNDP must also see to it that the development projects it supports do not have a negative impact on the country's population situation.

World Bank

Like other agencies and organizations that have close contacts with economic policy makers, the World Bank must ensure that the dialogue regarding all financial programmes--including structural adjustment as well as other negotiations regarding development--take appropriate account of

390

the population situation in the country. In this connection, the impact of other development sectors on population variables, as well as the impact of population on development sectors, must be considered. The World Bank should continue to increase its attention to population in its sectoral reviews and in its lending for the social sectors. Financial and technical resources devoted to population also must be increased.

United Nations Population Fund

In view of countries' frequent preference for multilateral assistance and of the major role UNFPA plays as a source of funding for population programmes, UNFPA should continue its role of adviser to Governments for in-country co-ordination of population assistance. It should also continue to help establish a programme strategy for such assistance. UNFPA also seems to be in a good position to oversee international co-ordination through the mechanism discussed above, serving as the focal point for co-ordination and overall analysis of policy and programme information and arranging the necessary meetings to discuss strategic programme issues.

Other United Nations agencies

United Nations agencies already active in the population sector undertake their population activities mainly with support from UNFPA. Even so, it is important that population be incorporated as an integral part of their regular activities. Such integration must manifest itself through heightened support for population policies and by further funding for population activities in these agencies' regular budgets. The agencies, being specialized, also have an important role in providing technical assistance to UNFPA country programmes. Better methodologies for providing such assistance have to be elaborated, both in terms of substance and administration. Other United Nations organizations, such as the United Nations Children's Fund (UNICEF), have mandates touching closely upon population issues, and some of them are beginning to acknowledge the importance of incorporating population concerns into their programmes. However, further efforts are needed, in particular to ensure complementary national assistance programmes.

Non-governmental organizations

The international NGOs, such as the International Planned Parenthood Federation (IPPF), have played a pioneering role in raising awareness of population issues, especially family planning, and in supporting innovative projects. In view of the continued sensitivities concerning population and the need to involve grass-roots organizations, these NGOs will have to continue to play a prominent role in both national and international awareness creation. These international NGOs will also be increasingly needed to assist local NGOs in the implementation of information or action programmes. Both NGOs and the private sector need to become more active in reaching particular groups and ensuring community participation.

The major implications--sectoral, national and international--raised in this chapter lead to recommendations for action for both the short term and the long term. Such recommendations will have to be tempered by the particularities of each country. The concept of strategic planning advocated in this chapter can be used by developing countries to incorporate, in a systematic way, substantive, administrative, managerial, institutional and financial elements of population programmes. It will also serve as a framework for the provision of co-ordinated assistance, technical and financial, by all parties involved in implementing a national population programme.

Annex

ANNEX - TABLE 1

DEMOGRAPHIC AND SOCIO-ECONOMIC INDICATORS IN 142 COUNTRIES

Country by Region	Population (000) 1989	Population growth rate (%) 1985-1990	Population "doubling time" (years)	Projected population 2,000	Total fertility rate 1985-1990	Crude birth rate 1985-1990	Crude death rate 1985-1990	Life expectancy (years) 1985-1990	Infant mortality rate 1985-1990	Maternal mortality rate 1980-1987	Lifetime chance of maternal death (1 in) 1980-1990	Contraceptive prevalence rate (%) 1971-1987	Urban population (%) 1985-1990	Female literacy rate (%) 1985	GNP per capital (US$) 1987
World	5,201,420	1.73	40	6,251,055	3.44	27	10	62	71	390	62	53	41	65	3,330
Developed countries	1,198,807	0.53	132	6,251,055	1.90	15	10	73	15	30	1,462	71	72	97	12,070
Developing Countries	4,002,198	2.10	33	4,988,573	3.92	31	10	60	79	450	48	48	31	51	670
Africa															
Angola	9,753	2.70	26	13,295	6.39	47	20	45	137	113	116	1	25	7	810*
Benin	4,594	3.15	22	6,561	7.00	51	19	47	110	1,680	8	9	35	16	300
Botswana	1,241	3.51	20	1,804	6.25	47	12	59	67	300	45	28	19	70	1,030
Burkina Faso	8,770	2.67	26	2,025	6.50	47	19	47	138	600	22	1	8	6	170
Burundi	5,297	2.88	24	7,283	6.31	46	17	49	112				6	26	240
Cameroon	10,957	2.60	27	14,787	5.79	42	16	51	94	140	103	9	42	45	960
Cape Verde	369	2.81	25	518	5.18	38	10	61	66	134	121	2	53	39	500
Central African Rep.	2,842	2.46	28	3,765	5.89	44	20	46	132	600	24		42	29	330
Chad	5,540	2.47	28	7,337	5.89	44	20	46	132	700	21		27	11	150
Comoros	503	3.11	22	710	6.19	46	15	52	73			1	25	40	380
Congo	1,941	2.73	26	2,635	5.99	44	17	49	73	1,000	14		39	55	880
Côte d'Ivoire	12,087	4.12	17	18,547	7.41	51	14	53	96			3	42	31	750
Equatorial Guinea	430	2.34	30	561	5.66	42	19	47	127				60		120*
Ethiopia	45,812	2.01	35	61,206	6.15	44	24	41	154	2,000	7	2	12	1	120
Gabon	1,131	3.45	20	1,620	4.99	39	16	52	103	120	139		41	53	2,750
Gambia	834	2.83	25	1,116	6.39	47	21	43	143				20	15	220
Ghana	14,556	3.14	22	20,418	6.39	44	13	54	90	1,070	13	10	32	43	390
Guinea	6,708	2.48	28	8,879	6.19	47	22	42	147				22	17	290*
Guinea-Bissau	967	2.08	34	1,244	5.38	41	20	45	132	400	39	1	27	17	170
Kenya	24,092	4.22	17	37,581	8.12	54	12	59	72	170	61	17	20	49	340
Lesotho	1,724	2.85	25	2,354	5.79	41	12	56	100	1,600	9	5	17	85	360
Liberia	2,474	3.18	22	3,543	6.50	45	13	55	87	173	75	6	40	23	440
Madagascar	11,605	3.18	22	16,562	6.60	46	14	54	120	300	43		22	62	200
Malawi	8,153	3.31	21	11,706	7.00	53	20	47	150	250	48	7	12	31	160
Mali	9,091	2.94	24	12,658	6.70	50	21	44	169			5	18	11	200
Mauritania	1,970	2.73	26	2,685	6.50	46	19	46	127	68	189	1	35	:	440

	(1)	(2)	(3)	(4)	(5)	(6)	(7)	(8)	(9)	(10)	(11)	(12)	(13)	(14)	(15)
Mauritius	1,089	56	1.25	1,240	1.94	19	5	69	23	99	434	75	42	77	1,470
Mozambique	15,254	26	2.65	20,445	6.39	45	9	47	141	300	44	:	19	22	150
Namibia	1,817	22	3.19	2,567	6.09	44	12	56	106	:	:	1	51	71	1,710*
Niger	6,898	23	3.01	9,750	7.11	51	21	45	135	420	28	5	16	9	280
Nigeria	109,202	20	3.43	159,149	7.00	50	16	51	105	1,500	8	10	31	31	370
Rwanda	6,990	21	3.40	10,144	8.29	51	17	49	122	210	48	:	6	33	310
Sao Tome & Principe	109	25	2.78	149	6.03	45	16	50	107	:	:	12	35	42	280
Senegal	7,174	26	2.69	9,668	6.39	46	19	46	128	530	25	:	36	19	510
Seychelles	68	70	1.00	75	6.74	48	17	50	116	:	:	4	37	60	280
Sierra Leone	4,049	28	2.49	5,399	6.50	48	23	41	154	450	29	:	28	21	3,180
Swaziland	763	20	3.43	1,116	6.50	47	13	56	118	:	:	:	26	66	300
Togo	3,349	23	3.09	4,727	6.09	45	14	53	94	84	163	1	22	29	700
Uganda	17,810	20	3.49	26,285	6.90	50	15	51	103	300	41	1	9	45	300
United Rep. of Tanzania	26,344	19	3.49	39,572	7.11	51	14	53	106	370	32	1	24	88	260
Zaire	34,867	22	3.67	49,349	6.09	46	14	53	98	800	18	:	37	46	220
Zambia	8,144	19	3.76	12,197	7.20	51	14	53	80	110	106	:	49	67	160
Zimbabwe	9,419	22	3.15	13,135	5.79	42	10	59	72	150	96	38	25	67	240
Asia and Pacific															
Afghanistan	16,127	27	2.63	26,608	6.90	49	23	42	172	640	19	2	19	8	220*
Bangladesh	112,547	26	2.67	150,589	5.54	42	16	51	119	600	26	25	12	22	160
Bhutan	1,484	33	2.67	1,906	5.54	38	17	48	128	:	:	74	5	:	150
China	1,119,876	51	1.39	1,285,894	2.37	21	7	69	32	44	801	:	21	56	300
Cooke Islands	20	97	0.72	22	5.08	34	17	71	26	:	:	:	32	:	:
Democratic Kampuchea	8,044	28	2.48	10,046	4.72	41	5	48	130	41	564	41	11	65	1,160*
DPR of Korea	22,402	30	2.36	28,165	3.61	29	11	69	24	47	556	34	64	:	80*
Fiji	737	44	1.60	834	4.31	27	7	70	27	500	39	48	41	81	760*
India	835,816	34	2.08	1,042,530	3.30	32	11	58	99	800	32	23	26	29	1,510
Indonesia	177,615	43	1.62	208,329	5.64	27	8	56	84	120	124	:	25	65	300
Islamic Rep. of Iran	54,666	20	3.45	74,460	4.53	42	6	65	63	:	:	:	52	39	450
Kiribati	67	57	1.22	77	4.82	32	3	70	30	18	961	:	34	:	3,610*
Kuwait	2,008	17	4.02	2,782	5.74	32	16	73	19	2	7,259	51	94	59	14,870
Lao PDR	3,970	28	2.49	5,134	3.50	41	6	49	110	59	404	:	16	76	160
Malaysia	16,944	30	2.31	20,870	4.72	29	12	70	24	:	:	:	38	66	1,800
Maldives	208	22	3.20	283	5.40	35	8	57	102	140	111	:	26	82	300
Mongolia	2,159	23	3.09	2,996	4.02	39	10	64	45	140	148	5	51	:	790*
Myanmar	40,814	34	2.09	51,129	5.95	31	5	60	70	850	17	14	24	56	180*
Nepal	18,675	28	2.47	24,084	5.08	40	5	51	128	:	:	:	8	12	160
Niue	3	7,000	0.01	3	4.53	34	13	71	26	:	:	5	22	:	1,030*
Pacific Islands	169	31	2.23	204	5.08	32	12	70	30	600	22	14	29	19	1,040*
Pakistan	118,509	20	3.45	162,467	6.50	47	6	57	109	1,000	15	5	30	35	350
Papua New Guinea	3,906	26	2.66	5,141	5.67	39	5	54	59	80	241	8	14	85	730
Philippines	60,878	28	2.48	77,447	4.33	33	10	64	45	34	1,226	4	40	81	590
Rep. of Korea	43,064	59	1.19	48,012	2.00	19	6	69	25	40	411	45	65	98	2,690*
Samoa	168	82	0.85	181	5.08	34	5	71	26	11	4,592	70	21	79	290*
Singapore	2,673	64	1.09	2,950	1.65	17	7	73	9	:	:	18	100	:	7,940
Solomon Islands	317	18	3.99	448	5.26	37	10	58	52	:	:	23	9	:	420

ANNEX - TABLE 1 (Continued)

DEMOGRAPHIC AND SOCIO-ECONOMIC INDICATORS IN 142 COUNTRIES

Country by Region	Population (000) 1989	Population growth rate (%) 1985-1990	Population "doubling time" (years)	Projected population 2,000	Total fertility rate 1985-1990	Crude birth rate 1985-1990	Crude death rate 1985-1990	Life expectancy (years) 1985-1990	Infant mortality rate 1985-1990	Maternal mortality rate 1980-1987	Lifetime chance of maternal death (1 in) 1980-1990	Contraceptive prevalence rate (%) 1971-1987	Urban population (%) 1985-1990	Female literacy rate (%) 1985	GNP per capital (US$) 1987
Asia and Pacific (Continued)															
Sri Lanka	16,983	1.32	53	19,385	2.67	23	6	70	33	90	348	62	21	83	400
Thailand	54,856	1.53	46	63,670	2.60	22	7	65	39	270	119	66	20	88	840
Tonga	118	1.92	36	140	5.08	34	5	71	26	..	..	..	20	99	720
Tuvalu	9	1.27	55	10	5.08	34	5	71	26	..	..	..	..	..	600*
Vanuatu	159	2.88	24	219	5.26	37	10	58	52	..	..	13	18	68	700*
Viet Nam	65,684	2.24	31	83,030	4.10	32	10	61	64	110	185	20	20	80	110*
Middle East and Mediterranean															
Algeria	24,585	3.12	22	33,247	6.05	40	9	63	74	130	106	7	43	37	2,760
Bahrain	497	3.65	19	682	4.14	28	4	71	26	19	1,060	..	82	64	10,620*
Cyprus	694	1.04	67	765	2.31	19	8	76	12	..	..	..	49	83	5,210
Democratic Yemen	2,416	3.07	23	3,430	6.66	47	16	51	120	100	126	..	40	25	420
Djibouti	395	2.96	24	552	6.60	47	18	48	122	..	..	..	78	9	770
Egypt	52,696	2.55	27	66,710	4.82	36	10	61	85	80	217	30	46	30	710
Iraq	18,272	3.48	20	26,339	6.36	43	8	64	69	..	..	14	71	87	2,850*
Jordan	4,105	3.94	18	6,329	7.18	46	7	66	44	..	..	26	64	63	1,540
Lebanon	2,903	2.12	33	3,603	3.38	29	8	67	40	143	173	53	80	69	810*
Libyan Arab Jamahiaya	4,381	3.65	19	6,500	6.87	44	9	61	82	80	152	..	64	50	5,500
Morocco	24,504	2.65	27	31,366	4.82	35	10	61	82	330	53	36	45	22	620
Oman	1,420	3.34	21	2,057	7.18	46	13	55	100	..	..	..	12	12	5,780
Qatar	353	4.15	17	499	5.64	31	4	70	31	19	778	..	88	51	12,360
Saudi Arabia	13,583	3.96	18	20,686	7.18	42	8	63	71	1,100	12	..	73	12	12,410*
Somalia	7,308	3.32	21	9,803	6.50	51	20	45	132	655	20	5	33	7	290
Sudan	24,480	2.88	24	33,610	6.44	45	16	50	108	280	44	20	21	14	330
Syrian Arab Republic	12,063	3.57	20	17,611	6.76	44	7	65	48	..	377	41	49	43	1,820
Tunisia	7,978	2.36	30	9,821	4.10	30	7	65	59	54	112	51	53	41	1,210
Turkey	54,521	1.99	35	66,622	3.55	28	8	64	76	210	..	..	46	62	1,200
United Arab Emirates	1,537	3.26	21	1,950	4.82	23	4	71	26	..	..	..	78	38	15,680
Yemen	7,777	3.04	23	11,145	6.97	48	16	51	116	..	..	1	20	3	580

Latin America and Caribbean

Anguilla	7	1.42	49	8	2.92	25	8	66	57						630*
Antigua and Barbuda	7	1.39	50	99	2.92	25	8	66	57			39	31		2,570
Argentina	31,913	1.27	55	36,238	2.96	21	9	71	32	85	332	74	85	95	2,370
Barbados	259	0.62	112	285	2.00	19	8	74	11	24	1,737	47	42	99	5,330
Bolivia	7,114	2.76	25	9,724	6.06	43	14	53	110	480	29	26	48	65	570
Brazil	147,285	2.07	34	179,487	3.46	29	8	65	63	150	161	66	73	76	2,020*
British Virgin Islands	13	1.36	51	16	2.92	25	8	66	57						2,600*
Chile	12,956	1.66	42	15,272	2.73	24	6	72	20	55	556	65	84	91	1,310
Colombia	31,172	2.05	34	37,998	3.58	29	7	65	46	130	179	70	67	87	1,220
Costa Rica	2,936	2.64	27	3,711	3.26	28	4	75	18	26	984	60	50	93	1,590
Cuba	10,247	0.75	94	11,189	1.71	16	7	74	15	31	1,575	49	72	96	1,910*
Dominica	80	1.32	53	93	2.92	25	8	66	57			50			1,440
Dominican Republic	7,012	2.22	32	8,621	3.75	31	7	65	65	56	397	44	56	94	730
Ecuador	10,485	2.79	25	13,939	4.65	35	8	62	63	220	82	47	52	77	1,040
El Salvador	5,151	1.39	36	6,739	4.86	36	9	66	59	74	232	31	43	80	850
Grenada	101	1.33	53	117	2.92	25	8	62	57			23			1,340
Guatemala	8,935	2.86	24	12,221	5.77	41	9	70	59	110	132	31	40	98	940
Guyana	1,022	1.74	40	1,197	2.75	25	5	55	30	100	304	7	32	47	380
Haiti	6,383	1.88	37	7,837	4.74	34	13	64	117	340	52	35	27	95	360
Honduras	4,977	3.18	22	6,846	5.55	40	8	74	69	82	184	52	40	35	780
Jamaica	2,483	1.52	46	2,886	2.86	26	6	69	18	100	292	53	49	58	1,820
Mexico	86,670	2.20	32	107,233	3.58	29	8	66	47	92	254	27	70	96	1,820
Montserrat	13	1.47	48	15	2.92	25	8	63	57			58			2,360*
Nicaragua	3,743	3.36	21	5,261	5.50	42	8	72	62	65	234	45	57	88	830
Panama	2,368	2.07	34	2,893	3.14	27	5	67	23	90	295	46	52	57	2,240
Paraguay	4,153	2.93	24	5,538	4.58	35	7	61	42	470	39	41	44	88	1,000
Peru	21,779	2.51	28	27,952	4.49	34	9	66	88	310	60	43	67	85	1,430
Saint Kitts and Nevis	49	1.41	50	57	2.92	25	8	66	57			42	45	78	1,700
Saint Lucia	135	1.32	53	156	2.92	25	8	66	57				40	98	1,370
Saint Vincent	109	1.33	53	127	2.92	25	8	70	57			53	18	98	1,070
Suriname	398	1.46	48	469	2.97	26	6	70	31	82	342		46	95	2,360
Trinidad and Tobago	1,263	1.59	44	1,480	2.68	24	6	66	30	81	384		64	90	4,220
Turks and Caicos	8	1.46	48	10	2.92	25	8		57				48	93	680*
Uruguay	3,105	0.76	93	3,364	2.61	19	10	71	27	56	570	49	85	94	2,180
Venezuela	19,226	2.61	27	24,716	3.77	31	5	70	36	65	340		88	85	3,230

Europe

Albania	3,187	1.83	38	3,795	3.00	24	6	72	39	22	1,994	76	34		910*
Bulgaria	9,000	0.11	631	9,071	1.90	13	12	72	16	12	4,085		66		2,350*
Greece	10,025	0.23	310	10,193	1.70	12	10	76	17	28	1,701	73	60	88	4,350
Hungary	10,571	-0.18	—	10,531	1.75	12	13	70	20	33	1,329		57	98	2,240
Malta	351	0.49	143	366	1.90	15	10	73	20	12	3,157	75	85	82	4,010
Poland	38,175	0.65	109	40,366	2.20	16	10	71	18	15	3,175	66	61	98	1,920
Portugal	10,259	0.25	279	10,587	1.75	14	10	73	15	180	216	58	31	80	2,890
Romania	23,162	0.48	147	24,346	2.15	16	11	70	22	27	1,583	55	49		2,350*
Yugoslavia	23,701	0.62	113	25,026	1.95	15	9	72	25				46	86	2,480

ANNEX -TABLE 1 (Continued)

DEMOGRAPHIC AND SOCIO-ECONOMIC INDICATORS IN 142 COUNTRIES

Source: Population, growth rates, total fertility rates, crude birth rates, crude death rates, life expectancy and urban population are from *World Population Prospects: 1988* (United Nations publication, Sales No. E.88.XIII.7), medium variant. Infant mortality rates are from *World Population Prospects: 1988* and also United Nations Children's Fund, *State of the World's Children 1989* (New York, 1989). Maternal mortality rates are from the World Health Organizations, Maternal Mortality Rates: *A Tabulation of Available Information*, 2nd ed. (Geneva, 1985); United Nations Children's Fund, *The State of the World's Children 1989*; and John A. Ross and others, *Family Planning and Child Survival: 100 Developing Countries* (New York, Columbia University, Center for Population and Family Health, 1988). Contraceptive prevalence rates are from *Levels and Trends of Contraceptive Use as Assessed in 1988* (United Nations publication, Sales No. E.89.XIII.4). Per capita gross national product (GNP) figures are from the United Nations Development Programme, "Statistics on 185 Countries and territories", unpublished.

Notes: An asterisk (*) indicates 1983 gross national product (GNP per capita.

Data for maternal mortality and contraceptive prevalence are the most recent available within the period indicated; the female literacy rate is for 1985 or the year closest to 1985.

ANNEX - TABLE 2

GOVERNMENT PERCEPTIONS OF DEMOGRAPHIC CHARACTERISTICS, 1987

KEY

Population Growth:	Mortality:	Fertility:	Migration:
1 Rate is too low	1 Acceptable	1 Too low	1 Appropriate
2 Rate is satisfactory	2 Not Acceptable	2 Satisfactory	2 Partially appropriate
3 Rate is too high		3 Too high	3 Inappropriate

Region/Country	Population Growth	Mortality	Fertility Level	Spatial distribution and internal Migration
Economic Commission for Africa				
Algeria	3	2	3	3
Angola	2	2	2	3
Benin	2	2	2	3
Botswana	3	2	3	3
Burkina Faso	2	2	2	3
Burundi	3	2	3	2
Cameroon	3	2	3	2
Cape Verde	2	2	2	3
Chad	2	2	2	2
Comoros	3	2	3	2
Congo	1	2	1	3
Central African Rep.	3	2	3	2
Côte d'Ivoire	2	1	2	2
Djibouti	2	2	2	2
Egypt	3	2	3	3
Equatorial Guinea	1	2	1	3
Ethiopia	3	2	3	2
Gabon	1	2	1	3
Gambia	3	2	3	3
Ghana	3	2	3	3
Guinea-Bissau	2	2	2	2
Guinea	2	2	3	2
Kenya	3	2	3	3
Lesotho	3	2	3	2
Liberia	3	2	3	2
Libyan Arab Jamahiaiya	2	1	2	3
Madagascar	3	2	3	2
Malawi	3	2	3	2
Mali	2	2	2	3
Mauritius	3	2	3	3
Mauritania	2	2	2	3
Morocco	3	2	3	3
Mozambique	2	2	2	3
Niger	3	2	3	3
Nigeria	3	2	3	3

ANNEX - TABLE 2 (Continued)

Region/Country	Population Growth	Mortality	Fertility Level	Spatial distribution and internal Migration
Economic Commission for Africa (Continued)				
Rwanda	3	1	3	3
Senegal	3	2	3	2
Seychelles	3	1	3	3
Sierra Leone	3	2	3	3
Somalia	2	2	2	3
Sudan	2	2	2	3
Swaziland	3	2	3	3
South Africa	3	2	3	2
Sao Tome & Principe	2	2	2	3
Togo	2	2	2	3
Tunisia	3	2	3	3
Uganda	3	2	3	2
United Rep. of Tanzania	3	2	3	3
Zaire	2	2	2	3
Zambia	3	2	3	3
Zimbabwe	3	2	3	2
Economic and Social Commission for Asia and the Pacific				
Afghanistan	3	2	3	2
Australia	2	1	2	3
Bangladesh	3	2	3	2
Bhutan	1	2	2	2
Brunei Darussalem	2	1	2	2
China	3	2	3	2
Democratic Kampuchea	1	2	1	3
DPR of Korea	1	2	2	2
Fiji	3	1	3	3
India	3	2	3	2
Indonesia	3	2	3	3
Islamic Rep. of Iran	2	2	2	2
Japan	2	1	2	2
Kiribati	3	2	3	3
Lao PDR	1	1	2	3
Malaysia	2	2	2	2
Maldives	2	2	2	3
Mongolia	1	2	1	2
Myanmar	2	2	2	2
Nauru	1	1	2	1
Nepal	3	2	3	3
New Zealand	2	1	2	2
Pakistan	3	2	3	3
Papua New Guinea	3	2	3	2
Philippines	3	1	3	3
Rep. of Korea	3	2	3	3
Samoa	3	2	3	3
Singapore	1	1	1	1
Solomon Islands	3	2	3	2

ANNEX - TABLE 2 *(Continued)*

Region/Country	Population Growth	Mortality	Fertility Level	Spatial distribution and internal Migration
Economic and Social Commission for Asia and the Pacific (Continued)				
Sri Lanka	3	2	3	3
Thailand	2	1	3	2
Tonga	3	2	3	2
Tuvalu	3	2	3	2
Vanuatu	2	2	2	2
Viet Nam	3	2	3	3
Economic and Social Commission for Western Asia				
Bahrain	2	1	2	1
Democratic	2	2	3	2
Iraq	1	1	1	2
Jordan	2	2	2	2
Kuwait	1	1	1	2
Lebanon	2	2	2	2
Oman	1	2	2	2
Qatar	1	1	2	1
Saudi Arabia	1	2	2	2
Syrian Arab Republic	2	1	2	2
United Arab Emirates	2	1	2	2
Yemen	2	1	3	2
Economic Commission for Latin America and Caribbean				
Antigua and Barbuda	3	2	3	2
Argentina	2	1	2	3
Bahamas	2	1	2	3
Barbados	3	1	3	1
Belize	2	1	2	2
Bolivia	1	2	1	3
Brazil	2	2	2	2
Chile	1	1	1	3
Colombia	2	2	2	3
Costa Rica	2	1	2	3
Cuba	2	1	2	2
Dominica	3	2	3	2
Dominican Republic	3	2	3	3
Ecuador	2	2	2	3
El Salvador	3	2	3	3
Grenada	3	2	3	3
Guatemala	3	2	2	3
Guyana	2	1	2	3
Haiti	3	2	3	3
Honduras	3	2	3	3
Jamaica	3	2	3	3
Mexico	3	1	3	3
Nicaragua	2	2	2	3

ANNEX - TABLE 2 (Continued)

Region/Country	Population Growth	Mortality	Fertility Level	Spatial distribution and internal Migration
Economic Commission for Latin America and Caribbean (Continued)				
Panama	2	1	2	3
Paraguay	2	1	2	3
Peru	3	2	3	3
Saint Kitts and Nevis	3	2	3	2
Saint Lucia	3	2	3	2
Saint Vincent	3	2	3	2
Suriname	2	2	2	3
Trinidad and Tobago	3	1	3	3
Uruguay	1	1	1	3
Venezuela	2	2	2	3
Economic Commission for Europe				
Albania	2	2	2	2
Austria	2	1	2	2
Belgium	2	1	2	1
Bulgaria	1	1	1	2
Byelorussian Soviet Soc. Rep	2	2	2	3
Canada	2	1	2	2
Cyprus	1	1	1	3
Czechoslovakia	2	1	2	2
Denmark	2	1	2	1
Finland	2	1	2	1
France	1	1	1	2
Greece	1	2	1	3
German Democratic Rep.	1	1	1	1
Germany, Federal Rep. of	1	1	1	3
Holy See	2	1	2	1
Hungary	1	1	1	1
Iceland	2	1	2	2
Ireland	2	1	2	2
Israel	1	1	1	2
Italy	2	2	2	2
Liechtenstein	1	1	1	1
Luxembourg	2	1	1	2
Malta	2	1	2	1
Monaco	1	1	1	1
Netherlands	2	1	2	1
Norway	2	1	2	1
Poland	2	2	2	2
Portugal	2	2	2	3
Romania	2	1	1	1
San Marino	2	1	2	1
Spain	2	1	2	2
Sweden	2	1	1	2
Switzerland	2	1	2	2
Turkey	3	2	3	2
United Kingdom	2	2	2	2

ANNEX - TABLE 2 *(Continued)*

Region/Country	Population Growth	Mortality	Fertility Level	Spatial distribution and internal Migration
Economic Commission for Europe (Continued)				
Ukrainian S.S.R.	2	1	2	2
United States of America	2	1	2	1
U.S.S.R.	2	1	2	3
Yugoslavia	2	2	2	3

Source: United Nations Department of International Economic and Social Affairs, Global Population Policy Data Base (New York, United Nations, 1987).

NOTES

Chapter 1
Introduction

1   All demographic information in this chapter is from *World Population Prospects: 1988* (United Nations publication, Sales No. E.88.XIII.7).

2   *World Population Trends and Policies: 1987 Monitoring Report* (United Nations publication, Sales No. E.88.XIII.3); "World Population Trends and Policies: 1989 Monitoring Report", ESA/P/WP.107 (New York, United Nations, 1989), mimeographed.

Chapter 2
Elements of Population Policy-Making

1   Review and Appraisal of the World Population Plan of Action (United Nations publication, Sales No. E.79.XIII.7).

2   UNFPA/UN Interregional Consultative Group of Experts on the World Population Plan of Action, "Final Report" (UNFPA/WPPA/20/Rev. 1), p. 17, in United Nations Fund for Population Activities, *Priorities in Future Allocation of UNFPA Resources*, DP/186 (New York, 1976), p. 12.

3   Much of this analysis has led to seminal publications including G. M. Farooq and G. B. Simmons, eds., *Fertility in Developing Countries* (London, Macmillan, 1985); *Proceedings of the Expert Group on Fertility and Family* (United Nations publication, Sales No. E.84.XIII.7); *Nuptiality: Selected Findings From the World Fertility Survey Data*, ESA/WP. 92 (New York, United Nations, 1986) (hereinafter referred to as *Nuptiality*); and John Cleland and Chris Scott, eds. *The World Fertility Survey: An Assessment* (Oxford, Clarendon Press, 1987).

4   "United Nations Fifth Population Inquiry", ESA/P/WP.102 (New York, United Nations, 1987), mimeographed.

5   *Nuptiality*.

6   W. P. Mauldin, "Measuring the impact of population policies and programmes on fertility", *Proceedings of the Expert Group on Fertility and Family* (United Nations publication, Sales No. E.84.XIII.7), pp. 365-340; A. Mason and others, *Population Growth and Economic Development: Lessons from Selected Asian Countries*, Policy Development Studies, No. 10 (New York, United Nations Fund for Population Activities, 1985).

7   National Academy of Sciences, *Population Growth and Economic Development: Policy Questions* (Washington, D.C., National Academy Press, 1986).

8   R. Repetto, "Population, resources, environment: an uncertain future", *Population Bulletin*, vol. 42, No. 2 (July 1987), p. 3; World Commission on Environment and Development, *Our Common Future* (Oxford, Oxford University Press, 1987); N. Sadik, "Safeguarding the future", *The State of World Population* (New York, United Nations Population Fund, 1988).

9   Mason and others, *Population Growth and Economic Development*.

10   M. Gendell, "Stalls in the Fertility Decline in Costa Rica, Korea and Sri Lanka", Working Paper No. 693 (Washington, D.C., The World Bank, 1985).

11   J. Cleland and C. Wilson, "Demand theories of the fertility transition: an iconoclastic view", *Population Studies*, vol. 41 (1987), p. 5.

12   Ronald Freedman, "The contribution of social science research to population policy and family planning program effectiveness", *Studies in Family Planning*, vol. 18, No. 2 (March/April 1987), pp. 57-83.

13   J. C. Caldwell, *Theory of Fertility Decline* (New York, Academic Press, 1982); P. T. Bauer, "Population scares", *Commentary*, vol. 84 (1987), p. 39.

14   S. H. Cochrane, *Fertility and Education: What Do We Really Know?* (Baltimore, Maryland, The Johns Hopkins University Press for The World Bank, 1979); R. E. Bilsborrow, "Priority areas for future research on demographic-economic interrelations", *Population and Development Modelling* (United Nations publication, Sales No. E.81.X111.2), p. 74-87; R. P. Shaw, "Appropriate population policy", chap. 4 in *Mobilizing Human Resources in the Arab World* (London and Boston, Routledge and Kegan Paul Ltd., 1985); J. Cleland and G. Rodriguez, "The effect of parental education on marital fertility in developing countries", *Fertility Determinants: Research Notes*, No. 19 (New York, The Population Council, 1987); J. G. Cleveland, "Socio-economic determinants of fertility: assessment of findings and implications", *Population Research Leads* (Bangkok, United Nations Economic and Social Commission for Asia and the Pacific, 1987); *Nuptiality*.

15   Cleland and Rodriguez, "The effect of parental education on marital fertility in developing countries".

16   Shaw, "Appropriate population policy".

17   J. Da Vanzo and others, "What Accounts for the Increase in Contraceptive Use in Peninsular Malaysia, 1956-75?--Development vs. Family Planning Program Effort", Paper presented at the Annual Meeting of the Population Association of America, New Orleans, April 1988.

18   J. Caldwell and P. Caldwell, *Limiting Population Growth and The Ford Foundation Contribution* (London and Dover, New Hampshire, Francis Pinter, 1986).

19   World Population Trends, Population and Development Interrelations and Population Policies, 1983 Monitoring Report, Vol. II (United Nations publication, Sales No. E.85.XIII.2); *World*

Population Trends and Policies: 1987 Monitoring Report (United Nations publication, Sales No. E.88.XIII.3).

20 C. Miro and J. E. Potter, *Population Policy: Research Priorities in the Developing World* (London, Francis Pinter, 1980).

21 Levels and Trends of Mortality since 1950 (United Nations publication, Sales No. E.81.XIII.3); *Model Life Tables for Developing Countries* (United Nations publication, Sales No. E.81.XIII.7); *Proceedings of the Meeting on Socio-Economic Determinants and Consequences of Mortality*, El Colegio de Mexico, Mexico City, 19-25 June 1979 (New York, United Nations; Geneva, World Health Organization); *Mortality and Health Policy: Proceedings of the Expert Group on Mortality and Health Policy*, Rome, 30 May-3 June 1983 (United Nations publication, Sales No. E.84.XIII.4); *Consequences of Mortality Trends and Differentials*, ST/ESA/Ser.A/95 (New York, United Nations, 1986).

22 J. Da Vanzo, "A household survey of child mortality determinants in Malaysia", in *Child Survival: Strategies for Research*, W. H. Mosley and L. C. Chen, eds., *A Supplement to Population and Development Review*, vol. 10, No. 2 (1984), p. 307-324; Shaw, *Mobilizing . . .*, chap. 4.

23 J. Hobcraft, "The proximate determinants of fertility", in *The World Fertility Survey: An Assessment*, Cleland and Scott, eds., pp. 796-837.

24 Da Vanzo, "A household survey of child mortality determinants in Malaysia".

25 *Ibid.*

26 Mosley and Chen, eds., *Child Survival . . .*, pp. 1-401.

27 *World Population Trends and Policies: 1987 Monitoring Report*; H. Ware, "Effects of maternal education, women's roles, and child care on child mortality", *Population and Development Review*, vol. 10, No. 2 (1984), pp. 191-214.

28 M. Nag, "Impact of social and economic development on mortality: comparative study of Kerala and West Bengal", *Economic and Political Weekly* (Bombay) 18, Nos. 19-21, Annual Issue (May 1983), pp. 877-900; J. Caldwell and L. T. Ruzicka, "The determinants of change in South Asia", in *Dynamics of Population and Family Welfare*, K. Srinivasan and S. Mukerji, eds. (Bombay, Himalaya Publishing House, 1985), pp. 281-332.

29 Mosley and Chen, eds., *Child Survival . . . .*

30   United Nations Fund for Population Activities, *Priorities in Future Allocation of UNFPA Resources*; United Nations Fund for Population Activities, "Report of the Executive Director on the Future Role of UNFPA: UNFPA in the 1980's", DP/530, 23 April 1981 (New York, 1981); The World Bank, *World Development Report 1984* (New York, Oxford University Press, 1984); United Nations Fund for Population Activities, "Research Requirements for Integrating Population Factors into Development Planning", paper prepared for Expert Group Meeting on Population and Development (New York, 1985); G. J. Stolnitz, "The Population Commission and demographic research: an overview", *Population Bulletin of the United Nations*, Nos. 19/20 (United Nations publication, Sales No. E.87.XIII.2), p. 27.

31   N. R. Shrestha, "Institutional policies and migration behavior: a selective review", *World Development*, vol. 15 (1987), p. 329.

32   R. P. Shaw, "Global and National Obstacles to Social Progress in Rural Development: Population Aspects" (New York, United Nations Population Fund, 1988), mimeographed.

33   C. P. Timmer, W. P. Falcon and S. R. Person, *Food Policy Analysis* (Baltimore, Maryland, The Johns Hopkins University Press for The World Bank, 1983).

34   Farooq and Simmons, *Fertility . . . .*

35   Food and Agriculture Organization of the United Nations, *Labour Migration and Agricultural Development in Southern Africa* (Rome, 1982); R. P. Shaw, "Population Problems and Rural Development in Africa: Essential Linkages", ARRD/AF/85/7 (Rome, Food and Agriculture Organization of the United Nations, 1985).

36   R. P. Shaw, "Women's employment in the Arab world: a strategy of selective intervention", *Development and Change*, vol. 12 (1981), pp. 237-272.

37   A. S. Oberai, *State Policies and Internal Migration* (London, Croom Helm, 1983); Shaw, "Population Problems and Rural Development in Africa . . ."; R. E. B. Lucas and O. Stark, "Motivations to remit: evidence from Botswana", *Journal of Political Economy*, vol. 93 (1985), p. 901.

38   Shaw, "Appropriate population policy".

39   R. E. Bilsborrow, A. S. Oberai and G. Standing, *Migration Surveys in Low-Income Countries* (London, Croom Helm, 1984); Lucas and Stark, "Motivations to remit"; Shaw, *Mobilizing . . .*, chap. 2.

40   R. P. Shaw, "On modifying metropolitan migration", *Economic Development and Cultural Change*, vol. 26 (1978), p. 677; United Nations, *Population and Distribution, Migration and Development*, ST/ESA/SER.A/89 (New York, 1984); Oberai, *State Policies . . .* and *Land Settlement Policies and Population Redistribution in Developing Countries: Achievements, Problems and Prospects* (New York, Praeger, 1988).

41   S. H. Preston, "Urban growth in developing countries: a demographic reappraisal", *Population and Development Review*, vol. 5, No. 2 (1979), p. 195.

42   Mason and others, *Population Growth and Economic Development* . . . .

43   R. P. Shaw, "Fiscal versus market variables in migration", *Journal of Political Economy*, vol. 94 (1986), p. 648.

44   *Oberai, State Policies . . .; Population Distribution, Migration and Development* (United Nations publication, Sales No. E.83.XIII.3) (hereinafter referred to as *Population Distribution*).

45   G. Standing, *Labour Circulation and the Labour Process* (London, Croom Helm, 1985); M. Prothero and M. Chapman, *Circulation in Third World Countries* (London, Meuthen, 1985).

46   R. P. Shaw, *Migration Theory and Fact* (Philadelphia, Pennsylvania, Regional Science Research Institute, 1975); M. P. Todaro, *Internal Migration in Developing Countries: A Review of Theory, Evidence, Methodology and Research Priorities* (Geneva, International Labour Office, 1976); *Population Distribution*.

47   S. Goldstein and A. Goldstein, *Surveys of Migration in Developing Countries: A Methodological Review*, Paper No. 71 (Honolulu, East-West Publications Institute, 1981); G. F. DeJong and R. W. Gardner, *Migration Decision Making* (New York, Pergamon Press, 1981); S. Findley, *Migration Survey Methodologies: A Review of Design Issues*, Paper No. 20 (Liege, International Union for the Scientific Study of Population, 1982); Bilsborrow, Oberai and Standing, *Migration Surveys in Low-Income Countries*; A. S. Oberai, "Migration, Urbanization and Development", Paper No. 5 in Development Training Paper Series (Geneva, International Labour Office, 1987).

48   Freedman, "The contribution of social science research . . .".

49   Population, Human Resources and Development Planning: The ILO Contribution (Geneva, International Labour Office, 1984), p. 19.

50   *Ibid.*

51   World Population Trends and Policies: 1987 Monitoring Report.

52   Report of the International Conference on Population, 1984, Mexico City, 6-14 August 1984 (United Nations publication, Sales No. E.84.XIII.8).

53   United Nations, *Projection Methods for Integrating Population Variables into Development Planning, Vol. I, Methods for Comprehensive Planning*, ST/ESA/SER.R/90 (New York, 1989).

54   United Nations Fund for Population Activities, "Report on Seminar on Population and Development Planning", New York, 26-27 September 1983, mimeographed, p. 1.

55   *Ibid.*

56   United Nations Population Fund, "Comparative Evaluation of UNFPA Support to Population and Development Planning", Presentation to the Programme Committee (May 1989); United Nations Fund for Population Activities, *Report of the UNFPA Expert Group Meeting on Population and Development Planning*, New York, 22-24 January 1985 (New York, 1985).

57   Report of the Informal Inter-Agency Expert Group Meeting on Methodologies for Integrated Population and Development Planning, Geneva, 21-24 May 1984 (Geneva, International Labour Office, 1984), p. 29.

58   *Ibid.*

59   B. M. Stamper, *Population and Planning in Developing Nations* (New York, The Population Council, 1977); R. E. Bilsborrow, "The integration of population in development planning: some methodological issues and suggestions", *International Population Conference*, Florence, 1985, vol. 3 (Liege, International Union for the Scientific Study of Population, 1985).

60   H. A. Sayed, J. M Stycos and R. Avery, "The Population and Development Program in Egypt: A Problem in Program Impact Measurement", Working Paper No. 8 (Cairo, Cairo Demographic Centre, 1984).

61   Stamper, *Population and Planning . . . .*

62   T. King, "Measuring the Demographic Consequences of Development Programs and Projects", paper written for a workshop sponsored by the Population and Human Resources Division, World Bank, 24-25 April 1979 (Washington, D.C.); R. Barlow, *Case Studies in the Demographic Impact of Asian Development Projects* (Ann Arbor, Michigan, University of Michigan, Center for Research on Economic Development, 1982);

K. Helmut, "Farm labor migrations in the Awash Valley of Ethiopia", *International Migration Review*, vol. 16, No. 11 (1982), p. 133.

63   R. E. Bilsborrow and P. F. Delargy, *Impact of Rural Development Projects on Demographic Behaviour* (New York, United Nations Fund for Population Activities, 1985).

64   E. Carrew, "Asia does poorly in integrating population with development plans", *Depthnews, Asia* (Manila, Philippines, 1987).

65   Bilsborrow, "The integration of population in development planning. .".

66   U.S. Bureau of the Census, *Popstan: A Case Study for the 1980 Census of Population and Housing, Part A, Program Considerations*, ISP-TR-4A (Washington, D.C., 1979).

67   Forrest E. Linder and Iwao M. Moriyama, *Improving Civil Registration* (Bethesda, Maryland, USA, International Institute for Vital Registration and Statistics, n.d.).

68   Manuel Ortega and Martin Vaessan, "Dissemination and utilization of findings and methodology within countries", in *The World Fertility Survey: An Assessment*, Cleland and Scott, eds., pp. 950-968.

69   Demographic Yearbook, Special Issue: Historical Supplement (United Nations publication, Sales No. E/F.79.XIII.8), pp. 7-11.

70   Principles and Recommendations for a Vital Statistics Systems (United Nations publication, Sales No. E.73.XVII.9); Linder and Moriyama, *Improving Civil Registration*; P. Padmanabha and others, *Urgently Needed Reforms in Civil Registration in Asian Countries: A Report for the Consideration of the Governments in the Region* (Bethesda, Maryland, USA, International Institute for Vital Registration and Statistics, Oct. 1986); United Nations, *Status of Civil Registration and Vital Statistics in Asia and the Pacific* (Bangkok, Economic and Social Commission for Asia and the Pacific, 1987).

71   Raul Urzua, "The uses of demographic knowledge for policies and planning in developing countries: issues and problems", in Raimondo Cagiano de Azevedo, *Population, Aid and Development* (Liege, International Union for the Scientific Study of Population, 1985), pp. 181-219; Donald Heisel, "Institutional arrangements and the use of demographic knowledge in the formulation of population policies", in International Union for the Scientific Study of Population, *International Population Conference, Florence, 1985* (Liege, 1985), vol. 3, pp. 331-343; C. Alison McIntosh and J. Finkle, "Demographic rationalism and political systems", in

International Union for the Scientific Study of Population, *International Population Conference, Florence, 1985,* vol. 3 (Liege, 1985); C. Miro and J. Potter, *Population Policy: Research Priorities in the Developing World,* Report of the International Review Group of Social Science Research on Population and Development (London, Francis Pinter, 1980); and United Nations Fund for Population Activities, *Comparative Results of UNFPA Evaluations* (New York, May 1986).

72   McIntosh and Finkle, "Demographic rationalism . . .".

73   Heisel, "Institutional arrangements . . .".

Chapter 3
Maternal and child health and family planning programmes

1   Preventing the Tragedy of Maternal Deaths, A Report on the International Safe Motherhood Conference, Nairobi, Kenya, February 1987, World Bank, World Health Organization and the United Nations Fund for Population Activities (New York, Family Care International, 1987), p. 6.

2   *Ibid.*, p. 10.

3   *Ibid.*, p. 15.

4   *Ibid.*, p. 16.

5   Christopher Tietze and Stanley K. Henshaw, *Induced Abortion: A World Review 1986*, 6th ed. (New York, The Alan Guttmacher Institute, 1986), p. 3.

6   Preventing the Tragedy of Maternal *Deaths*, p. 6.

7   International Encyclopedia of Population, vol. 1 (New York, The Free Press, 1982), p. 341.

8   Report of the International Conference on Population, 1984, Mexico City, 6-14 August 1984 (United Nations publication, Sales No. E.84.XIII.8), Recommendation 1, para. 14, p. 14.

9   J. Bongaarts, "Implications of future fertility trends for contraceptive practice", *Population and Development Review*, vol. 10, No. 2 (June 1984), p. 344.

10   John A. Ross and others, *Family Planning and Child Survival: 100 Developing Countries* (New York, Columbia University, Center for Population and Family Health, 1988).

11   Levels and Trends of Contraceptive Use as *Assessed in 1988* (United Nations publication, Sales No. E.89.XIII.4).

12   *Ibid.*

13   The figures are suggested by J. J. Speidel in an unpublished paper, "Resource Needs for Population and Family Planning Activities in Less Developed Countries", available from the author at the Population Crisis Committee, Washington, D.C. Somewhat lower estimates of current expenditures appear in Dorothy L. Nortman, "Family planning program resources: focus on funds",

413

Chap. 5 in *Organizing for Effective Family Planning Programs*, Robert J. Lapham and George B. Simmons, eds. (Washington, D.C., National Academy Press, 1987).

14 See, for example, *Population Briefing Paper*, No. 19 (Washington, D.C., Population Crisis Committee, October 1987). Additionally, see The World Bank, *World Development Report 1984* (New York, Oxford University Press, 1984), pp. 148-154.

15 The World Bank, *World Development Report 1984*, pp. 148-154.

16 World Population Trends and Policies: 1987 Monitoring Report (United Nations publication, Sales No. E.88.XIII.3).

17 Population and Family Planning Programs: A Compendium of Data through 1983 (New York, The Population Council, 1985).

18 Nortman, "Family planning program resources . . . ".

19 *Ibid.*

20 References to legal situations at country level are drawn from S. L. Isaacs and R. J. Cook, "Laws and Policies Affecting Fertility: A Decade of Change", *Population Reports* (The Johns Hopkins University), Series E, No. 7 (November 1984).

21 George B. Simmons, "Cost effectiveness and efficiency: the methodological issues", chap. 25 in *Organizing for Effective Family Planning Programs*.

22 Gunnar Myrdal, *Asian Drama: An Inquiry into the Poverty of Nations* (New York, Pantheon, 1968).

23 John Ross and others, "Community-based distribution", chap. 14 in *Organizing for Effective Family Planning Programs*.

24 M. Potts, J. J. Speidel and E. Kessel, "Relative risks of various means of fertility control when used in less-developed countries", *Risks, Benefits and Controversies in Fertility Control*, J. J. Sciarra; G. I. Zatuchni and J. J. Speidel, eds. (Hagerstown, Maryland, USA, Harper & Row, 1978), p. 28.

25 Lessons learned about operations of social marketing programmes have been extensively reviewed in *Population Reports*, Series J, No. 30 (July-August 1985), and in Amy Sheon, William Schellstede and Bonnie Derr, "Contraceptive social marketing", Chap. 15 in *Organizing for Effective Family Planning Programs*.

26 John Ickis, "Structural issues related to delivery systems", Chap. 6 in *Organizing for Effective Family Planning Programs*.

27   World Health Organization, *Alma-Ata, 1978, Primary Health Care: Report of the International Conference on Primary Health Care*, Alma-Ata, USSR, 6-12 September 1978 (Geneva, 1978), p. 20.

28   Ickis, "Structural issues . . .", pp. 150-151.

29   M. F. Fathalla, "Contraceptive Technology and Safety", Technical Background Paper, International Conference on Better Health for Women and Children through Family Planning, Nairobi, Kenya, 5-9 October 1987 (Geneva, World Health Organization, 1987).

30   D. B. Petitte, "A review of epidemiologic studies of vasectomy", *Biomedical Bulletin of Association for Voluntary Surgical Contraception*, vol. 5, No. 2 (July 1986).

31   "Depo-medroxyprogesterone acetate (DMPA) and cancer: Memorandum from a WHO meeting", *Bulletin of the World Health Organization* 64(3), 1986, p. 375.

32   "News Flash: Injectable Contraceptives Sterilization Alert" (Geneva, World Health Organization, Special Programme of Research, Development and Research Training in Human Reproduction, October 1987).

33   Royal College of General Practitioners, "Mortality among oral contraceptive users", *Lancet* 2, 8 October 1977, p. 727, and "Further analyses of mortality in oral contraceptive users", *Lancet* 1, 7 March 1981, p. 541.

34   B. V. Stadel, "Oral contraceptives and cardiovascular disease", *New England Journal of Medicine*, Part I, 305 (11), 10 September 1981, p. 612, and Part II, 305 (12), 17 September 1981, p. 672.

35   Royal College of General Practitioners, "Mortality . . ." and "Further analyses of mortality . . . ".

36   W. N. Spellacy and V. Wynn, eds., "Progestogens and the cardiovascular system", *American Journal of Obstetrics and Gynecology* 142 (6), Part 2, 15 March 1982, p. 717.

37   Royal College of General Practitioners, "Mortality . . .", and "Further analyses of mortality . . ."; D. Slone and others, "Risk of myocardial infarction in relation to current and discontinued use of oral contraceptives", *New England Journal of Medicine* 305 (8), 20 August 1981, p. 420.

38   P. M. Layde, H. W. Ory and J. J. Schlesselmann, "The risk of myocardial infarction in former users of oral contraceptives", *Family Planning Perspectives* 14(2), March/April 1982, p. 78.

39   J. Vana and others, "Primary liver tumors and oral contraceptives: results of survey", *Journal of the American Medical Association* 238 (20), 14 November 1977, p. 2154.

40   Potts, Speidel and Kessel, "Relative risks . . .", p. 28.

41   K. Treiman and L. Liskin, "IUDs--a new look", *Population Reports*, Series B, No. 5 (March 1988), p. 8.

42   *Ibid.*, p. 12.

43   *Ibid.*, p. 8, and H. W. Ory, "Ectopic pregnancy and intrauterine devices: new perspectives", *Obstetrics and Gynecology* 57 (2), February 1981, p. 137.

44   W. Parker Mauldin and Robert J. Lapham, "The measurement of family planning inputs", chap. 23 in *Organizing for Effective Family Planning Programs*.

45   "Operations research: lessons for policy and programs", *Population Reports*, Series J, No. 31 (May-June 1986).

46   S. C. Huber and P. D. Harvey, "Family Planning Programs in Ten Developing Countries", *Journal of Biosocial Science*, vol. 21 (1989).

47   Further information on cost strategies may be found in recent WHO work on financing primary health care and in an unpublished World Bank policy study, "Financing Health Services in Developing Countries: An Agenda for Reform".

48   See chaps. 17, 18, 19, 20 and 21 of *Organizing for Effective Family Planning Programs*; also, *Family Planning in the 1980s: Challenges and Opportunities* (New York, The Population Council, 1981).

49   For reviews of issues relating to community involvement see report of WHO Consultation on Policy Aspects of Community Participation in MCH/FP Programmes, Harare, Zimbabwe, 15-17 October 1986, available from Maternal and Child Health Unit, Division of Family Health, World Health Organization, Geneva, Switzerland.

50   Reviews of issues relating to incentives and disincentives appear in John A. Ross and Stephen L. Isaacs, "Costs, payments, and incentives in family planning programs: a review for developing countries", *Studies in Family Planning*, vol. 19, No. 5 (September/October 1988), and Henry P. David, "Incentives and disincentives in family planning programs", Chap. 22 in *Organizing for Effective Family Planning Programs*.

51   George B. Simmons and Robert J. Lapham, "The determinants of family planning program effectiveness", chap. 28 in *Organizing for Effective Family Planning Programs.*

52   "Operations research. . .".

53   Simmons and Lapham, "The determinants . . .".

54   Many of the assertions regarding training deficiencies mentioned in this section are documented in *Comparative Evaluation of Training in Maternal and Child Health/Family Planning Services: Common Issues and Regional Reports* (New York, United Nations Population Fund, 1989).

55   *Nuptiality: Selected Findings from the World Fertility Survey Data,* ESA/WP. 92 (New York, United Nations, 1986).

56   M. A. Khalifa, "Attitude of urban Sudanese men towards family planning", *Studies in Family Planning,* vol. 19, No. 4 (July/August 1988).

57   Report of the International Conference on Population, 1984, Recommendation 18(e), para. 22, p. 21.

58   Tietze and Henshaw, *Induced Abortion . . . .*

59   *Ibid.*

60   Preventing the Tragedy of Maternal Deaths, p. 16.

61   Tietze and Henshaw, *Induced Abortion . . .,* pp. 11-15.

62   Maggie Black, ed., *Better Health for Women and Children through Family Planning: Report on an International Conference held in Nairobi, Kenya,* October 1987 (New York, The Population Council, 1988), p. 39.

63   Report of the International Conference on Population, 1984, p. 21.

64   Black, *Better Health . . .,* p. 39.

65   John Bongaarts, "A Current-Status Method for Estimating Contraceptive Use-Failure Rates", an unpublished paper (IESA/P/AC.27/4) prepared for the United Nations Expert Group Meeting on Methodologies for Measuring Contraceptive Use Dynamics, New York, 5-7 December 1988.

66   Centre International de Recherche Medicale de Franceville (CIRMF), Rapport au Conseil Scientifique, Mai 1987 (unpublished data): Prevalence and type of infertility in Gabon, D. Schijvers,

417

A. Mehem, A. Dupont; Prevalence of Neisseria gonorrhoae infections, M. Peeters, E. Frost, S. Ossari; and Prevalence of positive serology for syphilis, A. Dupont, D. Schijvers, E. Frost.

67   *Ibid.*

68   Mauldin and Lapham, "The measurement of family planning inputs"; *Population Briefing Paper*, No. 19.

Chapter 4
Population Information,
Education and Communication

1   For example, the 1985 World Conference to Review and Appraise the Achievements of the United Nations Decade for Women: Equality, Development and Peace, which produced the Nairobi Forward-looking Strategies for the Advancement of Women (see *Report of the World Conference to Review and Appraise the Achievements of the United Nations Decade for Women: Equality, Development and Peace*, A/CONF.116/28/Rev.1 [United Nations publication, Sales No. E.85.IV.10]), and the International Conference on Better Health for Women and Children through Family Planning, Nairobi, Kenya, October 1987 (see Maggie Black, ed., *Better Health for Women and Children through Family Planning: Report on an International Conference held in Nairobi, Kenya*, October 1987 [New York, The Population Council, 1988]).

2   Review and Appraisal of the World Population Plan of Action (United Nations publication, Sales No. E.79.XIII.7), para. 87.

3   Report of the International Conference on Population, 1984, Mexico City, 6-14 August 1984 (United Nations publication, Sales No. E.84.XIII.8), Recommendation 29, para. 26.

4   *Ibid.*, Recommendation 74, para. 35.

5   Study of the Contribution of Population Education to Educational Renewal and Innovation in El Salvador, the Republic of Korea, Philippines and Tunisia (Paris, United Nations Educational, Scientific and Cultural Organization, 1980).

6   Personal communication from Sloan Wayland, 1988.

7   Personal communication from J. E. Jayasuriya, 1988.

8   Population Education: A Contemporary Concern; International Study of the Conceptualization and Methodology of Population Education (Paris, United Nations Educational, Scientific and Cultural Organization, 1978).

9   Policy Guidelines in Population Education (New York, United Nations Fund for Population Activities, 1986).

10   Population Education: A Contemporary Concern . . . .

11   "Family life education in Ethiopia", *World Education Reports*, No. 12 (New York, World Education, 1976).

419

12   J. H. Richards, "A Population/Family Welfare Education Programme for Workers" (Geneva, International Labour Office, n.d.).

13   Food and Agriculture Organization of the United Nations, "Integration of Population Education into Programmes for Rural Youth in Low Income Countries", INT/86/P66 (Rome, 1987).

14   To Operate a Set of Regional African Family Living Education Programmes for Parents, Adolescents and Men (New York, Margaret Sanger Center, 1987).

15   World Population Trends and Policies, 1987 Monitoring Report (United Nations publication, Sales No. E.88.XIII.3).

16   J. Senderowitz and J. M. Paxman, *Adolescent Fertility: Worldwide Concerns*, Population Reference Bureau, vol. 40, No. 2 (Washington, D.C., 1985).

17   Development of Out-of-School Population Education Programmes: A Synthesis (Bangkok, United Nations Educational, Scientific and Cultural Organization, 1980); and "Integration of Population Education . . .".

18   Training in Out-of-School Population Education (Bangkok, United Nations Educational, Scientific and Cultural Organization, 1982).

19   Paul Lengrand, *An Introduction to Lifelong Education* (Paris, UNESCO Press, 1975).

20   Report on the Inter-Agency Task Force Meeting on Project Follow-Up and Institutionalization (Geneva, International Labour Office, 1987).

21   Miriam T. Manisoff, ed., *Family Planning Training for Social Services* (New York, Planned Parenthood-World Population, 1971).

22   Personal communication from J. A. Johnston, 1988.

23   Everett M. Rogers, *Diffusion of Innovations* (New York, The Free Press, 1962); Snehendu B. Kar, "Communication for health promotion: a model for research and action" in *Advances in Health Education and Promotion*, vol. 1, Part A, 1986, pp. 267-302; and Kenneth R. McLeroy and others, "An ecological perspective on health promotion programs", *Health Education Quarterly*, vol. 15, No. 4 (1988).

24   Ronny Adhikarya and H. Posamentier, *Motivating Farmers for Action* (Eschborn, Federal Republic of Germany, GTZ, 1987).

25   This figure and those in the following sentence appear in "Radio: spreading the word on family planning", *Population Reports* (The Johns Hopkins University), Series J, No. 32 (September-October 1986).

26   The data on the Republic of Korea are from H. J. Park, "Use and relative effectiveness of various channels of communication in the development of the Korean family planning programme", *United Nations Economic Commission for Asia and the Far East, Report of the Working Group on Communication Aspects of Family Planning Programmes and Selected Papers*, Asian Population Studies Series 3 (Singapore, 5-15 September 1967), p. 69; the data on Pakistan are from B. Karlin and S. M. Ali, "The use of radio in support of the family planning programme in Hyderabad District of West Pakistan", *Pakistan Journal of Family Planning 2* (2) (July 1968), p. 1.

27   William O. Sweeney, *Population Family Planning Media Communications in Twenty-five Countries* (Honolulu, East-West Communication Institute, 1978).

28   Ronny Adhikarya and David Radel, "Problems and needs in population/family planning information, education and communication: an analysis of programs in Asia and the Middle East", *Country Programs and Future Needs for International Assistance* (Honolulu, East-West Communication Institute, 1975).

29   "Family planning programs--media communications in population/family planning programs: a review", *Population Reports*, Series J, No. 16 (March 1977).

30   *Ibid*.

31   "Research in family planning communication", *Report of Experts' Meeting held in Davao City, October 1972* (Paris, United Nations Educational, Scientific and Cultural Organization, 1972); Jack Glattbach, "Public information and mass media in population communication programs, *Population Communication Experience*, Paper No. 10 (Honolulu, East-West Communication Institute, 1977).

32   Alan Berg, *The Nutrition Factor: Its Role in National Development* (Washington, D.C., The Brookings Institution, 1973).

33   Kim Winnard, Jose G. Rimon and Julie Convisser, "The Impact of Television on the Family Planning Attitudes of an Urban Nigerian Audience: The NTA/ENGU Experience", for APHA Conference, The Johns Hopkins University Population Communication Services, Baltimore, 1987.

34   Guidelines in the Use of Video in Field Projects (Rome, Food and Agriculture Organization, 1987).

35   *Ibid.*

36   "Family planning programs--media communications . . .".

37   Evaluation Report of Clearinghouses in Asia, UNFPA Report (New York, United Nations Fund for Population Activities, 1977).

38   "Radio: Spreading the Word".

39   *Ibid.*

40   United Nations Educational, Scientific and Cultural Organization, *Folk Media and Mass Media in Population Communication*, Population Communication: Technical Documentation No. 8 (Paris, 1982).

41   E. C. C. Cernada, Y. J. Lee and M. Y. Lin, "Family planning telephone services in two Asian cities", *Studies in Family Planning* (4) No. 5 (April 1974), p. 111.

42   "Cooperative Media Development Programme in Support of Korean National Family Planning Programme", ICOMP Case Studies on Management of IEC in Population Programmes (Seoul, Planned Parenthood Federation of Korea, March 1986).

43   John Lawley, "Awareness is not enough", *People*, vol. 13, No. 2 (1986), pp. 8-11.

44   Nancy Yinger and Win Carty, "Kenya", *Population Today*, 15, No. 11 (November 1987), pp. 4, 9.

45   Adhikarya and Posamentier, *Motivating Farmers for Action*; Peter Spain, *Non-Formal Education in Human Sexuality Using Radio and Other Media: El Centro de Orientation Familiar, San Jose, Costa Rica* (Palo Alto, California, Institute for Communication Research, Stanford University, 1978).

46   Population Services International (Preethi Campaign), Spring 1976, p. 33, in "Family planning programs--media communications . . . ".

47   United Nations Educational, Scientific and Cultural Organization, *Folk Media and Mass Media . . . .*

48   "Traditional media", *Health Technology Directions*, vol. 7, No. 2 (Seattle, Washington, Program for Appropriate Technology in Health [PATH], 1987).

49   United Nations Educational, Scientific and Cultural Organization, *Folk Media and Mass Media* . . . .

50   Lawrence F. Salmen, *Listen to the People* (New York, Oxford University Press, 1986).

51   Murray Ross, *Community Organization: Theory and Principles* (New York, Harper and Row, 1955); Pearl S. Buck, *Tell the People* (New York, John Day Company, 1945).

52   Family Planning in the 1980s: *Challenges and Opportunities* (New York, The Population Council, 1981), p. 1.

53   Charles E. Basch, "Focus group interview: an under utilized research technique for improving theory and practice in health education", *Health Education Quarterly*, vol. 14 (4) (Winter, 1987), p. 411.

54   O. J. Sikes, "Family planning perspectives", *Populi*, vol. 9, No. 2 (1982).

55   Personal communication from Phyllis Piotrow, 1988.

56   Sikes, "Family planning perspectives".

57   Personal communication, Piotrow.

58   Report on the Inter-Agency Task Force Meeting on Project Follow-Up and Institutionalization, para. 6, p. 3.

59   Personal communication, Piotrow.

60   Allan Steckler and Robert Goodman, "How to Institutionalize Health Promotion Programs" (1988), unpublished paper.

61   Newlywed Kit, Caswell Family Planning Program (Yanceyville, North Carolina, USA, Caswell Family Planning Committee, 1967).

62   Arthur V. Greeley, *Facts and Fallacies about a Happy Marriage* (St. Louis, Missouri, USA, The Emko Company, 1966).

63   Mildred Z. Solomon, *Sexually Transmitted Diseases. A Clinic-Based Demonstration Project to Improve Patient Compliance* (Video) (Newton, Massachusetts, USA, Education Development Centre, Inc., 1986).

64   *Condoms for Couples* (San Francisco, San Francisco AIDS Foundation, 1988).

Chapter 6
Population Policies and Programmes
in sub-Saharan Africa

1   World Population Trends and Policies: 1987 Monitoring Report
        (United Nations publication, Sales No. E.88.XIII.3), p. 34.

2   *Ibid.*, p. 106.

3   World Population Prospects: 1988 (United Nations publication,
        Sales No. E.88.XIII.7), pp. 166-167, 190.

4   United Nations Population Fund, *1988 Report by the Executive
        Director of the United Nations Population Fund* (New York, 1988),
        p. 24.

5   World Population Trends and Policies: 1987 Monitoring Report,
        p.204.

6   D. Wulf, "The future of family planning in sub-Saharan Africa",
        International Family Planning Perspectives, vol. 11, No. 1 (March
        1985), pp. 1-8.

7   World Population Prospects: 1988, pp. 578-579.

8   The World Bank, *World Development Report 1988* (New York,
        Oxford University Press, 1988), and World Health Organization,
        "Evaluation of the Strategy for Health for All by the Year 2000",
        *Seventh Report on the World Health Situation, Vol. 2, African
        Region* (Brazzaville, WHO, 1987).

9   United Nations Population Fund, *1988 Report*, p. 22.

10   *Ibid.*, pp. 20-26.

11   United Nations Population Fund, *Annual Review of Population
        Law, 1985* (New York and Cambridge, Massachusetts, United
        Nations Population Fund and Harvard Law School Library), vol. 12,
        p. 140.

12   J. Peterson, "A new Africa dawning", *Populi*, vol. 13, No. 2
        (1986), pp. 4-19, and J. Karefa-Smart, "Health and family
        planning in Africa", *Populi*, vol. 13, No. 2 (1986), pp. 20-29.

13   Wulf, "The future of family planning in sub-Saharan Africa".

14   I. Palmer, *Impact of Male Out-Migration on Women in Farming*
        (West Hartford, Connecticut, Kumarian Press, 1985), and E.

Boserup, *Women's Role in Economic Development* (New York, St. Martin's Press, 1970).

Notes to Chapter 7
Population Policies and Programmes
in the Arab States

1   A. R. Omran, "Reassessment of the Population Problem in Egypt, 15 Years after Family Planning", Carolina Population Center papers (June 1981).

2   Mamdouh Salem (Prime Minister of Egypt), Press Release in Arab Youth Magazine, (February 1976), Arabic.

3   Central Agency for Public Mobilization and Statistics (CAPMAS), 1973, 1979, 1980.

4   World Population Trends and Policies: 1987 Monitoring Report (United Nations publication, Sales No. E.88.XIII.3), pp. 204, 207.

5   World Health Organization, *Maternal Mortality Rates: A Tabulation of Available Information* (Geneva, 1985).

6   A. R. Omran and C. C. Standley, *Family Formation Patterns and Health: An International Collaborative Study in India, Iran, Lebanon, Philippines and Turkey* (Geneva, World Health Organization, 1976), and A. R. Omran and C. C. Standley, *Further Studies of Family Formation Patterns and Health: An International Collaborative Study in Colombia, Egypt, Pakistan and Syria* (Geneva, World Health Organization, 1981)

7   A. R. Omran, "Health benefits of family planning for mothers and children", *World Health* (January 1974).

8   N. H. Wright, "Family planning and infant mortality rate decline in the USA", *American Journal of Epidemiology* 101 (1975), pp. 182-187.

9   World Fertility Survey data, 1984.

10   A. R. Omran, *Family Planning in the Legacy of Islam* (New York, United Nations Population Fund, forthcoming).

11   Omran and Standley, *Family Formation Patterns and Health*, 1976 and 1981.

12   D. Kirk, "A new demographic transition?" in *Rapid Population Growth: Consequences and Policy Implications*, National Academy of Science (Baltimore and London, Johns Hopkins Press, 1971).

13   M. Mahran, "Population Policy in Egypt", paper presented at the National Safe Motherhood Conference, Cairo, 1988.

14   For details see United Nations Population Fund, *Tunisia, Report of Mission on Needs Assessment for Population Assistance*, Report No. 45 (New York, 1981).

15   For details see United Nations Population Fund, *Morocco, Report of Second Mission on Needs Assessment for Population Assistance*, Report No. 88 (New York, 1986).

16   National Office of Family Planning and Population, *La Planification Familiale en Tunisie* (Tunis, March 1976).

17   Arab Republic of Egypt, "The National Charter" (Cairo, Government Press, May 1962).

18   United Nations Population Fund, "Comparative Evaluation of UNFPA Support to Population and Development Planning Project in the Middle East Region: Report of Mission" (1988), mimeograph.

19   Personal communication from Dr. Z. Hamza, Minister of Health, Jordan, during Regional Safe Motherhood Conference, Amman, 1988.

20   "The Amman Declaration about Population in the Arab World", issued by the Regional Conference on Population in the Arab World, Amman, Jordan, March 1984, *The Population Bulletin of ESCWA*, No. 24 (1984), Arabic.

21   "Recommendations of the Regional Safe Motherhood Conference", Amman, Jordan, 24-26 September 1988, mimeograph, Arabic.

22   "The Regional Arab Union of Fertility Care: a curriculum for medical education and training of physicians in fertility care services in the Arab world", Proceedings of a Meeting in Rabat, Morocco, 23-28 June 1986.

Notes to Chapter 8
Population Policies and Programmes
in Asia and the Pacific

1   World Population Prospects: 1988 (United Nations publication, Sales No. E.88.XIII.7), pp. 228-229.

2   World Population Profile: 1985 (Washington, D.C., U.S. Department of Commerce, Bureau of the Census, 1986).

3   Rafael M. Salas, *International Population Assistance: The First Decade* (Oxford, Pergamon Press Ltd., 1979), p. xvii.

4   Selected Papers, Third Asian and Pacific Population Conference, Colombo, September 1982, Asian Population Studies Series No. 58, ST/ESCAP/267 (New York, United Nations, Economic and Social Commission for Asia and the Pacific, 1984), pp. 121-123.

5   *Ibid.*, p. 123.

6   World Population Trends and Policies, 1987 Monitoring Report (United Nations publication, Sales No. E.88.XIII.3), p. 36.

7   *Ibid.*

8   Population Policy Briefs: The Current Situation in Developing Countries, 1985, Population Policy Paper No. 2, United Nations Department of International Economic and Social Affairs (New York, United Nations, 1986), p. 28.

9   World Population Prospects: 1988.

10   World Population Trends and Policies, 1987 Monitoring Report.

11   Dorothy L. Nortman, *Population and Family Planning Programs: A Compendium of Data Through 1983*, 12th ed. (New York, The Population Council, 1985).

12   The World Bank, *World Development Report 1988* (New York, Oxford University Press, 1988), table 29, p. 278.

13   *Ibid.*, table 30, pp. 280-281.

14   R. M. Fagley, "Doctrines and attitudes of major religions in regard to fertility", *Proceedings of the World Population Conference, Selected Papers and Summaries*, Vol. II (E/CONF. 41/3), Belgrade, 1965 (New York, United Nations, 1967), pp. 78-84.

15   Religious Attitudes Toward Birth Control, Population Crisis Committee, No. 6 (Washington, D.C., January 1977).

16   Population Perspectives: Statements by World Leaders, 2nd ed. (New York, UNFPA, 1985)

17   For a review of the specific constraints facing the Indian programme see The Population Council, *Population Policies and Programmes in India* (New York, 1987).

18   Comparative Evaluation of Training in Maternal and Child Health/Family Planning Services: Common Issues and Regional Reports (New York, United Nations Population Fund, 1989).

19   Selected Papers, Third Asian . . ., p. 294.

20   Report of the Asian Regional Conference on Women, Population and Development, Held in Beijing, People's Republic of China, 25-30 April 1985 (New York, United Nations Fund for Population Activities).

21   International Encyclopedia of Population (New York, The Free Press, 1982), vol. 1, pp. 209, 210.

Notes to Chapter 9
Population Programmes and Policies in Latin America and the Caribbean

1   *World Population Prospects: 1988* (United Nations publication, Sales No. E.88.XIII.7), pp. 218-219.

2   Pan American Health Organization, *Programas de Salud Maternoinfantil y Planificacion Familiar*, Documento para la XXXIIIa Reunion (Washington, D.C., 1988).

3   John A. Ross and others, *Family Planning and Child Survival: 100 Developing Countries* (New York, Columbia University, Center for Population and Family Health, 1988).

4   Pan American Health Organization, *Programas de Salud . . . .*

5   United Nations, *World Population Prospects*, pp. 218-219.

6   Ross and others, *Family Planning and Child Survival . . . .*

7   United Nations, *World Population Prospects*, pp. 218-219.

8   Differences in population growth rates between North America and Latin America have had important implications for the size of their respective populations. Latin America's population is now larger than North America's, as was the case before 1800 but not during the nineteenth century. See W. Mertens, "Population growth policies and food policies in Latin America", Proceedings Western Hemisphere Nutrition Congress III, Miami, 1972.

9   Albert O. Hirschmann, "The Political Economy of Latin American Development: Seven Exercises in Retrospection", *Latin American Research Review*, vol. 22, No. 3 (1987).

10   J. Wilkie, ed., *Statistical Abstract of Latin America* (Los Angeles, UCLA Latin American Center Publication, University of California, 1988), vol. 26.

11   The World Bank, *World Development Report 1988* (New York, Oxford University Press, 1988), table 30, pp. 280-281.

12   J. Sheahan, "Poverty, Repression and Economic Strategy", *Patterns of Development in Latin-America* (Princeton, New Jersey, Princeton University Press, 1987), p. 28.

13   Sheahan, "Patterns of Development . . . ".

14   Pan American Health Organization, *Programas de Salud . . . .*

15   United Nations Population Fund, *Report on the International Forum on Population Policies in Development Planning, 1987* (New York, 1987), p. 77.

16   Annual Report Fiscal Year 1987, Population Information Program, The John Hopkins University (Baltimore, Maryland, Population Communication Services, 1988).

17   Jairo G. Palacio, "La Educacion en Poblacion en America Latina" (Caracas, United Nations Educational, Scientific and Cultural Organization, 1989), mimeographed.

18   J. Wells, *Empleo en America Latina: Una Busqueda de Opiniones* (Geneva, PREALC, International Labour Office, 1987), pp. 6, 94 and 100.

19   S. R. Olivier, *Ecologia y Subdesarrollo en America Latina* (Mexico, Siglo XXI Editores, S.A., 1986), p. 134.

20   Alvaro Avila Bernal, *Corrupcion y Expoliacion en America Latina. Los Casos de Colombia, Venezuela, Brasil* (Barcelona, Grijalbo, 1987).

21   L. Morris, "Contraceptive Use and Reported Levels of Unplanned Pregnancies in Latin America", Paper, 14th International Congress of the Latin American Studies Association, Atlanta, Georgia, 1988.

22   Pan American Health Organization, *Programas de Salud . . . .*

23   Palacio, "La Educacion en Poblacion . . .".

24   J. E. Potter and others, "The influence of health care on contraceptive acceptance in rural Mexico", *Studies in Family Planning*, vol. 18, No. 3 (1987).

25   Pan American Health Organization, *Programas de Salud . . . .*

26   *Ibid.*

27   *Ibid.*

28   Comparative Evaluation of Training in Maternal and Child Health/Family Planning Services: Common Issues and Regional Reports (New York, United Nations Population Fund, 1989) and country notes for Latin America (1987), unpublished.

29   V. Ibarra, S. Puente and F. Saavedra, *La Ciudad y el Medio Ambiente en America Latina: seis estudios de caso* (Mexico, El Colegio de Mexico, 1986).

30   "Access to Birth Control: A World Assessment", *Population Briefing Paper*, No. 19 (Washington, D. C., Population Crisis Committee, 1987).

31   Pan American Health Organization, *Programas de Salud . . . .*

32   L. Morris, "Contraceptive Use . . . ".

33   *Ibid*.

34   Pan American Health Organization, *Programas de Salud . . . .*

35   M. Calvelo Rios, "Notas sobre la Estrategia de Informacion, Educacion y Comunicacion en Poblacion par la Region" (1988), mimeographed.

36   W. Mertens and others, *Reflexiones Teorico-Metodologicos sobre Investigaciones en Poblacion* (Mexico, El Colegio de Mexico, 1982).

37   A Summary of the Report on the Evaluation of MEX/79/P04 "Integration of Population Policy with Development Plans and Programmes" (New York, United Nations Fund for Population Activities, 1984), p. 10.

Definitions

<u>Age-dependency ratio</u> - The ratio of the combined child population under 15 years of age and adult population 65 years and over to the population of intermediate age, 15-64 years, per 100.

<u>Age-specific fertility rate</u> - The number of births occurring during a specific period (usually a calendar year) to women of a specified age or age group divided by the number of person-years lived during that period by women of that age or age group (usually by the mid-year population of women of that age).

<u>Average annual rate of growth</u> - The ratio of population growth per year in a given period to the mean population of that period. The rate is expressed as a percentage.

<u>Billion</u> - A billion is 1,000 million.

<u>Community-based distribution</u> - A mode of delivering services in local communities. With respect to family planning services, local residents are trained to provide information and some of the contraceptive methods.

<u>Contraceptive prevalence</u> - The proportion of all women 15-49 years old living in union who practise contraception.

<u>Crude birth rate</u> - The ratio of the number of live births per year in a population during a given period to the average size of the population during the period. The ratio is expressed per 1,000 population.

<u>Crude death rate</u> - The ratio of the number of deaths per year in a population during a given period to the average size of the population during the period. The ratio is expressed per 1,000 population.

<u>Dollars</u> - Dollars are U.S. dollars unless otherwise indicated.

<u>Economically active population</u> - The number of all employed and unemployed persons (including those seeking work for the first time). The term covers employers, persons working on their own account, salaried employees, wage earners, unpaid family workers, members of producer's co-operatives and members of the armed forces. The economically active population is also called the labour force.

433

Elasticity - An elasticity relates the percentage change in one variable, such as "children ever born", to the percentage change in another, such as the child mortality rate.

General fertility rate - The annual number of births divided by the mid-year population of women aged 15 to 49 years multiplied by 1,000.

Gross reproduction rate - A measure of the reproduction of a population expressed as an average number of daughters to be born to a cohort of women during their reproductive age, assuming no mortality and a fixed schedule of age-specific fertility rates. More specifically, it is the sum of age-specific fertility rates for the period multiplied by the proportion of the total births of girl babies.

Infant mortality rate - The number of infant deaths under one year of age per 1,000 live births.

Life expectancy (at birth) - Mean number of years to be lived by a newly born child, assuming the population is subjected to a fixed schedule of age-specific mortality rates. It is also called the expectation of life at birth.

Median age - The age that divides the population into two groups of equal size, one younger and the other older.

Pro-natalist - An individual attitude or a collective policy to increase the number of births.

Total fertility rate - The sum of the age-specific fertility rates over all ages of the child-bearing period. This measure gives the approximate magnitude of "completed family size", that is, the total number of children an average woman will bear in her lifetime, assuming no mortality.

Vital statistics - Demographic data on births, deaths, foetal deaths, marriages and divorces.

Sources: *World Demographic Estimates and Projections, 1950-2025* (New York, United Nations, 1988), pp. 2-3; *World Population Prospects: Estimates and Projections as Assessed in 1982* (United Nations publication, Sales No. E.83.XIII.5), p. 35; Arthur Haupt and Thomas T. Kane, *Population Handbook: International Edition* (Washington, D.C., Population Reference Bureau, 1980); and UNFPA Technical and Evaluation Division.

Glossary of Acronyms and Initials

ACP	African Census Programme
ADOPT	Asian-Pacific and Worldwide Documents on Population Topics
AIDS	Acquired immune deficiency syndrome
AMIDEP	Multidisciplinary Association for Population Training and Research, Peru
APLIC	Association for Population/Family Planning Libraries and Information Centers
ASEAN	Association of South-East Asian Nations
CAPMAS	Central Agency for Public Mobilization and Statistics, Egypt
CAPPA	Computerized Agricultural and Population Planning Assistance and Training System
CBD	Community-based delivery
CCU	Central Co-ordinating Unit, United Nations Statistical Office
CDC	Cairo Demographic Centre
CEDPA	Centre for Development and Population Activities
CELADE	Latin American Demographic Centre
CICRED	Committee for International Co-ordination of National Research in Demography
CLAP	Latin American Centre of Perinatology and Human Development
COF	Centro de Orientacion Familiar, Costa Rica
CONAPO	National Population Council
CPS	Contraceptive Prevalence Survey
DAC	Development Assistance Committee, Organization for Economic Co-operation and Development
DHS	Demographic and Health Survey
DMPA	Depo-provera
DOCPAL	Population Documentation for Latin America, CELADE
DTCD	Department of Technical Co-operation for Development, United Nations
ECA	Economic Commission for Africa, United Nations
ECAFE	Economic Commission for Asia and the Far East, United Nations
ECE	Economic Commission for Europe, United Nations
ECLAC	Economic Commission for Latin America and the Caribbean, United Nations
ECOSOC	Economic and Social Council, United Nations
EPI	Expanded programme on immunization
ESCAP	Economic and Social Commission for Asia and the Pacific, United Nations
ESCWA	Economic and Social Commission for Western Asia, United Nations
FAO	Food and Agriculture Organization of the United Nations

435

FELDA	Federal Land Development Authority, Malaysia
FP	Family planning
FPA	Family planning association
GNP	Gross national product
HIV	Human immunodeficiency virus
HRP	Special Programme of Research, Development and Research Training in Human Reproduction, World Health Organization
ICARP	International Committee for Applied Research in Population
ICCR	International Committee for Contraception Research, The Population Council
ICOMP	International Committee on Management of Population Programmes
IDEP	African Institute for Economic Development and Planning, Senegal
IDRC	International Development Research Centre, Canada
IEC	Information, education and communication
IFORD	Institut de formation et de recherche demographiques, Cameroon
IIPS	International Institute for Population Studies, India
IIVRS	International Institute for Vital Registration and Statistics
ILO	International Labour Organisation
IMR	Infant mortality rate
INANDEP	Andean Institute for Population and Development Studies, Peru
IPPF	International Planned Parenthood Federation
IPS	Inter Press Service
ISI	International Statistical Institute
ISPC	International Statistical Programs Center
IUD	Intra-uterine device
IUSSP	International Union for the Scientific Study of Population
JCGP	Joint Consultative Group on Policy
JOICFP	Japanese Organization for International Cooperation in Family Planning, Inc.
KAP	Knowledge, attitude and practice (of family planning)
LDC	Less developed country
MCH	Maternal and child health
MIS	Management information system
NFPB	National Family Planning Board, Jamaica
NGO	Non-governmental organization
NHSCP	National Household Survey Capability Programme
NPC	National population council
OAU	Organization of African Unity
ODA	Overseas Development Administration, United Kingdom of Great Britain and Northern Ireland
OPEC	Organization of Petroleum Exporting Countries
ORT	Oral rehydration therapy
PADIS	Pan-African Documentation and Information System
PAHO	Pan American Health Organization, World Health Organization

PDP	Population and Development Project, Egypt
PIACT	Program for the Introduction and Adaptation of Contraceptive Technology
PID	Pelvic inflammatory disease
PIDSA	Population Information and Documentation System for Africa
PISPAL	Programme of Social Research on Population in Latin America
PLAMIRH	Latin American Programme of Research in Human Reproduction
POPIN	Population Information Network, United Nations
PPFK	Planned Parenthood Federation of Korea, Republic of Korea
PREALC	Regional Employment Programme for Latin America and the Caribbean
RCGP	Royal College of General Practitioners, United Kingdom of Great Britain and Northern Ireland
RIPS	Regional Institute for Population Studies, Ghana
SIS	State Information Service, Egypt
STD	Sexually transmitted disease
TBA	Traditional birth attendant
TCDC	Technical co-operation among developing countries
TFR	Total fertility rate
UNDP	United Nations Development Programme
UNDTCD	United Nations Department of Technical Co-operation for Development
UNESCO	United Nations Educational, Scientific and Cultural Organization
UNFPA	United Nations Population Fund
UNICEF	United Nations Children's Fund
USAID	United States Agency for International Development
WFS	World Fertility Survey
WHO	World Health Organization
WPPA	World Population Plan of Action

Index

441

446

447

449

459

460

461